CANNING

Politician and Statesman

Peter Dixon

CANNING

Politician and Statesman

WEIDENFELD AND NICOLSON
LONDON

Weidenfeld and Nicolson
11 St John's Hill London SW11

ISBN 0 297 77061 6

Printed in Great Britain by
Willmer Brothers Limited, Birkenhead

CONTENTS

To 'The Crazy X' where much of this book was written

ACKNOWLEDGEMENTS

I would like to acknowledge the gracious permission of Her Majesty the Queen for quotations from the Royal Archives.

I would like to thank the Earl of Harewood for permission to quote extensively from the Canning Papers deposited in Leeds Record Office.

I would also like to thank the following for permission to quote from their manuscripts: The Trustees of the British Museum; The Keeper of the Public Record Office; The Trustees of the National Library of Scotland; The Keeper of the Records of Scotland; the University of Durham; University College London; Liverpool City Libraries; the William L. Clements Library, Ann Arbor, Michigan; Duke University Library, Durham, North Carolina; the Henry L. Huntington Library, Los Angeles, California; and Mr C. E. Wrangham, Rosemary House, Catterick, Yorkshire.

Unpublished Crown Copyright material in the India Office records transcribed in this book appears by permission of the Controller of Her Majesty's Stationery Office.

I
THE PROTÉGÉ OF PITT

The road to high office has always been strewn with the wreckage of greatness. Birth and wealth combined with the highest abilities can count for nothing against a small measure of bad luck or a moment of ill-humour. Conversely, the career of the aspiring statesman is one in which unpromising beginnings can develop far beyond the vision of the most clear-sighted.

In 1770 no prophet could have foreseen the future career of the infant George Canning, born without the advantages which wealth and inherited position bestowed upon his contemporaries and rivals. Canning's father, also named George Canning, was an expatriate Irishman and lawyer. His ancestor William Canynge represented Bristol in six successive Parliaments before his death in 1396. His two younger sons reached prominence as lord mayors of London and Bristol respectively. The eldest, John, fathered Thomas Canning who married the heiress of an estate at Foxcote in Worcestershire where they settled. A younger scion of this branch, another George Canning, received a grant of the manor of Garvagh in Londonderry from James I in 1618 and established another branch of the family there. The family were committed to the Protestant cause; one member of it was killed by the Catholic populace and another was attainted under James II.

The great-grandson of the original grantee was Stratford Canning. The eldest of his five children, George, fathered the subject of this biography. The family was prosperous, and George Canning could have looked forward to a valuable inheritance had he not alienated his father by his radical politics and a love affair, both of which met with parental disapproval. Cut off with only

£150 p.a. he entered the Middle Temple in 1757, but never practised at the Bar. In deepest penury, he was forced to alienate his inheritance to Paul, one of his younger brothers, in order to persuade his father to pay his debts. Soon in debt again in 1768 he nevertheless married one Mary Costello; beautiful, Irish and penniless. Though of gentle ancestry, she had no inheritance to look forward to; and the marriage, brief but happy, defied the contemporary axioms of practicality. After the marriage, George Canning set up as a wine merchant, but this project characteristically failed.

But for his famous son, George Canning would be known only to the obscurantist as a minor poet and pamphleteer. In 1763 he produced 'An Epistle from William, Lord Russell . . . to William Lord Cavendish, supposed to be written the night previous to his execution.'[1] Strongly anti-Catholic in tone, it also attacks the principles of monarchial absolutism, declaring

> *Of Right Divine, let foolish Filmer dream,*
> *The Publick Welfare is the law supreme.*[2]

Other works are moral and philosophical in tone. There is a set piece poem in Augustan couplets on love and chastity which sees the primal state of innocence as spoiled by a money economy and the consequent spread of vice. Classical antiquity is appealed to in an attack on the 'Progress of Lying' and his major work was a translation of Cardinal de Polignac's *Anti-Lucretius* written by the latter in 1747 as a refutation of *De Rerum Natura*. His use of Augustan couplets possibly influenced his son who preferred that style in all his poetry. Touches of ability appear, and there is real tenderness in the following lines, describing love, before it was marred by vice:

> *At night, when labour must to rest give place*
> *The happy pair enjoyed the warm embrace*
> *Clasped in each other's arms, enraptur'd lay*
> *And in soft transports breathed their souls away.*[3]

His son must nevertheless have winced at the general quality of his father's work. Unsurpassed in banality is the dedicatory epistle in his collected works, addressed to his former tutor:

> *When Popery high her bloody standard bore,*

> *And drenched Ierne's blushing plains with gore*
> *We boast of ancestors, with mutual pride,*
> *Who fought, who bled and (let me add) who died.*[4]

On 11 April 1770 George Canning's wife gave birth to the future statesman. Unable to provide the financial support necessary in the circumstances, he compensated with a poem to his wife entitled 'A Birthday offering to a young lady from her Lover'. A year later to the day, he himself died leaving his widow heartbroken and penniless. Few careers were open to the unfortunate lady and she had to make use of what contacts she possessed. Fortunately, her uncle was a gentleman usher; he approached Queen Charlotte with a request for an introduction to Garrick and through him she was able to start a theatrical career. On 6 November 1773 she appeared as Jane Shore; on 12 April 1774 she appeared as Perdita in *Florizel and Perdita,* a farcical version of *A Winter's Tale.* Unfortunately she was not a success, and after playing Mrs Beverley in *The Gamester* and Octavia in *All for Love,* she was relegated to minor roles, and departed for the provinces, playing Julia in *The Rivals* in Bristol in 1775.

By this time she was living with an actor-manager named Reddish, the son of a Frome tradesman. He had already enhanced an unsavoury reputation by marrying a Miss Hart 'who enjoyed an income derived from a degrading source'.[5] After spending her money he had left her. The affair with Mrs Canning was not a happy one but it kept her stage career going. Hannah More commented, 'this is the second or third wife he has produced at Bristol; in a short time we have had a whole bundle of Reddishes, and all remarkably unpungent'.[6] In the 1770s debt, drunkenness and madness finally closed his career and he died in York Asylum in 1785.

Paradoxically, it was the acting connection which saved young George Canning. His uncle Stratford, the youngest of the three brothers, was a London merchant of the firm of French, Burroughs and Canning, and by the 1770s had become successful and rich. The actor Moody had seen the extraordinary talents which the young George Canning possessed and setting these against his unsatisfactory background went to Stratford and told him that his young nephew was on the high road to the gallows. After much hesitation, Stratford agreed in 1778 to take charge of young

George's education. This was the turning point in the latter's life, for his environment changed completely. At his uncle's he met men of prominence amongst the opposition of the time – Burke, Fitzpatrick, Fox and Sheridan. The latter took a particular interest in the boy, soon seeing in his talents a future recruit to his party's cause. A small estate was settled on George, that of Kilbrahan, Co. Kilkenny which throughout his life was to provide a small and irregular income of about £200 p.a. He was educated first at Hyde Abbey School and then, on Fox's advice, sent to Eton. It was there that the boy whose life had previously been buffeted by chance began to display a degree of ability which marked him as a man who might shine in the highest stations of public life.

He did not break away from his mother, but wrote to her throughout his life and visited her when the opportunity arose. His letters to her are in an affectionate tone, and he described to her in great detail his daily life. Of Eton, he commented in October 1782, 'As to my distaste to Eton School I find it wears off as I grow more acquainted with the boys and as my station is pretty high I shall soon be able to be very easy here.'[7]

He can have heard little good concerning his mother from his relatives; Canning wrote to her that his uncle had 'expatiated upon your bad conduct and said he thought you had on all occasions rather consulted your own immediate pleasure and satisfaction than the interests of your family and me in particular'[8] – hardly an appropriate communication from a thirteen-year-old boy. She had meanwhile married a Mr Hunn, a Plymouth silk-mercer, by whom she had two daughters and a son, all of whom were later to be beneficiaries of George's generosity. The marriage was not a happy one and eventually they appear to have separated. In 1792 Canning wrote to his mother, 'Mr Hunn's behaviour is indeed extraordinary and fills me with astonishment and indignation. I hope it is capable of being explained in some way, though in what way I am at a loss to conjecture'.[9] In 1795 he wrote 'Mr Hunn's conduct is such as I turn with disgust from contemplating.'[10]

His mother was always in the background of Canning's life, viewed with affection but always something of a problem for him. Even at this early stage Canning was providing her with some financial support which, after his uncle's death in 1787, he raised from £20 to £50 p.a. To visit her he nevertheless needed his

uncle's permission and so his holidays were usually spent with
his father's side of the family. Besides his Uncle Stratford, Canning had another uncle, Paul, to whom the inheritance rightly
belonging to Canning's own father had fallen. He died in 1784
but his son preserved the connection with Canning, eventually
becoming Lord Garvagh.

Of his father's sisters, one was a spinster, but the other, Harriet,
married a wealthy clergyman, the Rev. William Leigh, later Dean
of Hereford, and she was of great importance in Canning's life.
Canning kept the closest contact with them and their family, often
spending his vacations with them first at Norwich and then at
Ashbourne Hall, twelve miles north-west of Derby, which they
leased from Sir Brooke Boothby. He never seems to have travelled
abroad at this time, but Stratford's financial interests took him to
Ireland on occasions and he accompanied Stratford there in 1785,
his first visit to the land of his immediate ancestors and apparently
his last for forty years.

At Eton Canning soon settled down and seems to have been
fairly happy. He was both studious and an extrovert, but, said
a contemporary, 'never played at any games with other boys'.
He was however 'fond of acting, decent and moral'.[11]

In 1786 a weekly paper appeared at Windsor which soon won
public acclaim. It was *The Microcosm*, which Canning produced
together with several friends who were contemporaries at Eton,
under the pseudonym of Gregory Griffin. Canning's main collaborators were John Hookham Frere, John Smith ('Easley') and
R. P. ('Bobus') Smith. Frere remained one of Canning's closest
friends. The son of John Frere of Roydon Hall, Norfolk, he was
born in 1769; and while undoubtedly a man of high literary ability,
indolence and 'an artless temper'[12] made him unsuitable for the
political and diplomatic appointments which Canning was later
to secure for him. John Smith too was to benefit from Canning's
patronage and when he died in 1827 he was Deputy Paymaster in
the Navy. 'Bobus' Smith was the eldest brother of Sydney Smith,
and later became Advocate-General in Calcutta, and subsequently
MP for Lincoln. An occasional contributor was Lord Henry
Spencer, son of the fourth Duke of Marlborough, who was to die
at the age of twenty-four when employed on a mission to Berlin.

Considering the ages of its authors, *The Microcosm* was a
remarkably polished work. Canning's own work, indicated by the

initial 'B', is mainly 'well-supported ironical pleasantry'.[13] Much
of his writing is morally improving in tone, but vices are attacked
in a way characteristic of the age of Addison and Steele and there
is no hint of the overriding need for moral reform which imbues
Sir Richard Hill's 'Address to Persons of Fashion'[14] or Wilberforce's *Real Christianity*.

The vices which Canning attacked are such as none would have
sought to defend; the 'noble art of swearing' is expostulated in
the second number; the promising novice delights 'the happy
parent [who] congratulates himself on the early improvement of
his offspring, and smiles to discover the promising seeds of manly
wit in the sprightly sallies of puerile execration'. Literary excur-
sions are suggested for the adept: 'The Complete Oath-Register;
or, Every Man his own Swearer'; 'Sentimental Oaths for the
Ladies' or 'Execrations for the year 1786'.[15] Clever word-playing
is frequent as in a supposed letter to G. Griffin from 'Nobody',[16]
and in the eleventh number Canning contributed a brilliant
example of the epic poem in the form of the nursery rhyme, 'The
Knave of Hearts'. Line by line we are shown the poem as posses-
sing all the characteristics of an epic – 'A beginning, a middle
and an end', 'one grand action or main design, conducive to
morality' and 'a hero', and the whole is subjected to a literary
criticism. This piece is hilariously funny and the dead-pan seriousness with which Canning describes the 'desponding melancholy'
of the lines

> *And – took them – quite away*

carries conviction even after two centuries.[17]

There are no politics in *The Microcosm*, and Canning's elaborate and witty intellectual exercises could win acclaim from all
sides of the political spectrum. Even where the subject was potentially emotive, as with 'The Slavery of Greece', Canning described
the 'glitt'ring tyranny of Othman's sons'[18] in much the same way
as he might have described that of Xerxes. Precocious brilliance
combined with political detachment won for *The Microcosm* a
fairly general acclaim. Even the King and Queen were amongst
its admirers and later told Canning 'that they hoped I had not
forgotten our old friend *The Microcosm* – for they had not'.[19]

Before Canning left Eton, his uncle and guardian died. His
uncle-in-law the Rev. Leigh declined the guardianship, and on

the advice of Lord Macartney, a family friend, this office passed to his late uncle's partner, Mr Borrowes. The job was by this time merely one of financial supervision, as Canning was determined to follow his uncle's wishes and go to Christchurch, though under pressure from the Rev. Leigh he abandoned the extravagent idea of going up as Gentleman Commoner. He was admitted on 17 November 1787.

Canning's politics, like those of his family circle, were staunchly Whig. 'You have heard, I suppose of the attempt against His Majesty's sacred life,' he wrote to his mother in 1786. 'Ministerials wanted to persuade all the people it was a plot laid by Fox and the D. of Portland – but thank God, nowadays everybody has sense enough to discover what degree of credit ought to be given to Ministerial papers – it has had a very bad effect however, as it has very considerably raised his popularity.'[20] Canning remained a Whig till after he had left Oxford.

Two of his closest friends, Hookham Frere and 'Easley' Smith, had gone to Cambridge instead, but Canning remained in close contact, particularly with Frere. Letters between them were in an extremely friendly style of informal banter, with frequent exchanges of Latin and Greek verses and letters in medieval English. Their poetic abilities were sometimes expended to their own despite; Frere wrote Canning a long poem on the sexual failings of their unfortunate friend:

> *Easley to sinful hours of Bam*
> *Well fondly doth retire*
> *The enchantress Siphilis him greets*
> *And sets him all on fire.*

'Schivious bubos' are amongst the side effects on which the poet lingers.[21]

This correspondence certainly shows that Canning was in no sense 'serious' as Evangelicals would have understood the term. While always a believer, religion never dominated Canning's life, and at Christchurch he regarded 8 am chapel as an imposition.[22]

On his arrival at Oxford Canning was elected to the Eton Club, which, like most university clubs of the time, had its own dress, including 'buff silk waist-coat and black silk inexpressibles'.[23] His peculiar background gave him a certain insecurity nevertheless, and he declined nomination to the Archer's Club, dreading 'the

idea of running even the smallest risque of a *black* ball'.[24] Instead
he projected the idea of a new club, along with fellow Etonian
and 'Microcosmopolitan' Lord Henry Spencer. This was a debating club limited to six members, the most prominent of whom
was Robert Banks Jenkinson, son of the President of the Board
of Trade, and later himself Prime Minister as second Earl of
Liverpool. Canning's first impressions of Jenkinson were favourable and he described him to his uncle as 'very clever and very
remarkably good natured',[25] though they were at that time dia-
metrically opposed in politics, Jenkinson being an ardent supporter
of Pitt. The other members of the club were John Newton, a
West Indian; William Drummond, later Ambassador at Constantinople; and Charles Goddard, future Archdeacon of Lincoln.
The club met on Thursday evenings at six. It boasted its own
uniform – a brown coat, velvet cuffs and collar, and buttons bear-
ing the initials of Demosthenes, Cicero, Pitt and Fox to demonstrate both political involvement and overall impartiality.

Even at this time Canning's mind was seriously turning to a
political career. He himself explained his being drawn into the
club as 'trying my strength with Jenkinson . . . and looking forward
to some distant period when we might be ranged against each
other on a larger field'.[26] For one with so little by way of financial
reserves and of so dubious a background, a political future was
a high ambition. The Dean of Christchurch, Dr Cyril Jackson,
a man who always retained Canning's highest respect and affection,
clearly thought that Canning's ambitions were running ahead of
his opportunities, warning him of the dangers to a professional
man, such as he would be, of avowing political views, and strongly
advising Canning to abandon his club. This Canning did, to the
dismay of his fellow members who unsuccessfully summoned him
to give reasons for his departure.[27]

Canning does not seem to have enjoyed his first year at Oxford,
and this, together with the departure of some older friends, made
him dread the following year. He wrote to the Rev. Leigh that
he looked forward 'with a sort of shuddering horror, to the dull
days which are to pass over my head this next term in that dun-
geon Christchurch. Nothing but the kindness of our gaoler, the
Dean, could make it tolerable'.[28]

In fact the subsequent year was more pleasant than he had
envisaged. In particular he became close friends with Lord Gran-

ville Leveson-Gower, son of the Marquess of Stafford, the Lord Privy Seal. This friendship helps to account for the political conversion which Canning was soon to undergo. Hitherto he had mixed in Whig circles – which he had originally met at his uncle's; he had been (and remained) a welcome guest at Crewe Hall, where Mrs Crewe, reigning toast of the Whigs (along with the Duchess of Devonshire), recognized his talents. At Trentham, home of the Marquess of Stafford, Canning began to meet men from the Government side in politics, though for the moment he remained a Whig.

Academically Canning was now being recognized at Oxford. Perhaps the transition from Eton, where he was established as one of the leading figures, to Oxford where he was a somewhat impoverished freshman, helps explain Canning's dislike of his first Oxford year. In his second he was able to surface from anonymity by winning the Chancellor's Medal with a long and somewhat tedious poem, 'Iter ad Meccam', a description of the Pilgrimage to Mecca in Latin verse. The poem is very much of a set piece, commencing with thoughts on Mecca and the tomb of Mohammed, proceeding via the places whence the pilgrims have come, conveniently providing endless scope for classical allusion, the dangers that beset the pilgrims, their prayers on arrival, and ending with a prayer to Christ and an explication of the superiority of Christianity. As a technical exercise the poem is excellent, but there is a basic lack of human insight and still more of feeling. No pilgrim would recognize himself in Canning's portrait. Lord Holland was to say of all Canning's writings that they 'excelled in splendour of diction and brilliancy of wit rather than in the expression of passion or truth of poetic feeling'.[29]

Romanticism in literature left Canning unmoved and he was later to exercise his satirical talents at its expense. Moreover this lack of empathy which was revealed in his writings also affected his oratory – often brilliant, always witty, but in the words of Henry Brougham, the Whig Lord Chancellor, 'it came from the mouth, not from the heart'.[30]

As one would expect, Canning also lacked the appreciation of Nature which characterized the Romantic Movement. As with many eighteenth-century gentlemen, his concept of a pleasant rural scene was a well-ordered garden. The beauty of the Lake District, which he visited in 1790 and which was at this time increasingly admired by his contemporaries, provided him with little to comment upon except the excessive rain,[31] though years later he was to come to appreciate it.

In 1789 Canning's talents were recognized by his election to a Studentship at Christchurch, as a Fellowship is termed. He wrote to his mother, 'The Dean of Christchurch has, without the smallest solicitation in my favour, given me a Studentship. I do not well know how I can explain to you what a Studentship is – but I am sure you will be glad to hear that it is also in some degree of pecuniary value.'[32]

The stipend was £20 p.a. Canning's other sources of income at this time were his Irish estate, worth £220 in English money, and an inheritance of £3000 which he received on his twenty-first birthday in 1791. This was money which his grandfather, persuaded to relent from his hostility before his death in 1786, now bequeathed to him. Of this £3000 he drew £1500 in 1791, leaving him with an income of £86 p.a. which diminished rapidly as the remainder of his capital was reduced to between £500 and £600 by the end of the following year.[33] Allowing for the £50 p.a. he paid his mother, Canning calculated in 1791 that he had £276 p.a. to spend.

As he himself rather facetiously pointed out, this was more than the per capita income of England and Ireland.[34] He also fully realized it was not enough to cope with the expenses of the professional and – *a fortiori* – political career on which Canning was now bent. Day to day expenses were great, and the cost of coach travel was enormous. On 2 March 1792, Canning recorded the expense of £3 3s for his journey from London to Oxford; on 21 June 1792, £3 13s 6d for the same trip. Even a coach to Wanstead[35] and back was £1 3s. As a bachelor he would frequently dine out and go to the play; the expense of 'Coaches – Play – and Supper' on one day in April 1792 was ten shillings.[36]

Unless he were to offer himself for holy orders (something Canning never seems to have considered) the obvious way for him to earn a living was at the bar. In the summer of 1791 he took his BA degree and then enrolled in Lincoln's Inn and took chambers in Paper Buildings. The initial expenses of getting started in the law were very great – when Spencer Percival, the Prime Minister, was assassinated in 1812, one of the most important justifications for the huge financial settlement bestowed by

Parliament on his wife and children was that the latter needed the money to enter the profession. Canning seems to have been reliant on the Rev. Leigh for several loans during this period. Canning was aware of the need to economize and spent many of the legal vacations at Oxford, reckoning to save about 8s 6d per day by this expedient.[37]

It must have been galling to the young Canning that his friends and contemporaries were free from these worries. Jenkinson could enter Parliament in 1792 with no thought of financial constraints, and as Canning thought of Jenkinson as a rival he smarted in his relatively impoverished position. Nor could Canning take a long tour of Europe as others among his friends did at this time. In March 1792 Granville Leveson-Gower and another friend of Canning's, Lord Boringdon, set out on a tour following a route from the Hague to Amsterdam, thence through Germany to St Petersburgh, returning via Moscow, Warsaw, Cracow, Vienna and Prague; a tour which took the full year.[38] Canning had to be content with a short tour of the Netherlands which he undertook after going down from Oxford in the summer of 1791.

Above all at this period Canning felt deeply humiliated by the lowly position of his mother. This certainly did not stem from any dislike of the theatre. He was often at the play and was an experienced critic, though, typical of the time, his criticisms were more often of the quality of the voices of the performers than of the plays. On Mrs Whitlock, whom he had seen in *Know Your Own Mind* at Chester, he commented, 'As for her boasted likeness to her sister, Mrs Siddons, I must own it rather disgusted than pleased me. She has all Mrs S's deep bass droning tones without any of her fine thrilling inflexions of voice, and emphasis.'[39]

Canning could not, however, bear to see his mother acting. He refused to travel from Crewe to Chester to visit her on one occasion, as he did not wish to see her 'in such a situation, and that while it was not yet in my power to rescue her from it'.[40] While at Eton he still took an interest in her profession; on her appearances at Beverley he had asked her: What sort of people do you perform before? Is your audience composed of mere country people or are they persons of taste and judgement who have any relish for theatrical diversions?'[41]

But after he had been at Oxford, and when a political career beckoned, he was mainly interested in inducing her to leave the

stage. In June 1791 he wrote, 'I should urge the trial of any line of
life in preference to the profession of the theatre.'[42] Five days
later he expressed his opinions more forcibly. Except for religion
and morality, he urged, everything in life takes its colour from
how it is regarded:

> Among these are *professions*; and there is perhaps no subject
> on which publick opinion decides more positively, than on the
> *respectability* or *disrespectability* of different pursuits and
> occupations. And when the profession of the theatre is in ques-
> tion need I hint to you, which side the Publick Opinion inclines?
> Whether in this case the world is just, or no – is nothing to the
> purpose – for when once its judgement is given, there is no
> appeal from it, and every individual must implicitly abide by
> its sentence.

Most unkindly, considering that he was in no position to
demand that his mother give up one of her means of livelihood,
he urged on her considerations of his own legal career and also
the position in society of his half-sister Mary. He portrayed people
in society as shunning her company because 'they do not choose
to have their daughters' manners and morals formed on the model
of the green-room'.[43]

However, it is to Canning's credit that he never used the allow-
ance he was paying his mother as a sanction against her continuing
on the stage, despite the harm he feared it would do to his own
career. Moreover, he was still responsive to her repeated requests
for financial assistance; in March 1794 he promised her £100
for August 1795, hoping that something would turn up to enable
him to pay it.[44]

Though Canning embarked on a legal career in 1791, it was
quite clear that he had set his heart on politics. Hitherto his
political associates had been Whig, though he was friendly to a
number of Pittites. It was shortly after this that he turned his coat
and became a Pittite himself. It was not only in his own eyes that
he was marked as a future holder of high office. Lord Lansdowne,
former Prime Minister and political mentor of Pitt, had pointed
him out at Oxford as a youth likely to become Prime Minister
himself.[45] In 1791 the Whigs were in a state of disarray; excluded
from office since 1783 by the hostility of the King, the French
Revolution was beginning to have a divisive effect on the party.

This eventually culminated in a schism between the committed reformers among them such as Fox, Sheridan and the young Charles Grey, and another group, which included many of the Whig peers and was headed by the Duke of Portland, whom Pitt was able to garner into his coalition in 1794. For a man as ambitious and impecunious as Canning the Whigs could hardly have offered any glowing prospects. Financial constraints alone made it inadvisable for him to rule out the possibility of office.

However, while self-interest might have impelled Canning away from the Whigs, it would be most unfair to suggest this as the only motive. Like most of his contemporaries, he had welcomed the French Revolution in 1789; in 1791 he was still basically sympathetic and approved of Mackintosh's reply to Burke's attack on the principles underlying it.[46] By 1792 he was nevertheless expressing doubts, and at a small London debating society of which he was a member, attacked the principles of Mirabeau, who had died some months earlier. 'To the steady eye of a sagacious criticism', he urged, 'the eloquence of Mirabeau will appear to be as empty and as vapid as his patriotism. It is like the beverage that stands so invitingly before you – foam and froth at the top, heavy and muddy within.'[47]

Canning was not merely disgusted by the excesses of the French Revolution abroad. He was also frightened they might happen in Britain. The story was later told that Canning was offered by Godwin the leadership of a possible British revolutionary party, and frightened by this, turned to the opposite extreme and offered his services to Pitt. This story is almost certainly false, but it conceals a grain of truth. The French Revolution had produced a noticeable effect in Britain; it was an age, declared an exuberant Scots Radical, when 'Farmers, ploughmen, peasants, manufacturers, artificers, shopkeepers, sailors, merchants are all employed in studying and reasoning on the nature of society and government.'[48] Politics were divided much more radically than at any time since 1660, and the choice for the aspiring politician between the Government and the dwindling but radicalized opposition was more momentous than it had been for years. Certainly organizations such as the extremely Radical 'Friends of the People' founded in 1792 must have frightened Canning, even though many of his former associates were involved with it.

Canning had sufficient Pittite friends that the transition was

not too difficult. With Frere smoothing the way, he wrote to Pitt
asking for a meeting. He stressed 'that however I may have been,
or may still be in habits of friendship and familiarity with some of
the most eminent men in Opposition, I am yet in no way bound
to them'.[49] Pitt replied in a friendly way, expressing 'the satisfaction which I shall feel in forming a personal connection with one
whom I have long known by Reputation, and whose talents I
sincerely wish to see exerted for the Benefit of the Public'.[50] The
connection was cemented when, following Pitt's invitation, the
two met on Wednesday 15 August 1792.

Lord Holland commented that Canning was unwise to put
himself under Pitt's auspices – that the law 'would have been a
more certain friend to him than the favour of a Prime Minister'.[51]
In fact, if Canning was really determined on a political career
he had made the wisest choice. Amongst the Whigs Canning
would have played second string to a number of well-established
orators and, had the Whigs achieved office, been passed over for
men with better family connections. Unable to plead the claims of
oligarchy, he was better advised in resting on the favour of the
Crown. Nor were the financial rewards of office, however slender
they might have appeared to some of his contemporaries, a consideration to be ignored by a man in Canning's circumstances.
Lady Holland commented on his conversion: 'Principle, I believe,
did not sway him much. He found the party in a desperate, lan-
guishing state, himself full of ambition and life, and that in that
party he must have contented himself with a very subaltern post;
whereas the reputation that Sheridan, in his overzeal, had anticipated for him made him an object worth getting to the others.'[52]

This is going too far, though it is difficult to disentangle the
political and personal reasons which impelled Canning to his
decision. But having formed his new political connection Canning's views certainly hardened. In December he sent a most
alarmist letter to his friend Edward Bootle Wilbraham[53] on the
state of Britain and Europe. His argument was partly philosophical: it is the right, he said, of any nation to pursue unhindered
the form of internal government it wills; France had unanimously
adopted 'a pure Representative Republic' into which our government, if ever it should change at all materially, would be most
likely to resolve itself. France had therefore made a useful experiment of general relevance, and Canning rejoiced 'in the disgrace

and defeat of the Duke of Brunswick[54] – not only as a liberal politician would rejoice in the repulsion of any attack upon the political liberties of a nation – but also as Walker the philosopher would rejoice in the punishment of any boy at Eton, who should have attempted to spoil his electrical experiments, by breaking one of his great cylindrical glasses'. But, Canning went on, the French by their treatment of Savoy and Genoa, and 'their system of impudent, savage and profligate warfare' compelled other nations to try to stop this threat. Meanwhile the danger had spread to Britain: '. . . in every quarter of the kingdom, there are societies formed for the reading, writing, talking and plotting destruction to every existing branch of the Government and to the peace and comfort of the country.' Canning went on to boast of the part he had played in preparing a persecution of a radical newspaper, *The Argus,* for seditious writings. He also dwelt on a reported outrage in Dundee 'where the insurgents have burned the custom-house . . . and hung an exciseman, and planted the Tree of Liberty with great solemnity and acclamation'.

The letter to Wilbraham shows that Canning shared the general concern at the political situation, even if he was able to smile at some of its manifestations: 'Some persons are providing themselves with muskets and swords, and others with horses and horse-pistols to scour the streets as cavalry. Jenkinson has resolved upon leading a corps of dragoons himself – in spite of my representations to him that his knowledge of musick better qualified him as a trumpeter.'[55]

Pitt clearly welcomed his new protégé. Canning was invited to stay with him at Addiscombe on 20 November 1792,[56] and Pitt set about trying to find a seat for him. As nothing was immediately available from Pitt, Canning made soundings about being returned for Newcastle-under-Lyme through his friend the Rev. John Sneyd of Keele Hall. He was however quite glad when this fell through, as the cost, even with very little opposition, would have been around £2,000.[57] Meanwhile his old Whig friend Mrs Crewe had been making enquiries for him. Like many other Whigs she had been frightened by the excesses of the French Revolution and was now much more sympathetic to the Government. She persuaded the Duke of Portland, who was fast moving away from the Whigs and was soon to join the Government, to offer one of the seats at his disposal to Canning. The latter nevertheless declined the offer – a bold step for one without family connections, even with Pitt's support. Clearly had he come in under the Duke's patronage, he would have been to a great extent bound by the Duke's opinions: perhaps Canning thought already that instead of belonging to a party, he should form one.

In fact he did not have to wait long for a seat. On 21 June 1793 Pitt wrote to him to say that he could replace Sir Richard Worsley, who was happy to return him for his own seat of Newtown on the Isle of Wight, and on 27 June Canning's election took place.[58] Representing a pocket borough had certain advantages even though it was not as prestigious as representing a county or a large town. The member for such a seat was only responsible to his patron for his parliamentary behaviour; there was no question of any obligation to obey instructions which town and county meetings sometimes imposed on their members. Furthermore, there was virtually no constituency work to take the member's time; later in his career Canning was to have to give a great deal of attention to the affairs first of Liverpool and later of Harwich but in a pocket borough the member would never even have reason to visit his seat. After his election, Canning wrote to the Rev. Leigh:

> The Newtonians, my Constituents, are not very numerous nor of such a disposition as to occasion any trouble. [They] will rest perfectly contented with knowing that they have a representative who will consider their interests as his own, for the time, and will therefore resist all wicked Reforms, that would take from this quiet and judicious set of men a suffrage, which they exercise with so much discretion and disinterestedness.[59]

At this period Canning's time was spent at his legal profession working in London and passing vacations either at Oxford or with his friends and relatives. In November 1793 he wrote to the Rev. Leigh, 'I for my part am going on in my usual Oxford way – living partly with grave tutors and partly with untutored boys – dining here, supping there, and canvassing politicks with the Dean night and morning.'[60]

Many of his friends were those he had known at Eton, and one among them was Charles Rose Ellis. A year younger than Canning he also was elected to Parliament in 1793. He was a wealthy Jamaica planter and Chairman of the Committee of West India

Planters and Merchants from 1810 to 1829. A cultured and civilized individual, he was a man of more liberal sentiments than many of his fellow planters and paid several visits to the West Indies partly to ensure the welfare of his slaves. He was not deeply involved in politics, confining his parliamentary speeches largely to West Indian affairs, where as a leading spokesman for the planters he opposed the abolition of the slave trade and later the immediate abolition of slavery. He and Canning were very close friends and Ellis had a strong influence on him.

Through Charles Ellis Canning met George Ellis, the former's cousin, also a West Indian planter. Though he was in Parliament from 1796 to 1802, George Ellis was not a House of Commons figure in any sense. He moved in literary circles and at his house, Sunning Hill, Canning met Sir Walter Scott, to whom he became a close friend. George Ellis was soon able to collaborate with Canning on an important periodical publication, *The Anti-Jacobin*.

Despite his political shift Canning did not abandon his old Whig friends. He was still on good terms with Sheridan and even Fox was never a personal enemy; Fox did not make enemies easily, and never willingly. Just before his first interview with Pitt Canning had stayed with the Foxes at St Anne's Hall and he played Casino with his hosts. Just after his change was final he stayed with Sheridan at Isleworth.[61]

Throughout the period Canning continued the studies in French which he had commenced at Oxford. It is more likely that he wished to acquire French out of its general usefulness than to suggest that at this early stage he had in mind his future appointments in the Foreign Office. But French being the language of diplomacy it nevertheless assisted him greatly in the first appointment which he was shortly to acquire, Under-Secretary for Foreign Affairs. He was certainly assiduous; typical entries in his diary read, 'Worked at French with Mr Guichard for 3 hours.'[62]

On 3 July 1794 Canning returned to Oxford to take his MA. This perhaps closes the first chapter in his life. He was now in Parliament and his academic and legal careers were drawing to a close. Technically he was still associated with Lincoln's Inn and occasionally chose to demonstrate his legal associations by dressing as a lawyer. In fact after he took his seat in Parliament on 21 January 1794 his career became a purely political one, a brave decision made possible for one so short of private means only by the reputation his name had already acquired and the patronage of the Prime Minister.

On 31 January 1794 Canning rose in the House of Commons to make his maiden speech. Parliamentary life was now dominated by the war with revolutionary France which had broken out a year earlier. The whole question of the advisability of the war split Parliament as much as the related question of the need to provide for internal security against infection by 'French principles'. The particular question on which Canning rose to speak was that of a treaty with the King of Sardinia whereby he was paid a subsidy to assist his own operations against France. The financing of continental allies was an appropriate policy for a country such as Britain with the wealth but without the manpower to engage in large scale military operations in Europe on her own. In 1759 a large subsidy treaty had been entered into with Frederick the Great to help him resist the combined onslaught of France, Austria and Russia.

Canning virtually ignored the details of the Sardinian treaty. Instead, he related it to the whole policy of the war, as 'growing out of, and inseparable from, a great connected, and comprehensive system – the system of general union amongst the powers of Europe, which had for its ultimate object the preventing the aggrandizement of the French Republic, and the checking the principles by which the aggrandizement was sought to be effectuated'. The argument that the activities of France were analagous to those of Britain's allies who had recently partitioned Poland was dismissed by Canning with the argument that it was only the former that involved Britain's security. Finally, he stressed the fruits of the war to date:

> . . . that we have still a government; that the functions of this House have not been usurped by a corresponding society, or a Scotch convention; that instead of sitting debating here, whether or not we shall subsidize the King of Sardinia, we are not rather employed in debating how to raise a forced loan for some pro-consular deputy, whom the banditti of Paris might have sent to receive our contributions; Sir, that we may sit here at all – These are the fruits of the war.[63]

Canning was pleased with his speech. He wrote to his mother that he had 'succeeded to the utmost of my expectations'.[64] The ministerial press gave the speech a warm welcome, though not unexpectedly, it was given a poor reception in the Whig *Morning Chronicle*. Fanny Burney praised Canning's 'excellent opening'.[65]

He quickly followed up with other speeches. On 10 April 1794 there was a further debate on the war, this time on the causes of the failure at Dunkirk and the evacuation of Toulon. As with his first speech, Canning quickly left the substantive ground of the debate and dwelt in general terms on what the state of the country would have been if the Opposition had been left to rule.[66] His speeches had removed any lingering doubts as to his affiliations; he had fully associated himself with the Government and its policy and shown himself a party man through and through. Warm praise came from Pitt, and strong abuse from Phillip Francis, John Courtenay, and the more violent Whigs.[67]

Dissenting from the general praise was Robert Jenkinson, and one is inclined to share some of his doubts as to the quality of Canning's early performance. In his speeches on the war he rarely attempted to show any deep grasp of the complex political and diplomatic factors involved, preferring to relate everything to more general principles and thus provide scope for the vigorous enunciation of his party viewpoint. Stripped of generalities his oratory was florid but conveyed very little.

Jenkinson's own early speeches were very different. His first, delivered on 29 February 1792, was against a motion by Samuel Whitbread which attacked ministerial policy in relation to the Russo-Turkish war. He made an able review of the entire diplomatic situation in Europe with a cogent justification of the government's actions – an extremely difficult task as Britain was so patently helpless in the face of the Russian capture of Oczakov.[68] Canning, generously acknowledged Jenkinson's 'amazing success'.[69] Even more notable was Jenkinson's speech opposing Wilberforce's motion for the abolition of the slave trade. Turning all the humanitarian arguments in favour of abolition on their heads, he argued that mortality on foreign slave ships was greater than in those of Britain and that it would therefore be an act of inhumanity to transfer the trade to the former. He went on to suggest two propositions which could eventually make the slave colonies self-sufficient through the natural increase of their population.[70]

A comparison of Canning's and Jenkinson's speeches is definitely to the detriment of the former, and the reliance on mere oratory in place of substantial argument was a defect to which Canning was continually liable. However, it must be stressed that polished and witty speech replete with classical allusion was much more congenial to parliaments of the late eighteenth century than to those of a subsequent period; certainly Canning himself felt that his speeches had made a good start to his political career. Fortunately Pitt shared his view.

The late eighteenth century was an age of excess. Politics were radically polarized in a way unseen since the previous century. In private life, excessive gambling and drunkenness was the norm rather than the exception. Charles James Fox was wont to pass from leading his party at Westminster to Brooks Club, where he would operate the bank at Faro. Heavy drinking was a normal social adjunct and scenes of drunkenness even occurred in the House of Commons. Indeed it is plausible to surmise a connection between the high-flown and grandiose oratory of Members of Parliament with the state of inebriation into which many would have passed after dining and drinking heavily. Against these excesses there were the beginnings of an equally violent reaction: the Evangelical Revival was already stigmatizing as vanity even such innocent social recreations as dancing.

Canning always preserved a golden mean between the two extremes. He drank, but not to excess, and it is rare to find him recording, as he did in 1794, that too great an 'attachment to the Madeira, Claret and excellent white Burgundy' had made him 'perfectly unfit to go to the Duchess of Gordon's' and also 'incapacitated from perceiving my own unfitness'.[71] He made no resolution, as Wilberforce and other Evangelicals did, to avoid gambling, and purchased tickets in the national lottery[72] which was still operated. However, he was never obsessed by it and later in life was to take a firm line against the heavy (and unsuccessful) gambling activities of his second son. While he enjoyed the company of women, with one possible exception Canning never formed any illicit attachments. Indeed, until 1799 he does not seem to have had any serious involvement with any woman, though his younger cousin Bessy Canning worshipped him for a time.

In religion he avoided both the Humian scepticism of Dundas and the 'seriousness' of Wilberforce. He retained a moderate attachment to the established church, and unlike his mentor Pitt, at times seems to have reflected on the state of his soul. In September 1793 he recorded, 'Went to Church – Received the Sacrament for the first time these four or five or perhaps six years. Made many serious resolutions in consequence, which I trust in God I shall be able to keep.'[73]

In politics too he avoided extremes. Where some of his contemporaries, notably William Windham who was amongst those Whigs who joined Pitt's Government in 1794, had been pushed by the French Revolution into opposition to all reforms, Canning was always able to take a calmer view. It was true that he gave strong support to the measures the Government took to prevent the spread of revolutionary principles in Britain. In May 1794 he spoke in favour of the suspension of Habeas Corpus. 'Good God!' he exclaimed, 'how could gentlemen oppose a measure that, at the present crisis was so absolutely necessary?'[74] However, when Thomas Muir, a founder of the Scottish 'Friends of the People', was sentenced to fourteen years' transportation for seditious speeches, he commented that it was 'a shameful trial'.[75]

The question of abolition of the slave trade and religious toleration also found him on the liberal side. He was in the minority in favour of abolition in the Division of 15 March 1796 and spoke against the trade in May 1797 and March 1799. Indeed so vehement were his views on this question that on one occasion he felt obliged to apologize to Robert Sewell, the Jamaica agent, for his language.

In supporting abolition he stood with Pitt and indeed with all the major orators in the House of Commons except Windham, who had changed his mind on the subject, and Jenkinson. On religious toleration he stressed that his views were different from those of Pitt and he supported the full repeal of the Test Acts, which still imposed certain disabilities upon non-conformists.[76] When in Parliament, however, expediency triumphed, and on a motion of Sheridan's to relieve dissenters and Catholics from the disabilities imposed by the Acts, he took Pitt's advice and absented himself.[77] Catholic Emancipation always had his support but the reasons for his views on this question were those of expediency. He saw it as necessary for the tranquillity of Ireland, with war or massacre as the alternative.[78] Canning was usually ready to listen to the case for reforms if it were made on grounds of expediency, but like Burke he was wholly unwilling to subject established institutions to a critique based on a merely speculative philosophy.

This helps to account for what some may see as an inconsistency in Canning's politics. As he grew older his opposition to parliamentary reform hardened, while his support, in principle, for Catholic Emancipation was steady. Canning saw the arguments for the former as stemming from general principles, the application of which to existing institutions he regarded as illegitimate. Arguments from expediency, which he might have considered, he felt did not apply, for Britain had 'the best practicable Government that the world has ever seen, that of America perhaps excepted'.[79] The effects of the French Revolution had cured him of applying philosophical abstractions to practical affairs.

While this philosophy in Canning's case did not lead to ultra-Toryism, it is fundamentally and by definition anti-Radical. What separated him from the ultra-Tory opponents of all reforms was a belief that expediency might on occasion dictate a change in the status quo. One might ask why Canning was not a right-wing Whig, and here Canning's personal circumstances weighed heavily. Unconnected with any of the great Whig clans he could never force himself on the Crown by means of aristocratic combination, and thus to justify his position he could only plead the favour of the Crown, and attack

> ... those principles, which maintain that *certain families* ought always to be at the top of the administration, that there is a sort of *descendible* right to posts of office and dignity, a kind of *hereditary* ministry in the Russells and Cavendishes, to the utter exclusion of all *plebeian* merit and *unconnected* ability – or at least to the exclusion of them from all offices, but such as they may hold *under* the Great Monopolising Whig corporation – these principles I have always held in ridicule and dislike as composing the most tyrranous, arrogant, and absurd system that ever was devised for the government of a free country.[80]

Lady Holland was half right when she said of Canning:

> He is, in his heart, the veriest Jacobin there is, and would, if he were not in power, manifest his principles in a most dangerous, innovating opposition. He abhors titles, and the aristocracy of hereditary nobility; the lowness of his own extraction first made

him envy then wish to destroy, those whom chance had raised above him.[81]

But it is not true he was a Jacobin at heart in the sense that the policies he favoured, even secretly, were of a radical nature. However, Windham's definition of Jacobinism as the revolt of the talents of a country against its property helps to illuminate Canning's position, for his career more than that of any of his contemporaries was an assertion of the claims of personal brilliance against inherited position. That underneath he felt the inferiority of his own origins is demonstrated by his attacks on those of his opponents – Whitbread's brewing interests and the Duke of Northumberland's 'Smithson' forebears were to be subjects for his wit. Had he never found patronage, disappointment might have driven him to Radicalism. As it was, he remained essentially a defender of a status quo which provided him, perhaps fortuitously, with the opportunities he sought.

Canning was not short of friends. In some ways this is surprising for he had a limited range of interests. He was always a theatre-goer, but music meant little to him, and at one time he refused the dedication of a piece of music, arguing that his acceptance of it 'would reflect some ridicule both on himself and on the composer'.[82] He had little interest in the fine arts in an age in which some of the great private collections were being built up. His appreciation of literature was largely confined to the ancient classics and his ideal form for poetry was the Augustan couplet. He urged Walter Scott to model himself on Dryden, whose metre was 'at once the most artificial and the most magnificent that the language affords'.[83]

As a result of this attitude contemporary literature was largely a closed book to Canning. Nor did he express any interest in the natural sciences; indeed on some subjects he was remarkably ignorant, as witnessed by Hookham Frere's anecdote that Canning was unaware that tadpoles turned into frogs.

Despite these limitations Canning was an excellent conversationalist. At Oxford he had been wont to stay up till the small hours deep in discourse, usually of a political nature, and simply to talk and listen (but especially to talk) remained perhaps the greatest delight in his life. It was undoubtedly the wit and originality he displayed in discourse which won him the ardent coterie of friends

and admirers he always possessed. Furthermore, he knew how
to put himself on good terms with people; he won the affection of
Lady Stafford when at one of their meetings he told her that what
most attracted him to their son, Granville Leveson-Gower, was
the affection with which the latter had 'uniformly spoken' of the
Marquess and herself. 'This', wrote Lady Stafford, 'pleased my
old Heart . . .'[84]

There were nevertheless those who disliked him. Among his
political opponents this was to be expected; Grey in particular
came to detest him, though his private friendship with Sheridan
survived the political breach.[85] However, he also appears to have
genuinely frightened some others, particularly women. If Canning
came to see her, wrote Lady Bessborough, Granville Leveson-
Gower's mistress,

> . . . what possible chance have I of escaping under the eye of a
> person who judges every one with severity, women particularly,
> and me perhaps more than any other woman? I know myself
> too well not to be certain that when tried by strict justice, I
> must be dislik'd and condemned. . . . As yet, whenever I have
> happen'd to see Mr Canning, I have appear'd before him as a
> criminal before his judge.[86]

The Dowager Countess of Erroll, who later married Canning's
close friend Hookham Frere, also disliked Canning. 'Do not open
this before that Canning man,' she wrote as a postscript to one of
her letters, 'I am afraid of him.'[87]

Some of the dislike for him may be accounted for by his anti-
feminist views. He did not believe that women had any place in
politics and it was hardly surprising that Lady Holland, for whom
politics was as natural an environment as the stage for a player,
disliked him. These views also caused difficulties with his Aunt
Hetty who held vehemently Whig views. At one time he wrote to
the Leighs that he thought she had at last come to her senses, and
'seen that a woman has no business at all with Politicks – or that
if she thinks at all about them, it should be at least in a feminine
manner – as wishing for the Peace and Prosperity of her Country;
for the success and credit of her Family (if she has any) who are
engaged in the practical part of Politicks'.[88]

Whereas Canning's brilliance and wit undoubtedly won him
many friends, it is nevertheless true that he was unduly conscious

of his own worth and disposed to resentment when the appropriate deference was not forthcoming. This aspect of his personality was to have drastic effects between 1809 and 1812 and accounts for his long subsequent exile from the highest offices.

The lighter side of Canning's nature was revealed in his love of practical jokes. On one occasion he and his friends arranged a hoax in which the victims, the Rev. Edward Legge and Lord Boringdon, were persuaded to visit a non-existent chapel in Cateaton Street to hear a Swiss preacher. The expedition was written up in verse and widely circulated.[89] Another practical joke caused a breach with Jenkinson. The latter had become a Colonel of Militia, and Canning and his friends wrote a bogus handbill inviting recruits to the regiment. Sitting up till 4 am at Lady Malmesbury's together with Charles and George Ellis, they produced the handbill which commenced:

> *To all Brave, aspiring, invincible Hero's*
> *No Republican Roundheads, but true Cavallero's —*
> *All right lads, who would wish for a fair opportunity*
> *Of defying the Frenchman with perfect impunity —*
> *All whose hearts are so warm, and whose limbs are so boney,*
> *As to love a good King, and to ride a stout Poney —*
> *Big bounties, strong beer, and good quarters and Glory!*
> *What a delicate prospect is open before ye!*
> *Come on, my brave Lads! not to bloodshed and murder —*
> *I vow from my thoughts there is nothing that's further;*
> *Tis the bold Colonel Jenkinson calls you to arm*
> *And solomnly swears you shall come to no harm.*[90]

The whole was accompanied by a picture 'of a Fencible Sergt. chasing sans culottes into the Water' prepared as from a printer and delivered to Jenkinson so that he would believe that such handbills were really distributed. Unfortunately Jenkinson did not see the joke and was deeply hurt by the ridicule, especially when the verses were read out by Edward Legge after they had been delivered to Jenkinson at dinner. Lady Malmesbury sat with him for two hours trying to soothe him. The Dean of Christchurch, Dr Jackson, arrived at the height of the incident and on learning the circumstances commented, 'Upon my word, for three members of Parliament as foolish a business as ever I heard ... why, Child, this is more nonsensical than you used to be at Christchurch, where you were quarrelling and making up again all day long – pretty people to govern a nation truly – I see what work you all make of it, as soon as you get from under my government.'[91] It was a fortnight after the incident before Canning and Jenkinson made up the quarrel.

Between 1770 and 1794 Canning had risen from a most unpromising origin to a position where he was patently on the verge of great opportunities. Apart from the fact that he was still not financially secure, the only real cloud on his horizon was indifferent health. His diary frequently records ailments, usually merely a cold, but the effects were often severe and led to fever and confinement to bed. Thus on 24 February 1794 he recorded the onset of an illness, probably a form of influenza, which by 30 March had forced him to take to his bed for nearly five days.[92] These illnesses were not so much serious as frequent, but later in his life in addition to these complaints he suffered severe gout, which was both agonizing and debilitating.

Politically, Canning had by 1794 reached a position from which he was not radically to deviate, though the shift of circumstances changed the emphasis in his ideas. He was a believer in the status quo, but as a workable arrangement rather than as an ideal. He was also prepared to redress real grievances where the demands of expediency, as in the case of Catholic Emancipation, or Christian morality, as in the case of the slave trade, demanded it. To a merely speculative political philosophy, whether tending to uphold or subvert the existing constitutional arrangements, he was an uncompromising opponent.

2
YOUNG CANNING
IN OFFICE

In his first year in Parliament Canning had consolidated his already considerable reputation. He had also shown himself a party man through and through and enhanced his prospects of advancement. Pitt thought highly of him and the two met frequently. As a mark of esteem, at the end of 1794 Pitt asked him to second the Address to the Throne. As Canning recounted the incident, this seems to have been a last minute decision on Pitt's part; he had discussed the question with Pitt two days before the speech and Pitt said he had not made up his mind on the question: then just after midnight he received a note from Pitt asking if he would be the seconder.[1]

The debate was essentially over the policy of continuing the war. Military misfortunes in the previous year had lessened its popularity, and some saw in the emergence of a more moderate government in France with the overthrow of Robespierre the opportunity of making peace. An amendment to the address was to be moved by Wilberforce which suggested that following the recent changes in France and the negotiations entered into by the Dutch States-General, it was expedient to 'endeavour to restore the blessings of peace to His Majesty's subjects, and to his allies, upon just and favourable terms'.[2]

Such an amendment might have been expected from the Foxites, but was more of a threat when made by the Evangelical Member for Yorkshire for he was a friend of Pitt, had a fair measure of prestige and was normally a supporter of the Government. To keep the country gentlemen from breaking ranks Pitt had chosen Sir Edward Knatchbull, the Member for Kent, to move the address. While a supporter of Government, he was not involved with it in any official way and it was clear that it was Canning's task to put the Government's viewpoint. He dismissed the suggestion that the rise of moderates to power in France radically changed the situation, for 'the hostility of the moderates towards this country was equal to that of the Jacobins'. Above all, he argued, Britain could not make peace with any government in France till she was convinced of its stability, otherwise she would be obtaining not peace, but a short and delusive armistice. As to the war, he looked to ultimate success through the exhaustion of French resources, while our own were 'not only unexhausted, but as yet comparatively untouched'.[3] The Original Address was carried by 246 votes to 73, and Canning could congratulate himself on his performance.

It was obvious that while Pitt's favour persisted, office could not long elude Canning. It was probably in his mind in a debate on 21 March 1795 when Fox had moved for a Committee of the Whole House on the State of the Nation. The general nature of the motion allowed Canning to range far and wide; in answer to opposition attacks on the scope of the patronage at the disposal of the Government, he was able to reply that the wages of office 'equalizes the classes of society, by enabling the state to avail itself of the talents of all its citizens; which opens as wide the doors of the senate-house and of the cabinet, to acquired eminence and plebeian worth, as to ancestral dignity and hereditary virtue'.[4] The reforms suggested by the Opposition, he went on, 'would go to unpopularize the constitution in the most eminent degree; to throw all power into the hands of the rich; and to exclude from situations of trust and service in the country all those whose talents or whose virtues might want the aid of birth and fortune to introduce them'.

It is difficult to believe that Canning did not have his own case eminently in mind when he said this. He still met regularly with Pitt to discuss parliamentary affairs in general,[5] and on 16 June they talked about the possibilities of Canning coming into office. Probably because of Canning's family connection with that country, Pitt suggested that eventually he should become Chief Secretary of Ireland after first taking minor office at home. However, the project of making Canning Under-Secretary at the Home

Office fell through when the Duke of Portland, the Secretary of State, said that the office was filled.[6]

This eventuality helped to shape Canning's career, for Pitt now turned to Lord Grenville, the Foreign Secretary, to get his consent to making Canning Under-Secretary at the Foreign Office. By 28 October Canning was able to write that everything was settled and that the only remaining task was to 'unfix' Mr Aust, the incumbent of the office, and find him a new place.[7] This proceeding being concluded by 2 November,[8] Canning was able to take office in the new year. He spent the second until the fifth of January with Lord Grenville at Dropmore and on the sixth put in his first morning's work at the Foreign Office.[9]

Canning's post was by no means a sinecure and he had to overcome what he confessed was his 'considerable inclination' to 'idleness'.[10] He was less than fair to himself; his diary records a very heavy load of work – in the morning he was at the Foreign Office receiving and answering despatches, meeting political friends in the afternoon and often attending the House of Commons in the evening. Wartime had increased the load on an office which even at the most lax of times was not one of ease. This sudden change in the pace of his life did not upset Canning for he was fundamentally a man of business. In August 1796 he wrote to his friend Lord Boringdon that 'the happiness of constant occupation is infinite'.[11] However, occasionally he showed signs of weariness; in 1797 he complained that couriers had succeeded each other from Lille, where negotiations with the French were being conducted, 'with such rapidity these three or four weeks, that I have been very little at liberty, and hardly a day free from anxious expectation'.[12]

What free time Canning had was usually shortly after the turn of the new year and again in the late summer when he visited friends in the country. He often visited Oxford where he liked to keep in close touch and very frequently travelled on to Derbyshire where he stayed with the Leighs at Ashbourne. These short respites were welcome: 'In the country for a fortnight,' he wrote gleefully to Auckland early in 1797, 'with a fixed determination to be so idle, that even these few lines written to you, are not written, without a sort of effort'.[13] Canning was clearly not of that class of politicians who are only happy when involved in business.

With the expiration of the 1790 Parliament Canning found a

new seat at Wendover in Buckinghamshire, obtained from Robert
Smith, a friend of Pitt and member of the West Indian interest,
who was soon to be created Lord Carrington. He wrote to the
Rev. Leigh in May 1796: 'I returned last night from Wendover
after a day of such noise and bustle and dust and dining and
drinking and smoking and halloing as I hope not to have to
encounter again for many years.'[14] Like Newport, Wendover
was a pocket borough and avoided the disadvantages which Canning attributed to open boroughs. No conscientious person, he
wrote, could prefer Coventry to Looe as the only 'advantages' of
the former were 'being concerned in a good deal of Riot, Bribery,
and Perjury, and having afterwards on all important questions to
surrender (one's) judgement to the instructions of some thousand
Ribband Weavers . . .'[15] As Member for Wendover, Canning was
responsible for his views only to Pitt.

As Under-Secretary for Foreign Affairs Canning was closely
concerned with the policy and direction of the war. Four cabinet
ministers were directly concerned with the war. His official head
was Lord Grenville, the Foreign Secretary. A former Speaker of
the House of Commons, he was a son of George Grenville who
had imposed the Stamp Act on the American colonies in 1765.
He represented the powerful Buckingham interest. His elder
brother, the first Marquess, was a large borough-owner. His
younger brother Thomas was a high-ranking diplomat who, together with their nephew, later the first Duke, was to hold office
under Lord Grenville from 1806 to 1807. Grenville was a strong
supporter of the war and as to policy believed in continental
alliances as the best way of limiting and eventually suppressing
the French danger.

Secretary for War – a new post created in 1794 – was Henry
Dundas. He wielded immense power as political controller of
much of Scotland, whose representative system was so limited as
to make that of England appear by comparison a paradigm of
democracy. His view of the war was rather different from Grenville's. A strong believer in colonial acquisitions as the best method
of draining France of resources, he always remained somewhat
cynical of continental entanglements. Perhaps he looked beyond
the immediate fortunes of the war to the future increase in Britain's
wealth and prestige which he believed were concomitant with
overseas possessions. Unlike Pitt and Grenville he was always a

strong defender of the West Indian interest and an opponent of the abolition of the slave trade.

The Secretary at War was William Windham. Originally in opposition, he had come into the Cabinet in 1794 along with the Duke of Portland and Earls Fitzwilliam and Spencer. His was a strangely brilliant though less strangely wasted mind. Such was his hatred of the popular wisdom that he supported the abolition of the slave trade when the cause had few supporters and was later found with as few last-ditch opponents of the measure. In 1800 he virtually on his own stopped a measure to prohibit bull-fighting, and paid the penalty for defying his constituents in this matter by losing his Norwich seat at the subsequent election. For him the war was a moral crusade against French revolutionary principles: the only way to destroy the infection, he believed, was to destroy it at its source. He was the liaison between the Cabinet and the French *émigrés* with whom he shared the undoubtedly misplaced belief that the best way to fight the war was cooperation with dissident elements inside France.

Holding the ring was Pitt himself, not so strongly committed to any individual strategy as the three Secretaries. Indeed, Pitt's interest was always devoted in the main to home affairs and House of Commons management. However, to him ultimately fell the co-ordination of opinions within his Cabinet and a major part of the decisions as to what the chief direction of the war effort was to be.

Privately as well as publicly Canning was a supporter of the war. In January 1795 he had written to his mother, urging upon her his views on the subject:

Consider that England was forced into the contest, by the manifest aggression and declared ambition of France and by the adoption of such principles of Government (I ought not to call it Government – but this language thank God affords no term to describe it) in that country, as, if suffered to prevail unchecked, must be ultimately subversive of all regular con-stitutions in every neighbouring nation.... [Though France] may *conquer here,* and triumph *there* – yet war exhausts her resources – and in the exhaustion of her resources, is our only hope of her being brought to a good disposition to maintain peace – or of her being unable to carry into full effect an evil disposition to the contrary.[16]

The subsequent year gave little additional cause for optimism. In March 1795 the remains of the Duke of York's army was forced to return to Britain after abandoning the Low Countries to the French. The coalition collapsed as first Prussia and then Holland made peace. Hopes of upsetting the French Government by supporting royalists inside France also came to nought. In June a force of *émigrés* was landed, on Windham's recommendation, in the Vendée, but the scheme failed and the force was annihilated. Worse disasters followed in 1796 with the French invasion of Italy. In a swift campaign Napoleon drove Sardinia and Naples out of the war and added fresh Austrian territory to the list of French conquests, which already included the Austrian Netherlands.

Canning was certainly not immune from the general gloom, though he did not share the feelings of Windham for whom the whole of civilization was tottering. In lighter vein he wrote to him:

> *Come Windham! Celebrate with me*
> *This day of joy and jubilee,*
> *This day of no disaster.*
> *Our Government is not o'erturned*
> *Huzza! – Our Fleet has not been burned*
> *Our Army's not our Master.*[17]

However, even Canning could not keep his spirits up when French successes on the Rhine were added to those in Italy. He wrote to Granville in July: 'The successes of the French upon the Rhine – or rather beyond the Rhine – for *upon* it is now a phrase that but imperfectly describes their progress – are quite disheartening. They are, I am afraid, beyond the power of one great battle to retrieve. . . . I repeat to you that I look forward to an Invasion – or an attempt at it, as almost certain.'[18]

The French successes in Europe which were beyond Britain's unaided power to counteract impelled the Ministry towards the consideration of peace. Also pushing them in this direction was a growing war-weariness in Britain which had already found expression in Wilberforce's amendment to the Address. Nevertheless, if Britain had been unsuccessful in campaigns on land, her maritime supremacy was still unshaken, and this provided security for peripheral activities. French gains in the West Indies in 1795 were reversed in 1796 though at a frightening cost in British losses from disease. In the East, Britain gained Ceylon and the Cape of Good Hope from the Dutch, with whom Britain was now at war. Consequently, Britain could go to the negotiating table not entirely without bargaining counters.

The prospect of negotiation was raised by the Government in the King's speech of December 1795. However, attempts to implement it through the British minister in Switzerland in the subsequent March failed when the French refused to alienate any territories they had annexed to the Republic. As these included the Austrian Netherlands, it was hardly possible for Britain to pursue the question further at that stage, as she was bound by treaty not to make peace without Austrian consent unless Austria's pre-war boundaries were restored.

The subsequent months witnessed several diplomatic setbacks for Britain. Spain moved steadily into the French orbit, signing a Treaty of Alliance at St Idelfonso on 15 August and declaring war on Britain on 5 October. Early in August, Prussia signed two Conventions of Amity. George Hammond, Canning's fellow Under-Secretary, left Berlin on 2 September without anything to show for the efforts of his special mission, and this failure increased the pressures for a renewed attempt at negotiation. Early in September Pitt travelled to Weymouth to discuss the subject with the King. Pitt wrote to his brother on the fourth: 'Hammond's mission has produced nothing effectual at Berlin. We therefore see nothing left (in order to bring the question of peace and war to a point) but to send directly to Paris. The step of applying for a passport will be taken immediately.'[19]

The Cabinet was fairly united on this step, though Windham was hostile to all dealings with the French Republic, being under the influence of Burke who had recently produced his *Letters on a Regicide Peace*. Canning was by no means such an extremist. In 1795 he had written to his mother that peace could be made as soon as a 'stable and intelligible Government' appeared in France,[20] a phrase which could clearly be interpreted as convenience dictated.

The British negotiator was Lord Malmesbury, a personal friend of Canning. George Ellis accompanied him in an unofficial capacity

at Malmesbury's own request. The reception of the negotiators
was by no means unfriendly, and Ellis wrote to Canning of their
good treatment.[21] At first Malmesbury was fairly optimistic. 'It is
undeniable', he wrote late in October, 'that the distresses of the
Directory are extreme, that the cry for peace is universal, that a
total disregard for the general wish might be fatal to them.'[22]

In fact his two months of interviews with Delacroix were singularly fruitless. In November Malmesbury wrote that the Directory
needed the war to continue to secure their internal position,[23] a
flat contradiction of his earlier assessment. By the end of the month
he believed the French Government to be convinced that the real
purpose of his mission was to make observations on the state of the
Republic's internal affairs.[24]

In fact, Britain was offering unrealistic concessions. Grenville
wrote on 11 December that Britain was ready to return all the
possessions she had taken from France in return for the restoration of the Austrian Netherlands and the Milanese.[25] Beyond this
Britain could not easily go because of her engagements to the
Austrians; yet this was not an adequate temptation for the Directory to be impelled towards peace.

There was moreover no agreement as to the status of the
negotiations. Britain wanted France to agree to enter into *pour-
parlers* as to the basis of the negotiations, so that an outline of the
terms could be communicated to their respective allies. France
wanted a clear exposition of the British terms as a basis for a
settlement without reference to the Austrians. By 27 November
Delacroix was complaining that they were moving in a *circle
vicieux*.[26] This correctly describes the negotiations as they proceeded for a further month until the Directory tired of the fruitless
exercise and presented an ultimatum in such terms that Malmesbury left Paris on 21 December.

Canning shared Pitt's desire for peace. In this he was much
more of one mind with the Prime Minister than with Grenville,
whose attitude to the negotiations was far more equivocal. Furthermore, his close relationship with Malmesbury and Ellis meant
that he could keep in touch with events independently of the
Secretary of State. This situation was to be repeated the following
year when the negotiations were renewed.

In April 1797 Pitt pressed upon the King the urgency of
Britain's financial difficulties as a reason for attempting a joint

peace negotiation with the Austrians.[27] The projected despatch of Hammond to Vienna to help secure this end was viewed optimistically by Canning,[28] and when the Austrians reached separate Preliminaries of Peace with the French at Leoben, the need for peace appeared more urgent. In May Canning recorded that he talked to Pitt 'upon the absolute necessity of a communication to Paris under the present circumstances'. Pitt agreed with Canning but stressed that others did not.[29]

The centre of opposition within the Cabinet was the Foreign Secretary, Grenville, while the King himself was hostile. Nevertheless, on 1 June Grenville wrote to Delacroix suggesting a fresh negotiation. The latter agreed, but in terms which Grenville found offensive. When the Cabinet agreed to the negotiations, Grenville expressed his dissent.[30] Pitt himself was a strong supporter of peace, feeling it his duty 'as an English Minister and a Christian to use every effort to stop so bloody and wasting a war'.[31] Canning observed the conflict. 'A Cabinet again at night', he recorded on 15 June. 'Great violence, Lord Grenville nearly going out.' A week later he recorded that a fresh note from the Directory had satisfied Pitt but Grenville was furious against it. Pitt insisted that Lord Grenville agree or 'get out. Lord G. agreed'.[32]

Canning was in a somewhat awkward position, being directly subordinate to Grenville but agreeing with Pitt as to the necessity of ending the war. On 13 July he wrote to George Ellis:

We cannot and must not disguise our situation from ourselves. If peace is to be had, we must have it; I firmly believe we must, and it is a belief that strengthens every day. When Windham says we must not, I ask him, 'Can we have war?' It is out of the question, we have not the means – we have not, what is of all means the most essential, the *mind*. If we are not at peace, we shall be at nothing. . . . For my part, I adjourn my objects of honour and happiness for this country beyond the grave of our military and political consequence, which you are now digging at Lisle. I believe in our resurrection, and find my only comfort in it.[33]

The negotiations were conducted in secrecy. The full story was known in Britain only to Pitt, Grenville, and the two Under-Secretaries, Canning and Hammond. To achieve this, Malmesbury sent from Lille two sets of despatches of which only one was for

general cabinet consumption. Of the replies, only Hammond's
were circulated to the Cabinet in the hope that his execrable handwriting would disguise the true situation from minor members of
the Cabinet. This extraordinary proceeding was, according to
Canning, 'devised by Lord Grenville to *tie up Pitt's tongue alone,*
whom he suspected of communicating with other persons, and
fortifying himself with out-of-doors opinions against the opinions
which might be brought forward in Council by those with whom
he differed in his general view of the Negotiation'.[34]

Britain was prepared to offer the French a restoration of all the
colonial territories she had taken from France, while keeping the
Cape of Good Hope and Trinidad, taken from the Dutch and
Spanish respectively. France wanted first the settling of three
points: a renunciation by Britain of any financial claims upon
Belgium for loans made to the Emperor; a restoration of, or compensation for, ships taken at Toulon; and a renunciation of the
claim still nominally made by the English king to be King of
France.

Surprising as it may seem, Canning treated the last claim as a
serious question with many legal implications. Pitt took a different
view of this – 'I could only get him to make jokes (and those for
the most part bad ones) at dinner today', complained Canning.[35]
However, it was divergences of opinion amongst the French
Government that made for slow progress, though the prospect of
peace brightened when Talleyrand became Minister of Foreign
Affairs in place of Delacroix in July. In Britain, Grenville still
dragged his feet. He disliked the new French conditions and was
extremely pessimistic when an agreement was reached between
the Portuguese minister in Paris and the French, though this was
later repudiated. 'We are still feeling our way', was all he would
concede in a letter to the Russian ambassador.[36] His brother
Buckingham pressed upon him a much more militant viewpoint;
he did not wish him to sign peace except with Louis XVIII, whose
restoration he foresaw in six months time.[37]

At Lille Malmesbury was a tough negotiator. 'I pledge myself',
he wrote to Canning, 'to fight desperately every inch in the East
and West; to cavil at the ninth part of a hair; to wrangle till I am
hoarse for titles, dignity, treaties, ships and what not; nay to live
on patiently at Lisle for the sake of maintaining the smallest portion of either of these.'[38] He was however realistic. In the Austrians

he placed no faith whatever. 'If we again commit ourselves with the Court of Vienna', he wrote, 'we shall be like an old Dutch ambassador with whom I was acquainted, who, after having divorced his wife for the most notorious misbehaviour, intrigued with her and ruined his constitution.'[39] Nor did he have any unrealistic view of favourable political changes in France; what changes had been wrought by 'patience and temper on our part' and by events, made 'the principle on which we set out practicable and by no means whatever justifies our rising in price'.[40]

This posture which combined firmness with conciliation was not assisted by Grenville. In August Malmesbury complained to Canning,

> You must have perceived that the instructions and opinions I get from the Minister under *whose orders I am bound to act* accord so little with the sentiments and intentions I heard expressed by the Minister *with whom I wish to act* that I am placed in a very disagreeable situation ... if I am only to remain here in order to break off the Negotiation creditably, and not to terminate it successfully, I, then, instead of resigning my opinion, must resign my office.[41]

Malmesbury had gone on to express the hope 'that the war party in the Cabinet have not *surprised the religion* of the *pacific* one'. In fact, it was the triumph of a more militant group in France that ended the negotiation. Instead of the expected victory of the Council and Assembly which Maret had assured Malmesbury was imminent,[42] Barras and other Directors engineered a *coup d'état* on *18 Fructidor* (4 September). New representatives arrived at Lille with demands for the return of all English conquests and an additional demand that Malmesbury return to England to secure sufficient powers to negotiate on this basis within twenty-four hours. A step of such impropriety left Malmesbury no alternative but to leave Lille, which he did on 18 September. On 5 October he sent a formal note to the French plenipotentiaries breaking off negotiations.[43]

The failure of a final attempt at peace involving a British offer of bribes to Barras and his friends brought immediate hopes to nought. Malmesbury dwelt on the unluckiness of events, for peace had been very near.[44] These events helped to swing Canning towards the view that treating with the French in their present state of political turmoil was impossible. 'You must be under no apprehension of our secret negotiations leading to anything', he wrote to George Ellis in October, 'I am sure you will be glad to hear . . . that we have but the one plain way before us.'[45] Meanwhile Austria made peace with Bonaparte at Campo Formio – a treaty to which Paris had to accede. Lombardy and Belgium were ceded to the French Republic, while Austria took the now suppressed Republic of Venice in lieu.

The year certainly marked a low point in Britain's fortunes in continental Europe. But though her strategies lay in ruins and her allies were dispersed, Britain's naval supremacy still stood. In February 1797 Admiral Jervis defeated the Spanish Fleet at Cape St Vincent, and in October the Dutch fleet succumbed to Admiral Duncan at Camperdown. The greatest triumph was reserved for the following year. In September 1798 news reached the Cabinet of Nelson's overwhelming victory over the French Admiral Brueys at the Battle of the Nile. Sweeping away the gloom which had been occasioned by Bonaparte's occupation of Egypt, it assured British maritime supremacy in the Mediterranean. Canning wrote in his diary: 'The Victory occupies all our thoughts. It is impossible to talk, write, or think of anything else.'[46]

Yet if Britain were to successfully oppose the French in Europe she could only do so together with her former allies, and of them she remained deeply suspicious. In October 1798 Pitt wrote that even if Austria were to re-engage herself with Great Britain, 'I see no reliance to be placed on such an engagement which would justify the payment of any subsidy to that Court'.[47] When Austria entered the war again in 1797, Canning went so far as to say that he did not care if they were beaten.[48] Both he and Windham remained suspicious of Russian co-operation as well. Unless a 'universal co-operation' could be entered into with the Russians, they felt it better for Britain to 'remain as it is, upon a pure defensive'.[49]

If Canning mistrusted European allies he certainly did not adopt the alternative policy of making peace with France. He was convinced that this was impossible until the opportunity of 'a safe compromise' arose.[50] The prerequisite of this was a stable government in France. The European stalemate, combined with 'the disagreeableness'[51] of his position under Grenville, wearied him of the Under-Secretaryship. In October 1798 Canning wrote to Pitt

saying that he was sick of his present office and asked to be
relieved of it,[52] and so on 1 April 1799 he left the Foreign Office,
thanking Grenville for his 'kindness and understanding'.[53]

Canning was a loyal supporter of Pitt's policies, even when they
were unpopular. In 1795 he wrote to his mother trying to reconcile
her to the new taxes just imposed on the grounds that they pressed
'so lightly upon the lower Orders of the Community'.[54] He was
nevertheless not uncritical, particularly where he felt Britain's
internal security was threatened. After the naval mutiny at the
Nore in May 1797 he called on Pitt and 'recommended vigorous
measures – Parliamentary Declaration, etc., etc. He promised a
Cabinet – No such measure taken. All concession – All silence in
Parliament'.[55] On 26 May he wrote, 'Grey's motion for Reform in
Parlt. Pitt spoke early – and not as he ought to have done – not
stout and scouting the whole thing as a Jacobin question – but
argumentation – and flatly. This made it impossible for others
to speak aftds. *on principle*.'[56] In Parliament Canning supported
all the Government's measures for preserving security by suppressing traditional liberties: in 1795 he spoke in favour of the
Seditious Meetings Bill[57] and in 1798 and 1800 he spoke in favour
of the continuance of the act suspending Habeas Corpus.[58] His
opinions on these matters are also revealed by an incident which
occurred in 1798. He learnt that a man had been trying to see him
for some days. 'Of course,' wrote Canning, 'I did not see him –
especially as my Servant mentioned his being an Irishman, and
I have more than once found the information coming under such
circumstances to relate exclusively to the state of the informer's
finances, and his desire for immediate and lucrative employment.'[59]
In fact as it turned out the man was connected with the Irish rebellion, but Canning did not betray his confidence when he discovered this, even though it technically made him guilty of
misprision of treason.

Canning played a full part in parliamentary life, speaking on a
variety of subjects. Office brought personal attacks, and in 1797
Fox argued that the provision of a place for Mr Aust in order
to free the Under-Secretaryship for Canning was a corrupt practice.[60] Such accusations were commonplace, though more extreme
was the unfounded suggestion in *The Morning Chronicle* that
Canning was using his inside knowledge for purposes of stock-
jobbing. As Lord Grenville was in the House of Lords, Canning

was called on to speak on questions of war policy, though this was
rendered somewhat less arduous by the secession from Parliament
of Fox and his leading friends. In December 1798 Canning had
to answer Tierney's motion for peace with France. He reverted to
the more general arguments on European security which the
Government had used at the outset of the war, proclaiming that
'we can be but precariously safe, as long as there is no safety for
the *rest of Europe*.'[61] The speech was a success, though it clearly
demonstrated that Canning shared some misconceptions with the
rest of his colleagues as to the state of European opinion. Clearly
inspired by the *émigrés* was his sympathy for 'the people of the
Netherlands driven into insurrection and struggling for their
freedom against the heavy hand of a merciless tyranny'.[62] This
attitude was to lead to the disastrous Anglo-Russian expedition
to the Helder the following autumn.

Despite his ministerial and parliamentary activities, Canning
had time to lend his literary talents to the defence of the established order. From November 1797 till midsummer 1798 he
collaborated with J. Hookham Frere, George Ellis, and William
Gifford (later to become the first editor of the *Quarterly Review*)
to produce a weekly publication *The Anti-Jacobin or Weekly
Examiner*. This was published every Monday during the parliamentary sitting, defending the Government and its politics, and
above all attacking the whole philosophy they saw as underpinning
Jacobinism. Canning took the exercise very seriously; in 1795 he
had attacked 'an evil more poisonous than plague or famine, I
mean the propagation of Principles subversive of all social order
and all human happiness'.[63] *The Anti-Jacobin* minced no words.
The twentieth edition included an 'Ode to Jacobinism' which
began:

> *Daughter of Hell, insatiate Power,*
> *Destroyer of the Human Race . . .*[64]

The Anti-Jacobin was at once the attack of the conservative
against the current radical ideology, of the traditional moralist
against subjectivist ethics, and of the classicist against German
Romanticism. The prospectus underlined its general philosophy:

We have not yet learned the modern refinement of referring in
all considerations upon human conduct, not to any settled and

preconceived principles of right and wrong, not to any general and fundamental rules which experience, and wisdom, and justice and the common consent of mankind have established, but to the internal admonitions of every man's judgement or conscience in his own particular instance ... we do not dissemble – that we reverence Law – we acknowledge USAGE – we even look upon PRESCRIPTION without hatred or horror.

The journal mixed argument and satire. The first issue commenced with a dissection of 'the Jacobin poet' who would sing paeans of praise for the victories of Bonaparte, embellished with such scenes as 'phalanxes of Republicans shouting victory, satellites of Despotism biting the ground':

But let his own country triumph, or her allies obtain an advantage; straightaway the 'beauteous face of war' is changed; the 'pride, pomp and circumstance' of victory are kept carefully out of sight – and we are presented with nothing but contusions and amputations, plundered peasants and deserted looms. Our Poet points the thunder of his blank verse at the head of the recruiting Serjeant, or roars in dithyrambics against the Lieutenants of Pressgangs. ...'[65]

The first issue also contained Canning's classic satire on Southey's 'Inscription for the Apartment in Chepstow Castle, where Henry Marten the Regicide was imprisoned thirty years'. Southey had written:

For thirty years secluded from mankind
Here Marten linger'd. Often have these walls
Echoed his footsteps, as with even tread
He pac'd around his prison – not to him
Did nature's fair varieties exist;
He never saw the sun's delightful beams,
Save when through yon high bars he pour'd a sad
And broken splendour. Dost though ask his crime?
He had rebell'd against a King, and sat in judgement on him;
for his ardent mind
Shap'd goodliest plans of happiness on earth,
And peace and liberty. Wild dreams! but such
As Plato lov'd; such as with holy zeal

Our Milton worshipp'd. Blessed hopes! awhile
From man witheld, even to the latter days
When CHRIST shall come, and all things be fulfilled.[66]

In parody, Canning wrote an 'Inscription for the Door of the
Cell in Newgate, where Mrs Brownrigg, the Prentice-Cide, was
confined previous to her execution'.

For one long term, or e'er her trial came,
Here Brownrigg linger'd. Often have these cells
Echoed her blasphemies, as with shrill voice
She scream'd for fresh Geneva. Not to her
Did the blithe fields of Tothill, or thy street
St Giles its fair varieties expand;
Till at last in slow drawn cart she went
To execution. Dost thou ask her crime?
SHE WHIPP'D TWO FEMALE PRENTICES TO DEATH,
AND HID THEM IN THE COAL-HOLE. For her mind
Shap'd strictest plans of discipline. Sage schemes!
Such as Lycurgus taught, when at the shrine of the
Orthyan Goddess he bade flog the little Spartans;
such as erst chastised
Our Milton when at College. For this act
Did Brownrigg swing. Harsh laws! But time shall come,
When France shall reign, and laws be all repeal'd![67]

Much of the Journal's efforts was devoted to attacking the
opposition press. Misrepresentations were exposed and the
Government was congratulated when it withdrew its advertisements from *The Morning Chronicle, The Morning Post* and *The
Courier*.[68] Effort was also devoted to explaining and defending
such government policies as its new plan of finance.[69] It supported
the Government during the Irish crisis by printing the 'Loyal
Address of the Citizens of Derry to Earl Camden' and unearthing
such facts as that at Ballinderry all the Catholics had signed an
address attacking the rebellious United Irishmen.[70] Whig leaders
were attacked. The leading article in the thirteenth issue rejoiced
over the dismissal of the Duke of Norfolk from the Lieutenancy
of the West Riding of Yorkshire;[71] Fox's birthday celebrations
were made a subject for mirth[72] and the third issue contained a
spurious account, supposed to be by *The Morning Chronicle*, of

a speech to be made by Fox after the Revolution justifying various despotic measures.[73] The latter was by Frere, but Canning was delighted with it, specially recommending it to the Rev. Leigh.[74]

The satire was by no means always kind. Mockery was made of the Duke of Northumberland's less than noble lineage in a poem which perhaps reveals Canning's underlying distaste for those of a higher birth than his own. 'Duke Sm-ths-n [Smithson] of N-rth-mb-rl-nd' was portrayed as declaring:

> *No drop of Princely Percy's blood*
> *Through these cold veins doth run;*
> *With Hotspur's Castles, blazon, name,*
> *I still am poor Sm-ths-n.*[75]

The fact that the strongly pro-slave-trade Member of Parliament for Liverpool, Banastre Tarleton, was still at that time a Whig, gave *The Anti-Jacobin* review further opportunity for satire, when at a supposed 'Meeting of the Friends of Freedom', an altercation was caused when Tarleton gave the traditional Whig toast of 'The Cause of Freedom all over the world', 'only to be interrupted by Olandah Equiano, the African, and Henry Yorke, the Mulatto'.[76]

Only occasionally was *The Anti-Jacobin* stylistically similar to the old *Microcosm*, though one exception was a long and very elaborate mathematical, philosophical and only at the end political poem on *The Loves of Triangles,* replete with a vast amount of mathematical imagery.[77]

In the thirtieth issue there began *The Rovers* on which Canning, Frere and Ellis co-operated. Much of this play was an attack on current German literature, with the very strong implication that in rejecting the classical mould one was automatically associating with Jacobinism. Typically, the play was extremely humorous. Rogero's song contained the immortal lines:

> *When e'er with haggard eyes I view*
> *This dungeon that I'm rotting in,*
> *I think of those companions true*
> *Who studied with me at the U———*
> *———niversity of Gottingen*
> *———niversity of Gottingen.*[78]

'Young Pottinger' pleaded his plight:

Oppressed by the tyranny of an abbot, persecuted by the jealousy of a count, the betrothed husband of my sister languishes in loathsome captivity. Her lover is fled no one knows whither – and I, her brother, am torn from my paternal roof, and from my studies in chirugery, to seek him and her, I know not where – to rescue Rogero, I know not how. Comrades, your counsel! – my search fruitless – my money gone – my baggage stolen! What am I to do? In yonder abbey – in these dark dank vaults, there, my friends – there lies Rogero – There Matilda's Heart.[79]

Matilda herself is positively Gilbertian:

Dinner – it is taken away as soon as over, and we regret it not! It returns again with the return of appetite. The beef of tomorrow will succeed to the mutton of today, as the mutton of today succeeded to the veal of yesterday. But when once the heart has been occupied by a beloved object, in vain would we attempt to supply the chasm by another. How easily are our desires transferred from dish to dish! Love only, dear, delusive, delightful love, restrains our wandering appetites, and confines them to a particular gratification![80]

This play was not without its effect in Germany. It aroused the fury of the German historian Niebuhr, who regarded Canning as 'a sort of political Cossack'.[81]

It was probably the poetry of *The Anti-Jacobin* that was most effective as it was both witty and readily memorable. This was largely by Canning; none would forget the famous satire on 'The Friend of Humanity and the Knife-Grinder' in which the former grieves at the wrongs he supposed the other had suffered, either from 'the squire, for killing of his game? or Covetous parson, for his titles distraining? Or roguish lawyer, [who] made you lose your title All in a lawsuit?'

Philanthropy evaporates when the friend of humanity discovers that the knife-grinder wants nothing to do with politics but only sixpence to drink a pot of beer.[82] Most remembered of all is the poem on the 'New Morality' which was put in the final issue. It began by proclaiming its aim:

> *From mental mists to purge a nation's eyes*
> *To animate the weak, unite the wise,*

> *To trace the deep infection, that pervades*
> *The crowded town, and taints the rural shades.*

One by one the evils of revolutionary philosophy are enumerated.
First, there came the man imbued with French philanthropy:

> *What, shall a name, a word, a sound control*
> *The aspiring thought, and cramp the expansive soul?*
> *Shall one half-peopled island's rocky round*
> *A love, that glows for all Creation bound? . . .*
> *No narrow bigot he –* his *reason'd view*
> *Thy interests, England, rank with thine, Peru!*
> *France at our door, he sees no danger nigh,*
> *But heaves for Turkey's woes the impartial sigh;*
> *A steady Patriot, of the world alone,*
> *The friend of every Country – but his own.*

Next, Canning attacked 'sensibility', as distorted by Rousseau,
that feels

> *For the crush'd beetle* first – *the widow'd dove,*
> *And all the warbled sorrows of the grove;*
> *Next for poor Suffering Guilt – and* last *of all,*
> *For Parents, Friends, a King and Country's Fall.*

French Justice and Candour were also to be eschewed. An alternative philosophy was then proclaimed.

> *I love the bold uncompromising mind,*
> *Whose principles are fix'd, whose views defined;*
> *Who scouts and scorns, in canting Candour's spite*
> *All* taste *in morals, innate sense of right,*
> *And Nature's impulse, all unchecked by art,*
> *And feelings fine that float about the heart;*
> *Content, for good men's guidance, bad men's awe*
> *On moral truth to rest and Gospel law.*
> *Who owns, when Traitors feel the avenging rod,*
> *Just retribution at the hand of God.*

Having dealt with principles, Canning then attacked individuals,
both in France and Britain, including a famous hymn based on
Milton, inviting English Radicals to worship Réveillère –
Lepeaux, who was attempting to promote a new revolutionary

religion. In the middle of a long list of supposed worshippers
came

> *Couriers and Stars, Sedition's Evening Host,*
> *Thou* Morning Chronicle, *and* Morning Post,
> *Whether ye make the Rights of man your theme,*
> *Your Country libel, and your God blaspheme,*
> *Or dirt on private worth and virtue throw*
> *Still blasphemous or blackguard, praise Lepeaux!*

Canning presents us with a procession of Romantics and Radicals,
lambasting them together, and ends up with a warning to Britain
that if, untrue to herself, she became 'French *in heart*'

> *– the victory crowns our brow*
> *Low at our feet, though prostrate nations bow,*
> *Wealth gild our cities, commerce crown our shore,*
> *London may shine, but England is no more.*[83]

In the middle of 1798 *The Anti-Jacobin* ceased publication in
that form; its work, as its authors declared, done. Apart from any
political effects, it had re-established Canning's reputation for
wit and literary prowess which he had first earned in the days of
The Microcosm.

Before 1799 it would appear that Canning had never been involved in any deep relationship with a woman but now he became
deeply involved with a married woman, and it would seem highly
plausible that this was Caroline of Brunswick, the Princess of
Wales. The relationship between her and the future George IV
had turned, almost on acquaintance, from mutual distrust to
hatred, and the Princess was no more loath than her husband to
supply the consequent deficiency in her life with extra-marital
relationships.

Canning was introduced to her and her Blackheath circle by
Lord Malmesbury. Always attractive to women, he was her life-
long friend and sympathizer. Later in life this was to force his
resignation from the Cabinet. She would appear to be the most
plausible candidate to fit references in his letters to Granville of
1799. In August he wrote: 'I am this moment returned from my
visit. The keeper left us for a few minutes. And the thing is too
clear to be doubted. What am I to do? I am perfectly bewildered.'[84]
In a further letter he wrote of 'the abundant and overpowering

temptations to the indulgence of a passion ... which must have been dangerous, perhaps ruinous, to her who was the cause of it, and to myself. ...' Also, 'the day of the last dinner was not quite so blameless as I promised you it should be. I have had one other interview, in which I took leave for a long time, for the Keeper is going on a visit to her friends in the Country, and during her absence I have said I cannot possibly call at the r.T. or elsewhere. This gains two or three months.'[85]

It was in August 1799 that he gained relief from this passion whose indulgence would have been high treason. Staying at Walmer Castle, occupied by Pitt by virtue of his being Lord Warden of the Cinque Ports, he met Miss Joan Scott. This lady was wealthy and of a well-established family. Her paternal grand-father was David Scott of Scotstarvit, Fife. By profession an advocate, he represented Fife in Parliament from 1741 to 1747 and Aberdeen Burghs from 1751 to 1766. After Walpole's death, he transferred his allegiance from the Opposition to the Government. The family was well connected: his half-nephew was the Earl of Mansfield; his wife was Lucy, daughter of Sir Robert Gordon whose family were premier baronets in Scotland; his brother-in-law, also Sir Robert Gordon, was MP for Caithness after being forgiven his part in the 1715 rebellion. According to the *History of Parliament*, he was renowned for cruelty to his tenants. David Scott's second son was John Scott. Like his rela-tives, he became an MP, representing Caithness from 1754 to 1761, Tain Burghs from 1761 to 1768 and Fife from 1768 to 1775. By profession he was a soldier; in 1762 he became Colonel of the 26th Regiment of Foot and in 1770 he became a major-general. In 1769 he visited America with his regiment.

Financially John Scott started with very little. The position of colonel was one that could be turned to personal profit due to the system of paying the colonel a block sum for the maintenance of his regiment. However, the main foundation of his fortune was gambling. Horace Walpole recorded that in 1755 Sir John Bland lost £32,000 'to a Captain Scott who at present has nothing but a few debts and his commission'.[86] When he died in 1775, George Selwyn wrote to Lord Carlisle: 'The place of Nickster which is in the Devils gift and vacated by John Scott is not disposed of. We go into mourning on Thursday. The waiters are to have crepes round their arms and the dice to be black and the spots white, during the time of wearing weepers, and the dice box unmuffled.' He also suggested a motto *Sic Dice Placuit*.[87]

Gambling was indeed the foundation of his fortunes. It was an age in which fabulous sums could change hands in a frighteningly short period, and Scott was amongst that group known as 'hounds' whose main function was to deprive those of a higher social status of the means to maintain it. Money having obtained for General Scott his social position, he established his seat at Balcomie near Crail in Fife. Indeed Sir Walter Scott described him as the head of the clan.[88]

On the 6 November 1770 General Scott married Lady Mary Hay at Craighouse, the Forfarshire seat of her father Alexander Lockhart. On her mother's side she was of good Jacobite stock; her great-grandfather the fifth Earl of Linlithgow was attainted after the 1715 rebellion, and her grandfather was the fourth Earl of Kilmarnock, executed in 1746.

But the marriage was not ordained to last, and herein lies a tale in the best tradition of eighteenth-century farce. The scene changes to the Red Lion Inn at Barnet where on 4 October 1771 Lady Mary Hay arrived in the company of Captain James Sutherland of the 26th Foot, who ordered the innkeeper to 'get a bed ready with all haste'. After dining on mutton chops and port wine they retired to bed at 9 pm. At 2 am General Scott arrived in the company of friends and inquired as to the presence of a lady and gentleman of the description of his wife and her lover.

The General walked upstairs and rapped on the appropriate door, which Captain Sutherland opened, candle in hand, and immediately slammed in the General's face. Outside the ostler was putting away the horses, when he was surprised to see an upstairs window open and a man dressed only in shirt and night-cap jump out and run into the neighbouring fields whither he and others unsuccessfully pursued him.

Meanwhile upstairs, General Scott had ordered the bedroom door to be broken. Inside the room was a frightened Lady Mary Hay, totally naked, who fell on her knees and begged the General not to kill her. The bed was investigated and it was found 'that the sheets were very much rumpled, and there were several spots on the said sheets as if a man and woman had lain together therein'. The General and his wife returned to Scotland; divorce proceedings were instituted and the marriage was dissolved by the Edinburgh consistorial court on 18 December 1771. Nothing was seen of Captain Sutherland till he returned to the inn, dirty, tired and torn by brambles on the evening of 5 October. He revealed he had spent the entire day hiding in a haystack.[89]

Though doubtless chastened by the experience, General Scott remarried in 1773. His new wife was Margaret, daughter of Robert Dundas of Armistone, by his second wife Ann Gordon. This marriage brought Scott in contact with the powerful Dundas clan. Robert and William Dundas, MPs, were his wife's half-nephews. Most significantly, her brother was Henry Dundas, later to be Secretary of State, friend of Pitt and through family and governmental interest, political controller of most of Scotland. General Scott's new wife quickly bore him two daughters – Henrietta in 1774 and Lucy in March 1775. In December 1775 General Scott died and Joan Scott was then born to him posthumously on the 14 March 1776. *The Scots Magazine* commented: 'So the general's issue is three daughters, and, according to the London papers, he died worth upwards of £300,000 in money, besides a considerable property in land.'[90]

As the children were left fatherless, though wealthy, other members of the family played a part in their upbringing. It was because Joan Scott was Henry Dundas' niece that she was at Walmer at the same time as Canning. By this time her mother had died and Joan was assisted in her affairs by her brother-in-law, though being an heiress in her own right she was independent of his control. Her eldest sister Henrietta had married the Marquess of Titchfield in 1795. He was the son of the third Duke of Portland whose title he was to take on the latter's death in 1809. Her other sister Lucy had married Lord Doune, heir to the Dukedom of Moray, but she died in 1798. It was consequently to be with the Marquess of Titchfield that Canning carried out his negotiations.

A lady of Joan Scott's wealth and position was never without suitors.[91] She had recently broken off an affair with Arthur Paget,[92] the second son of the Earl of Uxbridge. An heiress of her means could certainly expect to marry both aristocracy and wealth. Since Canning was merely a rising young politician of small means and dubious origins, in pursuing his intentions towards Joan Scott he was risking a humiliating rebuff. He used his friend Granville's sister Susan as an intermediary, and he was certainly conscious

of the problems involved. On 15 August 1799 he wrote to Susan
describing how

> ... in about ten minutes I had confessed to you a passion con-
> ceived in less than ten days for a girl with God knows how many
> thousand pounds, the sister of one who had recently blended
> her name with a Dukedom – and imposed upon you the task
> of finding out her disposition towards me. I cannot but feel
> some apprehension lest you should have fancied that you saw
> something of sordidness and vanity in the whole proceed-
> ing ...[93]

He had ample time to make himself known to Joan Scott as
he contrived to ask Dundas to press him to stay on at Walmer.
It is evidence of his close relationship with Pitt that he was one of
the few people in whom at this stage he confided. Meanwhile Lady
Susan raised Canning's case with Joan herself and informed Canning of her response. The latter's reply revealed all the anxieties
of the lover; he referred to 'that part of your first conversation in
which she declared that she had found me very different from
what she expected. I dare not conjecture in what this difference
may have consisted.'
Joan Scott had spoken of her desire that the man she should
marry would have at least a competency to join to her fortune –
and she knew of the hazard in which such a competency would be
placed by politics. Canning in reply hinted of various political
offices he might receive from Pitt which would help to compensate
for the disparity of fortunes. On one point Canning was adamant:
'My hopes and desires and taste and turn of mind are bent, I fear,
irrecoverably to public objects: and I should certainly look for,
in a wife, a mind which at least would not revolt from what must
form the subject of my thoughts. . . .'
Canning kept up the pressure. He did not let himself be
deterred by Joan's comment that the 'fancy of a week would very
soon pass away' and rejected Lady Susan's advice not to revisit
Walmer for a while. On 20 September he wrote to Lady Susan:
'Facts (so far as you state them) are discouraging; but your infer-
ences from them (vague and general as they are) have something
consoling in them.'[94]
In fact the relationship flourished. The Marquess of Titchfield,
Joan's brother-in-law, was also a friend of Canning, and he allowed

his early reservations to be overborne. By May 1800 Canning was able to write to Lady Stafford that Joan had finally decided to be his.[95]

The wedding took place at half past seven on the evening of 8 July 1800 at Brook Street. The Rev. Leigh officiated. Only a small party was present. Canning, Leigh, Frere and Pitt shared a coach to the ceremony. On the way an observer exclaimed, 'What, Billy Pitt! and with a parson too', to which Frere replied, 'He thinks you are going to Tyburn to be hanged privately'.

Pitt was so nervous at the wedding that he could not sign as a witness. 'Had Canning been Pitt's own son,' wrote Frere, 'I do not think he could have been more interested in all that related to this marriage.'[96]

Canning was indeed fortunate in his choice of bride. He was now freed from many of his financial worries and could thus look on a political career with an assurance that only an independence of fortune can provide. Had he tarried his case could well have been otherwise. Within a few months of his marriage Canning was, along with Pitt himself, out of office. Lady Malmesbury wrote: 'Canning is in luck to have married in 1800, for from what I hear by well-informed persons, he would have stood a much worse chance for Miss Scott and her £80,000 in February 1801.'[97]

The marriage was also fortunate from the point of view of Canning's personal happiness. Charles Ellis wrote to him shortly after his wedding: 'I doubt not your Happiness will be complete, and greater Happiness you will find it, not only than you can have ever known, but greater than you have ever fancied to yourself.'[98]

This certainly seems to have been the case. Throughout his life he would write daily letters to his wife during his absences. These were not short notes but long letters with full descriptions of current public business. On his first night of separation he wrote to Joan from Huntingdon saying how much he missed her 'and how much stranger still it will be when I get across the passage to bed to find nothing there to welcome me – but, all cold, and solitary, and comfortless.' Five days later he wrote: 'Adieu, my Dear Dear Dear Dearest Love – I feel, like you, how few and weak words there are to say how much I love you.'

His early letters are filled with references to the 'Little Thing' soon to become his eldest son George, for by this time his wife was pregnant. Joan is invited to talk to the 'Little Thing' as soon as it can understand, 'which I suppose it can when it begins to jump about'.

On 3 December he is blaming the Post Office for the late delivery of his letter: 'Stupid People – They fancied they were only neglecting public business which would not be minded and did not know that under Hammond's cover to Ld. T(itchfield) was a precious letter to my own little love, which was more important than a hundred despatches.'[99]

Canning's private life was thus established on a firm footing. What problems remained were those concerned with his own family – these he called his 'plagues'; the first was his mother herself, 'the second is my cousin George, who is in despair, and calls here hourly . . . The Devil! Here he is again – no, not he – somebody who is not let in. . . .'[100]

It is ironic that at the same time as his personal life had entered a period of calm and sunshine, storms were gathering that threatened to blight his political career.

3
'A STATE NEITHER OF PEACE NOR OF WAR'

Canning wrote, 'I always determined to be a Privy Councillor at thirty.'[1] This ambition was fulfilled in 1799 after he resigned as Under-Secretary to Lord Grenville; for, by the end of the year, he held no less than three positions; he became a Member of the Board of Control for India, a body established by Pitt's India Act of 1784 to exercise an overall supervision of British India; he was made Joint-Paymaster-General of the Forces; and finally, he was given a £500 p.a. sinecure as Receiver-General of the Alienation Office, a position he continued to hold even after losing office in 1801. In addition, he joined the Privy Council.

Thus despite his parvenu background, Canning was now firmly established in politics, if not wholly popular with those of more respectable lineage. In 1800, when new arrangements were under discussion, the Duke of Buckingham was most distressed to see his brother 'put by for such animals as Steele and Rider and Canning.'[2]

Canning still owed much of the dominance of his position to his oratory. On 5 February 1800 *The Times* declared: 'Mr Canning every day confirms the sanguine hopes entertained by him. No man transfuses his character more naturally into his speeches. That of Monday was a just mixture of wit and argument, and a happy compound of information, modesty and good-humour.'[3] He was nevertheless reliant on Pitt for his position until his marriage provided him with financial independence. Afterwards he could more easily afford to disagree with Pitt. In 1799 Pitt had written, 'On all the main practical points we are perfectly agreed'.[4] Within a year this had changed.

The international setting was a complex one. The immediate aftermath of the British victory at the Nile was not as favourable to Britain as might have been expected. The *Guillaume Tell* and the *Genereux* had escaped the wreckage of Aboukir Bay and were supported by a number of smaller craft. In Italy the situation had worsened. Urged on by his wife Maria Carolina as well as by Nelson and Lady Hamilton, King Ferdinand had marched on Rome. The rabble which passed for his army were no match for the French under Championnet, who pushed them back and occupied Naples in January 1799, establishing the Parthenopean Republic.

Nevertheless, elsewhere in Europe the Second Coalition – the alliance of Britain, Russia and Austria – was beginning to be successful. In March 1799 the Austro-Russian troops under Suvarov commenced their march across northern Italy which culminated in the battle of Novi on 15 August 1799. This French defeat confined French power in Italy to Genoa – still held by Massena. In the process, Naples had been evacuated by the French and royal power re-established there. This change in allied fortunes was not to last. On 25 September the allies were defeated at Zurich, and Suvarov, arriving from Italy, was too late to retrieve the situation and had no choice but to retreat East.

The Czar Paul blamed the Austrians for letting his Russians down – a charge with a great deal of substance. The impetuous nature which had impelled this lunatic Russian emperor to join the war largely because of his election to the headship of the Knights of St John who had been evicted from Malta by the French, now inclined him to change sides. Impelling him further in this direction was the failure in November of the Anglo-Russian assault on Holland. This ill-conceived and badly-led expedition had failed through a typical mis-assessment of continental attitudes. The Dutch, expected to rise to greet the Anglo-Russian force as their liberators, in fact gazed upon the scene as passive spectators of events with which they had no concern. The combined force, after making minor incursions down the Helder peninsula, eventually evacuated under humiliating terms. By early 1800 Paul had intimated to the French that they had no more to fear from him. By the end of the year, the Convention of Armed Neutrality had put Russia and the other northern powers in a state of hostility to Britain as in 1780. Had Paul not been assassin-

ated in March 1801 the future course of Anglo-Russian relations
would have been very difficult to predict.

The other theatre of operations, the Rhine, saw little activity.
The Austrian commander there was the Archduke Charles. He
was a good tactician of the eighteenth-century school of limited
warfare but not really suited to an age when peoples rather than
dynasties clashed.

If 1799 was a year of mixed fortunes, 1800 was disastrous.
Napoleon had returned from Egypt to France late in 1799 and
in November executed the *coup d'état* which made him First
Consul. In 1800 he returned to the scene of his triumphs of 1796
in Italy, where on 9 June he won one of his greatest victories.
This, the defeat of the Austrian commander Melas at Marengo,
was followed by the Armistice of Alessandria. Combined with the
Armistice of Parsdorf which ended hostilities on the Danube, it
temporarily removed Austria from the war. The resumption of
hostilities in November was followed by the overwhelming French
victory at Hohenlinden. The peace of Luneville in February 1801
established French power on the left bank of the Rhine, and
Austrian power in Italy was confined to Venetia. Meanwhile
Naples was forced to a humiliating treaty which excluded British
ships from her ports.

Only two events relieved the gloom of the war from Britain's
point of view. In April 1801 the threat presented to Britain by the
Armed Neutrality was ended by Nelson's destruction of the Danish
fleet at Copenhagen. Clearly, however ineffective British power
in continental Europe, her navy was still supreme. This enabled
her to deal with one threat which had hung over from Napoleon's
Egyptian expedition – the existence of French power in the Middle
East, wholly cut off from reinforcement from metropolitan France.
In 1800 Britain turned away from the policy of direct continental
involvement which Grenville favoured because the destruction or
secession of her allies made such a policy unrealistic. She turned
back to her traditional policy, favoured by Dundas, of using sea-
power to isolate enemy outposts overseas. In 1800 an expedition
was prepared to deal with the problem of Egypt. It embarked from
Gibraltar in December and by the middle of the following year
had defeated Menou's depleted contingent of Frenchmen and
occupied Cairo and Alexandria. It was ironic that news of this
substantial British victory arrived too late to affect the negotiations

for peace with France which Britain had entered into and which were concluded at Amiens in the following year.

In 1798 Canning had declared the official Government attitude: 'We can be but precariously safe as long as there is no safety for the rest of Europe.'[5] He remained an enthusiastic supporter of the war and was no less immune than his colleagues from the illusions that led to the errors of the subsequent year. He had referred to 'the people of the Netherlands driven into insurrection and struggling for their freedom against the heavy hand of a merciless tyranny'.[6] He consequently supported the unwise Helder expedition, though eventually, like his colleagues, he was forced to face the reality of the situation and accept withdrawal as 'we had better have our army without Holland than Holland without the army'.[7]

In November 1799 Bonaparte came to power in France. Canning wrote to Grenville in delight:

> The destroyer of the National Representation of the French Republic is a public benefactor to Europe. I care not whether he restores a King or becomes himself a Despot, so that he be bloody and tyrannical enough. Heaven prosper all his projects against French liberty and Republican principles, whatever other may be. But as to peace – peace with a Government six weeks old! No no-no![8]

It is evidence of the important position held by Canning that despite his resignation from the Foreign Office he played a large part in drafting the reply to Napoleon's peace overtures. In a letter to Pitt he discussed them. The best course of action was still to try to get Austrian and Russian co-operation and unite forces to shake 'this expiring Republic and infant despotism to its centre'. However, Canning fully realized that their own political friends in the country would not long endure a separate war 'if moderate terms should be offered, and Bonaparte's Power should appear to establish itself firmly and on Principles that can be distinguished from Jacobin'. In the first instance, nevertheless, there was no difficulty in rejecting the overtures. Pitt agreed that while there was still a reasonable prospect of constructing a great continental alliance against France, then 'all Notion of Peace but with Monarchy will probably without difficulty be set aside'. Furthermore, he argued somewhat optimistically that France was likely to sink under increasing embarrassments, particularly that of paying the armies. Nevertheless, were Bonaparte to establish himself as a military despot, a situation could be envisaged in which it would be impossible to refuse to treat. Consequently, Britain ought never to treat with a Jacobin Government, but neither ought it to commit itself to the restoration of royalty as the *sine qua non* of peace.[9]

Pitt and Canning were at this stage fully agreed. Canning himself was delighted at the reply to Bonaparte which he had played a large part in drafting. It was nevertheless fairly rash to slight a newly-established despot. The form of the letter did not even address Napoleon but was written rather as if it were a personal letter to George III. While no insistence was made on the re-establishment of the French Royal Family, it was pointed out that this would be regarded as the best guarantee of France's peaceful intentions.[10]

The reply to these overtures became the subject of a parliamentary debate later in the month. It fell to Canning to defend the Government's policies. He referred to the failure of the negotiations at Lille and asked 'Was the mere fact of an experiment having been tried, and failed, of itself a sufficient inducement to try it again?' He went on to rebut the suggestion that Britain was insisting on the restoration of the French royal family, attacked Bonaparte, whose intercepted correspondence from Egypt (which Canning edited and published) shows 'fraud, perjury, treachery, and deliberate breach of faith'. He ended up by giving a fairly optimistic view of the situation, and the Government's case was sustained by 265 votes to 64.[11]

In fact the Government almost certainly blundered in not entering into negotiations when the allies were in a strategically strong position with Italy in their hands. Within the year Canning realized that blunder, for he wrote to Frere of how prudent it would have been to enter into negotiations with Bonaparte early in 1800.[12] But this was Canning being wise after the event. The previous December he had written

I like the tone of everything that I hear today, better than I ever did before. And I am persuaded that the whole game is in our hands now, and that it wants little more than *patience*, to play it well, to the end.[13]

In August 1800 Canning sent an assessment of the general

C

situation to his friend the Earl of Mornington, who was Governor-General of India. He still justified the refusal to treat with France the previous January on two fairly orthodox grounds. The first was the difficulty of reconciling the safety of the country and the tranquility of Europe with the predominance which peace at such a time would leave to France, and secondly, he also stressed the danger to all governments if the example of successful usurpation was allowed to stand. The second argument was later to underlie the philosophy of the Holy Alliance – the principles of which Canning has been portrayed as the leading opponent. The first argument, if valid in January, was still more so after Marengo. Nevertheless, Canning also argued that there was no case now for not entering into a negotiation with France, except the prospect of a new general combination of all the principal powers on better terms than previously. This he realized was a forlorn hope. He added the opinion that the general expectation in Paris was of the eventual restoration of royalty, but it was the domestic political situation that really impelled Canning towards the necessity of negotiation. While he felt the force of the second argument for continuing the war – the dangerous example of successful usurpation – he accepted that such a position could no longer be sustained in the House of Commons.[14]

Canning thus supported Britain's peace initiative of August 1800. This was an intimation to France through the Court of Vienna that Britain was now ready to join in a general negotiation for peace. The French reply appalled him: it was an offer of naval armistice – in effect an invitation to Britain to sheath her only weapon while still engaged in combat. This offer put Canning back onto the side of those who opposed any dealings with France, and this led to his first major political difference with Pitt. He was scathing. He wrote to Frere,

Is it possible ... that we can so far overlook the insolence of this proposal as to begin treating gently about a modification of it? ... our offer not having been accepted, we have nothing more to say, and will have no armistice on any condition at all. If we argue, and remonstrate and distinguish, and set right what has been mis-stated – in short, if we do not show that we feel the contempt and ridicule with which they have treated us, and are heartily ashamed of having given so much room for it – there is an end. Do people hold up their heads? And does the Cabinet meet by daylight? Who kicks them individually as they go into the Cabinet. . . ?[15]

'Canning,' wrote Windham a few days later, 'furious against the armistice, and still more at the idea of reverting to it now'.[16]

Canning was clearly in a fury, and adopted a policy of not speaking but merely voting on government questions. It was his friend Granville who told him not to be so foolish. 'Is it possible', he asked, 'that because some measures . . . are pursued in direct contradiction to your opinion, you are to abandon every idea of Improvement, and Reform upon which you used to talk with the greatest eagerness and upon which I remember you used to say you felt very confident your zeal would not relax?' Was this the way Canning was to repay Pitt's kindness?[17]

The negotiation in fact came to nought, but it damaged relations between Pitt and Canning. This was confirmed when Pitt rejected Canning's arguments against communicating papers in this and other aspects of foreign politics to Parliament.[18] Canning was concerned at this breach and in November wrote to Pitt asking if there had been a 'sensible estrangement' between them. Pitt gave a conciliatory reply,[19] and Canning resumed his parliamentary role, defending the Government's war policy on the twenty-seventh.[20]

The whole incident was perhaps little more than a storm in a tea-cup. It did demonstrate however that Canning, now financially secure, was prepared to act more independently of Pitt and even, as he was soon to do, to defy his wishes. Meanwhile the end of the possibility of negotiations and the deteriorating war situation left the Government in the difficult position of being forced to defend a policy which seemed doomed to failure. In November Canning wrote: 'My only hope is that people may be so much occupied with the question of scarcity as to pay little attention to that of Peace.'[21]

Where decisive action was concerned Canning was usually in the forward party. The problem of the Danish fleet and the possibility of its being used against Britain hung over the Cabinet in 1800. Canning urged his colleagues to 'strike and strike quickly'.[22] This would demonstrate to Europe the principles on which Britain would make peace.[23]

At the beginning of 1801 Britain had two projects on which she was engaged and in which she was acting unilaterally. Canning thought that if both of these went successfully the war could speedily be brought to conclusion 'on high ground'. In the meantime, doubtless for political reasons, he accepted that Britain should not refuse 'a fruitless negotiation . . . tho I do not look to its future with any hope of its leading to a long continuance of the war'.[24] Clearly Canning's unfettered inclinations were far more sympathetic to the war than the policy he saw as politically necessary.

At this stage other events intervened and the ending of Britain's part in the 'war of the Second Coalition' was to be the work of another ministry. The political horizon was clouded then, as so many times before and since, by the problem of Ireland. This Catholic country, suppressed a hundred and fifty years earlier by Cromwell's soldiery, was Britain's Achilles Heel. Statesmen were haunted by the vision of Ireland dominated by a continental enemy. The country itself was seething with discontent. Its Parliament had achieved a great deal of autonomy in 1782 but it was wholly Protestant in an island which was overwhelmingly Catholic. The seed-bed of discontent was suitable for the flowering of French principles and in 1798 Britain had to cope with a rebellion which, though finally crushed at the battle of Vinegar Hill in June, nevertheless determined English statesmen to attempt a final solution to the problem. This took the form of organic union between Britain and Ireland in which, within the context of the new Parliament of the United Kingdom, dominated by the Protestant majority in the country as a whole, Catholics could be allowed participation in Parliament.[25] If statesmen needed any bolstering of their convictions on this point, it was provided by an abortive French invasion of the country in August 1798. Pursuing through the Viceroy Cornwallis and the Chief Secretary Castlereagh a dual policy of holding out promises of future reforms to the Catholics and buying out the borough-owners with honours and money, the Government achieved its desired end when in 1800 the Irish Parliament voted away its own existence.

Canning was a full supporter of the Government's policy in this regard. He immediately reacted to the news from Ireland, writing from Ashbourne that *now* was the best moment for Irish union, with the only alternative being 'an eternal unextinguishable

conflict between the different parties in Ireland.[26] He was nevertheless aware of the problems, which he expressed in a typically
humorous letter to Windham:

> Chap. 1: Lord Clare's[27] arrival in London. Ld. C. himself very
> reasonable. Confesses he fears nothing himself from the Catho-
> lics having *everything* but it is impossible to carry the point in
> Ireland. Protestant Union practicable. High Protestant party
> would fain make it a fundamental Article of the Union that
> nothing farther should be done for the Catholics hereafter.
> This to be absolutely rejected – and the whole question reserved
> – and with a full determination to do what is right upon it at a
> future season. Reasons for being satisfied with this sort of
> Union. Task of carrying it. Committee of Privy Council of both
> kingdoms to prepare it. Message to the English and Irish Parlia-
> ment at the same time (not till after Xmas). How many
> members from Ireland – 100 too many. Pitt thinks not. Peers
> to be chosen for life? or by families? or as in Scotland? how
> many? thirty? Bishops and Archbishops ex officio? Free Trade
> – Apostrophe to Lord Liverpool. Conclusion. Drunkenness at
> Bellamy's. Duel.[28]

It fell to Canning to help defend the Government's policy in
the House of Commons in January 1799 and he tried unsuccessfully to get round Sheridan's point that the Settlement of 1782
meant a 'final adjustment' of Irish status. He then went on to
defend Union as the 'middle term' to reconcile Catholic with
Protestant. Furthermore, it would redress the great social deficiency in Ireland – the lack of a 'middle class of men'. He doubtless
believed all this but could hardly have been speaking honestly
when he declared that the measure was not being forced upon
Ireland, 'but given for the consideration, for the mature and
deliberate judgement of the Irish Parliament. . . .'[29] 'Do not', he
urged three months later, 'let us be led to imagine that the Irish,
however spirited and quick in feeling, are creatures of passion
only.'[30]

The union with Ireland itself had the unanimous support of
King and Cabinet, but this was not the case with Catholic
Emancipation. In the latter part of 1800 several cabinet ministers,
especially Loughborough, the Lord Chancellor, schemed against
the measure and found the support of the King. On 28 January

1801 the King told Dundas that he would 'reckon any man' his 'personal enemy who proposes any such measure'. Against such adamance from the throne Pitt could not present the opinion of a unanimous Cabinet. On 31 January he offered his resignation. None were fully aware of what this might mean. Canning had been the first to know of Pitt's intention to resign, being by this time as much in Pitt's confidence as anyone else, yet he said on 2 February 'You need not be frightened, Pitt is not out, nor likely to be so.'[31]

Malmesbury felt that the resignation was tactical. On 7 February he wrote: 'It looks at times to me as if Pitt was playing a very selfish and, in the present state of affairs a very criminal part; that he goes out to show his own strength, and under the certain expectation of being soon called upon again to govern the country, with uncontrollable power.'[32]

In fact, Pitt's conduct was not governed by ulterior motives. After 31 January he stressed his readiness to support any administration formed on the same general principles as his own. The King acknowledged this and put the blame elsewhere. On 13 February he wrote: 'Lords Camden and Castlereagh and Mr Canning are the persons that led Mr Pitt to the rash step he has taken, and . . . his own good heart now makes him, by exertion in favour of my service, take the line most to his own inclination as well as honour.'[33]

Canning was in Pitt's confidence at this time. On 15 February Pitt wrote to him, 'It will be a real relief and comfort to me to talk with you (as we have been always used to do) on every thought in either of our minds. . . .'[34]

However, this turn of events led to something of a break between them. Pitt wished all his old followers to remain in office under the King's new choice of first minister, the Speaker of the House of Commons, Henry Addington. Canning had no intention of doing so. On one hand he advised Pitt to withdraw his resignation urging that the former must concede on the Catholic question what, after all, had to be conceded.[35] On the other hand if Pitt were to go, he was determined to follow. On 6 February he made Addington aware of his resolution on this question[36] though at this stage he did not express hostility to the possible new Government, telling his friend John Newbolt that he did not want to dissuade him from giving the new Government all the support in his power.[37] Many of Canning's friends shared his views. Charles Ellis wrote of Canning's motives 'that when Pitt, the only man in his opinion fit to be minister goes out, he follows his Example – and that is the choice between following that Example or serving under the Person who has the foolish vanity to think he can replace him. . . .'[38] Granville Leveson-Gower wrote that 'Pitt is the object of my political idolatry and it is impossible to have any opinion of any Government of which he is not at the head, and more especially when everything like ability withdraws with him. . . . In short, the dregs of Government cannot make a respectable administration.'[39]

Canning was not a man to suffer fools gladly, and the new administration earned his unrelenting contempt. Indeed, it was hardly impressive. It lacked Grenville, Windham, Spencer, Cornwallis and Castlereagh. Only four among the cabinet ministers had sat in a Cabinet previously, and Addington included in the lower ranks of his Administration his brother, two brothers-in-law and a cousin. Canning felt he clearly could not follow Pitt in giving the Administration his support, and yet he knew if he did not this would create great difficulties for the latter, as he was universally known as Pitt's protégé. Any view he expressed would be widely taken as Pitt's real views which he did not dare declare publicly. Lady Stafford wrote to her son Granville:

It is reported that Mr Pitt holds this new Administration in great contempt, talks of it in that style, and not of a *certain great person* with more respect. Upon this being combatted, and one saying that they should like to hear the Person say that *they had ever heard* Mr Pitt talk in that way either of [the King] or of this New Administration, it was answer'd, 'Mr Canning does in all Companies, and he is supposed to speak Mr Pitt's sentiments'.[40]

This situation caused difficulties between Pitt and Canning as soon as the new Administration was formed. As early as April Pitt complained that Canning misunderstood him.[41] He tried suggesting to Canning that he take office under Addington, but Canning was adamant; he could not consider as his rivals in the Administration nonentities such as 'Nicholl and Sir Christopher Hawkins and Jeffreys the Silversmith', and he held this attitude despite his belief that he might be long excluded from government, for 'Addington's power is established for this reign at least'.[42]

The facts were that Canning could now afford to take an independent line. Pitt had given him his start in political life but his wife's fortune enabled him to build on this foundation on his own. His principles were unaltered. His hostility to unproved innovation even led him to oppose a measure to prohibit bull-baiting. 'The amusement', he declared, 'is an excellent one. It inspires courage, and produces a nobleness of sentiment and eleva-tion of mind.' Furthermore, 'the natural instincts and antipathies of animals had ever been made a source of amusement to man, and notwithstanding all the laws that would be made, would continue to be so.'[43]

Canning was as hostile to intellectual innovation as to that in the realm of politics. The founding of the Royal Institution in 1800 drew such scornful wit from him that even Lady Holland was pleased.[44] A long satirical poem included the lines:

> 'Tis time at length that abstract science
> With useful art should form alliance
> Should quit her academic leisure
> To dig, and spin, to gage and measure
> Turning the abstract law to practical
> Should teach mankind in strain didactical
> The art of mending chairs and mats,
> Of frying sausages and sprats:
> How shining ploughshares turn the ground up
> How watches make a noise when wound up.[45]

Clearly Canning was not a child of the new industrial era.

The new Administration's main unsettled problem was that of the war. In September 1801 negotiations between the British and French began in earnest, and in October the Preliminaries of Peace were agreed. The terms were not favourable to Britain. She was required to evacuate the Cape, Egypt and Malta, and places of strategic importance on the route to India. In the West Indies the islands of Martinique and Tobago were restored to the French, while the mainland territories of Demerara and Berbice, with their enormous potential for sugar cultivation, were returned to the Dutch along with Curaçao. The only positive gains were Trinidad and Ceylon, taken from the Spanish and Dutch respectively. On the continent French influence was left supreme in Nice, Savoy, Piedmont, the Netherlands and the left bank of the Rhine. The terms seemed so unfavourable to Britain on the face of it that the Austrian Ambassador thought there must be better terms which had been kept secret.[46]

Negotiations dragged on over the succeeding months. Britain relied upon promises given in private conversations on such issues as the presence of French troops in Holland and the claims of the King of Sardinia. In fact nothing came of these and the lengthy negotiations between Cornwallis and Joseph Bonaparte led to no new concessions on the French side. For Britain the choice was to stand firm and withdraw from the negotiations or accept the terms of the Preliminaries fundamentally unchanged. She adopted the latter course and on 25 March 1802 peace was signed at Amiens. Whitworth went to Paris as British Ambassador and Andreossy came to London as his counterpart. France meanwhile consolidated her position, and in January 1802 Napoleon became President of the new Italian Republic in northern Italy.

The peace fulfilled all Canning's worst fears. France was clearly retaining the dominant position in continental Europe while Britain was abandoning much of her Mediterranean supremacy with the promise to evacuate Malta. At the same time Britain was not being wholly faithful to her friends. Boundary settlements were made against Portuguese interests and the claims of the House of Orange were passed over. Canning was 'astounded and dismayed' by the terms.[47] 'God forgive Pitt', he wrote, 'for the hand he has had in them.'[48] Such a peace, he argued, could not last six months unless Bonaparte changed his system or was overthrown.[49] Canning clearly toyed with the idea of outright opposition to the peace. He and Granville discussed this in October, encouraging each other by the terms in which they reprobated it. On reflection, political factors intervened. Granville had never seen anything to produce as much pleasure on the faces of 'farmer, labourer or manufacturer'. The advantage of opposition would be merely that of a brilliant speech and a 'triumph over Jenky'.[50]

Pitt's views on the peace, in public at least, were wholly different. He asserted it was such a peace as he would have signed himself. Canning hoped that Pitt would not ask him to support the peace but said he would do so if requested[51] even though he saw it as 'what to the best of my judgement I heartily disapprove.'[52] Pitt simply replied with a strong letter in defence of the peace.[53]

Windham was even more implacably hostile to the peace than Canning. The latter urged him not to bring the Treaty to a vote in the House of Commons as people would be found to commit themselves in its favour and Pitt would speak warmly for it. It would be better to leave it possible for Pitt to say the Preliminaries promised well, but the Treaty did not live up to them. Addington must not be able to say that 'the Treaty was my work to be sure but you, all of you, approved it.'[54]

But Windham was not the man to agree with such a weak line. He drafted a reply to Canning attacking Pitt as 'the author of the ruin of this country, by the false conception which he originally formed of the great game which he had to play. . . .'[55] He did in fact bring the Treaty to the vote. Pitt spoke in favour of ministers, and Windham's motion was lost by 276 votes to 20. Canning absented himself but his friends the Ellises and Lord Morpeth voted against the Treaty.[56] Canning afterwards conceded that 'perhaps . . . it would not have been brave and gentleman-like to have shirked a division'.[57]

Throughout the proceedings Canning was not merely acting alone. Already he had attached to himself a sizeable group of friends who were also political associates. Lady Holland had seen the process starting earlier and took a jaundiced view of it. In 1798 she wrote that Canning 'has made a little party out of the great party, that peculiarly belong for him! Over them he exerts an almost despotic sway, not only in their votes but their opinions and conduct in the minutest concerns, such as who they must see and live with.' This little set she scornfully described as relying on old jokes and witticisms common to themselves. The marriage of Charles Ellis, she felt, had been a blow to Canning's power, for 'he ventured not only to fall in love, but to make his proposals without a previous consultation with the young Cato, the authority of whose little Senate was infringed upon by such an overt act.'[58]

The accusation was not without substance. Canning was a loyal friend, but would not accept partial loyalty as reciprocation. He closely scrutinized the political conduct of the ten to fifteen Members of Parliament who were closest to him and was disinclined to sustain personal friendship in the face of political difference. Closest to him were Charles Ellis, Lord Granville Leveson-Gower and later William Huskisson. There were also John Hookham Frere, who left Parliament in 1802, William

Sturges (later Sturges-Bourne), Lord Binning, Lord Boringdon, Lord Morpeth, Robert Smith, Edward Bootle Wilbraham and John Dent, known as 'Dog Dent' because of his bill for taxing dogs. At times as many as fifteen members were attached to Canning.

As early as 1797 Canning complained bitterly of Morpeth's conduct. 'That *cursed brothel*,' he wrote, '(these are hardly decent words to *read out*, so you must skip to) Devonshire House has gained its point, and Morpeth last night gave his first vote to opposition. . . .'[59] Indeed, after 1804 political differences were to lead to a more lengthy estrangement with Morpeth. Difficulties were to arise with several other friends. Boringdon approved of the Preliminaries of Peace in 1801 and wrote to the Foreign Office Under-Secretary congratulating him. This exercised Canning's ire. In 1807 Granville returned from St Petersburgh to associate himself with the Talents Ministry. Canning wrote to him that this must most certainly 'abate those habits of confidence, which it certainly would have been no small happiness to me to have preserved unabated to the end of our lives'.[60]

Canning liked to adopt a paternal relationship to his disciples. In 1798 he wrote elaborate instructions to Granville as to how to write a speech.[61] He wrote detailed criticism of his friend Frere's despatches from Lisbon[62] and promoted his interests despite the latter's fundamental inefficiency. In return he demanded that his friends shared his opinions, particularly that relating to his own importance.

His wife's fortune, his party and after 1802 his personal ownership of the seat he represented in Parliament (Tralee), all enabled Canning to take up an attitude to the Addington administration that was different from what Pitt would have wished. His mind was quite made up. Addington was a man 'utterly unfit to fill the station in which he is placed'. Consequently, a

> temperate and mitigated Opposition in Parliament, in which one should judge and act fairly upon *measures* as they arose, contending however uniformly all the while and upon every occasion that the MAN was utterly the fool he is, and that it is mischief and madness to trust the country in his hands – might do a great deal of good, and presents a highly respectable line of conduct, not to say a very amusing one. . . .[63]

Canning was certainly not prepared to give the Addington Ministry any chance to prove itself. That such measures it took might prove popular – the peace itself, and the repeal of income tax in the same year, merely gave him further cause for gloom. His whole effort was devoted to securing the return of Pitt by the dual methods of attacking the Government and scheming amongst Pitt's old friends. The unwillingness of Pitt himself to bow to the wind raised by his protégé merely caused him exasperation. In a bitter letter to Granville, he described Pitt's conduct: how the Government

> give him a bit to eat, and show him half a dog's ear of a despatch from Lord Cornwallis. With this discipline he is become as tame as a chaplain ... he begs pardon ... and feels bona fide that every thought of resistance or self-assertion into which he has suffered himself to be betrayed or goaded has been an act of treachery and Leze-Medecine which he cannot too much atone for by increased devotion, blind obedience and self-abasement. And yet this is the mind that governed the World, and might have saved it![64]

Pitt in fact played an honourable role. He regarded himself as morally committed to the Addington Government. In 1801 he reprobated Canning for a plot to engineer his return to office saying that he 'thought the project utterly improper, and that [he] would hold no intercourse with those who would not concur in a strenuous support of the New Administration; nor should [he] think those persons friends to [himself] who croaked about their instability.'[65]

Pitt did not actually break off intercourse with Canning but the relationship was maimed by his exasperation at being dragged along a road marked out by his own protégé. As for Canning himself, he veered from extreme pessimism to jubilation as Pitt's attitudes alternately shifted. In 1802 he complained to Frere that Pitt was lost. Nothing but a new war could restore his importance in the country, and this Britain would submit 'to all sorts of baseness to avoid – and with his full countenance and encouragement'.[66] It was nevertheless only a month later that Canning's famous poem in praise of Pitt 'The Pilot that Weathered the Storm' was read and applauded at the Merchant Taylor's Hall by the 820 persons present.

If hush'd the loud whirlwind that ruffled the deep
The sky, if no longer dark tempests deform,
When our perils are past, shall our gratitude sleep?
No! – Here's to the Pilot who weather'd the storm!

At the foot-stool of Power let flattery fawn
Let faction her idols extol to the skies
To virtue in humble retirement withdrawn
Unblam'd may the merits of gratitude rise.

And shall not His memory to Britain be dear,
Whose example with envy all nations behold;
A statesman unbiass'd by int'rest or fear,
By Pow'r uncorrupted, untainted by gold.

Who, when terror and doubt thro the Universe reigned,
While rapine and treason their standards unfurl'd,
The heart and the hopes of his country maintain'd,
And one kingdom preserve'd midst the wreck of the world.

Unheeding, unthankful, we bask in the blaze,
While the beams of the sun in full majesty shine,
When he sinks into twilight, with fondness we gaze,
And mark the mild lustre that gilds his decline.

Lo! Pitt, when the course of thy greatness is o'er
Thy talents, thy virtues, we fondly recall!
Now justly we prize thee, when lost we deplore,
Admir'd in thy zenith, but lov'd in thy fall!

O! take then – for dangers by wisdom repell'd
For evils by courage and constancy brav'd
O! take for a throne by thy counsels upheld,
The thanks of a people thy firmness has sav'd.

And O! if again the rude whirlwind should rise!
The dawning of Peace should fresh darkness deform,
The regrets of the good, and the fears of the wise,
Shall turn to the Pilot that weather'd the storm![67]

What particularly pleased Canning was that the last verse was
called for over and over again.[68] To preserve balance Canning
also produced a poem for Addington's birthday. Entitled 'The
Bird of Today', it was 'supposed to be written *bona fide*, by an

Admiring Fool' and to be recited at Apothecary's Hall.[69] On several other occasions Canning exercised his poetic wit at the expense of the Addington Administration. 'The Grand Consultation' suggested that Addington be joined in his great work of doctoring Britain to death by other eminent physicians. The 'Ode to the Doctor' implied that only his relatives saw merit in Addington; an insight explained by their being

> *Lodg'd and fed at public charge. Their job?*
> *When his speeches hobble vilely*
> *What! 'Hear him' burst from brother Hiley,*
> *When the faltering periods lag,*
> *Hark to the cheer of brother Bragge.*

Addington's unfortunate phrase that 'to doubt is to decide' gave Canning great scope to point the First Minister to the desired line of conduct:

> *... say, Addington, if France*
> *New ways inflict, fresh claims advance,*
> *To humble England's pride;*
> *Wilt thou thy Country's right forego?*
> *Behold he doubts – he does not know*
>   *'To doubt is to decide' ...*
>
> *If Pitt would hear his Country's voice*
> *Say, wouldst thou point thy Sovereign's choice*
> *To worth and talents tried?*
> *Shake not thy empty head at me –*
> *Thy modest doubts too plain I see –*
>   *'To doubt is to decide'.*[70]

Pitt's own attitude in these years is very difficult to read retrospectively. In general one can say that he started out with little intention of making any assault on the Addington Administration until growing disillusion made him first waver, and then finally commence something like opposition. The latter was largely influenced by the renewed outbreak of war in May 1803.

As early as August 1802, Canning was becoming more hopeful. Pitt, he said, was 'much better in opinion than I had ever seen him – disgusted with the Doctor and his system as much as one could wish, but – but – but – as to *acting*, no hopes of that yet'.[71]

What perhaps really infuriated Canning was his opinion, at least in his more optimistic moments, that Pitt could, if he wished, control the situation. He was not alone in this view. In November 1802 the Duke of Buckingham expressed the view that Pitt could go to the head of the government tomorrow if he wished.[72] It was at this time Canning tried to engineer a plot to get rid of Addington. He visited Lord Malmesbury to try to persuade him to use his influence on this subject with the Duke of York and through him with the King. At the same time Cartwright, the Member for Northampton, was nominally to hand a petition to Addington asking the latter to resign. George Rose, a friend of Pitt, learned of the scheme which Canning had sponsored along with Granville, Morpeth and Sturges-Bourne, and Pitt himself put a stop to it.[73] Canning also tried to inveigle Pitt into a specific issue by asking if he thought a naval estimate of 50,000 men to be sufficient. Pitt refused to judge the situation.[74]

Canning still did not abandon hope. In December 1802 he flatly declared that Pitt 'cannot withdraw himself from the following of a nation; he must endure the attachment of a people whom he has saved'.[75] Pitt, however, still preached forbearance, and strongly objected to the fact that people thought 'they could collect my intention from the declarations of persons whose relation to me in no degree justified such inference'.[76] Nevertheless, the attitude of the Addington Government was causing him some concern. In December 1802 The Times published a leading article praising the Ministry and attacking Pitt for not rallying to its support. Addington's brother Hiley was thought to be responsible. The budget of 1803 was seen by Pitt as criticizing his own handling of affairs.

The most important factor was nevertheless the steadily worsening situation in Europe. The occupation of Switzerland, the French re-armament and the exclusion of British exports frightened the Addington Government. Pitt joined his voice to those urging the Government not to give up Malta.[77] Canning urged Pitt to stronger measures. In February 1803 he painted a very gloomy view of affairs, particularly in regard to Holland and described the Government as being 'as magnanimous as a mouse'.[78] Indeed, in a letter to Frere on 2 February he saw no hope that Holland would not follow Switzerland.[79] Pitt's replies were equivocal. His mind, he said, was made up as to the line required by the present crisis, but for unspecifiable reasons he could not enter into any explanation on the subject.[80]

The reasons for Pitt's silence were that he was at that moment listening to schemes for a possible junction with the Government. Pitt was no longer deterred by consideration of the Catholic question, though he had recently talked of the importance of finding 'if possible, such a solution as might be satisfactory to His Majesty, and at the same time not inconsistent with the maintenance of our public characters'.[81] Various proposals were made. Pitt unequivocally rejected the suggestion that he might be prepared to serve under Addington. In March a proposal was made by Addington that they both served under Pitt's brother Chatham, but Pitt rejected this, stressing the importance of having a real First Minister. The final proposal that Pitt himself be Prime Minister failed because of the unwillingness of Addington's party to admit the Grenvilles into the Government.

Canning seems to have played little part in this process despite his long letters to Pitt on the state of the country. Nothing could better illustrate that his real power base, apart from a few friends, rested on little more than oratory inspired by indignation. Some nevertheless blamed him for the failure of the junction. Speaker Abbott wrote: 'It was believed Canning had been principally instrumental in working upon Mr Pitt to the temper of mind which had produced this end of the transaction.'[82]

Meanwhile the Government, contrary to Canning's view, was acting vigorously. The militia was called out, additional men were requested for the navy, and Malta was not evacuated despite the terms of the Treaty of Amiens. Finally, on 18 May, Addington declared war.

Under Addington's regime, England had passed from war to peace and back to war. Throughout this period, Canning had not been inactive in Parliament. One issue he used to embarrass the Government was the cultivation of Trinidad, a former Spanish colony kept by Britain after the Peace of Amiens. Despite his friendship with the West Indians Charles and George Ellis, Canning had always supported the campaign for the abolition of the slave trade.

'I *do* feel (you know I do)', he wrote to Frere, 'a conscientious conviction and duty upon the question of the slave trade, which has pushed me sometimes almost to extremities with P. himself . . .'[83] Despite the fact that it was, as Canning said, 'a subject which has nothing of party politics in it,'[84] the hostility towards abolition shown by most members of the Government brought the campaign for abolition to a halt for three years, for its leaders preferred to work through government influence.

Trinidad was a related subject because the large amounts of uncultivated land on the island clearly provided great scope for a huge development of the slave trade. Canning's aim was to secure a government promise that no land grants be made without a guarantee that they should not be cultivated by slaves imported from Africa. On this question Canning undoubtedly acted under Pitt's instructions both in raising and dropping the question,[85] for Pitt himself felt certain obligations on the subject. Canning's speech was not particularly incisive and his suggestion that Trinidad be cultivated by free white labour was absurd.[86]

The question was nevertheless an embarrassing one, for Canning could rely on the enemies of the Government and the Abolitionists. Furthermore there were many West Indians who, being possessed of property in the older colonies, feared competition from more fertile lands elsewhere. Canning himself wrote to Wilberforce that his friends who did not agree with him on the slave trade question as a whole would, on the question of the New Cultivation 'not only agree, but would some of them I hope take an active part with me'.[87] For Canning it was also a very useful stick with which to beat the Government; as he wrote: 'This Slave Trade – Trinidad – Question is delightful. He [Addington] writhes and kicks under it every time that it is renewed by a hint or enquiry, in the most amusing and preposterous manner.'[88]

Canning looked for other issues on which to embarrass the Government, accepting Frere's view that Pitt should not be allowed to prevent him 'pulverizing' the Government.[89] He planned to follow up a motion thanking the Ministry for the Peace of Amiens with one thanking Pitt. The latter objected but it was successfully moved by Sir Henry Mildmay at the end of the day.[90] Other opportunities were not lacking. Canning spoke on the Address of Thanks in November 1802. Englishmen, he said pointedly, must rejoice at the spirit and love of independence shown by Switzerland in face of the French as they 'know not how soon they might be called upon to exercise the same virtues'.[91] In November it was said that 'The Grenville party with the Canningites threaten Mr Addington with a system of violent opposition.'[92] Canning's speech on the army estimates shortly afterwards certainly seemed to justify this. He attacked ministerial policy towards Russia and Sardinia; he warned that 'Providence itself . . . can scarcely save a people who are not prepared to make a struggle for their own safety.' Above all, he roundly and pointedly declared:

> Away with the cant of 'measures, not men!' the idle supposition that it is the harness and not the horses that draw the chariot along! No, Sir, if the comparison must be made, if the distinction must be taken, men are everything, measures comparatively nothing. I speak, Sir, of times of difficulty and danger; of time when systems are shaken, when precedents and general rules of conduct fail. Then it is, that not to this or that measures, however prudently devised, however blameless, in execution, but to the energy and character of individuals, a state must be indebted to its salvation.[93]

The ending of what Canning called 'a state neither of peace nor of war'[94] by the renewal of the war brought Pitt back actively into the House of Commons. On 24 May he urged that Britain could not pursue a weak and timid policy[95] and in the following month had his first open disagreement with ministers.

On 3 June 1803 Colonel Peter Patten-Bold, the Member for Newton, moved five resolutions denouncing the French and attacking ministers for their whole course of conduct towards them during the peace, for deceiving Parliament and in particular criticizing the decision to evacuate the Cape. Canning had worked out the format for these resolutions together with Tom Grenville.[96] Pitt took a middle line. He argued that he could neither applaud ministers nor concur in the full extent of the resolutions, and so he moved the Orders of the Day. Canning spoke emphatically in favour of the resolutions. Ministers clearly could tolerate neither the resolutions nor Pitt's alternative, as the latter would leave criticism suspended over them.[97] Ministers defeated Pitt by 333 to 56 votes whereupon Pitt and several of his friends left the House. The Foxites refused to support the resolutions, for as Fox said, though they could not approve the conduct of ministers, their successors might be even more objectionable. Indeed, the war was clearly opening the fundamental cleavages within the forces opposed to Addington. Historically the Foxites had been opposed to the war, and on 24 May 1803 sixty-seven of them had supported Grey's pacifically-inclined amendment to the Address.[98] When Pattens' resolutions came to the vote they found thirty-four supporters against 275 Government men. Canning acted as a teller along with Earl Temple, nephew of Lord Grenville, and his brother Tom.[99] The minority consisted of Grenvillites and such Pittites as were inclined to Canning's views,[100] together with three members of Fitzwilliam's connection and a few stragglers.

On paper the Government had survived this brush with Opposition very well. Nevertheless, the combined minorities plus the Foxites totalled about 150 MPs. Furthermore, Pitt himself had begun to show his hand. In May he had complained that no one did his cause so much disservice as Grenville in the House of Lords except Canning in the House of Commons.[101] Still, he was being slowly dragged in the direction desired by Canning and Grenville. The Speaker blamed them for poisoning Pitt's mind against Addington, who had in fact played perfectly straightly. They had used, he said, the King's hasty expressions when the Prince of Wales and Lord Moira exasperated the King against Pitt, and blamed the King's attitude on Addington.[102]

Canning himself saw that much had been gained. The great project for the session of evicting Addington had failed. Nevertheless, 'the next best object is fully attained. P. is completely, avowedly, *unmistakeably* and irrecoverably separated from A. and if not in direct hostility to him, restrained from being so only by consideration for the K[ing].'[103] Shortly afterwards Canning spent a politically agreeable week with Pitt, though he was worried that there seemed no reason why the Addington Administration should not hobble on.

Meanwhile the international situation darkened further. In France invasion preparations were well in hand. In Britain the Government mishandled the levying of a volunteer force intended for the contingency. Pitt watched with concern. In September additional reasons were provided for inclining him against the Government when a pamphlet appeared under the superscription of 'A Near Observer', probably Hiley Addington, which attacked Pitt and praised the Ministry. Canning was denounced in the pamphlet as 'a mere partisan and stickler for the House of Grenville ... an instrument of Mr Windham, and an auxiliary of Mr Cobbett'.[104] Canning was undoubtedly pleased at the growing

breach between Pitt and the Government. He wrote to Pitt re-
peatedly for guidance and had the effrontery to declare that he
wished 'to regulate myself not in exact imitation of your conduct
but in strict conformity to your views'.[105] Pitt certainly had some
strong criticisms of the Government. He itemized the handling of
the volunteers, the inadequate defence of maritime counties, the
slowness of naval preparations, the non-embargo on certain items
of naval equipment passing into French ports, and policy towards
Spain. However, he did not promise to come to London himself
to take part in any attack on the Government and warned against
'any harrassing opposition'.[106]

This lack of positive intentions on Pitt's part disgusted Canning
and at the same time grounds for personal offence arose. Pitt had
commissioned a reply to the Government pamphlet of September.
At first he had thought of Canning for its author, but thinking the
latter's style would be too recognizable, he approached a Mr
Courtenay who wrote it as 'a more accurate observer'. This
pamphlet declared that 'Mr Pitt disapproved highly of Mr Canning's Parliamentary conduct.'[107] Canning complained bitterly to
Pitt of the statement's 'propriety, its justice, and its truth'. He
asked Pitt:

> Have I failed to resort to you and to put myself into your hands?
> not for a pitiful dole of counsel from day to day, but for such
> an enlarged comprehensive plan of instructions as should pre-
> scribe my course, and define my end: leaving me, no doubt . . .
> with that freedom in subordinate parts, without which every
> action must be mere puppetry, and every word echo and imita-
> tion.[108]

Pitt excused himself in reply, and the two arranged to meet before
the end of the year.[109]

In January 1804 Grenville approached Pitt to suggest they link
forces to get rid of Addington. Canning backed up the suggestion
in verse.[110] Pitt, however, refused. Canning felt that he had thrown
away the greatest situation offered him, and blamed the influence
of Lord Camden.[111] At the same time Canning described to his
friend Granville the attitude of Pitt to himself. Lady Hester
Stanhope, Pitt's niece, with whom he was living, told Canning
that Pitt was attached to him 'in a way unlike what he feels about
anybody else'. Canning then recalled that that was probably in

the past tense, and again quoted Pitt, via Lady Hester, as to Canning's 'ungovernable ambition and impatience of idleness and obscurity'. Clearly the relationship had changed radically since 1794. Pitt had, however, explained his own future actions. It was, he said, only when Government had shown themselves determined to reject his suggestions that he should pronounce them unfit for their situations, and the country, in his opinion, not safe in their hands.[112]

In 1804 Canning participated in a sustained onslaught on the Government. On 7 March he supported Sir John Wrottesley's motion for an inquiry into the conduct of the Irish government. 'If such was refused,' he declared, 'I must repent of the vote I gave, as an English member for the Union, and now, as an Irish member, protest against this apathy in the House towards the interests of Ireland.' The motion was lost by 178 to 82. Creevey's motion for documents on the war in Ceylon, lost by 70 to 47 votes on 12 March, found Canning again in the minority. On 15 March Pitt himself came to Parliament and moved for papers comparing the state of the navy in 1803 with that in 1801, as the navy stood high in Pitt's list of priorities. This time the motion was lost by 201 to 130. On 19 March there was a minority of 56 against 173 on a motion for re-committing the Volunteer Consolidation Bill. On this the Pittites nevertheless felt obliged to support the Government. In total, 169 MPs voted against the Government in one or more of these divisions.[113] A combination of Foxites, Pittites and Grenvilles, they were gradually growing into a formidable force.

In April 1804 the onslaught was renewed. Pitt was highly worried by the military situation, and on the ninth wrote to Canning of the need for a general arming of the maritime counties.[114] Canning continued to denounce the Government. 'Ministers', he said, 'had nothing consistent or uniform in their views. They knew not what they proposed, and they took no effectual means of carrying any of their plans into effect. They were subject to eternal variations of opinion. They never advanced boldly to any object. "They lightly waddled to the end in view." ' Canning was in two further minorities on the Irish Militia Bill.[115] On 23 and 25 April the Government had to face virtual censure motions, the first from Fox being defeated by only fifty-two, the second from Pitt losing by only 240 to 203. On the same day Canning's friend Dent carried a procedural motion against the Government by 100 to 76. It was, however, Pitt's motion which was decisive. It arose from his general objections to the Government's mishandling of the defence of the country, and in particular to the Army of Reserve Suspension Bill.[116]

Already Pitt had been negotiating with the Lord Chancellor, Lord Eldon, who represented those members of the Government who were unhappy with the way things were going. After the votes of the twenty-fifth Addington realized he could not longer sustain a defence against all the opposition forces uniting against him. All he could look forward to was more and more waverers deserting him as the idea of Pitt's return to office grew plausible. On 30 April Eldon told Pitt that Addington had resigned. Pitt was now certain to return as First Minister. The only question was the sort of Government he would head.

The period from 1801 to 1804 was unusual in Canning's life insofar as he spent most of his career as a supporter of Government. One finds him in this period fundamentally masking private feelings with public principles. He was appalled that a nonentity such as Addington should replace Pitt, and he was frightened that this would blight his own prospects. In the early part of the period there can be little justification for his attitude. He received little harm at Addington's hands, yet stopped at nothing to render the latter contemptible. His relations with Pitt were thus badly damaged by these three years. Pitt felt a certain obligation to Addington and failed to see why his own political conduct should be dictated by a man who owed everything to him. Relations with Canning were then very strained, and at one time the latter thought their intercourse 'closed for ever'.[117] It was essentially Pitt's view of international affairs which eventually forced him into activity. This was easier because by 1803 his own and Addington's closest supporters had created a degree of enmity between them which the principals had not desired. Canning and his friends could not understand Pitt's attitude. They were always convinced that Pitt was on the verge of stepping back into the political arena and they moved back and forth between jubilation and gloom. Had Pitt still not stepped forward in 1804 they would have been driven frantic. Frere said that if Pitt could turn out the Doctor and refused, the ruin of the country was to be laid at his door.[118] As it was, Pitt at last lived up to the expectations of his most ardent supporters and they waited eagerly to see the shape of his new Government.

Canning's personal life in this period was highly satisfactory. He was deeply in love with his wife and wrote to her constantly when absent, keeping her in touch with events. This was probably just as well for his personal mental balance, as the concept of retirement as something which might have to be borne was in his mind at this period.[119]

In 1801 his eldest son was born after a protracted and painful labour. He was christened George Charles Canning, the middle name being a tribute to their friend Princess Caroline, who was a godmother and who came to stay with them in September.[120] The young boy was described by Canning as 'plump, good-humoured, lively, full of health and vigour and spirits ...'[121] In fact he was to suffer from lameness and perpetual ill-health and to meet a premature death in 1820. In December 1802 another son was born, William Pitt Canning, who enjoyed excellent health but who was later to cause his father much anguish through his unsuccessful gambling. In 1804 a daughter Harriet, later Lady Clanricarde, was born.

In June 1801 the family moved to South Hill, near Bracknell. Canning dabbled in farming and by 1802 was losing £100 per year in this pursuit. Altogether, he was now firmly established domestically. His financial position had been transformed, but even his enlarged resources were feeling something of a strain from sudden expenditures. In 1802 he told Frere that he had sold two diamond snuff-boxes to a Jew 'for £300 – Guineas – I should say, I beg the Jew's pardon'.[122]

Canning's domestic circumstances can be learned from his six-monthly tax return. The £68 1s 9½d[123] he paid at Michaelmas 1801 included an assessment for ten male servants, two four- and one two-wheeled carriages and a dog.[124] This was not outstanding wealth, but it was comfortable and more than Canning could have expected three years earlier.

Thus well-established as a family man and happy with the return of Pitt as the fulfillment of all he had worked for during the past three years, Canning must have viewed his world in May 1804 as not falling far short of his greatest ambitions ... so far.

4

THE PITTITE INHERITANCE

Canning's hopes were not to be realized. In his previous sixteen years in office Pitt had built up an almost unbeatable coalition of parliamentary factions. One of the results of the 1801 crisis was the dispersal of this coalition, and by 1804 Parliament was in a more fluid state than it had been since the death of Rockingham in 1782. Could Pitt manage again to form a Government from the factions whose only common ground was their dislike of the Addington Administration? He could and did, but to Canning's utter amazement there was one glaring omission from the new Cabinet: himself.

The opposition to Addington had been incredibly heterogeneous. It included exiled Pittites of various hues, the Grenville political-family connection and orthodox Foxites. On the face of it there would appear to be little hope of co-operation among these groups to act as a whole. The most important political issue upon which they argued among themselves was, of course, the prosecution of the war.

Canning never despaired of attempts to draw European coalitions together to crush what he saw as a threat to British security. Windham, bitter in his dislike of the Addington Administration, was also bitter in his denunciation of Fox, for whom the war was a mistake to be ended as quickly as possible. In 1803 when the Foxites had divided alone on a resolution for peace, Fox had said:

> Let no man now look to his holding a pound without giving possibly fifteen shillings of it to Government towards the prosecution of the war ... and all this for what? For Malta!

Plain, bare, naked Malta, unconnected with any other interest.[1]

It might seem unlikely that such an opposition could unite with Pitt in a new government; nevertheless, those who in 1803 looked to the rapid termination of the Addington Government hoped for just this. The idea of the junction was not universally popular. Speaker Abbott wrote of the general dissatisfaction amongst Pitt's friends and among the public at the prospect of Fox's inclusion.[2] Canning, however, regarded it as desirable for he saw the necessity of Pitt's new government basing itself firmly on a parliamentary majority. Clearly, his personal distaste for the Addingtonians exceeded his purely political distrust of the Foxites. Grenville was even more firmly committed to an alliance of this sort.

The project was never brought to the test. The King had long hated Fox and was most unwilling to have him take any part in administration. Perhaps Pitt could have compelled the King to yield by threatening to remain in opposition, but he was fearful of such a step. The King was generally regarded as being only precariously sane and Pitt was prepared neither on this nor the Catholic issue to risk provoking a relapse. Besides reasons of humanity, there was the prospect of the Prince of Wales as Regent and Pitt had a long-standing fear of decisive action. He might in Canning's words have once 'weathered the storm' but usually he was more inclined to seek the nearest port, however insalubrious, whenever the wind blew hard.

The port into which Pitt was blown when he formed a Government in May 1804 was not to Canning's liking. The Cabinet included six members of Addington's. These were the Earl of Westmorland, the Duke of Portland, Lord Eldon, Lord Hawkesbury, Viscount Castlereagh and the Earl of Chatham. Apart from Pitt, Canning could acknowledge little quality in most of this Cabinet, though he always respected Viscount Melville, as Henry Dundas had become, and impartial observers acknowledge the talents of Hawkesbury and Castlereagh.

Canning's exclusion from the Cabinet was something of a surprise. Pitt argued that cabinet office would be injurious to Canning himself as he would not be thought ready for it.[3] In fact it is more likely the real reason was that Pitt's enthusiasm for Canning had waned considerably and that there were other men who could be of better use in the Cabinet. Seeing the way things were going

Canning set off for South Hill telling Pitt that he was prepared to
return to town at an hour's notice if wanted. Pitt replied to Canning conceding his arrangement was not the best, but asserting
that it would be efficient and strong. Meanwhile he had left the
offices of Treasurer of the Navy and Secretary at War vacant for
Canning to choose.[4]

On 13 May Canning accepted the office of Treasurer of the
Navy, whose function was management and control of the finances
of the navy. It had been held by Melville in Addington's day,[5]
but it was not the cabinet office that Canning had wanted. What
galled him further was the inclusion in the Cabinet of Hawkesbury
(Jenkinson) and Castlereagh. This was far worse for Canning than
the non-serious office holders such as Lord Mulgrave and the
Duke of Montrose. The former pair were Canning's rivals for
the most valuable political prize in prospect – the ultimate leadership of the Pittites. Canning saw it as his by right of superior
intelligence. Hawkesbury was eventually to win it only to see his
re-grouping of the Pittite coalition crumble in the hands of his
successor and rival.

In addition to this disappointment Canning objected to the
principles on which the Cabinet was based. He described it as a
'shabby narrow Government'[6] and the quality of its leadership he
regarded as deplorable. 'It is sad work – such a Cabinet to be
under.'[7] In addition, he was not feeling particularly well at the
time as he had recently had a severe fall riding in which his mare
had trodden upon, and severely injured, his leg.

In such a Government Canning could not be expected to feel
at ease. The tension boiled over on 18 June when Canning, speaking in favour of the Additional Force Bill, felt constrained to
deliver a strong attack on the former Administration. Hawkesbury
felt, not unreasonably, that this was directed toward himself, for
he had been Foreign Secretary at the time. Hawkesbury's father,
the first Earl of Liverpool, who disliked Canning, claimed to have
letters showing that Pitt had offered to dismiss Canning for this
attack but that Hawesbury had not insisted on this.[8] The story,
embellished with humble apologies from Canning, was spread by
Hawkesbury himself[9] and appeared in the press. Canning was
naturally angry and spread his own version[10] claiming Pitt's, and
finally Hawkesbury's, agreement that the story was false. The
story has interesting features. Clearly Canning convinced his

friends. 'The Pope', said Lady Bessborough, who always referred to Canning in this way, 'was delightful and staid with me till past six, but making my blood boil at Lord Hawkesbury's unheard of shabbiness (which he does not know the extent of as well as I do)'.[11] Fox himself was convinced as to Canning's integrity in the matter. Canning wrote to his friend John Sneyd. He claimed to have a minute in which Hawkesbury accepted that Canning never agreed to apologize for his speech. 'But', said Canning, 'he is a lying shuffling hound and therefore I keep the minute to come in aid of this, in case it should be necessary.'[12]

Interestingly enough, the only matter that Canning was formally pursuing was the 'point of honour' involved in the question of apology. Neither Hawkesbury nor Pitt denied in public that the latter had offered to dismiss Canning, and so the accusation that Canning was in the Government by grace and favour of his rival was a very serious one and could certainly be regarded as a point of honour. Pitt's prevarication on the issue, of which Canning complained, is a hint that he probably did offer to dismiss Canning. Hawkesbury's original complaint must, after all, be regarded as justified and Pitt might well have lost patience. Canning was certainly called on to explain his words, but that he had stopped short of a humble apology gave him an issue on which to stand firm and hope that the whole would be regarded as false whose part was overstated.

The highest offices continued to elude Canning. Late in 1804 it became clear that poor health would not long allow Harrowby to continue as Foreign Secretary. Thomas Grenville wrote accurately to his brother, 'Canning, if there was likely to be a question of him is, I am informed, not thought to be in high favour in Downing Street.'[13] The new Foreign Secretary was, to Canning's disappointment, Lord Mulgrave. Worse news awaited. Since its inception it had been clear that Pitt's Government needed more parliamentary strength. The vote on the Additional Force Bill on 18 June had only been carried by 265 to 223 votes. New strength for the Government was found in January 1805, when Addington became Lord President of the Council as Viscount Sidmouth.

Wilberforce called Pitt's treatment of Addington 'one of the noblest exercises of true magnanimity that was ever exhibited to the admiration and imitation of mankind'.[14] Canning could hardly be expected to see it as other than a bitter blow, for he now had to serve under a Cabinet filled with men he despised and including a man whom he had recently denounced for 'systematic opposition' to Pitt.

On 4 January Frere visited Canning to persuade him not to resign.[15] On the sixth he wrote that he had tendered his resignation but would probably not go out. 'The Doctor's business', he had groaned, '. . . now appears in its naked horror.'[16] On 1 January he had written to Lady Hester Stanhope, 'I cannot face the House of Commons or walk the streets in this state of things, as I am,' and complained of Pitt's unkindness in not consulting him.[17] In fact Pitt took some pity on him. Canning visited him on the eighth in town at Pitt's request. The latter begged him to stay in office, talked of the necessity of getting strength for the Government through the admission of Addington and offered him the Irish First Secretaryship if he preferred it to his present office. Canning dined with Pitt on the ninth and the fourteenth, finally deciding against becoming Irish Secretary on the fifteenth after discussing it with others.[18]

If Canning had acquiesced on the arrangement, he was certainly not happy with it. On 25 February he wrote to Granville regretting that a party of Pitt's friends out of office had not originally been formed. Again he complained of 'the miserable colleagues whom he [Pitt] had thought fit to associate to himself'. But his own relationship with Pitt had improved slightly. He wrote a speech for Pitt on military defence though he still could not talk to him on many questions. However, he managed to tell Pitt that he ought to make it clear he was supreme in the Administration so that 'these people will sink into their intrinsic nothingness'. He also told Pitt that he would do nothing which would make it inconsistent 'to oppose them, with fire and sword' in the event of Pitt's separation from Addington. As for the rest, Canning told Granville, he looked 'with the most perfect indifference on all that passes in Parliament in which I am not personally concerned'.[19] Nor was there, as far as Canning could see, any real compensatory advantage in the terms of a real increase in parliamentary strength. In April he wrote that 'P. is weaker than the Dr ever was.' All he could do was to stay in office. Canning again attacked those who had originally urged Pitt to acquiesce in the construction of his Government on a narrow base.[20]

All the hopes Canning had nurtured when out of office now lay in ruins. In some ways the situation was worse, for at least then there had been hopes of improvement. Now Canning saw his patron drifting away from him into a political connection whose narrowness he detested.

Amongst other things, it nevertheless fell to Canning to defend the military policy of the Government. In February 1805 he had to answer a motion from Windham asking for a committee on the defence of the country. He tried to show that the disposable forces available for Britain's needs were 20,000 more than at the same time in the previous year. In April he defended the Militia Enlisting Bill and in June he answered a motion by Grey, declaring that 'Lord Nelson's fleet was more than adequate in every respect, to the French Fleet'.[21] To illustrate Canning's life style at this time one can take a week from his diary. On Monday, 22 April 1805 he went to South Hill alone. On Tuesday he stayed there, dining with George Ellis at Sunning Hill nearby. On Wednesday he returned to town. He and Joan dined in a large party at the Mildmays and then went to the play. On Thursday he went to the office and then to Parliament where he spoke for three to four hours. He also supped with Pitt. On Friday he again went to the office and to Parliament, dining with the Dents. Saturday he spent at the office and Sunday he called on Lady Bessborough and dined with Lady Mulgrave. The record shows a fairly active mixing of social and political life, though the latter appears to be less arduous than in his previous period as Under-Secretary or subsequently as Secretary of State for Foreign Affairs.

One major incident of 1805 affected Canning greatly. In February the Commissioner of Naval Enquiry revealed that while Lord Melville was Treasurer of the Navy, Mr Trotter, the Paymaster, had transferred funds to his private account. It was also revealed that Melville, apparently rather confused, had agreed to these transfers. The issue was a serious one. The practice of mixing public funds in one's private account had been common in the mid-eighteenth century – on such had the fortune of Henry Fox been based. But by the turn of the nineteenth century it was viewed as corruption, and in this case it affected one of Pitt's closest associates, now First Lord of the Admiralty; moreover, Canning was involved by virtue of his tenure of the office in question. Ironically he had on his appointment thanked Trotter for his invaluable help![22] Canning did not shirk the task of defending Melville. Lady Bessborough considered that no one had done well in the affair except he, though perhaps Canning's own views are best gained from her comment that while she was sorry for Melville, 'I suppose it is very bad since even the Pope [Canning] says so.'[23] Canning himself felt he had acted honestly in giving Melville and 'my unfortunate paymaster' time to defend themselves.[24]

In the Commons Samuel Whitbread had moved a strongly-worded censure motion on Melville on 8 April. Canning asked if it were 'fair to call on the house to convict the party without a hearing, which had not yet been had?'[25] The case put the Government in a tricky situation. The *coup de grace* came with a speech from Wilberforce. In the early 1780s he had been Pitt's closest friend, but his religious conversion led to a gradual breach. A decade later the Government regarded his voting record with suspicion, looking on him as a man who was always with them, except when he was needed. Rarely could his help have proved more timely than at this moment, but he had prayed long on the subject and felt obliged to join in the censure of Melville on what was a moral as well as a political question. He certainly swayed a large number of votes, such that the tally stood at 216 on each side. White-faced, the Speaker voted to keep the question before the House and as the motion was declared carried, Pitt, humiliated, collapsed in tears surrounded by his friends while the hard core of the Opposition cried out in jubilation like huntsmen after a view.

The resignation of Melville and the dismissal of Trotter was not enough for the Opposition. On the tenth Whitbread moved a strongly-worded address designed to preclude his return. 'I cannot, Sir,' replied Canning, 'refuse to the honourable gentleman the praise of Spartan inflexibility, or more than Roman virtue, but while humbly and at a distance I admire the exertion of these high qualities in him, I pray to Almighty God to spare me the pain of being ever called upon to imitate his example'.[26] Essentially his speech was a plea for mercy, but like Pitt he conceded that Melville had effectively excluded himself from the King's councils.

On the eleventh Canning called on Pitt and found him 'sadly cast down'.[27] The matter was by no means cleared up for the Opposition had tasted blood. Grey asked for the printer of a pro-Government journal, *The Oracle*[28] to be called before the House for his 'libellous' words that Melville had 'fallen a victim to confidence displaced; to prejudice misjudged and to indignation misapplied'. Canning defended him as merely showing intemperate zeal but he was nevertheless summoned and censured.[29] To add to the Government's troubles, Sidmouth (Addington) started putting forward the pretensions of his group for a greater say in the Government, at the same time questioning the handling of the affair. Canning was bitter. 'That rascally Doctor, that scoundrelly Doctor. . . . He must have his grievances forsooth, and his pretensions and his opposite opinions – and must state them too, and threaten to go out upon them – when? Just at the moment when P. was in distress. . . . Who was right all along? Who knew this man from the beginning? Who advised against trusting him?'[30]

Relations with the Sidmouth group worsened. On 11 June a member of the Sidmouth party, Nathaniel Bond, supported by Hiley Addington, carried a motion by nine votes to substitute a criminal prosecution for an impeachment of Melville.[31] At the same time they used fairly intemperate language. The Marquess of Buckingham wrote, 'The violence of Pitt's friends against Addington cannot be described.'[32] Canning of course went out of his way to make the breach as final as possible but even Pitt himself could no longer contemplate office for Hiley Addington in particular. The Sidmouth group had thus scuppered their own ambitions by at least a misinterpretation of the freedom of action they were allowed.[33] Perhaps also they desired to demonstrate their importance by playing a balancing role between parliamentary factions which seemed evenly balanced. From Canning's point of view the subsequent resignation of Sidmouth himself on 5 July was a great point gained, even if it did weaken the Government further. The subsequent cabinet shuffles did not, however, favour him. The aged Lord Barham replaced Melville at the Admiralty and Camden became Lord President in the place of Sidmouth. Castlereagh took Camden's office as Secretary of State for War and the Colonies in plurality with his existing position as President of the Board of Control (for India). Harrowby returned to the Cabinet as Chancellor of the Duchy of Lancaster.

Canning spent the summer in the south and west, leaving town on 24 July. Part of the time he spent with Sturges-Bourne at Weymouth where at one point he saw the King on the Esplanade and talked to him for a long time. Afterwards he went to Christchurch (Hampshire) where the days passed 'in a most quiet and uneventful uniformity' with his family. He wrote letters, bathed and walked on the beach. A letter to his mother recounts one incident, describing

> ... the result of my interference last year in behalf of a poor girl, whom, when I last spoke to you of her, flattered myself I had rescued from destitution: Alas! it turned out otherwise. After she had been at home about ten days, I called at her Aunt's house and she was gone. A miscarriage had relieved her from her burden, and as if she had only waited for that relief she had in the course of a few days taken her leave, announcing her resolution to return to her former way of life. At first I suspected harsh treatment on the part of the Aunt ... (but this not the case) ... yet I am persuaded her first repentance was sincere. Her second I am afraid, will be a bitter one poor girl.[34]

The end of the summer saw no brightening of the political horizon for Canning. Pitt again tried to broaden the base of his Government and even visited Weymouth to press his views on an obdurate monarch. However, Grenville had recently presided over the Stowe fete where a public demonstration of attachment to the Prince of Wales had made the King dislike him as much as he disliked Fox.[35] The Hanovarians were never famous for domestic concord, and politicians had to choose sides within the Royal Family carefully.

As the prospect of a broadening of the Government faded, Canning felt desperately frustrated with politics. Eventually at dinner with Pitt in late October he complained bitterly of his own position and grievances of the previous eighteen months. Pitt seems to have promised that Canning could be raised to Cabinet rank without changing his office and, while the latter told Pitt he would have preferred a more responsible post, he no longer felt he had legitimate cause for complaint. Certainly by late November, Canning was convinced that he would be added to the Cabinet in the New Year. There were nevertheless other views. George Rose could not conceive that 'it could ever have entered Mr Pitt's mind for a single moment ... such a sudden advancement would have given much offence, and would, I am sure have been generally disapproved of.'[36] However, it must be pointed out that at this stage relations between Pitt and Canning were more friendly than they had been for some years. This may partly have arisen from Pitt's ill-will towards Sidmouth as a result of the Melville affair.

Meanwhile the skies were darkening over Europe. Trafalgar had, as Canning said, brightened 'the prospect of public affairs',[37] but Britain's power to direct a blow at the power of Napoleon in Europe was reduced considerably by the defeat of the Austrian and Russian Forces, first at Ulm in October then at Austerlitz in December. The Russians withdrew, the Austrians signed humiliating terms at Pressburg and the Prussians accepted Napoleon's offer to cede them Hanover, part of George III's dominions. Furthermore, Britain was forced to withdraw an expeditionary force she had despatched to north Germany in October.

Canning was fully aware of the seriousness of the situation. Before the event he had declared that he could not 'believe in the separate peace and nothing else is fatal or irretrievable'.[38] When this eventuality was upon them, Canning was not alone in blaming the breakdown of Pitt's health on the international situation. Throughout December Pitt had remained at Bath ill through gout. It was here that the news of the Franco-Austrian armistice reached him and as he headed back to his home at Putney he was already a sick man. On 8 January 1806 Canning wrote to Sneyd that 'if he fails, all is up, to be sure.'[39] and wrote to Pitt to persuade him to come and rest at South Hill. Pitt in fact returned to Putney where Canning visited him on the fourteenth at Pitt's request conveyed through Lady Hester. He wrote, 'The change since Bath dreadful! and his appearance such as I shall never forget.'[40] Despite this, to Canning's horror, Lord Chatham saw Pitt on business on the fifteenth.[41] On the eighteenth there seemed to be better news[42] but in fact Pitt was slipping quietly away in the presence of his family and Bishop Tomline of Lincoln. On the twenty-second Canning again visited Putney, but Pitt was too ill to see him, and on the twenty-third Canning received final news of his death. 'But five hours dead!' he wrote, 'nay, not five, not so much! and to be mentioned already merely as a fact. Alas.'[43] Charles Ellis described Canning's condition as 'dreadful': 'He could not cry or speak; he had been sanguine enough to hope to the very last, and the blow came unbroke upon him.'[44] Canning was not alone in these feelings. Melville wrote, 'The fatal blow

D

which overwhelms us admits of no comfort.' The Russian Ambassador, he added, was 'quite overwhelmed with grief and despair'.[45]

Canning at least had the consolation that he had remained loyal to Pitt the last two years, however unpleasant at times.[46] The blow was nevertheless a hard one. On the day of his funeral he wrote: 'How solitary and dismal everything appears now that he is out of this world.'[47] Although Canning would not have appreciated it, there is black humour in the chronological death column printed in his own diary for 1807:

> Miss Mary Ann Grove, of Fern House, Wilts., by her clothes catching fire – The Right Hon. W. Pitt, First Lord of the Treasury, and Mr G. Adrey, ensign in the 60th regiment in consequence of drinking near a quart of rum for a wager.[48]

The death of Pitt marked the death of an administration and the temporary interment of a political system created twenty-two years earlier. There were rumours that Marquess Wellesley and Canning might try to patch up the Administration, but it would have been impossible, even if they had had the will to try. At a critical point in British history, the ship of state was to be manned by a fresh crew.

The King had long resisted the inclusion of Fox and his supporters in his Government. He remembered the bitter struggle he had had with them in 1783 before dismissing them over the India Bill. Now he was faced with a situation where no Pittite was willing or able to form a Government. He was left with no choice but to turn to Lord Grenville.

'The loss of P.', wrote Canning, 'has necessarily thrown the K. into the hands of the united opposition'. Grenville, he said, had *carte blanche*.[49] Fox became Foreign Secretary. Charles Grey, tainted with Jacobinism by his erstwhile membership of the 'Friends of the People', was First Lord of the Admiralty. Windham was the new Secretary of State for War and the Colonies. Lord Henry Petty, a man of 'advanced' principles in both politics and religion, became Chancellor of the Exchequer. Fitzwilliam, notorious as the former pro-Catholic Lord Lieutenant of Ireland, represented with Spencer the great Whig houses. Sidmouth re-appeared in the Cabinet as Lord Privy Seal.

For the King, Sidmouth alone must have appeared as a glimmer of light in a galaxy of darkness. Canning was horrified. The new arrangements he said, 'are more disgusting than it was possible to believe.[50] ... The proscription of Pitt's friends is complete without a single exception.'[51]

The party of Pitt had always regarded itself as the party of the King and the party of Government. This had been the rationale of its creation and now, excluded as a body it was not immediately clear to them what their course of action should be. They met frequently and on 8 February Canning called on Lord Lowther and had a long discussion on 'the state of public affairs and the conduct fit to be pursued by P's friends'. Later he was visited by Castlereagh and Perceval for the same reason. The latter was a rising star amongst Pitt's party. A lawyer, he had entered Parliament for Northampton in 1796 and quickly distinguished himself for the depth of his evangelical convictions and implacable opposition to reform in Church and State. Under Addington he had been first Solicitor- and then Attorney-General. Canning had not yet learnt to view him as a rival and so favoured his pretensions over those of Castlereagh and Hawkesbury.

On 17 February a huge party of Pitt's friends met at Castlereagh's for dinner and again on the twentieth at Camden's. There was one equivocal element in the attitude of this group, and that was their attitude to Grenville, with whom many had had friendly connection and whom they clearly distinguished from his associates. Canning wrote a scathing poem on the members of the new Administration which ended:

> *But if amongst this motley crew*
> *One man of real parts we view*
> *With mind for highest station fit,*
> *The colleague, friend, yet foe of Pitt,*
> *He, to whose merits all men granted,*
> *That Pitt's last list, one great name wanted,*
> *He, who with every talent shone,*
> *Except consistency alone,*
> We smile, if such a man there be
> *But weep, if Grenville should be he.*[52]

In February Castlereagh and Hawkesbury decided that Pitt's friends should stay together and not oppose except where the Administration was subversive of Pitt's principles. They were also to be ready to aid Grenville against Fox. Canning could hardly object to this, but he was very angry at the pretension of Castlereagh and Hawkesbury to set the direction for Pitt's friends. He certainly would acknowledge no leader in the House of Commons, especially not Hawkesbury with whom Canning had 'pointedly declared he would never have any intercourse'. Canning therefore suggested that they should look up to someone such as Lawther or Beaufort as a *point d'appui* for the party. His alternative was the extraordinary suggestion that the party should combine a vigorous opposition to the Government with looking up to Grenville as the real leader of the party:[53] Canning was therefore prepared to see a nonentity or a political enemy in charge of the Pittites, but on no account was he prepared to brook a rival.

In March Canning told his mother that his sense of duty required 'a watchful attendance, if not an active interference in Parliament'.[54] The first debate of the new session in which Canning intervened concerned the payment of Pitt's debts. It provided an opportunity for Canning to boast 'the most vehement source of hostility' to the Ministry. The first major parliamentary assault upon the new Government came in March when the Opposition attacked the inclusion of Lord Chief Justice Ellenborough in the Cabinet. Canning spoke in favour of Spencer Stanhope's motion attacking the appointment, rejecting in particular the Government's argument that there was no such thing as a cabinet as a legal fiction.[55] The Government carried the day by 282 to 64. Castlereagh and Perceval were with Canning in the minority. The result showed clearly the parliamentary strength of the Government. On 23 February Rose and Canning had analyzed the composition of the House of Commons and considered it favourable.[56] They could not have envisaged a defeat of these proportions.

The Opposition nevertheless refused to yield. One issue of which much was made were the military reforms of William Windham, who had a perverse genius which Canning had recently learned to detest. Windham wished to change the military system to base it upon a regular army in which the soldiers benefited from improved conditions and limited terms of service. Canning wrote:

> Next W--dh-m, *metaphysic elf*,
> *Who all things knows – except himself;*

Three tedious hours who raves and talks
Of all that in his cranium stalks;
Whose regular ideas fear
Militia much, more volunteer,
A wild inapplicable genius,
Scarce versed in policy's quae genus,
In Syntax yet more scantly read,
Without one concord in his head.[57]

Certainly Windham's plans were incompatible with the military system operated under Pitt, and especially the volunteer system as expanded by the Additional Force Act of 1804. Canning misquoted Pope and described the whole as 'a mighty maze and all without a plan'[58] and genuinely bewailed the fate of the volunteer system.[59] In Parliament he spoke regularly on the subject, and on one occasion unsuccessfully moved a destructive amendment, strongly supported by Castlereagh.[60] Canning was particularly hostile to what he considered to be the dangerous provision for limited periods of service. When the bill went to the House of Lords he went with Charles Long and William Huskisson to see the result, which turned out to be a victory for the Government by 97 to 40.[61] Huskisson was now one of Canning's closest associates. Born like Canning in 1770, he had entered Parliament in 1796 when already Secretary to the Admiralty. He had resigned with Pitt in 1801, and thereafter his career was closely linked with that of Canning.

A variety of other issues arose before the summer recess which the Opposition could use to attack the Government. In May Canning opposed the Vote of Thanks to Earl St Vincent, the Whig Admiral and First Lord of the Admiralty, and in June he joined Castlereagh in opposing the Chelsea Hospital Bill to provide veterans with a hospital facility, which they felt, would encourage indiscipline by bestowing on soldiers as a right what they might expect as a boon.[62] In July Canning spoke sarcastically of 'this wonderful government, from whom so much were expected'.[63] At the end of the month he wrote to the Rev. Leigh:

Our Campaign is closed – and with such a speech from the Throne!! as if there was no continent, no ally, no Russia, no Turkish Fleet, no Cape of Good Hope in the World – not a word of Duckworth's victory – not a word of negotiating jointly

with our allies! O! shame – and nothing but trumpery about
auditing public accounts forsooth! and such twopenny-half-
penny matters.[64]

The Government was surprised at the vehemence of Canning's
opposition, especially as they knew of his unhappiness under
previous arrangements and how bad his personal relations were
with many of the Opposition. Lady Bessborough asked, 'Why,
why is the Pope so violent? All was in so far a way, yet perhaps
it gives him a fairer opportunity of speaking well, but is everything
to be sacrificed to a speech!' Canning, she felt, was 'frittering
away his talents in a fruitless opposition against people he thinks
well of, and with those he opposes'.[65] There were those in the
Government, though by no means all, who would have welcomed
Canning's accession. Grenville in particular wanted to see Canning in his Government. The European situation, the need for
effective speakers in the House of Commons and his personal
respect for his former Under-Secretary led him to make an
approach through the agency of the Marquess of Wellesley in
late June. Canning consulted Castlereagh, Perceval and Hawkesbury, who would only consider any proposition in the light of a
total re-casting of the Government. A fresh approach in August
met a similar response, and though Grenville's brother urged that
if standing firm would make the Pittites negotiate separately,
Wellesley's reports that they had determined to stick together were
accurate.[66]

Despite his interest in having Canning, Grenville was determined not to take a large number of Pittites into his Government.
His allies would not have tolerated it, even had it been his own
inclination. Canning found this attitude unreasonable and was
not prepared to take a step which would irrevocably separate him
from his own political allies, however mixed his feelings to many
of them were. He was also determined to see that his own political
followers did not take any step apart from him. Granville in particular was very inclined to take office and this led to an estrangement, both political and personal. 'I cannot agree with you', wrote
Granville in exasperation at Canning's high-handed mixture of
dictation and silence, 'as to the degree of influence which you
think politics must have upon the habits of private friendships.'[67]

An important factor which underlay the politics of 1806–7

was the attitude of the King. His hostility to the Administration was an open secret. In March Princess Caroline told Canning 'that the K. had been with her – quite well, and in pretty good spirits – hating these people – and she says talking of me much more kindly than he ever did before.'[68] It is quite clear that in June and July he was intriguing with the opposition leaders, though still unable to take open action.

Internationally the Administration faced a very gloomy situation. They had had hopes of being able to make peace with Napoleon – Canning described Fox as being 'headlong for peace – even a separate peace', adding 'but the K. I trust against it'. Such projects came to nought and the Earls of Lauderdale and Yarmouth, who went to France on a pacific mission during the summer, returned empty-handed. The French military dominance on the continent became unshakeable. The Prussians, eventually goaded into war by French activities in northern Germany, were crushed at the twin battles of Jena and Auerstadt in October. The army bequeathed by Frederick the Great would clearly not match the technique of mobility and concentration with which France had changed the face of war. Canning was bitterly critical of the Government's handling of relations with Prussia.[69] Britain's own military ventures in southern Italy and Buenos Aires also ended in fiasco.

Canning's summer was dominated to a large extent by personal affairs. A worsening in a condition of lameness which afflicted his eldest son forced him to move to Hinckley in Leicestershire to be near a prominent healer, though in the event it proved that little could be done for his son, whose health remained a constant anxiety to his parents till his death in 1820. The move to Hinckley entailed longer absences from his family. Canning felt these deeply, and in February 1807 wrote to his wife: 'Three-sevenths are very near indeed to half – and today three-sevenths of my absence from my own dearest and best of loves expires.'[70]

Early in September 1806 Charles James Fox died to the grief but hardly the surprise of his friends, for he had been ill most of the year. Thus one year had removed the two main lights of the political system. Fox and Pitt had crystallized a particular division in British politics and epitomized the ideals of many of their followers. Their own individual positions had been largely responsible for the form party political groupings took in the con-

fused years between 1801 and 1806: Pitt, because of his attitude
to the Catholic Question in 1801; and Fox, because of the loyalty
of new friends in 1806. For Canning, the magnetism which Pitt
exercised over his followers was an example to be followed, and
his fight for the Pittite inheritance was one of the main determin-
ing factors in his career.

The followers of Fox had found themselves in Government
at last with the death of Pitt. Now they saw their beloved leader
removed, and lacked anyone of the same stature to replace him.
However, the Whigs were still far too strong to be removed
simply because of Fox's death, and it required their own actions
over the next nine months to destroy them.

Meanwhile, a government re-shuffle was necessitated. Charles
Grey, later Viscount Howick and then Earl Grey, stepped into
Fox's place as Foreign Secretary and leader of the House of
Commons. The need for strength in the Commons impelled the
Government to ask for a dissolution, which the King could
scarcely refuse. The amount of patronage at the disposal of the
Government had been waning for thirty years, but it was still
sufficient to be decisive in many seats, even without the King's
private contribution, which he reserved for Governments to which
he was more favourably disposed.

Perhaps because the Whigs were less used to managing the
patronage machine at elections, the results were somewhat mixed.
Thomas Coke carried William Windham with him to victory over
the Tory in Norfolk; but in Norwich, William Smith, a radically-
inclined independent Whig, lost his seat. Nevertheless they had
the satisfaction of seeing William Roscoe, an anti-slave-trading
Whig returned for Liverpool. Canning himself could no longer
use Tralee and had to pay dearly for the privilege of again representing Newport in the Isle of Wight. The reactions of the
Opposition were nevertheless rather gloomy. Bathurst said that
'Whatever the King's real sentiments are, the dissolution of
Parliament has so strengthen'd the Ministry that he would not
be able to overthrow it, tho' Canning, Perceval and Lord Castlereagh may make it difficult for them to go on without gaining
some of them'.[71] Canning commented that the ministers had
'obtained a new lease, and they have put it out of the K. power
to have again recourse to the same expedient [a dissolution]'.[72]
Their future line of conduct was expressed by Perceval who

stressed the importance of making as good and united an appearance at the beginning of the session as possible, without risking a division at that time. He also gave an assurance that there was no truth in a rumour that the King had told Portland that those who considered themselves his friends should not oppose his 'present servants'.[73]

In early September while Fox still lay dying Grenville had made fresh approaches to Canning, which they discussed in the course of two long country walks. Canning insisted that arrangements must be generally acceptable and raised three substantial points. As regards the negotiations with France, he could give no pledge of support in the event of peace. The King's agreement to his accession was essential, and, at that time, the question of Fox's health had still to be settled. On the seventh Grenville agreed with Canning that nothing could be done till the outcome of both Fox's illness and the Paris negotiations were known. Nevertheless on the eleventh a renewed offer was made, embracing cabinet office for Canning, the Privy Council for another nominee, and a law office for Perceval.[74]

On Saturday 13 September the prospect of agreement vanished, Wellesley telling Canning that the difficulties arose from 'his numerous pretensions'. Canning himself suggested that if Grenville had further offers to make, he put them to the Duke of Portland, who was now regarded as the figurehead for the opposition.[75] It was on the evening of that day that Fox died, thus increasing the need for fresh recruiting to the Government.

On the sixteenth Canning wrote to Wellesley saying he had thought of a mode of arrangement which might lessen what appeared to be insuperable difficulties.[76] The essential problem was that while Canning wanted to bring several other Pittites with him into the Government, most of the Whigs wanted Canning to join alone. Grenville was not prepared to go much further than his original offer to provide a law office for Perceval. Canning again told him to negotiate through Portland and lamented that Grenville should have lost so favourable an opportunity to gain that ascendancy which a connection with Pitt's friends would give.[77] The ascendancy to which Canning referred was of course that over Grenville's own colleagues of a more radical persuasion. Lady Bessborough blamed Canning for his attitude and was glad that Granville did not join him 'in an

opposition so hopeless and so useless as this is likely to be', and
this with Hawkesbury and Castlereagh 'both of whom, as long
as they were ministers, abus'd and treated him [Canning] as ill as
it was in *their little power* to do'.[78] By October it was clear to
Grenville that Canning had bound himself by certain commitments to the Opposition,[79] and thus it was that the Government
had looked to another source of fresh strength – a dissolution.
All that was left of the negotiation was discussion between Grenville and Canning as to an agreed version of events the latter
could give to his friends.[80]

One further attempt to get Canning to join the Government
was made. In February 1807 Grenville's own family urged on
him the desirability of the junction. They were particularly
worried by the possibility of the first Earl Grey's death and the
consequent elevation of Charles Grey, Viscount Howick, to
the House of Lords, for they would lose his speaking ability in
the Commons.[81] This made a recruit such as Canning doubly
welcome.

According to Canning, Tierney, the President of the Board of
Control, considered his accession 'to be purchased at any rate'.[82]
The negotiations were opened by the Government, using Grenville's nephew Earl Temple as an intermediary. Canning was
aware of certain weaknesses in the Government's position. Grenville was disliked by the King and had quarrelled with the Prince
Regent. He was disliked by many of the Foxites. Furthermore the
Cabinet was badly split on the Catholic question. Canning nevertheless gave the proposed junction serious consideration. He
drew up an elaborate chart of leading Pittites in order to analyze
whom it would be best to bring into the Cabinet with him, supposing he were allowed only one:

	1	2	3	4	5	6	7	8
Lord Eldon		+	+	+		O		
Lord Castlereagh							O	O
Lord Mulgrave	+		+		+			
Sir William Grant			+	+	+			
Sir Charles Yorke		+	+	+	+	O		
Earl of Chatham	+	+		+		O		O
Earl Bathurst	+	+		+	+			

(1)   who would carry most of Pitt?
(2)   who would bring or satisfy most people?
(3)   who would feel the most obliged to *me*?
(4)   who would the King like best?
(5)   whom would Lord G[renville] like best?
(6)   Inefficiency
(7)   Unpopularity
(8)   'Mischievous intrigue'.

Having thus analyzed his colleagues, Canning added, 'Perhaps Lord Bathurst is the best of all.'[83] It is perhaps interesting that the only person on the list who was really a threat to Canning, namely Castlereagh, was rated much lower than anyone else.

Negotiations continued. On Friday 6 March, Grenville and Canning met at Hampstead and the former expressed a strong wish that the latter become Chancellor of the Exchequer. They arranged to meet again on the Monday. A further problem had now arisen. Grenville felt obliged to make Whitbread Secretary at War when General Fitzpatrick, a superannuated friend of Fox, vacated the office. Furthermore, Howick, (Charles Grey) would insist that this carry a cabinet seat. Whitbread was one of the more extreme Foxites, and Canning refused to sanction the appointment but said he would not regard it as an insuperable bar to union if it were done first.[84]

On the whole Canning's friends were unsympathetic to his commitments to the other leading figures in the Opposition. Charles Ellis urged him to negotiate as an individual rather than for a full coalition, for then he could have the following offices: First Lord of the Admiralty, Chief Justiceship of Common Pleas; Attorney General, Governorship of Madras and Jamaica, Lordships of the Treasury, and the Admiralty, one Secretaryship of the Admiralty. There would also be the promise of the first vacancy in the Cabinet, the Privy Council and the India Board. Canning could offer Jamaica and Madras to Chatham and Castlereagh respectively. Perceval could be offered the Attorney Generalship and Grant the Chief Justiceship. Huskisson and either George Rose jun. or Robert Dundas (Melville's son) could have the minor Lordships. Ellis agreed that Canning would then have done more than anyone for Pitt's friends.[85] Canning conceded the truth of much of this, but still quibbled that he would so like Windham's removal, while Whitbread 'spoils all'.[86]

It is interesting to speculate whether or not Canning would have accepted office under Grenville. Dramatic repercussions would certainly have followed in that Britain would not have been governed by the pure 'Tory' Ministries which were soon to be in the ascendant for so long. In fact, the very day Canning wrote to his wife of the degree of power that was in his grasp, he learned from Portland of a major crisis between the King and the Government over the Catholic question.

Nine days of uncertainty followed in which it was unclear what would eventuate. On 14 March 1807, Canning wrote that in the event of Grenville's staying, he would not accept an offer so narrow as that hitherto offered, but would insist on the expulsion of Sidmouth 'and so forming a Cabinet of *two parties* only, in which his own and mine (being one and the same) shall be the strongest. Any other junction would be folly and ruin.'[87] Meanwhile Canning urged Grenville to give in to the King and remain in office. On the sixteenth he believed they had done so, but on the nineteenth he received definite information that the Ministry was turned out. The negotiations with Grenville were thus wholly aborted.

While Canning was negotiating with Grenville, he had not felt bound to offer them support in the Commons. The new Parliament had met in December 1806, and there were immediate differences between Government and Opposition. Canning immediately moved a very long-winded amendment to the Address which enabled him to review the perilous international situation before withdrawing it so as not to cause a division. He again returned to the international situation in a debate in January on the breakdown of the negotiations with France. His support for the Government was double-edged for he was prepared to join in expressions of regret at the breakdown only because of the prevalence of the 'shameful opinion' that nothing was so chimerical as a renewed confederacy against France.[88]

The Opposition were by no means clear as to the degree of co-operation amongst themselves that would be appropriate. They met regularly over dinner to discuss policy measures such as Castlereagh's financial resolutions of February, but Canning remained suspicious of the desire of his associates for 'a complete understanding' as he feared this would entail a pledge for his future political conduct.[89] One further obstacle that the minority were conscious of was the hostility of the press. *The Courier* was friendly and *The Morning Post* was equivocal, but the rest were actively hostile.

Early in 1807 the Opposition found themselves as a body opposed to the Government's financial plans. Castlereagh drew up an alternative which Canning thought highly of, until Huskisson discovered it to be filled with errors. Castlereagh attempted to salvage his plan, but Canning would have nothing to do with the operation, though he did go to Parliament to attack the Government's own scheme. The Opposition also acted together in the case of Caroline, the wife of the Prince of Wales.

In 1805 Lady Jane Douglas, Princess Caroline's former Lady of the Bedchamber, had accused her of illicit relationships and of having had an illegitimate child. Unofficial inquiries were made by the Opposition in November, for they were sympathetic to the Prince on political grounds. With the introduction of a Whig Government, an official enquiry was undertaken by Grenville, Erskine, Ellenborough, Romilly and Spencer.[90] Among those accused was Canning himself. In June 1806 he asked Lady Bessborough if she had heard of the allegation, and when she replied 'Yes', she said Canning 'neither own'd nor denied, but on the whole I am staggered and afraid it is in great part true'.[91]

It is difficult to come to any firm conclusion on the matter except to point to his friendship with the Princess and the dangerous relationship he had acknowledged before his marriage. The Prince of Wales himself told Canning in 1820 that he had scratched his name out of the record,[92] but in practice, suspicion of Canning in this respect played a role in the Prince's attitude towards him for many years. In the face of these allegations, the Princess turned towards the Opposition where she found strong support, particularly from Spencer Perceval, who called her a 'much injured lady' and declared 'to the scaffold in such a cause'.[93] It is ironical that the allegations of 1805–6 found the Whigs opposed and the Tories supporting the Princess, whereas in 1820, when the allegations were renewed, the situation was entirely reversed to a large extent due to George IV's shift of politics.

In fact the 'Delicate Investigation', as it was called, acquitted the Princess on the main charges but censured her for frivolous conduct. Her supporters found this an inadequate exculpation, especi-

ally when the King reneged on the promise he had given that he
would receive her at Court. In September Perceval began work
on a 156-page answer to the allegations. Early in 1807 the
Opposition met regularly to discuss their conduct. On 16 February they met at Perceval's, on the twenty-first at Lord Eldon's and
on the twenty-seventh at Bathurst's. On the latter occasion they
decided that the King must agree to receive the Princess. If not
'The Papers are in the press, and ready for publication. The
experiment is a frightful one, but the threat having been made, it
must be executed.'[94] However, they were agreed that Perceval
extend his deadline from the second to the fourth of March, and
in the meantime Lord Eldon would go to see the King to warn
him of the harm publication would do to the Royal Family. As
it happened, the King was not prepared for a confrontation with
the Opposition at this stage, as he needed them for his own
purposes. So by 11 March Canning was able to tell his wife that
the King had promised the Princess would receive a communication in a short time. Canning was confident it would be 'tolerably
satisfactory'.[95] Before the end of the month the Pittite Opposition
were in Government. On 21 April the new Cabinet acquitted the
Princess of all charges and advised the King to receive her. They
were left with the embarrassing task of buying back such copies
of Perceval's book as had already been distributed, and were
forced to pay highly-inflated prices.

In the last days of the Talents Ministry, as the Foxite-Grenville
coalition was called, one long-standing political issue was finally
ended with the abolition of what remained of the slave trade.
Already the Government had introduced a measure abolishing the
trade to foreign and newly-conquered territories, thereby dividing
the sugar-growing West Indian interest. In 1807 they took over
Wilberforce's self-appointed task, and exerting full Government
pressure, carried the abolition by an over-whelming majority,
something Pitt had always been unable or unwilling to do. Canning strongly supported the abolition,[96] to which Hawkesbury,
Castlereagh, Eldon and Bathurst were strongly opposed. There
were rumours that the new Government would reverse the abolition, but any attempt to do this would unquestionably have driven
Canning and Perceval from the Government. In February Canning had the opportunity to declare his underlying political
principles. The occasion was the Freehold Estates Bill, which

Canning opposed. He conceded that veneration for every institution of our ancestors should not be carried to excess and bigotry. Nevertheless,

> If we were to look generally at the fitness of things he would undertake . . . to prove to the conviction of speculative men and many others, that there was nothing that had been hither to held venerable in our law that did not require reformation. He could prove that the right of primogeniture ought to be abolished, and that it was improper to leave almost the whole to lazy drones of elder brothers, and leave the rest to make their way in the world as they could. If you began with these notions, there was no end to them.[97]

This unwillingness to subordinate facts to ideas is the hallmark of Canning's philosophy. It at once reconciles his hostility to Jacobinism with his willingness later in life to accept the reality of successful revolt in Latin America and not to wish to suppress it on general and speculative grounds.

Meanwhile, one must review the events which brought the Talents Ministry to an end after fifteen months of office. In March 1807 Grenville, in the words of Wilberforce, ran his ship aground on a rock above water. The Government had planned to re-enact a 1792 Act which allowed Catholics in the army to serve in all ranks under Brigade General. The King's support was obtained for this, only for him to find that the Government had decided to extend this to opening the army and navy indiscriminately to Catholics and Dissenters. Even the position of Commander-in-Chief was not exempt. On 4 March the King realized what was happening and told Howick that he could not sanction the arrangements. On the fifth Canning recorded that something was boiling up in Cabinet on this question but Grenville did not mention the problem to Canning when he met him on the sixth. The King had meanwhile got in touch with the Opposition and on the eleventh Portland was able to tell Canning of the crisis. Canning was forced to consider his own attitude and told Portland that despite his support for Catholic Emancipation, he was of the same opinion as in 1804; namely, that discussion should be kept back on subjects where the King's conscience was 'really and painfully alive'. There were those in the Opposition who took a much harder view. Perceval replied to Sidmouth that 'we' should tell the Catholics 'that as we found you at the Union, so we will keep you, but beyond that situation we will not advance you'.[98] Canning himself promised Portland that he would ask Grenville for renewed assurances of the King's support of the measure, in default of which he would say that it went far too far, and would oppose it. Meanwhile opposition to the measure within the Cabinet had come from Sidmouth who proceeded shamelessly to betray his colleagues. The King had been in contact with him and told Portland of his attitude, but on the eleventh Perceval received a communication directly from Sidmouth suggesting a meeting to concert measures against the Catholic bill. On the fourteenth Canning wrote to his wife explaining the situation. He would, he said, oppose the bill and join any administration formed by Portland provided Sidmouth played no significant part in it. In the latter eventuality he would take a separate stand with his friends in the House of Commons and await events.[99] Such antipathy was reflected by Sidmouth, whose attitude at this juncture was determined partly by the possible inclusion of Canning in the Cabinet. He had already told Howick he would not sit alongside Canning despite the former's stress on the urgency of the inclusion.[100]

The Opposition could only wait to see what would happen. There were voices, such as that of Melville, which urged that Pitt's friends should unite and that 'the only avowed object of the union must be a total overthrow of the present Administration. . . .'[101] In fact the whole game was now in the hands of the King. Ministers attempted to withdraw the measure but in such a way as to save their own faces. In reply the King demanded that the Government undertake in writing not to put forward further concessions for Catholics. The Ministers had no choice but reject this staggering impropriety and this gave the King the opportunity to dismiss them. Thus in 1807 as in 1783, George III demonstrated his ability to get rid of a Ministry which he disliked. Then he had turned to Pitt; now he turned to the remnants of Pitt's party led, ironically, by the nominal Prime Minister he had turned out in 1783.

Considering possibilities on the 17 March, Canning was not terribly enthusiastic about Portland, except as an alternative 'for the Dr would be the Devil'. On the nineteenth he finally learned that Portland had been asked to form a Government with the assistance of Lords Lowther and Chatham. One problem was the attitude of Wellesley who kept alternately accepting and rejecting the post of Foreign Secretary. Canning was worried about the position of Castlereagh. If they were both Secretaries of State, he told his wife, he could not concede his having the lead in the House of Commons. On the twenty-third Wellesley retracted his refusal of the Foreign Office and it appeared that Castlereagh would become Secretary for War and Canning First Lord of the Admiralty. He was unclear whether he preferred this or the Foreign Office but a letter from Joan decided him for the latter when Wellesley changed his mind yet again. On the twenty-fifth he wrote from the Foreign Office, 'I had a battle to fight, and an intrigue to defeat and [I had] to assert myself boldly – which I did – and here I am.' In addition he had had an interview with the King, which he hoped had dispersed something of the bad opinion the latter had of him. On the twenty-eighth he received all the foreign ambassadors one by one, and settled down to his new ministerial career.[102]

The years 1804 to 1806 saw vicissitudes in Canning's career. They had opened with the disappointed hope that Pitt would be able to found a firmly-based Ministry, which had passed into despair with the death of Pitt himself in 1806. Yet Canning was not pleased when those whom he had hoped to see serve under Pitt formed the Talents Ministry to the exclusion of many Pittites immediately afterwards, and the best interpretation of his vacillation between January 1806 and March 1807 is that he was uncertain of the future and unwilling to bind himself too closely with any side until he saw more clearly what would happen. The King's action settled the uncertainty, and Canning felt no embarrassment in berating the Ministry with which he had so recently negotiated. In a superb example of his gift for satire he wrote an epitaph for the Talents Ministry, called

All the Talents:
When the broad-bottom'd Junto, with reason at strife,
Resign'd, with a sign, its political life.
When converted to Rome, and of honesty tired,
They gave back to the Devil the soul he inspired.
The Demon of Faction, that over then hung,
In accents of horror their epitaph sung,

While Pride and Venalite join'd in the stave,
And canting Democracy wept at the Grave.

'*Here lies in the tomb that we hollow'd for Pitt,*
Consistence of Grenville, of Temple the wit.
Of Sidmouth the firmness, the temper of Grey,
And Treasurer Sheridan's promise to pay.

Here Petty's finance, from the evils to come
With Fitzpatrick's sobriety creeps to the tomb,
And Chancellor Ego, now left in the lurch,
Neither dines with the Jordan, nor whines for the Church.

Then huzza for the Party that here is at rest,
By the Fools of a faction regretted and blest,
Though they sleep with the Devil, yet theirs is the hope,
On the downfall of Britain to rise with the Pope.'[103]

5
FOREIGN SECRETARY

The new Cabinet contained no members of its predecessor. As Prime Minister, Portland was no more than a *point d'appui* for the opponents of the Talents Administration. Six other members of the Cabinet – Westmoreland, Camden, Eldon, Mulgrave, Chatham and Bathurst – represented the Government in the House of Lords. Portland himself headed the Government as a matter of duty, and did not regard personal parliamentary activity as one of his obligations. Apart from Canning there were three cabinet members in the Commons – Castlereagh, Perceval, and until his father's death in 1808 (when he became second Earl of Liverpool), Hawkesbury. The leadership of the House of Commons went to Perceval along with the Chancellorship of the Exchequer and the Duchy of Lancaster, the latter being intended to compensate him for loss of his legal income. Canning did not at this stage regard Perceval as a rival in the same way as Castlereagh or Hawkesbury. Had Castlereagh been given the leadership in the Commons, he would probably not have served.

At the Foreign Office Canning had as his under-Secretaries George Hammond, who had worked with Canning under Grenville, and Viscount Fitzharris, son of the Earl of Malmesbury, though the latter soon resigned to be replaced by Charles Bagot. Despite their past differences of opinion in opposition Canning was soon reconciled to his old friend Granville Leveson-Gower, whom he eventually persuaded to take over as ambassador in St Petersburg, provided he was free of his ties with the Opposition.[1] Like all his colleagues, Canning was immediately beset with a vast number of letters begging for some of the patronage at the

disposal of his office. These came from political friends, but far
in excess of Canning's ability to satisfy. Often they would be
powerfully supported; for example, Melville backed up Earl
Aberdeen's request to be British Minister in Sicily.[2]

In wartime, the nature of the Foreign Secretary's job was per-
force altered. Co-operation with the purely military departments
of government was clearly essential, and unfortunately this meant
co-operation with men for whom Canning had scant liking or
respect. The Master-General of the Ordnance was the Earl of
Chatham, whom Canning regarded as ineffectual and certainly not
suitable for a post supplying a large proportion of Europe with
necessary arms. Canning had originally spoken highly of Lord
Mulgrave, who took the Admiralty, believing he possessed the
same opinions and intentions Canning himself would have carried
there.[3] Relations did not remain good, and in 1808 Canning complained bitterly that no matter the manner in which he approached
the Admiralty for ships, he was unable to avoid giving offence.[4]
At the War Office, Castlereagh was a rival regarded by Canning
with some respect but little liking. Canning's relationship with
these men with whom he had to work closely on vitally important
issues gives some indication of the causes of the breakdown of
the Government in 1809.

The most immediate problem for the Government on taking
office in 1807 was the parliamentary situation. The King's conduct in turning them out was regarded by the Opposition with
great hostility, and on 13 April Thomas Brand moved that it was
unconstitutional for Ministers to restrain themselves from giving
advice on any subject. This was a clear reference to the King's
demand that the Catholic question not be raised, and ministers
were forced to oppose it. The outcome of the debate was difficult
to foretell. The Sidmouth group were supporting the new Government and already many of those who believed in supporting any
Government had changed sides, but it was with great relief that
the Government managed to defeat the motion by 258 to 226
votes, despite the presence in the opposition lobby of many of the
non-party country gentry. Canning spoke in the debate, roundly
declaring that 'the late ministers had by their own acts rendered
their dismissal unavoidable'.[5] Within a month of negotiating with
them, Canning was driving a thick wedge between himself and
the Whigs. Grenville's brother Buckingham strongly reprobated

his tone in the House of Commons and his 'military grasp for power both in England and in Ireland'.[6]

The Government faced a Parliament that had been elected under the auspices of their opponents and wanted a safer majority. At the end of April, a dissolution was granted by the King. 'There is an end of this damned Parlt,' commented Canning.[7] Already preparations were under way for buying up boroughs and bringing Treasury pressure to bear where possible. Canning had forwarded to Portland offers from the proprietors of Gatton, Shaftesbury and Wexford, which the Government could have in return for certain favours. In the latter case, this was a Tellership of the Exchequer. Canning himself was returned for Hastings, a privilege for which he and his co-member paid the proprietor nearly £5000.[8]

There was a great deal of popular feeling in favour of the Government at this election. On the one hand it could be portrayed, as in 1784, as a case of King against upstart ministers. Wilberforce considered the issue the same as in that year. Moreover, the new Government had anti-Catholic sentiment running for them. 'No Popery! No Slavery' urged a placard in favour of Wilberforce and Lascelles in Yorkshire.[9] The result was nevertheless not so favourable to the Pittites as the analogous election of 1784 had been. In that year the greatest landowner in Yorkshire, the Whig Earl of Fitzwilliam, had to withdraw his candidates in favour of two Pittites because of popular sentiment. There in 1807, his son Viscount Milton secured election alongside Wilberforce. Nevertheless, local influence was insufficient to return Grey for Northumberland and he had to flee to a pocket borough, while the brief Whig interlude at Liverpool came to a sudden end. The exact complexion of the new Parliament was not known till it met late in June, when the Address of Thanks was carried by 350 to 155. Canning called the division 'beyond all expectation'.[10] King and Government could both congratulate themselves on a highly satisfactory state of affairs.

The preservation of good relations with actual and potential European allies was one of the first aims of the new Government. Early in April Canning asked the King to write a personal letter of flattery to the Russian Czar, and later in the month he insisted that it should not appear to be Britain that rejected the Austrian offer of mediation.[11] In the Near East, the new Government was

faced with the failure of Britain's attempt to intervene in force
to mediate between the Russians and the Turks who were under
the influence of the French minister Sebastiani. Great hopes were
put in a joint Anglo-Russian blockade of the Bosphorous and
Dardanelles. 'Hunger at Constantinople', wrote Mulgrave, 'will
soon turn the Sovereign People there against the French Minister
and His faction.' In fact, the city was supplied overland. At the
same time Britain was worried that the Turkish war would divert
Russia from the French war while underneath was the realization
that Russia had 'unavowed and indefensible designs upon the
Turkish Empire'.[12] Meanwhile Britain's pre-emptive occupation
of Alexandria spread doubt about her own motives.

In northern Europe the public Russian position was strong.
She proclaimed herself to be fighting against 'Bonaparte, the
enemy of all Nations and against those who style themselves his
subjects'. At the same time Canning expressed his worries to the
Russian Ambassador about recent and possibly hostile changes in
the attitude of the Russian Cabinet, and was puzzled by the exact
role of the Duke d'Antraigues, a French exile given dual status
with the Russian minister Alopeus in London.[13] The former he
considered able but indiscreet. Britain meanwhile proceeded with
her policy of military co-operation against the French in northern
Europe. A formal request for aid from the Swedish minister
Rehausen on 1 June was met with the despatch of an expedition
to Stralsund later in the month.

As so often before in the war, Britain's hopes were shattered
at a blow. A decisive victory by Napoleon over the Russians at
Friedland on 22 June shattered the morale of the Czar and made
up his mind that he was better pursuing his own ambitions in
Finland and Turkey than a lost cause against the French. The
two Emperors met on a raft in the River Niemen and signed the
Treaty of Tilsit on 7 July 1807. Even before Canning had a full
report of the terms, alarming despatches were received as to the
cordial atmosphere at the meeting.[14] All this coincided with a
worsening of Anglo-Danish relations provoked partly by a genuine
fear amongst the Danes of French power and also a resentment
at the British pretension to prevent trade between neutral powers
and France, albeit that this aspect of warfare had been initiated by
Napoleon the previous year. From Copenhagen Garlike, the
British minister, was sending news of the ill-will of the Danish

Cabinet to Britain, while Canning's relations with Rist, his counterpart in London, could hardly have been worse. More worrying than this was a report received on 9 July from the British consul at Altona that France intended to occupy Holstein.[15] Behind this lay the deeper worry that France might go on to upset the naval balance in the Baltic by securing the Danish fleet. The precedent from 1801 pointed to strong action to prevent this, and on 14 July the Cabinet accepted Canning's memorandum urging a strong augmentation of British naval force in the Baltic.

The Treaty of Tilsit went much further than Britain could have envisaged at worst. France gained heavily at Prussia's expense and also set up the Grandy Duchy of Warsaw. Most of European Turkey was to be left to France and Russia jointly while the Czar was to be allowed to pursue his ambitions in Finland. France's ambitions in the Mediterranean were bolstered by Russia's agreeing to give her the Ionian Islands. Russia was to force her mediation on Britain and go to war if it was refused. In the immediate crisis, one secret article was more important than all these. This was for the formation with Denmark and Portugal of an anti-British naval league. Warning of this came to Canning on the evening of 21 July. It was sent to Canning *'Pour vous seul'* from the Duke D'Antraigues at Richmond, Surrey. His wife had received the information from one of his closest friends, a general, placed close to the Russian Emperor. It had been sent via Altona and forwarded to his wife from thence on 11 July.[16] This information immediately affected Britain's relations with Russia and Denmark. As regards the former, Canning did not alter the opinion he expressed earlier on the twenty-first that the Emperor had been overreacting to hide his disgust at his own behaviour. He would come back to his friends.[17] Canning was therefore circumspect and when officially informed by Alopeus of some of the Tilsit terms merely replied that he wanted more information and hoped they were such that an honourable peace could be obtained.[18]

But as for Denmark, the new information quickened a resolve already virtually made. Nevertheless, from Denmark, Garlike was denying some of the alarmist reports Canning had transmitted. It was not true, he said on the twenty-fifth that the Danish fleet was being equipped. On the twenty-eighth he denied reports that France had demanded Holstein, adding that if France tried to close either of the Danish ports to the British flag, she would be considered at war with Denmark.[19] In fact, he had already been ordered by Canning to Prussia, and envoys with stronger instructions were on their way. Neither Brooke Taylor nor Francis Jackson who attempted to negotiate with the Danes in early August had any success in their aim of securing the Danish fleet and were forced to withdraw.

In Britain, military preparations to invade Denmark were hastened in late July and the first contingent sailed on 30 July 1807. After the failure of Jackson's mission a landing was made and the investment of Copenhagen begun. Canning was naturally anxious. On 31 July he wrote to his wife, 'The measure is a bold one, and if it fails, why we must be impeached I suppose – and dearest dear will have a box at the trial.'[20] On 1 August he wrote of his renewed conviction of the morality and political wisdom of the step taken due to fresh information as to 'the French being actually about to do that act of hostility the possibility of which formed the ground work of my Baltic plan'.[21] A possible failure in execution nevertheless kept him from sleeping well. Throughout August and September he waited for news, firstly of whether or not force would in fact be necessary, then for news of the actual military operations. At the same time knowledge of what the Opposition could make of a fiasco and unease at the King's strong objections to the morality of the venture, which Canning tried to treat jocularly, contributed to his disquiet.[22] On 11 September he wrote to the Rev. Leigh, 'No news yet from Copenhagen – but it must come in a day or two now – and it must be good. See what care we take of you parsons and your families. But for this expedition you would have had an invasion from the north – and Plumstead bombarded.'[23]

Meanwhile in Denmark the military operation had gone smoothly. On 2 September a naval bombardment of Copenhagen was commenced and after three days in which considerable damage was done to life and property the Danes asked for a truce. On the seventh they agreed to give up their fleet, and Britain agreed to evacuate their forces from Denmark. The peril of increased French naval strength was removed. This, said Canning, was 'an answer to timid politicians'.[24]

The problem of Russia remained. On 12 August Canning instructed Granville that unless the secret article was revealed or disavowed he should call on Admiral Gambier for a naval demonstration off Revel or Cronstadt.[25] Appropriate instructions were sent to Gambier.[26] Meanwhile Granville saw the Czar who denied that Tilsit had contained a secret article hostile to Great Britain. At the same time the Czar mused that Copenhagen 'was to be justified on principles which might possibly at that moment occasion a similar enterprise against Russia'.[27] Meanwhile Britain forebore from any directly hostile act against Russia. Canning believed in the existence of a pro-British party at St Petersburg and hoped for a change of policy there, which an open humiliation might thwart.[28] Canning had, however, seen a letter from Czartoryski in St Petersburg to D'Antraigues in which the account of the Emperor's weakness was 'almost incredible'.[29]

In fact Czar Alexander was still under Napoleon's influence, and immediately made new promises to France to mediate for peace with Great Britain. If Russian mediation were to be refused, she was to declare war on Britain. While Britain had desisted from overt action against Russia in the Baltic, a further problem presented itself in the shape of the Russian fleet sailing northwards from the Mediterranean. On 13 September Canning told the Admiralty that this must be prevented by force from proceeding beyond Portugal,[30] save to a British port, and, over Chatham's fears of premature acts of hostility,[31] secured agreement for this. Force was in fact unnecessary as the Russian fleet wintered in the Tagus, but the precaution was well-advised, for in December Russia declared war in terms which the King felt might have been dictated by the Paris '*Moniteur*'.[32]

Meanwhile, to add to Britain's problems, Austria took a hand. In November their Ambassador Prince Stahremberg stressed how 'highly inconvenient and dangerous' the war was to other European powers. The threat of war implicit in the representation made the King remark that he trusted every Englishman's blood would boil when powers attempted to threaten Britain to act against her interest.[33] In January Stahremberg demanded that Britain send plenipotentiaries to Paris to treat for peace, and when it was revealed that he had done this on his own authority and not on that of his Government, he was impelled to ask for his passports. Austria thus joined Prussia and Russia in the list of powers, so recently allies of and subsidized by Britain, who were now at least nominally her enemies.

Since 1806 Napoleon had pursued a policy of excluding British
trade from the continent. Britain replied in kind with a policy
originally recommended by James Stephen in his work *War in
Disguise*. He was a close friend of Perceval who was essentially
the author of this policy as expressed in the Orders in Council of
November 1807. These insisted that all ships which were to visit
a port from which British ships were excluded must first visit a
British port to pay duty. For the neutrals this meant that they
could not avoid falling foul of either Britain or France, as Britain's
control of the sea matched France's power on land – a classic
geopolitical confrontation between the whale and the elephant.
Canning was a strong supporter of the Orders in Council. On one
hand he had no doubts as to their justice,[34] and on the other he
argued that Britain had in her own resources and those of her
colonies 'ample means of self-existence'.[35]

In fact, the effects of the trade war were two-fold. The closing
of British export markets on the continent produced a progressive
depression of trade with concomitancies of economic distress and
ultimately political disturbance. It also worsened relations with
neutral powers, especially the United States, which put an
embargo on trade with both Britain and France in December
1807. In March 1808 Canning nevertheless joined Castlereagh,
Mulgrave, Bathurst and Westmoreland in opposing a memorandum of Perceval himself suggesting a relaxation. He argued that
he had an apprehension of a war with the United States and that
Pinckney, the American minister, was of the same opinion.[36]

The Danish fleet was not the only maritime problem troubling
Britain in the middle of 1807. The secret article of Tilsit had also
mentioned the Portuguese fleet. Canning wrote in August, 'We
have more work upon our hands. Lisbon *ought* to be another
Copenhagen. Would our fleet and army were come back and
ready to start again.'[37] The Portuguese Regent was under
continual pressure. France wanted Portugal to close her ports to
British ships and declare war. Britain wanted to escort the
Portuguese Royal Family with their fleet to Brazil. A period of
confusion followed till late in October the Regent declared war
on Britain at the same time as Napoleon, running out of patience,
ordered the French Marshall Junot to occupy Portugal. In
London, Canning had meanwhile signed a convention with the
Portuguese minister Souza which allowed Britain to occupy

Madeira in the event of the closure of Portuguese ports. Britain was to assist, if desired, in taking the Portuguese Royal Family to Brazil. She was also to be allowed to trade with Brazil. Canning didn't know whether this treaty would prove to be 'dupery' or 'forebearance'.[38] Certainly he told Strangford, Britain's envoy-extraordinary to the Regent, that he hoped the latter did not imagine that the King could 'consent to suffer any nation to declare war against him with impunity. . . .'[39] Strangford was fairly gloomy about the likelihood of his persuading the Regent to flee. Canning stepped up the pressure by authorizing a direct attack on the Portuguese fleet in Lisbon harbour, or if this was impossible, a blockade of the Tagus. The Portuguese were warned of this.[40] At the same time, orders were issued to take over some of Portugal's overseas possessions. Before these were cancelled, Goa was taken with the full co-operation of the Viceroy.[41] On 26 November Sir Sidney Smith was given orders to blockade the Tagus with force equal to the Portuguese and Russian squadrons, unless the Royal Family escaped French influence by going to Brazil.[42] Finally, on the twenty-eighth, with French troops virtually on the outskirts of Lisbon, Strangford persuaded the Regent to go. The following day the fleet sailed for Brazil under British escort. Canning was delighted. 'Huzza, Huzza, Huzza,' he wrote to Leigh . . . 'Denmark was saucy and we were obliged to *take her* fleet. Portugal had confidence and we have rescued her's.'[43] Britain had at the same time, as Bathurst pointed out, acquired a new outlet for her cotton and muslin goods.

Despite maritime success, Britain could hardly have faced the opening of 1808 with confidence. On the continent her enemy was triumphant and most of her old allies hostile. Peripherally Britain could still act with Sweden and Sicily and indulge in schemes to put a Pretender on the Persian throne.[44] But her main European objectives were as far away as ever.

Canning nevertheless looked on the cheerful side. He wrote to Granville: 'We have now what we have had once before and once only, a maritime war in our power – unfettered by any consideration of whom we may annoy – or whom we may offend – And we have (what would would to God poor Pitt had ever resolved to have!) determination to carry it through.'[45] Negotiation he nevertheless felt, could not be refused if offered, and later in the year he argued that this must be on the basis that neither Britain nor

France could be expected to give anything up.[46] On the other hand, the optimistic view was that if they could keep the war alive 'the smothered feelings of the Continent may yet break forth.'[47] Furthermore there were those who argued that Britain had much of national interest to gain from the war. Mulgrave was against any negotiation with France because it would be 'so injurious to our great and brilliant prospects in South America'.[48] He clearly saw a new area for British commercial and territorial expansion.

Britain still had allies in Sweden and Sicily, the latter important for the preservation of Britain's naval power in the Mediterranean. Relations were not altogether easy, as the Sicilian Court was a centre of intrigue, much of it pro-French.[49] Britain's relations with Sicily also brought Canning into a conflict with the law officers of the Crown. The Sicilian Ambassador Prince Castel-cicala had complained of a book that reflected badly on the Sicilian Government, notoriously one of the worst in Europe, and Canning asked for a prosecution. The law officers refused because 'so much freedom has been long exercised, and perhaps too largely allowed to discussions of this nature, and juries are always found so unwilling to restrain it'.[50]

If Sicily was a political, Sweden was a military liability. In November 1807 Baron de Wetterstadt on behalf of the Swedish Government instructed their Ambassador in London to ask Britain for the help of her army and navy, and for subsidies.[51] Of major concern was Russia's ambition to occupy Finland, and it was suggested that Britain help Sweden by naval demonstrations against Reval and Cronstadt whilst occupying Denmark's over-seas possessions.[52]

Britain's immediate response was merely to sign a subsidy treaty in February, but as Russia and Denmark made a concerted attack later in the month, this response seemed inadequate. In April 1808 an expedition under Sir John Moore was authorized. When this arrived, however, the Swedes only wanted to use it to occupy the Danish province of Zealand. Permission to land the troops at Gothenburg was refused, and after Moore himself was at one time put under arrest by the Swedes, the expedition returned fruitless to England in July. The whole series of events illustrate the problems involved in Britain's co-operation with nominal allies on the continent with different aims from herself.

In this case the problem was enhanced by the mental instability of the Swedish King.

Despite the breakdown in formal relations with Prussia, Austria and Russia, Britain had kept open her lines of communication with them,[53] waiting for a change of heart. She held back from a decisive act such as issuing letters of marque against Austrian vessels in the Mediterranean even though it was used for purposes of enemy trade, and Britain had an undoubted legal right to act.[54] By the middle of 1808 this policy was paying dividends, and overtures made to the Austrian Minister Count Stadion in Vienna in July and August 1808 were favourably received. The prospect of renewed Austrian participation became more and more realistic and with it came the requests to Britain for financial assistance. 'I am afraid', wrote Canning in November, tongue-in-cheek, 'a subsidy of six millions a year is a little beyond the mark. . . .'[55] A treaty was nevertheless agreed in April 1809 but Austria's invasion of Bavaria was quickly countered by Napoleon's occupation of Vienna. Despite success at Aspern in May, Austria was once more driven from the war by the French at Wagram in July.

Britain's hopes for anti-French resistance in northern Europe were even more forlorn. On 11 March Canning saw a Prussian officer charged by various persons in Germany who wanted to take advantage of the Austro-French war to stage revolts in Westphalia and Lower Saxony. Britain was worried that these insurgents might not have the support of the King of Prussia, and before any formal arrangements were made, revolts which had broken out prematurely in Westphalia and Prussia were crushed. In July Canning heard of a revolt that was about to break out in Hanover and urged that Britain give all the aid in her power. Nothing came of this either.[56]

Alliance with popular forces in Germany was never a successful part of the British war strategy. In the Iberian peninsular, however, the opposite proved to be the case. In April 1808 Napoleon solved a dispute over the Spanish throne between Charles IV and the future Ferdinand VII by placing upon it his own brother Joseph. Spontaneous revolts broke out throughout Spain and Portugal and in the former political control passed into the hands of local juntas. French attempts to subdue the country quickly were rebuffed at Baylen in July where their army was surrounded and forced to surrender. The insurgents naturally turned to Britain for assistance, and delegates from the province of Asturias arrived on 8 June, soon to be followed by others from Galicia and Seville. They were met with a wave of popular enthusiasm from all sides of the political spectrum. Canning fully shared these feelings, even though he objected to references to the 'Patriots of Spain' as being too like the language of the Whig *Morning Chronicle,* preferring the term 'Loyal Inhabitants'.[57] The Cabinet decided to make the following reply to the Asturias delegates: that Britain would give them every assistance, would recognize the Junta and use her navy to give all possible help to the Spanish provinces.[58] The latter was felt to be particularly useful as regards the protection of Catalonia, and it was even hoped that British activity here might cause a wave of revolts in southern France.[59] On top of this determination came the good news from Baylen of the French surrender. Lady Bessborough nevertheless objected to Canning's 'indecent tone of exultation at the massacre of the French troops by the peasants, after they had surrendered'.[60]

On 12 July 1808 an army was despatched under Sir Arthur Wellesley, soon to be followed by Moore and his troops just back from Sweden. On 21 July the Cabinet renewed its commitment to furnish prompt and adequate assistance to Spain and Portugal, and the despatch of 100,000 muskets was soon agreed.[61] Meanwhile success attended British arms in Portugal. On 21 August Wellesley, who was marching to Lisbon, a hundred miles south of where he had landed, decisively defeated the French Marshall Junot at Vimeiro. It was fortunate that the battle occurred as early as it did, for Wellesley had been superseded in his command of the army by Sir Hew Dalrymple, Governor of Gibraltar, and Sir Henry Burrard, his second-in-command. The appointments represented a victory for the abstract principles of seniority over the practicalities of war. They also owed something to the Duke of York, the King's son, who was Commander-in-Chief. After the battle was won Dalrymple and Burrard arrived in time to prevent Wellesley from capitalizing on his victory by thoroughly routing the French. When shortly afterwards the French asked for an armistice, they agreed.

The Convention of Cintra is one of the most extraordinary acts of generosity ever made by a victorious army. Perhaps, as Lady Arden suggested in jest, the British generals really could not read

French.[62] When Clauswitz argued from his experience of the Napoleonic Wars that the destruction of the enemy's armed forces was the 'first-born son of war', he could hardly have been thinking of Cintra, except perhaps as a counter-example. Under its terms, agreed between Dalrymple and Kellerman, Britain was to transport the French army back to France in her own ships. There was no prohibition on these troops re-entering the war. The French were guaranteed their property, which meant the fruits of their plunder, and any reprisals against the pro-French party in Portugal were forbidden.

In Britain the news of Vimeiro was greeted with understandable rejoicing, which soon soured as the scarcely believable news filtered in from Cintra. Ministers heard of some of the terms through the Portuguese minister but refused to believe them until confirmation came from Dalrymple himself on 15 September. Canning was at Hinckley, and learned of the news through a letter from Perceval the following day. He was appalled, describing the Convention as 'ruinous and disastrous'. He could not understand the legal point that the King 'cannot undo a Convention . . . if signed by a man who has a sword by his side'.[63] Indeed there could be little doubt that the ministers were bound by the commitments of their generals, except as regards the amnesty for Portuguese collaborators which was probably *ultra vires*. They could only fulminate. Canning was particularly appalled by the guarantee given to the property of French soldiers, which was certainly the most dishonourable clause. Meanwhile Castlereagh, who, said Canning, had been 'working night and day to get transport to convey our own Troops' now had to find it for the French army![64] Canning was in no doubt where the blame must lie – all the generals, including Wellesley, fell under his ire. 'We must judge them, or the Public will judge us.'[65] Particularly frightening were the possible effects within Spain and Portugal. 'What more could Bonaparte have wished for?' asked Huskisson, who expected the Portuguese to 'relapse into their former imbecility'.[66] Canning felt that the Convention 'exposes us to more mischief . . . than would have been hazarded by our not sending to Portugal a single man'.[67] Britain must probably expect 'the surrender at no very distant time of Portugal itself to the Enemy from whom we have delivered it'.[68] Perceval was virtually alone in seeing one practical gain in the release of British troops for action in northern Spain.

They could clearly be brought more quickly to the centre of war than the French army, which would first be shipped back to France.[69]

There was little the Cabinet could do. An original despatch to Dalrymple was stopped so Canning could be consulted, but he still objected to the tone of its replacement as being too mild. Over Canning's objections, for he blamed all the generals, including Wellesley, the Cabinet decided that only Dalrymple be recalled. As to the Convention itself, Canning wrote a long letter to the King disagreeing with the view of his colleagues that there was no reason not to implement Cintra. He could not believe that a commander-in-chief had unlimited powers to act in the King's name.[70] In fact Cintra was now merely a problem in British politics. In December a Court of Inquiry considered the Convention and in February Canning had the delicate task of defending the Government in Parliament on the issue.

After the optimism of Vimeiro, Cintra provoked fresh ministerial pessimism. Nevertheless, they were still resolved to continue the war. In October Napoleon and the Czar put forward jointly a peace proposal. Mulgrave wrote to Canning that he left to him the 'management of the strong and popular grounds' on which Britain either declined the invitation or insisted on impossible conditions.[71] Canning in fact insisted on the admission of his Spanish allies to the negotiations – a demand which was clearly unacceptable to the French.

Meanwhile in Spain, the French were gradually being pushed northwards until Napoleon took a hand by re-inforcing his forces with veterans and taking command in the theatre personally. Perhaps because of Cintra, Britain had redoubled her efforts in the peninsular in order to persuade the Spaniards she was still in earnest. From Portugal Sir John Moore marched into the interior to link up with forces under Sir David Baird from Corunna. Moore was not beloved of ministers, partly because of his Whig principles and partly because of difficulties they had experienced with him in Sicily and Sweden. Moore himself certainly included Canning especially when he wrote of his two or three enemies in the Cabinet.[72] However even Portland conceived an unfavourable view of Moore when he first knew him, because of his 'disposition to Intrigue and Duplicity of Conduct'.[73] Castlereagh told his colleagues that Moore had raised every objection to the plan to link up with the forces from Corunna and had parted from him with a prediction of certain failure. 'Good God!' replied Canning, 'and do you really mean to say that you allowed a man entertaining such feelings with regard to an expedition to assume the command of it?'[74]

As Moore marched into Spain he received news of Spanish defeats which eventually made him decide that he had no choice but to return to Portugal. Canning disliked the decision. 'I had rather a bloody battle and a defeat than safety at such a price by running away,' he wrote.[75] However, despatches from Frere, who was now envoy to the Spanish Junta, begging for assistance, together with some indications that Madrid might yet be held against the French, changed his mind. Reinforced with the artillery under Hope Moore again marched northward. On 20 December 1808 he linked up with Baird and secret information enabled him to win a victory over Soult in a minor cavalry engagement on the twenty-first. Nevertheless, fresh information that Napoleon himself was moving in his direction and that his lines of communication with Portugal were cut determined him to retreat to Corunna. Losses on the march were considerable, though the army successfully reached the coast on 11 January 1809. Moore himself was killed in an engagement on the sixteenth but the embarkation of his troops was completed. The French were now dominant through most of Spain.

Ministers followed these proceedings with some dismay. Canning denounced Moore for 'running away'. Madrid, he felt, could have been saved by quick action on his part. He also expressed his shame that Government 'so pusillanimously shrank from the inconvenience of removing him'.[76] 'I have just read Moore's despatch,' wrote Canning on 7 January. 'He is, as usual, in full retreat.'[77] 'The truth is', he told Bathurst, 'that we have retreated before a rumour – an uncertain speculation – and Moore knows it.'[78]

Canning's disappointment is hardly surprising. The peninsular venture seemed to be ending in total disaster despite Spanish and British successes. Whether or not it was fair to blame Moore is another matter. Moore had a low opinion of the Spanish army as allies at best, and now on all sides he learned of fresh defeats inflicted upon them. His own forces were insufficient to match

E

the French if they brought their full weight against him, and
when this seemed likely to occur it is difficult to conceive of an
alternative to withdrawal. Ministers did not see it this way. In
England they made it clear that his conduct did not meet with
their approval. Canning strongly attacked the claims of 'Sir John
Moore's friends who are our enemies' and set himself to rebuff
what he called the 'misrepresentations' of Lord Grenville and
The Morning Chronicle.[79]

The retreat from Corunna threw into question the security of
Portugal. Canning felt that it might still be saved, and asked for
a Cabinet on 11 February 1809 as 'No subject can be of greater
importance and urgency'.[80] Britain nevertheless still had obligations towards Spain, and Canning saw the possible refusal of
Spanish permission for British troops to occupy Cadiz, held by
the loyalists, as providing an excuse for pursuing what might have
been Britain's best policy from the beginning; namely, 'The
accumulation of a considerable force in Portugal to be used first
for the defence of the Kingdom – and not to move into Spain,
except on some special call, and for some adequate and definite
object'.[81] The Spaniards did in fact refuse permission, ostensibly
because it would make it appear that British troops were sheltering
there after their defeats in Galicia,[82] but probably for fear that
Cadiz might become another Gibraltar. Meanwhile in London a
treaty of peace and friendship was signed between Canning and
Don Juan de Apodaca, the Spanish plenipotentiary.

In Portugal Arthur Wellesley was put in charge of the British
forces, which were raised to 23,000 in April. In Spain Canning's
friend Frere was recalled. He had become the Opposition's scape-
goat for Moore's failure, and certainly Canning himself could not
justify his pretensions to interfere in military policy. He was
replaced by Arthur Wellesley's brother the Marquess Wellesley,
who left England on 25 July. Canning had prevented his taking
his mistress Mrs Leslie with him. On 11 August he arrived in
Seville. Canning told him to tell Frere, who felt deeply injured
by his recall, that the Government approved of the substance of
his conduct, but that some of his language was indefensible.[83]
The military situation was meanwhile changing. Arthur Wellesley
had marched into Spain and on 22 July joined forces with Spanish
troops under Cuesta. On 27 and 28 July they beat off an attack
by the French at Talavera, and Wellesley went off in pursuit of

the French Marshall Soult. Unfortunately the Spaniards abandoned Talavera, and Wellesley was eventually forced to withdraw to Badajoz on the border. Wellesley called the Spaniards 'children in the art of war'. Others were more scathing, particularly about Cuesta's retreat from Talavera. Canning said, 'The abandonment of our wounded will never be forgiven.' Furthermore, he felt that feeling in Britain would be such 'that I am persuaded we shall never be able to keep Parliament and the Country up to the support of the Spanish cause unless we can secure some signal reparation'.[84] Despite the removal of General Cuesta on grounds of 'ill-health', it was also clear that the Spanish army could not be improved in time to allow Arthur Wellesley to resume offensive operations at any early period.[85]

Canning's position was difficult. On the one hand he had to pay lip-service to the 'irrepressible force of a nation determined to shake off a foreign yoke and establish its independence'.[86] On the other he had to co-operate with the Spaniards as they really were. To some extent Canning cut this Gordian knot by leaving the war in the hands of the two Wellesleys, whilst taking full responsibility for their decisions. He nevertheless hinted that while Arthur Wellesley might wish to use his 30,000 men in offensive operations in Spain, he might well decide that nothing more than the defence of Portugal could be achieved.[87] The Marquess Wellesley had a lower opinion of the Spaniards than Canning, and he urged that no British army could safely co-operate with Spanish troops until a great change occurred 'in the conduct of the military resources of Spain'. He instanced the battle of Talavera, where 'Sir Arthur Wellesley witnessed the flight of whole corps of Spanish troops who after having thrown away their British arms and clothing, plundered the Baggage of the British Troops, at that moment bravely engaged with the enemy.' He blamed the inchoate nature of the *ad hoc* governmental system, and in particular the dispersion of power in an assembly too numerous 'for unity of Council or promptitude of action'.[88]

Canning could nevertheless not evade the problem. He was faced with perpetual requests for arms from the Spaniards. 'In this war,' he complained to de Garay, 'we have supplied by turns almost the whole continent with arms – Russia, Prussia, Sweden,

Portugal, Sicily and Spain – while at the same time our own
military establishments are *sixfold* what they formally were . . .'[89]
At the same time, the Spaniards were suspicious of British motives.
It was, for example, both impossible to get permission to take
over the Spanish ships at Ferrol and also unwise to seize them for
fear of a diplomatic breach.[90] Cadiz was kept firmly out of British
hands. Relationships with some Spanish officials were uneasy as
in some cases their loyalty was suspect. It was said that 'everything
was French' about the Spanish Viceroy in Buenos Aires – 'the
Dresses – the French hairdressers, tailors, shoemakers, etc., etc.'[91]

Difficulties arose in putting Anglo-Spanish relations on a firm
footing. Canning saw the need for a definite treaty with Spain,
laying out mutual obligations[92] but was disappointed in the response. 'At present,' he wrote, the Spaniards 'think they are sure
of us; and that they have a right to us; and that instead of every
assistance that we afford them being another matter of fresh
acknowledgement, every point upon which we hesitate is an injury, and a breach of Engagement. This tone of theirs is offensive,
and becomes irksome to me.'[93]

The Spanish proposals for a treaty appalled Canning. In return
for general assurances, Britain was to guarantee to Ferdinand VII
Spain and the Indies and to 'place at the disposal of Spain a large
British army, to be employed in Europe or America, at the will of
the Junta, and to pay a large subsidy, and supplies of all kind
besides. . . .'[94] Spain's offer of declaring war on Denmark came
long after it could have been of any use, and Canning wearily
commented, 'If they have a fancy for it, I see no harm in it.'[95]
Indeed the Spanish alliance, which had seemed so promising
when the Asturian delegates first arrived, had paid few military
dividends when Canning left office. It did assist Britain's monetary
position at a time of potential crisis by providing a source of
supply for silver. Otherwise Canning could only seek solace in
the shipment of merino sheep he and Charles Ellis had received
through the delegates.

The final adventure whilst Canning was Foreign Secretary was
an expedition to the Scheldt, with the aim of occupying the island
of Walcheren and making an attack on the French naval preparations at Flushing and Antwerp. It was 'a most dangerous under-
taking'[96] and any possible success depended on speed, as Canning
had urged in March.[97] When the expedition eventually sailed on

28 July, the armament was formidable in size but the element of surprise was lost. Chatham, who commanded it, was dilatory, and the expedition fell victim to the disagreements and crossed counsels which befell so many combined army-navy operations. The French withdrawal up the Scheldt, which Mulgrave hailed as a good sign,[98] merely gave the French time to prepare their fortifications. The capture of Walcheren Island and eventually of Flushing itself proved to be barren conquests. When the expedition returned later in the year it had achieved nothing and had suffered badly through losses of personnel.

Throughout his period as Foreign Secretary, Canning played an active role in Parliament, particularly in defending the policy of the war. He did not spare the previous Administration. On 30 June 1807 he strongly attacked it for providing jobs for its own friends. Canning's defence of the Prussian and Swedish subsidies was intended to 'account completely to the Continent for our not having helped them and throw the blame where it ought to rest – on the shoulders of our predecessors'.[99] This attitude infuriated the Opposition, with whom, after all, Canning had only recently been negotiating. Grey became a bitter enemy and Grenville was astonished, attacking Canning for an 'ungenerous abuse of power' after the latter had refused his nephew a permission which was a mere formality.[100] As his relations with Opposition worsened, he was nevertheless still unpopular in certain Tory circles, and at one stage Portland had to apologize for an injurious sally made against Canning by Lord Chancellor Eldon.[101] At the same time, his parliamentary abilities were winning renewed fame. His speech on the Committee for Inquiry into public economy was described by Perceval to the King as 'one of the most brilliant speeches which either he or any other man ever delivered'.[102] Boringdon, admittedly a follower of Canning, said that 'in the Commons, it is clear *consensu omnium* that Canning is beyond comparison the first man on his own side of the House.'[103]

In 1808 the Opposition renewed their attack on the conduct of the war. Howick had gone to the House of Lords as Earl Grey, and George Ponsonby now led the Commons Whigs with Samuel Whitbread heading their more radical elements. In February Canning had to defend the expedition to Copenhagen and he did so in a speech Palmerston described as the most brilliant and convincing he had ever heard.[104] The debates on Spain gave Canning an opportunity for the enunciation of high-sounding general principles such as he loved. 'Any nation in Europe,' he declared, 'that starts up with a determination to oppose a power which, whether professing insidious peace or declaring open war, is the common enemy of all nations . . . becomes instantly our essential ally.'[105] So much government business involved the war that it might have seemed, as Lady Holland remarked, that Canning had assumed the lead in the House of Commons.[106]

Canning, along with Castlereagh, held pro-Catholic principles in contrast to their colleagues. He was angry with the decision to reduce the grant to the Catholic seminary at Magnooth in April 1808 and again with the decision to appoint Dr Duigenan, an extreme Protestant, to the Irish Privy Council. He particularly objected to the kind of argument used by the Government to justify its policy.[107] He nevertheless refused to support Grattan's motion for a committee on Catholic claims, arguing, on purely expediential grounds that there was a 'strong prevailing sentiment' in the country against further concession.[108] At this stage, he also regarded himself, in the tradition of Pitt, as being bound not to force the isue of Catholic representation in Parliament on an unwilling King. Grattan's motion was lost by 281 to 128.

Early in 1809 the Government had little military success to offer the Commons. In February Canning had to defend it against a censure motion from Petty on the terms of the Convention of Cintra, in which he blamed Ministers. Canning replied in a balanced speech which the Whig, W. H. Fremantle, described as 'a reproof both to ministers and generals'.[109] The motion was lost by 203 to 153. When the campaign in Spain was debated three days later Canning threw the blame for some of the mistakes on Moore himself.[110] In defending the increasingly unpopular Orders in Council, he demonstrated their initiation by the Talents, and claimed that the Government had pursued a conciliatory policy towards America.[111]

In all these issues, the Government found itself on the defensive, and this also became the case in domestic matters. Early in 1809 Gwyllym Wardle, MP, charged that the Duke of York, the King's son and Commander-in-Chief of the armed forces, had given commissions on the advice of Mrs Clarke, his mistress, who was paid by the recipients for these favours. The matter was naturally blown up in the press, and for a time 'Duke or Darling' replaced 'Heads or Tails' as an appeal to chance. Canning argued that the Duke should resign and feared that in defending him, the Government might have to use the King's name, which should not be thus devalued when the time might come in which it was 'the only stay in the Country'.[112] In debate he nevertheless drew a distinction between the moral guilt, which was admitted, and the political guilt, which had not been proved in that there was no evidence that the Duke knew of these transactions.[113] Fortunately, the Duke himself resigned three days later, and the House passed a resolution that it was not necessary to proceed to further measures. The word 'now' which had preceded 'necessary' in Lord Althorp's original resolution was removed by a government majority of 113.

As if one scandal was not enough for the session, in April Castlereagh had to face a censure motion from Lord Archibald Hamilton. As President of the Board of Control, Castlereagh had placed an East India Writership, a highly profitable position for a young man, at the disposal of Lord Clancarty to obtain a seat in the House. The Government escaped on the technical ground that the transaction had never been completed. The irony was that in securing the consent of the Irish Parliament to vote itself out of existence nine years earlier Castlereagh had been guilty of far worse.

The Parliament which had seemed so favourable to the Government when elected in 1807 was gradually slipping out of control. In 1808 Canning had described it as 'troublesome'[114] and it was becoming more so. In that year the Government had not dared to use its influence in the Commons to throw out a bill prohibiting the grant of offices with reversion, as the right to hand on an office was known. In 1809 they were faced with a bill from J. C. Curwen to prohibit the purchase of parliamentary seats, and had to confine themselves to amending it. Canning blamed the Castlereagh affair, on the grounds that the Curwen bill was 'a bill which no Government whose strength had not been impaired by disgrace, could, or would have submitted to entertain'.[115]

The parliamentary session of 1809 was not a happy one for Canning. Life in Parliament was increasingly difficult, the war was going badly and he was having problems with his colleagues.

In addition he was tired with 'such overwhelming accumulation of business as has literally occupied each moment of my days'.[116] All these problems were to have an important influence on his role in a major political storm which was just about to break – the worst political crisis of his career.

6

THE DUEL WITH
CASTLEREAGH

At the best of times Canning had scant respect for most of his colleagues. With the war going badly they were, in his eyes, obviously to blame. He objected to the lack of system in Britain's military operations as a whole, and lack of vigour in putting them into execution. With the cleaning up of the Duke of York affair he felt able to put his views before the Duke of Portland. He objected to three things in particular. The first was the conduct of the Government in accepting the Convention of Cintra, and especially the taking of this decision during Canning's absence at Hinckley. The second was the Spanish expedition of Sir John Moore in which he had reluctantly concurred. The third was the delay in strengthening Portugal in the spring. In general he criticized the lack of decision in the Cabinet and especially the fact that he had been unable to press the question of Portugal in the previous two months. When Castlereagh learned of Canning's letter to Portland months later, he very reasonably pointed out that the Government had had little alternative but to accept Cintra, defended Sir John Moore, and denied undue delay in the reinforcement of Portugal.[1] But Canning persisted, 'No man can shut his eyes to the plain fact that the Government has sunk in publick opinion since the end of the last session of Parliament.' He finally demanded changes in the Government, failing which he must resign.[2]

Nine days elapsed between the writing of the letter to Portland on 24 March 1809 and its despatch on 2 April. Perhaps Canning was summoning up the courage to send it. On 4 April Portland replied inviting Canning to join him at his seat at Bulstrode.[3]

Several days of discussion followed in which Canning confined himself to one specific demand, the removal of Castlereagh from the War Department. Portland took his difficulties to Lord Bathurst, the President of the Board of Trade. On his advice, he went to discuss the matter with Lord Camden who was Castlereagh's uncle. Camden agreed that the best plan would be for Castlereagh to change office and also go to the House of Lords.[4] However, none of them really dared broach the subject. Meanwhile Canning's impatience grew, and the termination of the debate on Spain, he argued, removed his moral obligation to remain in the Government. Portland replied the same day, urging that hardly an hour had passed without his considering the problem, only to receive a reply from Canning which used the charges of corruption recently levied against Castlereagh to strengthen his case. The latter should retire, he argued, as 'an atonement to the feelings of the Publick'.[5]

Unable to think of any other course of action, and convinced that Canning was necessary to the stability of his Government, Portland offered his resignation to the King. The latter asked for an explanation, and Portland told him the nature of the problem.[6] In response to renewed pressure from Canning, the King himself suggested that the functions of the War Office be split, leaving the colonies exclusively with Castlereagh. Canning would thus get much of the direction of the war, while to compensate Castlereagh for the loss of power, the King suggested he also become President of the Board of Control for India.

Canning never claimed to like the plan, but he finally agreed to accept it because it was the King's idea.[7] Portland assured Canning that he had asked Bathurst and Camden to help him urge Castlereagh to take India, begging Canning not to take any precipitate step, as the Government would not recover from his resignation.[8] On 21 June the Cabinet approved the Walcheren expedition, which Castlereagh totally ignorant of the situation, was preparing. This provided an additional excuse for delay. More members of the Cabinet were now aware of what was going on; and Perceval, the Chancellor of the Exchequer, wrote to Canning on 25 June that it was very hard to drive Castlereagh from the Government while the expedition was proceeding.[9] Canning conceded the point in a letter to Portland, but urged that arrangements must be hastened.[10]

Meanwhile the other members of the Cabinet had still not summoned up the courage to tell Castlereagh. Late on 27 June Canning learned to his surprise that Camden had still not informed him of the King's desire that he give up the management of the European war. Portland replied, excusing Camden, and urging that a fortnight's delay was the maximum conceivable. The Government did not wish to provoke Castlereagh's resignation in the middle of the expedition.[11] The King's plan had been worked out when only Portland, Bathurst, Eldon, Camden and Canning himself knew of the situation. Gradually other members of the Cabinet learnt and did not like it. Perceval now objected to the fundamental principle of dividing up the War Office's responsibility.[12] In this atmosphere of confusion, worsened by Camden's unwillingness to tell his nephew of the situation, the plan gradually died.

The time was ripe for a new plan. On 4 July Portland saw Canning and suggested that Camden resign his office of Lord President of the Council, apparently voluntarily. Consequently Castlereagh could fill the vacancy and the Marquess Wellesley could be brought into Castlereagh's office. This was perfectly agreeable to Canning as he and Wellesley shared a common viewpoint on the direction of the war.[13] On the twelfth, Canning wrote confidently to his wife that Camden was going to see the King that day. He was agreeable to the change being postponed till after the outcome of the expedition on the personal assurance of the Duke. Then, if it failed, Castlereagh would be told that this and earlier misfortunes made it highly expedient for him to give the war into other hands. Conversely, if the expedition was a success, the change would be represented as strengthening the Government.[14]

However, problems were cropping up behind the scenes. The view that Canning was essential to the Government was not unique to Portland. Canning himself shared it, of course, but so did Liverpool, then Home Secretary, who urged the King that Canning must be preferred to Castlereagh on political grounds. On the other hand Castlereagh, he argued, had begun the expedition, and Liverpool could not reconcile himself to the 'manifest cruelty and injustice' of dismissing him now. As Canning's resignation would be followed by that of the Government, Liverpool asked the King to treat his own office as being at his disposal to facilitate arrangements.[15] On 13 July Perceval, unknown to Canning, wrote to Portland promising to try and persuade Castlereagh to resign, but explicitly refusing to help insist upon it.

Portland was now faced with a situation in which all eventualities seemed to be leading to the dissolution of his Government. From a personal point of view this was not unwelcome to him, for he was old and ill. On the other hand, the King clearly wished him to try to keep the Administration together, and Portland, who boasted virtues rather than abilities, had loyalty high on his list.

By 14 July, Canning saw that something was wrong. Typically, he demanded a decision *now*, and two days later asked that it be bolstered by the King's promise. On the seventeenth, still with no answer to his question as to what arrangements were to be, he insisted that there must be a plan. Two already, to which he had agreed, had been withdrawn without explanation. On 18 July he drew Portland's attention to Castlereagh's continuing ignorance of the situation, refusing to complain, as it had been sanctioned by the King, but wanting his objections to it remembered when it was urged 'as an act of injustice towards Lord Castlereagh'.[16] Portland finally replied, promising always to acknowledge that the reserve towards Castlereagh originated with himself. The new offer to Castlereagh was to be the Lord Presidency of the Council and the Privy Seal. If he refused, he was still to be removed and an opening made for Wellesley.[17] Clearly, Portland was hoping that the new offer would prove sufficiently attractive to Castlereagh, for he must have known that he risked the departure of Perceval and probably Liverpool if he enforced the arrangement. Canning himself found the new plan satisfactory, and asked permission to tell Wellesley of the arrangement immediately. This was a typical example of Canning pushing his luck well beyond the strain it would bear. The King was furious at this new request, arguing that the concessions made to Canning had been 'unprecedented in the whole of His Reign' and expressed his utter repugnance. Canning for once saw he had gone too far and 'cheerfully' withdrew his request.[18]

In August 1809 the situation was changed by Portland's sudden illness. The question under discussion therefore became that of a total restructuring of the Government. On the twenty-fifth Perceval wrote to Canning saying it was doubtful that Portland could long hold his present situation and would be willing to renew his preferred resignation. One advantage of the new arrangement, he stressed, was that it would enable them to conceal from Castlereagh the cause of his removal. 'I am satisfied', he urged, 'that at this moment, he has not the least suspicion upon the subject.'[19] In reply Canning tried to find out who was behind the letter. When Perceval stressed it was his own initiative, though he had spoken to Harrowby, Canning refused further discussion. Perceval then revealed that Liverpool had spoken on the question with the King at the latter's initiative, though this confession rather contradicted his statement that there had not been other consultations. Canning felt free to put forward his own ideas on the future shape of Government. He urged that there must be a Prime Minister in the House of Commons. This clearly could only be himself or Perceval, and just as he wouldn't expect the latter to serve under him, so he wouldn't serve under Perceval. Canning had thus put forward a claim to be Prime Minister or nothing. Perhaps he greatly overestimated how essential he was. In this one might argue that Portland was much to blame for being over-ready to concoct plans to suit Canning's requirements, thereby accepting Canning's self-assumed eminence at face value. Canning himself may have been encouraged in this course of madness and arrogance by a visit earlier in the month of Robert Dundas, who had promised to resign with him. The Dundas family controlled the votes of a high proportion of Scottish MPs and only a very bold ministry could defy them. Perceval sent a fairly reasonable letter in reply, agreeing with Canning in principle, but saying that as he did not wish to be Prime Minister, he looked to find one from the other House.[20]

On 2 September Canning wrote to Portland that the time had now come for Wellesley to become Secretary for War. Portland replied on the third, stalling on the general issue and raising the question of his own resignation. Canning immediately withdrew his demand and asked to resign with Portland. In this crisis, Canning received letters urging moderation. Perceval argued that a third person as Prime Minister was better than the total overthrow of the Administration. On the seventh, Portland, who had resigned the previous day but was remaining in office till a successor could be found, asked Canning to withdraw his resignation and attend the Cabinet that day.[21] Canning did not attend and his absence made Castlereagh inquisitive as to its cause. Eventually he dragged the truth from his uncle, offered his resignation to the King the next day and withdrew from public view for twelve days to nurse his injury. Thus, paradoxically, Castlereagh learned the truth of the plotting behind his back just at the moment when it had become unnecessary that he ever learn.

In this situation Liverpool and Perceval clarified their positions to Canning. Liverpool removed the impression that he would only acquiesce in Castlereagh's removal as part of a general rearrangement of the Government, but Perceval confirmed it. In particular he drew to Canning's attention the contents of the letter he had written to Portland on 13 July.[22] Increasingly Perceval was emerging as the spider at the centre of the web. He had effectively scuppered two plans which would have accommodated Canning and now, by a show of reasonableness, was attracting to himself those who disliked the forwardness of his rival. Canning himself paid tribute to the candour, manliness and modesty of his behaviour.[23]

On 12 September Canning sent his sentiments to Portland re-iterating his view that there must be a Prime Minister in the House of Commons and that he would not serve under Perceval.[24] The next day Canning had an audience with the King in which he repeated this view. There was, he urged, no substitute for Portland, for 'he is not one of a species, he is an individual, the last of his species – there is nothing like him to be found'. As to alternative Prime Minister in the Lords, Chatham, who would once have seemed obvious, was ruled out by his apparent mishandling of the Walcheren expedition. He renewed his threat to retire if Percevel was chosen, but told the King that if the Government failed to stand he would have an alternative in Canning and his friends. The King told Perceval later that this was 'the most extraordinary' conversation he ever heard. Edward Cook, Castlereagh's Under-Secretary, called it 'the most insolent proposition that was ever obtruded upon a Monarch by a presumptuous Subject'.[25] The King meanwhile instructed Perceval to consult with other members of the Cabinet on the contents of Canning's letter to Portland. On the fifteenth Canning wrote to his wife that 'constant meetings and co-jobberation . . . are going on at P's [Perceval's]. Castlereagh has disappeared as through a trap-door.' He then went on to discuss who would have office with him. Charles Long, he felt, was certain, but was worried that Huskisson had not been quite explicit.[26] Meanwhile it was becoming obvious that the Government was falling apart. Colonel MacMahon wrote to the Prince of Wales on 15 September that all the members of the Cabinet were scheming against one another and that Grey and Grenville would be approached to form a ministry from the Opposition.[27]

Perceval was in a difficult position. Charles Arbuthnot, one of the ablest of political managers, wrote to Huskisson, 'The holding together the present Administration seems impossible, for Canning, as you know, has pretensions which his colleagues will not agree to, and without him the business of Parliament could not be carried on'.[28] On 16 September Canning put a shot across Perceval's bow when he explicitly denied a statement made by George Rose that he had promised 'to support in Parliament any Government which you and the rest of your Colleagues might form'.[29] Ideally Canning still wanted to be summoned himself. For Perceval he wanted the woolsack. As its intended recipient wryly commented, 'However he attempted to gild and decorate the ornament, I am persuaded that he meant only to put an extinguisher on my head in the shape of a coronet.'[30] Canning's own confidence was exaggerated. Not all his supporters approved of his course of conduct. In particular, George Rose was under pressure from his family. On 17 September his daughter-in-law wrote a strong letter denouncing Canning's 'vaulting ambition'. He, she said, had clung to Rose just to climb the ladder and given nothing in return. 'I cannot bear,' she added, 'that the King or Country should suppose you quit office because Mr Canning is not first Minister.'[31]

On 18 September the Cabinet came to a decision. The Government strength in the House of Commons, they felt, had last session been inadequate. Canning's secession would weaken them even further, so they could not recommend the King to pick a ministry from amongst themselves. They stressed, nevertheless, that Canning would face similar difficulties and thereby ended Canning's hopes of an early consummation of his ambitions.[32] This minute preceded the first of several attempts made between 1809 and 1812 to form a ministry jointly with the Opposition. An approach to Grey and Grenville followed.

Meanwhile Canning received a letter from Castlereagh denouncing his conduct.

You continued to sit in the same Cabinet with me, and to leave me not only in the persuasion that I possessed your confidence and support as a colleague, but you allowed me, tho' thus virtually superseded, in breach of every principle both public and private to originate and proceed in the Execution of a new Enterprise of the most arduous and important nature, with your apparent concurrence and ostensible approbation.

Castlereagh concluded by challenging Canning to a duel.[33] Canning felt he had little option but to accept the challenge. In his reply he spoke of 'misrepresentations'[34] but the story was too complicated for Canning to explain without a seeming show of cowardice. Furthermore, any explanation would have to throw blame on Portland and the King, and Canning was unwilling to do that. It must be said that Portland and Camden were more to blame than Canning for Castlereagh's injury. No-one who knew of the negotiations was blameless, but as Canning was prime mover in the whole operation, it is difficult to keep from censuring him merely because he had made other men guardians of his own conscience. As for Castlereagh, it is impossible to say whether he sought restoration of diminished honour or merely revenge.

Charles Ellis became Canning's second, and attempted to give such explanations to Lord Yarmouth, who was acting for Castlereagh, as would be consistent with his honour.[35] This attempt failed, and Canning set about to prepare for his own possible demise. To his wife he wrote a touching letter of farewell. 'I could do no otherwise than I have done. God bless my own best and dearest love – a better and a dearer never did God give to man.' He discussed his own family. For his eldest son George he did not advise politics, for then he would 'feel and fret, and lament, and hate, and despise – as much as his father'. He advised the life of a scholar, or, if he wished it, a clergyman. The second son William he described as 'unamiable, selfish and singular', but stressed that he had been less loved, and perhaps affection would alter his nature. Of Harriet, or 'Toddles' he had nothing ill to say. He then described his financial affairs, drawing Joan's attention to the affairs of the Alienation Office which Canning kept in his own hands. Lest he appear a defaulter he had borrowed £2,000 from Charles Ellis. He made a point of asking Joan to give his mother £2,000, or £300 per year, which was less than the income from his Irish estate. Everything else went to Joan. He concluded, 'I hope I have made you happy. If you have been a happy wife – and if I leave you a happy mother, and a *proud* widow, I am content. Adieu, Adieu.'[36]

The following day Canning and Castlereagh met at Putney Heath at 6 am. A final effort by Ellis to end the affair amicably failed, and the combatants walked twelve paces and fired. The first shots missed, but on the second attempt Castlereagh shot Canning through the 'fleshy part' of his left thigh. Honour being satisfied Castlereagh helped Ellis to take Canning to Yarmouth's house nearby where a surgeon was waiting. As Canning told his mother, he was not seriously hurt and a fortnight on a couch would be sufficient for a full recovery.[37] He was in sufficiently good spirits – mainly, no doubt, through sheer relief, to write an amusing account to the Leighs of how the ball had passed through his thigh and 'nankeen breeches', and recommending Lord Castlereagh as the operator should they be inclined to repeat the experiment.[38]

News of the duel quickly became public and the papers of 22 September carried the story. *The Morning Post* at first confined itself to reporting, but the Whig *Morning Chronicle* naturally drew political conclusions. 'To suppose it possible,' it declared, 'after the disgusting exhibition they have made, to form out of their dispersed and disordered ranks a Government that could stand, is the height of absurdity.' Nearby was an example of disorderly behaviour lower down the social scale when a linen-draper's shopman, when indicted, went into the dock with a placard, 'No Italian depravity or French duplicity – native talent and the old prices.'[39]

The King himself was shocked at the news. Canning wrote to him explaining that it was impossible to decline satisfaction to Castlereagh, but the King refused to reply.[40] Meanwhile recriminations began about who had been responsible for the concealment from Castlereagh of the plans for his removal. Portland offered to take it upon himself to explain the delay.[41] Canning sent his correspondence with Castlereagh to Perceval, from whom he received an acknowledgement that Canning was 'no passive or unremonstrating accomplice in that concealment'. Later

Perceval seemed to go back on these words and a bitter correspondence followed.[42]

Both Castlereagh and Canning were anxious to justify themselves. Castlereagh sent his defence to the King on 1 October.
The King relented to Canning sufficiently to tell him that he
could do no other than accept the challenge 'tho' he mortally
disapproves of Duels'.[43] Nevertheless, despite the fact that Castlereagh was more unpopular with the public than Canning, he got
the better of the debate in a concerted attempt to make people
believe that what had occurred stemmed from Canning's 'monkey
tricks to make himself premier'.[44] Grey, who disliked both, said,
'It is impossible to defend Canning's conduct either in a public
or a private view.'[45]

Canning found himself in a dilemma. If he failed to answer
Castlereagh's accusations he could be thought to be acquiescing in
them. On the other hand, if he did, he might anger the King by
revealing the workings of his Government.[46] To Sheridan, with
whom he retained something of his former friendship, he argued
that any account which did not give the full facts must be
fallacious. He nevertheless submitted to this injustice because of
the King and Portland, 'who, however unluckily he may have
mismanaged the business I am sure meant all for the best'.[47] To
Sturges-Bourne he was more explicit: 'The dilatoriness of the
poor old D of P – and the something worse – of Lord Camden
have been the cause of all that has happened.'[48]

Controversy over the rights and wrongs of the situation
appeared in the press. Canning wrote to Perceval asking that the
'nonsense and the calumnies which I have seen for the last week
in the ministerial papers' should subside,[49] but felt obliged to
answer 'An Accurate Account' which appeared on 2 and 3 October
putting Castlereagh's view. On the fourteenth Canning's reply
stressed that he had not designed the concealment and at one
time had even been ignorant of it.[50]

Privately he complained bitterly that his enemies knew he
could not make a true defence 'without expressing names that
ought never to be mentioned'.[51] By the twenty-seventh he felt he
had no alternative but a full printed defence, and further 'foul
misrepresentations'[52] in mid-November sharpened his resolution.
Later in the month his 'Letter to Lord Camden'[53] appeared, a
copy of which he sent to the King to avert royal disfavour.

The result of the controversy was to baffle the public and embitter politics. Huskisson described Castlereagh's friends as having acted 'like ruined spendthrifts'.[54] Canning delighted in a malicious anecdote from Bristol where the toast of 'Lord Camden and the Navy' was mistaken for 'Lord Camden and his Nephew' and a cry of 'No Castlereagh' started.[55] The bitterness persisted for years. The public bewilderment on the whole settled into a belief that Castlereagh was the wronged party. Grenville wrote in mid-December that Canning was deeply depressed, feeling the unfavourable impression that his own conduct, and still more his published defences had caused.[56] The whole affair was good meat for the satirists. The author of 'The Battle of the Blocks' described the conflict between 'Mister Canting' and 'Lord Castaway'. The whole is seen as the former's plot to blame Castaway for the Government's failings and at the same time become Prime Minister, for 'Me, for that station all acknowledge fit'.

Little is more contemptible than overweening ambition which is seen to have failed. This was certainly the light in which Canning was seen, except by his nearest associates. There was little more he could do about the events of mid-1809, and very wisely with the new year he refused to say anything further on a subject which for him was best consigned to oblivion.

Throughout this period, the Government was being re-formed. Before the duel the old ministry had decided it could not stand on its own, and Perceval discussed the situation with Portland on 20 September. The duel made matters worse. Perceval called it 'Terrible . . . for public impression. It must end in an attempt to form an united government with our opponents.'[57] Liverpool wrote that it would be 'vain' to attempt an exclusive Administration. Consequently, Perceval had received the King's permission to approach Grey and Grenville in an attempt to form a united Administration. Liverpool considered the experiment worth a 'fair trial'.[58] George Ellis was convinced that the old Government would 'unite with anyone, and submit to everything provided they can prevent Canning's attainment of that ascendancy in the House of Commons to which his own Talents have long since obviously destined him'.[59]

The Whigs refused the offer. Lord Holland wrote that it was foolishness to think that it could have succeeded,[60] but in reality it was Grey's obduracy that prevented any junction. He was not, he asserted, prepared to join any administration which would comprehend any of the leading members of the late or present Administration. Above all, he detested Canning whom he considered 'worse than any of his late colleagues'. He had never forgiven the latter's turncoat conduct from 1804: 'his immediate acceptance of office upon the principle of the late Administration, his conduct towards us the moment we were in power and all that has happened since has made so deep an impression on my mind that I could not now bring myself either in or out of office, to act with him'.[61] When Canning became his political opponent Grey had expected hostility, but also fairness and common liberality, yet 'instead he had met with the grossest misrepresentation, the most ungenerous and unprecedented attacks. . . .'[62] Grey also had an exaggerated view of the weakness of an administration which he did not believe could take office without power to settle the Catholic question.[63]

On 4 October Perceval kissed hands as Prime Minister. The following day Canning was able to walk and a week later he submitted his seals of office to the King. He was not to receive them back for thirteen years. There were few powerful voices urging that renewed attempts should be made to get Canning into the Administration, though one voice raised in his support was the Princess of Wales who wrote to Perceval on the subject calling him 'so eminent a speaker and statesman and a man of such unshaken integrity'.[64] Perceval was unmoved. Since he had originally learned of Canning's objections to Castlereagh he had played a quiet role behind the scenes and was at last at the front of the stage. Canning had originally trusted Perceval but by the end of the year called him a man 'whose conduct has been such as appears to my mind irreconcilable with any principle of good faith, public or private'. In particular he complained that Perceval, having got Canning's opinions as to the formation of a new Government, had circulated them without permission to Harrowby and Liverpool so that it should be thought his resignation was not due to Portland's refusal to implement his promise to remove Castlereagh but to the refusal of his colleagues to agree to his ideas on the formation of a Government. Furthermore, Portland's resignation, of which Canning learned later than his colleagues, confirmed this impression.[65] Conversely, Perceval, arguing his case to the Princess of Wales, stressed the number of attempts that had been made to get Canning to agree to a third person to head the ministry.[66]

Neither Perceval nor Canning were telling the whole truth. Canning's resignation was directly due to the failure to remove Castlereagh, but he knew of the likelihood of Portland's own resignation and therefore invited misinterpretation. Furthermore, he had made it clear that a Prime Minister was required in the House of Commons, and as he would not accept Perceval, this had to be himself. Canning had, nevertheless, not refused point-blank to serve under a peer, though he had raised a strong general objection. Whatever the motives of the protagonists, the desirability of having Perceval without Canning grew on his colleagues, and soon had fairly general support.

Canning expected his non-participation in the Government to be more devastating in its effects than it in fact proved. Loyal to Canning, Granville Leveson-Gower, who had been admitted into the Cabinet in June as Secretary at War, resigned; but the rest of the Cabinet stood firm. In junior offices Huskisson and Sturges-Bourne left with Canning, but Wellesley-Pole and Charles Long did not. Robert Dundas, who in August had promised to resign with Canning, in fact joined the Cabinet as President of the Board of Control. George Rose too decided to stay. 'Old Rose came to me today,' wrote Canning, '*cried* and *remained* Treasurer of the Navy.'[67] Rose explained to his daughter-in-law that he thought Perceval's offer of agreeing to serve under Canning's choice of three peers a fair one. After explaining his final decision to Canning he had hoped they would remain friends, but later when he held out his hand to Canning it was received very coldly.[68]

Canning never liked deserters. The biggest blow of all was Marquess Wellesley's decision to serve as Foreign Secretary. He had left Canning his own letter of resignation to be used alongside Canning's own, but Perceval pre-empted this by offering Wellesley the Foreign Seals on 5 October. At first Canning thought Wellesley would refuse but then he heard rumours that Wellesley was being told by the Administration that they had proposed him as Prime Minister but Canning had opposed it. He wrote angrily to Perceval that he would have worked with Wellesley, but it was pointed out in reply that this was merely a misrepresentation of Canning's general objection to the plan for another peer as

Minister, in which context the names of Harrowby, Bathurst, Liverpool and Wellesley had all been mentioned.[69] In late November Canning wrote gloomily to Charles Bagot that Wellesley was 'decided to accept at *all* hazards, and *any* thing.'[70] In October Canning had been able to write gleefully about 'the distress to which P. is reduced'.[71] By December his attitude had changed, and he wrote that 'with P. in his present situation my return to office is impossible'.[72]

Thus had ended one chapter in Canning's life which began with his determination to remove Castlereagh and grew into a determination to become First Minister. As regards the interminable delays in securing the implementation of Portland's promise, he had reason to complain of his colleagues. Indeed, as Liverpool later confessed, they had simply hoped that something 'might occur'[73] in the course of the Walcheren expedition to obviate the difficulties. But the fact remains that Canning had been his own worst enemy.

The establishment of the Perceval Government left Canning in an equivocal position. Grenville was clear that Canning could not act with the Opposition because of questions to do with the war, and particularly differences of opinion about relations with America.[74] When he eventually reflected on his position Canning decided to act independently of any of the existing parties, upholding this and any other government against reformers, but opposing them without scruple where he considered them wrong.[75]

In late 1809 no-one knew in which direction Canning would move. There were those who thought he might move towards opposition and rumours of this which appeared in *The Morning Chronicle* in October angered him intensely.[76] On the government side, Lonsdale thought it a strong possibility[77] and even his friend and ally J. W. Ward, later Viscount Dudley, thought he would join the Opposition if they treated him well.[78] Despite his sense of isolation at a time when everyone seemed 'against him except his own particular cronies',[79] Canning lost nothing of his arrogance.

In November J. H. Frere arranged a reconciliation with Wellesley, who wanted to see a ministry in which he and Canning shared the offices of Foreign Secretary and Prime Minister.[80] Canning wrote to his wife that though annoyed with Wellesley, he should not condemn him as Perceval wished, nor could he refuse to have anything to do with all those who would not acknowledge his claims to be Prime Minister. On the other hand, Canning went on:

> it is not with anger – but with contempt that I must treat W. when he is actually in my office. If my object was to take the chance of preventing him from taking it (the Foreign Secretary-ship) – perhaps the other would have been the better chance – but I believe he was pledged – folly and rascality I grant you – but so pledged I was to make him as inconvenient to them as I could. Does my own love think it would be no vengeance to turn the Perceval down again and then, not to take office with W? – or failing that to leave W. with the impression that nothing but Perceval's pertinacity in his office prevented him from being at the head of a strong government.[81]

These are clearly the words of an embittered egotist.

The year 1810 was filled with rumours of a change in government, as Perceval's parliamentary strength was regarded as inadequate. According to Thomas Grenville, Carlton House, where the Prince of Wales' circle met, was talking in March 1810 of Wellesley at the Treasury, Canning as Foreign Secretary, Granville at the War Office and Huskisson at the Exchequer.[82] Such a rumour was unrealistic but illustrates the atmosphere of confusion. In the Easter recess the Government approached Canning, Castlereagh and Sidmouth to ask them if they would serve under Perceval together. Canning merely declined to answer abstract questions, but the arrangement never came to anything as Sidmouth refused to work with his old enemy.[83] Canning was hoping to work through Wellesley to make his return inevitable, though he was somewhat worried at the latter's apparent ineptitude in office. He told his wife gleefully that there was a prevailing wish to see him back at the Foreign Office, 'and what I confess pleases me (and will please my own love still more) is that Wellesley's Premiership is never mentioned except as a means for that end'.[84] He nevertheless felt that Wellesley's pressure, to be effective, should be accompanied by a tender of resignation.[85]

Canning was certainly asking much of someone he rather despised. Wellesley acted honourably. In June he offered his resignation if Canning could step into his place, but this was rejected by the Cabinet, who clearly wanted an overall arrangement.[86] Can-

ning felt they were merely trying to delay this.[87] On 23 July
Wellesley pressed on Perceval the urgency of getting Canning into
the Cabinet[88] and the matter was discussed in Cabinet three days
later. On Wellesley's insistence, Sidmouth was left out of consideration, but a joint offer was made to Castlereagh and Canning.
The plan involved giving Canning and Castlereagh the Home
Office and the Admiralty to apportion between them, and was
flatly rejected by Castlereagh.[89] Canning wrote to Perceval stressing that the only post he was prepared to accept was that of
Foreign Secretary, only to receive a curt reply from Perceval that
he had hoped Canning would be prepared to accept a post more
in keeping with the interests of the Government. Canning even
pressed his luck further by saying that he had always thought
the office of Chancellor of the Exchequer disposable in any
arrangement. He clearly wanted this for Huskisson, who, he had
told his wife in March, could 'take care of the House in my
absence'. Perceval merely replied that this was not settled.[90]

Canning had now been out of office a year. The Opposition
watched him with interest. Buckingham described him as 'most
unhappy, and with a lust for office not disguised and most insati-
able'. Thomas Grenville agreed 'that the restless intriguing spirit
of the ex-Minister will not rest till somehow or other he shall get
his real boxes again'.[91] In this atmosphere the political world was
shaken by the madness of the King brought on by the death of
his daughter Princess Amelia. It soon became clear that the Prince
of Wales would become Regent, and he had been a life-long
friend of the Whigs. In December a Regency Bill was brought in,
based on that introduced by Pitt when the same situation had
arisen in 1788. The Bill contained certain limitations on the
Regent's power. Canning shocked many Pittites by joining in
the Whig opposition to these restrictions. He argued that the
executive authority should be unimpaired, but one cannot avow
the suspicion that he was trying to mend his fences with the future
George IV. Certainly he was later to regard the Regent's treatment
of him as a sign of base ingratitude.[92] On some votes the Government was defeated and Canning's role in these was certainly
decisive.[93] The Government had nevertheless successfully carried
the bill by January and the question immediately arose of whether
or not the Regent would replace his ministers.

The Whigs certainly thought that their hour had come. Lord

Grenville was urged by his brothers to include Canning in any Administration. Grey was angry at this, refusing to work with Canning and speaking sarcastically of 'this upright and powerful statesman'.[94] The Regent himself, while hinting at the grounds of his own personal dislike of Canning 'viz, his intimacy with the Princess',[95] nevertheless almost suggested a coalition with him and condemned all exclusion of persons. In fact a combination of the Regent's natural dilatoriness and fear of his father's recovering to find the Whigs in office stayed his decision. Throughout the year prospects of the King's recovery faded and the political world was filled with rumours. Canning was not sure what to think. In June he wrote that he did not believe the Government would change; that the Regent would go on so long that in the end he would lack the courage or power to do it. On 25 July he thought that an offer to Grey and Grenville would be made, which would mean in effect that the Government had fallen into their hands. Four days later he wrote that the Opposition would not come in as a party, even on the King's death, but that a partial arrangement would be made. He continued to believe this and warned Huskisson not to be too disparaging about Wellesley for the latter was praising Canning and was the only person round whom a Government not entirely Percevalist or Opposition could be built.[96]

The Opposition were equally puzzled. Early in August Tom Grenville was conveying reports from Brighton of intrigues with Wellesley and Canning, only to write later in the month that they had all blown over.[97] Nevertheless, as the year went on and the day on which all the restrictions on the Regent expired approached, the political temperature rose still further. Would the Regent change the Government or would he abandon his old friends? Furthermore, what would his attitude be to concessions to Catholics?

The New Year found Canning still in a state of uncertainty. On 9 January he wrote that nothing had changed his view of Perceval remaining uppermost.[98] In February he wrote, 'As to P. his power is confirmed for ever . . . as to office *adieu* to it for this reign'.[99] On the other hand, four days later he considered the possibility of the Regent being driven to extremity. He envisaged an 'intermediate ministry of which the Mog (Mogul – i.e. Wellesley) and I should be the basis'.[100] As to the components of the ministry, Canning was increasingly inclined to Opposition, justifying his view on the grounds that they might recant on their basically hostile views to British activities in Iberia. On the other hand, he could never work with Perceval 'unless he recants his anti-catholic violence'.[101]

Meanwhile Canning had a long conversation with Wellesley in which he stressed his objections to the Government. It was not, he said, constituted 'in such a way as to be fit for the time'. Perceval, 'with a thousand good qualities' was 'wholly unfit' for the job. Canning himself did not covet the position, but 'there were many persons under whom I would serve. . . .'[102] Perhaps encouraged by this conversation Wellesley resigned from the Government on 19 February, the day after the restrictions expired, objecting to the narrow scale of operations in the Iberian peninsula.

The Whigs were also considering the state of affairs. Buckingham urged his brother that he could not take office without Wellesley and Canning. The Regent's view of Canning was reported that he found him useful and brilliant, but 'insincere and intriguing'.[103] The Government changes that occurred came as a surprise. Sidmouth and Castlereagh were added to the Government, the latter in Canning's old position of Foreign Secretary. Perceval was now confirmed in office and with additional parliamentary strength which devalued Canning's own importance. The only place he could drift was towards Opposition but still he stood aloof from any formal commitments. Furthermore, no one was quite sure what game the Regent was playing. In May, Canning's notice for a motion on the Catholic question was regarded by Auckland and Grey as 'a case of Prince versus Perceval'.[104]

In practice the conclusion that the Regent had finally committed himself to Perceval must be accepted. The hypothesis, however, became unprovable on 11 May 1812 when a bankrupt Russian merchant, who blamed Government policy for his losses, shot Perceval dead in the lobby of the House of Commons. In the face of such a tragedy what hostile feelings he had had for the late Prime Minister died and Canning was one of those called in by the speaker to discuss provision for Perceval's family. All political prospects now became wrapped in a deep mist.

Canning's absence from Government removed some of the constraints from his parliamentary conduct. He certainly saw the advantages he could obtain by playing a balancing role. His first speech of the 1810 session was made in support of Government on an amendment to the Address, which was lost by 264 to 167. Canning considered his own speech to have been a 'brilliant one'[105] though his friend Ward thought it below average and saw it as evidence that Canning was depressed at his sense of having incurred public disapprobation.[106] The major question of the new session was the failure of the expedition to the Scheldt. Canning had already identified it as a question on which an effective mischief could be done to the Government.[107] When Porchester moved for a Committee of Inquiry early in the session Canning opposed it on a technicality, but did not bestir his followers. He supported an opposition motion that the submissions made by Chatham to the King in the course of the expedition be laid before the House,[108] and on the 6 March he opposed Government during the debate on Whitbread's resolution. 'Huzza – huzza – huzza,' he wrote to Joan, 'my own love will be satisfied I think with the transactions of the night. In primis – Govt. was beaten by 33 – 188–221. Secondly I beat them. More voted with me, I am confident, than would have turned the question.'[109] In the end, Canning strongly supported the policy of the Scheldt expedition, for he was much closer to Government than to Opposition on issues connected with the war.[110] The importance of the whole proceeding was nevertheless the demonstration of Canning's power as an arbitrator in a Parliament where Government lacked a safe majority.

In general, Canning could be relied on where questions of the war were concerned. The vote of Credit Bill of June gave him an opportunity to reiterate his strong support for the war and draw attention to Spain, where 'from the ashes of their slaughtered countreymen, and from the smoking ruins of their cities and their hamlets has burst forth a renovated flame, kindling anew their ardour and enthusiasm....'[111] Perceval told the King that Canning had answered Whitbread so successfully that he himself had not felt it necessary to say anything.[112]

On domestic questions Canning felt no such obligation to Government, and he could play a balancing role. In the *Weekly Register* of 24 March 1810, Sir Francis Burdett had denounced the action of the Commons in imprisoning a Radical activist, John Gale Jones, for a libel on the House. Canning had originally thought Burdett should be proceeded against at law, but the

Speaker persuaded him otherwise, and on 5 April he joined Government in insisting on the House's 'imperious duty' to maintain their privileges 'with firmness and jealousy'.[113] Burdett's imprisonment was therefore ordered by a resolution of the House. Days of rioting in London followed, as the Serjeant-at-Arms attempted to effect the resolution. This came before the House when an investigation was requested into the shooting of a civilian by an unknown life-guardsman, against whom the coroners' jury had returned a verdict of wilful murder. Canning acquiesced in the refusal of this investigation. On the other hand, he did support the release of Gale Jones himself, opposing Government on this issue with the argument that he had been punished enough.[114] To his wife he wrote: 'I wonder whether my own love will be more surprised or amused at my speech and vote of last night. It was a piece of mischief....'[115]

A further opportunity for Canning to oppose Government arose in March on a resolution of Bankes to abolish sinecure offices. Anticipating the arguments of his opponents Canning conceded that 'the fabric of monarchy could never be maintained except the throne was surrounded, not merely by a decent, but a gorgeous splendour.' On the other hand, the resolution did not in fact entrench on the prerogative of the Crown.[116] In practice the steady pressure from Parliament for the reduction of the patronage of the Government served severely to undermine its ability to control the political situation.

Canning dealt with other issues as they arose. He opposed referring Grattan's petition for Catholic Emancipation to a committee, but in a very moderate speech. On the other hand, he was vigorous in his denunciation of a measure for parliamentary reform as being a motion to declare the House inadequate for the performance of its functions. Rather he said, 'Let the venerable fabric, which has sheltered us for so many ages, and stood unshaken through so many storms, still remain unimpaired and holy, sacred from the rash frenzy of that ignorant innovator who would tear it down, careless and incapable of any substitution.'[117] To offset this witness to conservatism, one might nevertheless set Canning's support for Samuel Romilly's bill to remove the death penalty for stealing more than forty shillings from a dwelling. Typically for Canning when espousing the cause of change, he eschewed arguments of principle and relied on the evidence that juries perjured themselves in such cases in order to avoid a conviction.[118]

The tantalizing uncertainty of Canning's position underlay the negotiations for his re-entry to the Government. Despite Canning's general support, Perceval could not rely on him. On the other hand, Opposition did not trust him. In 1810 Lady Holland said of Canning: 'Faithless and unprincipled are the leading traits in that gentleman's character.'[119] Whitbread attacked him in Parliament for his recall of D. M. Erskine, son of a leading Whig and Minister-Plenipotentiary in the United States.[120] Canning himself seemed at that time to be uncertain of which way he was going, confining himself to telling his wife early in 1810 that he could not be in opposition till the following year. At the commencement of the following session he was sent the Tory whip and returned it, implying it must have been a mistake.[121]

Two main issues dominated the session of 1811. Canning opposed the restrictions which the Government sought to impose upon the Regent's exercise of power. Along with Castlereagh and Wilberforce he helped to defeat a government resolution to give the Queen full control over the Royal Household. Canning's triumph of the session came on the bullion question. Under the financial exigencies of war, the Bank of England had suspended the right to draw bullion in lieu of notes. There had consequently been an effective devaluation of the paper as against cash and a parliamentary committee sat under the chairmanship of Francis Homer to find a remedy. When it reported it attacked the excessive issue of notes by the Bank of England and demanded a return to cash (i.e. gold) payments within two years. The Government rejected this conclusion, and put forward a resolution 'that a note and 1/-d were in public estimation equal to a guinea of full weight'. This was clearly an abject falsehood, but one with the albeit forlorn intention of effecting what it purported to describe.

Canning had been considering the question for some time. Huskisson, author of a work on bullion, had been advising him throughout 1810, recommending the Report of the Bullion Committee while insisting that it was not the existence, but the excess of paper circulation to which he objected, pointing to the evils of superabundant credit in a period of rising prices.[122]

In Parliament Canning took a middle course. He attacked the Government and in particular tried to pour scorn on Castlereagh who had intervened in the debate with his concept of a 'sense of value'. He went on: 'As well might you pretend to fix a limit on the shore and bid the flowing oceans advance no further, as attempt by the interposition of a statute to stop the tide of the precious metals in whatever direction it is made to flow by the influence of commercial necessity and commercial demand.' Canning nevertheless concurred with Vansittart, speaking for the Government, that the practical resolutions of the bullion committee should not be adopted.

This splendid compromise enabled Canning to participate in the general scorn being poured on Government for a position which was not only wrong but contradicted by their own actions,[123] and also to avoid the inconvenience which would have been imposed on the war effort by a sudden return to cash payments. As it was, he could safely ask for a mere record to be made of the principles of the monetary system as laid down by the bullion committee,[124] though the Government defeated Canning on this issue. Cash payments were restored in 1819.

Canning's intervention in this question was generally regarded as a *tour de force*, and won him prestige. It was nevertheless not within his main field of concern. He had already written to Wellesley that he intended to go into the country as soon as parliamentary reform, 'the only question that I foresee in which I take any interest', was disposed of.[125]

In 1812 the gap between Canning and the Government widened. The Orders in Council were by now having a strongly deleterious effect on British trade and manufactures. Perceval and Stephen were still committed to the full implementation of the policy and in 1811 there was a dramatic decline in the number of licences issued to allow ships to go to ports under blockade, from 3,186 in 1810 to 588.[126] In March 1812 Henry Brougham moved for a Select Committee to enquire into the Orders. Canning agreed with him, arguing that while he had approved of them in their original form, he disliked certain amendments which had been introduced.[127]

The other major issue of early 1812 was the Catholic question. It first arose in the form of a motion for a committee on the state of Ireland, but Canning opposed this as he strongly disapproved of confusing the two issues.[128] He nevertheless followed this up with support for Turton's motion on the state of the nation because he disapproved of Government conduct on the Catholic question. In April Gratton consulted him on the shape of a motion on the subject and when the latter moved for a committee he gave it full support. On 4 February Canning had written to his wife that he was pleased with his speech of the previous day because it showed it was possible to be for the Catholics in substance, but against yielding at that time.

On 24 April he was far less equivocal. He reviewed the harshness of the old penal laws and justified his previous silence with the deference he had felt was owed to the old King's opinions. Pitt, he urged, would have concurred. The motion was lost by 300 to 215, but on 6 May Canning gave notice of his own motion for an Address to the Regent to take the question into consideration. It was fixed for 28 May.[129] In addition, Canning had worsened his relations with Government by supporting a sinecure offices bill which was carried against Government by 134 to 123 on 4 May.[130] A week later Perceval's death revolutionized the situation.

The immediate and fairly general reaction to Perceval's assassination was that a major change of Government was inevitable. Ward took it for granted that Wellesley and Canning would come in, but whether with ministry or opposition for their associates he was not sure.[131] It fell to Liverpool to attempt to keep the old Government in business. On 17 May he saw both Canning and Wellesley, expressing the disposition of all his colleagues to work with Wellesley and offering to accommodate Canning's friends. Castlereagh was nevertheless to have his position preserved and the suggestion was put forward of his taking the lead in the Commons. As to the two issues of policy which Canning and Wellesley raised, Liverpool insisted that the views of his colleagues on the Catholic Question were unchanged and that an extension of activities in the Peninsula was impossible.[132] It was not an offer such as Canning could accept and Wellesley had refused to serve without him. It may indeed have been so designed. Canning had observed on the sixteenth that Government could only stand without a new accession of strength on showing that it had tried to obtain it and been unreasonably refused. 'They would unquestionably prefer the latter ground, and I should wish that we could avoid furnishing it.'[133]

In practice the Government could not conjure up a parliamentary majority with such ease. On 21 May Stuart Wortley

proposed a Commons motion for an Address to the Regent for
a strong and efficient Administration. Canning spoke in favour
of the motion and defended himself from accusations based on
his own communications with Liverpool. He stressed that he
would not take office if forced to leave his views on Catholic
emancipation in abeyance.[134] The 'previous question' was defeated
by 174 to 170 and the address carried without opposition. Wellesley was invited to explore the possibilities of a new Administration.

From Canning Wellesley received a promise of cordial assistance for an Administration based on serious consideration of the
Catholic question and a full military effort in the Peninsula. The
only thing Canning would not accept would be the pressing of
unacceptable personal pretensions. Acting for Wellesley, Canning
approached Liverpool on these terms. The latter felt it unnecessary to discuss principles as all his colleagues felt bound not to
join an Administration under Wellesley. They particularly
objected to the language he had used about Perceval and respect
for the latter's memory thus created an 'insuperable obstacle'.
Canning curtly asked if this was an objection that would stand up
before the country. Melville, as Robert Dundas had become,
nevertheless stressed the same objection to Wellesley as such.[135]

Wellesley met Grey and Grenville at the former's house on
23 May and asked them if they would participate in such a
Government. On the twenty-fourth they produced a guarded
memorandum agreeing as regards Catholic emancipation but not
liking the Peninsula commitment, regarding it as one which
should be directed by changing circumstances. In particular they
entertained 'the strongest doubts of the practicability of an increase in any branch of the public expenditure'.[136]

Wellesley's soundings have thus been most unpromising. On
26 May Canning met Melville and asked him if his colleagues
considered Wellesley's assignment as being ended. The following
day he got the reply, from Liverpool via Melville, that the Regent
considered it so.[137] But Liverpool was being premature, for the
Regent had not made up his mind. In fact he turned back to
Wellesley on 1 June with a formal authorization to approach
Grey and Grenville.

The approach was made immediately. As regards policy the
basis was still the minute of 23 May. Now a specific basis for
office was presented. Grey and Grenville could nominate four

Cabinet members; Wellesley was to nominate four, and the Regent himself would choose Wellesley, Canning, Moira and Erskine.[138] The Opposition had had a week to consider the situation. Grey was the crucial figure, for despite a long personal association with Wellesley, Grenville had made it quite clear that he would not serve without Grey.[139] The latter really believed in an exclusively Whig Government. Apart from his dislike of Canning he was also frightened at the state of the nation, the blame for which he laid in large measure at the Government's door. Throughout his political career there lay a deep fear of popular revolution, the appeasement of which he regarded as essential. If reminders of this were wanting, he had recently been frightened at the almost universal satisfaction amongst the lower orders at the death of Perceval.[140]

Consultations nevertheless went on among the Whigs, and on 2 June, Grey asked Wellesley for more time.[141] On the third Grey and Grenville finally refused. The style and formation of the Cabinet they said, was incompatible with Wortley's motion. In particular 'it is to the principle of Disunion and Jealousy that we object: to the supposed Balance of contending interest, in a Cabinet so measured out by preliminary stipulation'.[142]

This ended Wellesley's attempt to form a Government. The Regent turned to his friend Lord Moira to see what he could do. Canning learned of proceedings on the fifth and sixth by rumour, and declared his inclination not to participate in such an Administration if it was formed substantially from the Opposition.[143] At dinner on the sixth he learned that these negotiations had broken down.[144] A tentative approach was made by Moira to Canning but the former gave up the attempt and the Regent turned back to Liverpool, who commenced his fifteen-year premiership.

On the face of it, such a Government looked fairly weak, and Canning could certainly expect an approach. His friend Frere urged him to stand firm against any inadequate proposition and above all to insist on the lead in the House of Commons. The Cabinet, he urged, would regard Canning's accession as a disaster from which they would attempt by any means to extricate themselves, but the country gentlemen, responsible to a wider electorate, wanted it so they could have such a Government as they could support at election time.[145] Canning probably did not require advice in order to overplay his hand.

F

Parliamentary life still went on. Canning explained the negotiations surrounding Wellesley's abortive ministry in the context of a fresh motion from Stuart Wortley. In this, he renewed an old line of attack on the Whigs. There were those on the other side, he urged, who believed that the great families and connections of Great Britain had a right to interfere in the nomination of ministers. 'He himself who was so very humble an individual who could not boast of any of these high connections, and who, perhaps, though unknown to himself, was influenced by those circumstances of his humble rank, did not certainly believe in the existence of any such right or pretension in the aristocracy.'[146] Indeed, had Canning but known it, the Whig diarist Creevey had already recorded his contempt at two landless figures such as Canning and Wellesley attempting to dictate to Grey, the Russells and the Cavendishes.

Meanwhile Canning's motion on the Catholic question was due. In a very moderate speech he laid down three basic principles. As a general rule citizens had, *prima facie,* equal rights. There was a need for identity of interest among all groups in a community. Where a great cause of political discontent was outstanding, the state should take it into consideration.[147] His motion, which called for consideration of the state of affairs next session, was carried by 235 to 106 votes. He had asked Liverpool for his views and got a fairly measured reply, albeit hostile to the general question.[148] Castlereagh and Vansittart supported him nevertheless, as did many Irish office holders who were not under government pressure and chose to please their constitutents. In the Lords, a similar motion by Wellesley was lost by only one vote. There were doubtless those who regarded the speedy carrying of some measure of emancipation as inevitable. If they had recalled the lesson of the slave trade campaign they would have realized how easy it was to prevent the enactment of any measure which merely had the general consent of Parliament. It was in fact inconceivable that a measure of that magnitude could have been passed without the full-hearted backing of Government. With Lord Liverpool as Prime Minister this was unobtainable.

The Government still felt the addition of Canning to be necessary for their parliamentary strength. Their weakness was demonstrated by Brougham's successful campaign for the repeal of the Orders in Council, and on 4 July Canning wrote that he was expecting an approach, and was alive to the dangers of accepting or rejecting an inadequate offer.[149]

The approach came on the eighteenth. Castlereagh was to keep the lead in the House of Commons, which he had assumed on Perceval's death, but was to give Canning the Foreign Office. On the nineteenth Canning wrote to Liverpool saying he would serve *with* but not *under* Castlereagh.[150] On the twenty-second Liverpool replied. As Chancellor of the Exchequer, Castlereagh, he urged, would have two-thirds of Commons business in the nature of things. Furthermore, five further posts would be available to assist arrangements[151] – in other words, for Canning's friends. In conceding Castlereagh the lead, he was not, said Liverpool, conceding supremacy. Canning replied dismissing all arrangements which might disparage him in public estimation, suggesting that Castlereagh should stay at the Foreign Office and manage connected business. Canning would take the rest. He was, he said, still prepared to consider a third person, in which context the name of Nicholas Vansittart, the Chancellor of the Exchequer, had already been mentioned.

Castlereagh was shown this letter, and perhaps because he felt he had been generous enough in conceding the Foreign Office to his old rival, or perhaps, as was urged by Charles Arbuthnot,[152] because he did not express himself well, he insisted that one person must have the lead in House of Commons business. Canning took strong exception to this letter, and when he learned the correct version of it from Huskisson, told Liverpool that Castlereagh would always be able to deny he had accepted the principle of equality.[153]

The Prince Regent attempted to keep the negotiations going. A second letter from Castlereagh was sent by way of explanation, but this failed to satisfy Canning and the Regent grew angry that he seemed to be raising his price as he was wooed. He 'takes as much courting as a woman, and a good deal more than most'.[154] The Duke of Cumberland visited Canning, but the latter discouraged any attempt to preserve the negotiation.[155] He was conscious that he had sacrificed the interests of his friends for a point of personal honour,[156] but they in fact helped to urge him on, Granville in particular declaring that any concession by Canning made the Government think they could have him on their own terms.[157]

In effect the negotiation ended there. Canning wrote to Granville that he was convinced he had had a 'great escape',[158] but in reality he had again grossly overplayed his hand by an exaggerated belief in his own importance to Government. He was to come to bitterly regret that he had sacrificed the reality of power for something of the format. At the same time, the urgency of Canning's admission was greatly eased by the ending of the Parliament and the hopes entertained by ministers of removing some of Canning's friends from its successor. Furthermore, Wellington's victories in Spain were at last justifying the Government's war policies.

For Canning 1812 can be seen as the culmination of the events of 1809. Throughout the period he had gambled with his genuine claim to very high office for a position in which he could dictate his own terms to the Government. The gamble was lost and Canning went into the political wilderness for four years; and only to return afterwards to a much humbler abode than that he had previously occupied. Gone was the opportunity, which Castlereagh was to inherit, to assist in the conclusion of the peace settlement and the re-drawing of the map of Europe. Gone was the patronage with which to build up and consolidate a faction. The parliamentary eminence remained, but as the Regent became more and more committed to the Liverpool Administration and less and less inclined to intrigue with its opponents, Canning could not play the balancing role which enhanced his power earlier. It was some time before the full realization of what he had done dawned on Canning and taught him, if nothing else, something of the humility which had hitherto been singularly lacking.

7
RETREAT TO LIVERPOOL AND LISBON

Liverpool was a wealthy, self-confident port. An 1802 election song summed up the atmosphere well:

> Peace or war, there's no port on earth can come nigh us
> Manufactures, wealth, credit and plenty abound.[1]

Though nearly twenty years in Parliament, Canning had never experienced a contested election. In 1812 this deficiency was supplied when he was elected Member for Liverpool.

A very small port in the early eighteenth century, by 1784 it had engrossed five-eighths of the British slave trade and three-sevenths of that of all Europe. The relative importance of the slave trade had nevertheless declined prior to abolition, although the commerce of the port continued to grow.[2] In 1788, 3,677 vessels entered the port of Liverpool; in 1801, 4,746; and by 1824 this had become 10,001, with a tonnage of nearly 1.2 million.[3] Apart from the slave trade Liverpool developed a large trade to the West Indies in sugar, to America in cotton, and after 1813, a trade to the East Indies commenced following the relaxations of the Charter of the East India Company in that year.

Liverpool enjoyed a vigorous political life, for it had a large number of electors. The franchise was bestowed upon the Freemen of the city and the Freedom could be acquired by birth, apprenticeship or gift. In the election of 1710 there had been approximately a thousand votes,[4] but this number grew throughout the century as the town increased in size and importance. The bestowal of the Freedom was essentially in the control of the Corporation, but once given could not be retracted. Only a small percentage of the population possessed voting rights, but the absolute numbers were such as to lead to serious contests. The 2,345 Freemen who voted in the election of 1806 represented 3 per cent of the 1801 population of 77,653.[5] The 4,335 who voted in 1830 were 2.6 per cent of the population.[6]

The majority of resident voters were connected with the maritime trades. Of 2,502 resident voters in the 1818 election, over half fell in the categories of shipwrights, blockmakers, ropers, sailmakers, coopers and other miscellaneous occupations connected with the sea and foreign trading. A fair variety of other occupations were represented. Bathlayers, slaters, plasterers and masons numbered 120 in 1818. There were seventy-three painters, plumbers, and glaziers, and 289 voters were connected with furniture-making and joinery. Only thirty-three voters were recorded as 'Labourers'. At the upper end of the social scale there were 366 persons recorded as 'Gentlemen, Merchants and Brokers'.[7]

The voting population of Liverpool was thus fairly heterogeneous. There was a randomness in a Franchise which deprived William Roscoe, man of letters and briefly MP for the city, of the vote, and yet gave one to his gardener. It is nevertheless a gross exaggeration to say, as did the diarist Greville, that the electors of Liverpool were 'the lowest rabble of the town . . . a pack of venal wretches'.

There were three basic political groupings in Liverpool. The first was the Corporation interest which turned from simple Pittite to ultra-Tory. The second consisted of gentlemen and merchants of more independent principles, but bound together by the dislike of a corporate influence which they did not wield. The third party consisted of more genuine Whigs and Radicals.

In the eighteenth century the struggle was essentially between the Corporation interest and the others. 'Glorious 1761' had witnessed the victory of Sir William Meredith over the former, and thereafter the Corporation usually only put up one candidate of their own, though they would sometimes give their support to one of the others.

In 1790 the Corporation candidate was Bamber Gascogne, the independent was Lord Penrhyn, Charles Ellis' predecessor as Chairman of the West India Planters and Merchants, and the Whig was Banastre Tarleton. The election was vigorously fought. Candidates outdid each other in their support for the slave trade, recently threatened by Wilberforce's motions. To the tune 'Hearts of Oak' was sung:

If our Slave Trade had gone, there's an end to our lives
Beggars all we must be, our children and wives
No ships from our ports, their proud sails e'er would spread
And our streets grown with grass, where the cows might be fed,
Heart of oak is our Bam
Heart of oak are his men
Be always ready, steady boys steady
And vote for our Gascogne again and again.[8]

The election was a triumph for the Whig, Tarleton. Originally the Corporation had given support to Penrhyn alongside Gascogne, but in the last stages of the election they hastily abandoned him to secure the election of their own nominee alongside Tarleton who was well clear at the head of the poll.

In the 1796 election, Bamber Gascogne was replaced by his brother Isaac, who remained MP for the city for thirty-five years, till punished by his constituents for moving a successful amendment to the Reform Bill in 1831. Like his brother, Isaac had the full backing of the Corporation. Tarleton, who stood again in 1796, easily held off the challenge from his brother John, a Pittite to whom the Corporation gave some backing. By 1802 Tarleton had 'turned his coat to his King' and abandoned the Foxites. For the next three elections he fought alongside Gascogne with support from the independent and Corporation interests.

In the years after 1802 the Whig influence in the city grew and attached to itself part of the old independent interest. Powerfully backing them were the two biggest local magnates, the twenty-first Earl of Derby and his son Lord Stanley, and the second Earl of Sefton. With a Whig Government, the 1806 election presented them with a great chance of victory. Money was not wanting to the Whig cause, and it was said that £11-£12,000 was spent by the Whigs, compared with £3,000 by Gascogne's friends and £4,000 by those of Tarleton.[9] The Whig candidate was William Roscoe, and uniquely for a Liverpool candidate, he opposed the slave trade. Despite leading in the poll for five days, the Generals (Gascogne and Tarleton) had clearly outrun their strength by the sixth. As in 1790 the Corporation support for the more independent of the two candidates was

removed as they hastened to ensure the return of Gascogne alongside the victorious Whig.

The subsequent election reversed the verdict of 1806. The
Pittites were back in government and the contest could be described as 'The Grand Appeal of a beloved Monarch to the Voice
of his People'.[10] Roscoe fought a half-hearted campaign and was
bitterly attacked for having 'preferred his new fangled notions of
liberty, and modern philosophy, to the interests of his constituents.'[11] This, of course, referred to his support for abolition of
the slave trade. The Generals drove home the point by sending
little black children round the town in their own colours, to which
the Whigs replied with a procession of black men carrying plac-
ards, 'We thank God we are free.' The victory of the Generals
was quickly assured and though the poll was kept open by a Free-
man called Thomas Green, who later became prominent in Whig
circles in the city, there was never any doubt as to the result.
Roscoe obtained only 379 votes, as against 1,461 for Tarleton and
1,277 for Gascogne.

One point that emerges from the elections in Liverpool prior
to 1812 is that the political divisions in the town paralleled
economic divisions. The West Indian and slave trades were always
on the Corporation or independent side, whilst the American
traders strongly supported Roscoe in 1806 and 1807. It is interesting to note that while John Gladstone was purely an American
trader his politics were Whig and his religion Non-conformist.
As his economic interests led him to the East and West India
trades, his politics became Tory and his religion Church of
England.

One major change which occurred between 1807 and 1812 was
the elimination of Tarleton as a serious contender. He had always
been very dilatory as regards constituency duties, he had annoyed
many by accepting the sinecure of Governor of Berwick, and
he had taken a sudden lurch towards the Radical side in politics,
supporting Brand's motion on the state of parliamentary representation in 1810. Above all, he had left the election bills for
1807 unpaid.[12] The Corporation still had their own candidate in
General Gascogne, but the independent interest looked around
for a co-member.

Early in 1812 several merchants considered Canning as a
possible MP. Out with the Government, he nevertheless had

prestige and oratorial power which could serve the interests of Liverpool well. Among those promoting his candidacy was John Bolton, a West India merchant of enormous wealth. In 1821 in the island of Santa Cruz alone he was owed £80-£100,000.[13] There was Joseph Hibberson, soon to be a leading East India merchant, and other prominent merchants of the town including William Ewart, H. B. Hollinshed, and John Drinkwater, jun. Later in the year these were joined by John Gladstone, father of Gladstone the Prime Minister, and himself involved in a variety of trades and also immensely wealthy.

Tentative approaches reached Canning early in the year, but he delayed his reply as he did not know whether or not he was to be in office. On 24 February 1812 he replied that he would like to be MP for Liverpool, but would not put himself at any expense.[14] He confirmed this resolution to his wife the following month, perhaps to allay her fears,[15] for many a fortune had been wrecked in this period through unwise electioneering. Canning preserved his connection with Liverpool, and this led to an embarrassing incident in May when his friend Granville subscribed £50 to a Liverpool fund for Mrs Bellingham, wife of the assassin of Perceval. Perhaps Granville felt some obligation, as he had been Minister in Russia during the period Bellingham, as a Russia merchant, had gone bankrupt. In effect, Granville's letter was used by a radical faction in Liverpool to promote what Canning called their 'outrageous and abominable doctrines'.[16]

Contacts persisted, and in August Canning was told he would be requested to stand because of the Opposition's attempts to impose two candidates on the city. He told Granville that he had no violent desire to be in Parliament again, and that above all he would not engage 'to defray one single obolus'.[17] This declaration he reiterated to his Liverpool supporters in mid-September.[18] Late in September he heard the encouraging news that Gladstone was going to support him.[19] On the twenty-seventh he was not so sure, and wondered if his supporters had been put off by his refusal to bear any of the expenses.[20] His fears were unnecessary as news reached him at Ellis' home at Mamhead in Dorset in early October that he would be asked. He was also informed that £6,000 of the required £10,000 was already subscribed.[21] The other side did not have financing of this order. By the tenth they had only £4,000 subscribed, most of which was spent on bringing

non-resident voters from London.[22] As for Canning, he was able
to boast that the election had 'not cost me a farthing'.[23]

Canning had been moving round the country through the
summer, mainly visiting political associates such as Huskisson
at Eartham, Dent at Barton Lodge and Blackford on the Isle of
Wight. He finally received the requisition requesting him to stand,
'signed by 80 or 90 of (I am told) the most respectable names in
Liverpool' on Sunday, 4 October. He replied at once, accepting
their offer and promising to be constant in his political principles.[24] Canning set out on the fifth and, after calling in on his
mother at Bath, reached Liverpool on the seventh. With him he
took his younger son William, and every so often his diary records
a gift of £5 or so to him. William was not yet ten.

As Canning approached Liverpool he was met by his supporters. Thomas Creevey, one of his opponents, recorded that
at Warrington the Canningites were out in force and inclined to
treat him roughly. He considered himself lucky to get safely away
considering the violence and drunkenness.[25] On arrival, Canning
lodged with Gladstone.

The refusal of William Roscoe to stand again for Parliament
forced the Whigs to look for new candidates. They approached
Henry Brougham, a rising young lawyer and orator who was
particularly welcome to the American merchants at that time
because of his opposition to the Orders in Council. He welcomed
the idea of standing, as the Duke of Bedford had sold Camelford,
the pocket borough which he represented, and, unlike his patron,
he was loth to break Curwen's Act, which had just made such
traffic in Parliamentary seats illegal. It was also put to him that
the prospects of success were good.[26] The other candidate was
local – the Whig diarist and camp-follower, Thomas Creevey.
He was popular with merchants in the out-posts because of his
attacks on the monopoly of the East India Company. Of Canning
he wrote that 'never fellow deserved exposing more. He is a
frothy, unfeeling imposter, full of words and epigrams and without any solid reasoning or a bit of heart. A true disciple, in short,
tho' in an inferior way, of the Arch villain Pitt.'[27]

The Whigs started the campaign with a public dinner for
Brougham early in September, at which the Earls of Derby and
Sefton and Lord Stanley were present.[28] On the twenty-ninth a
very large election dinner was held at a cost of 2s 6d for Freemen

and 5s for others. Two whole sheep, fifty rounds of beef of the largest size, one barron of beef, thirty legs of mutton, 1,500 loaves of bread, two cart loads of potatoes, and twenty-three barrels of ale and porter were consumed.[29] The dinner commenced at 1.30 in the afternoon, and the company sang:

> *Give a long pull, boys*
> *Give a strong pull, boys,*
> *A pull all together for Creevey and Brougham.*[30]

More than in any previous election at Liverpool, the factions were separated by genuine cleavages of ideology. Roscoe wrote to the Duke of Gloucester that 'In the present feeling of the nation to advocate the indefinite continuance of the war and to assert the inexpediency of all reforms whatever is to destroy all sympathy with the people and to drive them on to lengths which would otherwise never have been thought of.'[31] There spoke the voice of the true reformist Whig.

The local press was divided. The *Liverpool Courier* supported the Tories, but *The Mercury* was bitterly hostile. 'Let the Freemen of Liverpool elect him', it declared, 'and they will have the satisfaction of seeing him, a *placeman*, and one of the old firm too, carrying on the business of war and finance to the speedy ruin of Old England.' It goes on to quote the bitterly sarcastic views of Sydney Smith as Peter Plymley: 'He sweats and labours and works for sense, and Mr Ellis seems to always think it coming, but it does not seem to come; the machine cannot draw up what is not found in the spring. . . . Providence has made him a light, jesting, paragraph-writing man. . . . When he is jocular he is strong, when he is serious he is like Samson in a wig. . . .'[32]

The election commenced on 8 October. Canning was proposed by John Gladstone and a poll was demanded. At the end of the first day's voting Canning had 139, Brougham 137, Creevey 135, Gascogne 117. Tarleton himself received only five and he rode away from the town in anger.

The election was an exhausting one. Brougham went round the clubs and in the eight days polling lasted, made 160 speeches. Canning described a typical election day. At 10 am, twelve gentlemen came for breakfast. After that, he repaired to the hustings until 5.30. There followed a procession, dinner and a canvass of the clubs which lasted till eleven or midnight.[33] On one occasion he addressed 10,000 people from a window.

The early polling looked rather black for Gascogne. However, when the Whigs rejected a compromise offer of electing Canning and Brougham, the election turned into a struggle to demonstrate who really controlled Liverpool politics. The Canningites joined forces with the Corporation party. On the sixth day of the contest Brougham and Creevey were still ahead of Gascogne but their strength was on the point of exhaustion. The seventh day proved crucial. Canning polled 285, Gascogne 273, Brougham 75 and Creevey 64. In desperation the Whigs tried to delay proceedings by enforcing the long oath of supremacy and abjuration upon the voters. They apologized to the Catholic voters for thus disfranchising them.[34] The stratagem was of no avail. On the eighth day the Whig vote collapsed and victory was conceded to the Tories. Canning had 1,631 votes, Gascogne 1,532, Brougham 1,131 and Creevey 1,068. In all 2,726 Freemen had voted. All but fifty-five of Canning's votes were split, the over-whelming majority of these with Gascogne.[35]

A whole range of political issues were raised in the election. Canning confessed that he had some difficulties because of his pro-Catholic views.[36] On parliamentary reform he felt no inhibitions, declaring roundly 'I deny the grievance. I distrust the remedy.'[37] Above all, he firmly defended the Government's war policy. As for the foundation of his political principles, he proclaimed: 'To one man, while he lived, I was devoted with all my heart and with all my soul. Since the death of Mr Pitt I acknowledge no leader.... I have adhered and shall adhere to [his] opinions as the guides of my public conduct.'[38]

Canning's well-known allegiance to Pitt gave Brougham the opportunity for one of the finest pieces of oratory of his career. 'Gentlemen,' he declared,

I stand up in this contest against the friends and followers of Mr Pitt, or as they partially designate him, the immortal statesman now no more. IMMORTAL in the miseries of his devoted country. Immortal in the wounds of her bleeding liberties! Immortal in the cruel wars which sprang from his cold miscalculating ambition! Immortal in the intolerable taxes, the countless loads of debt which these wars have flung upon us – which the youngest man amongst us will not live to see the end of. Immortal in the triumphs of our enemies, and the ruin of our allies, the costly purchase of so much blood and treasure. Immortal in the afflictions of England, and the humiliation of her friends, through the whole results of his twenty-years reign from the first rays of favour with which a delighted court gilded his early apostasy, to the deadly glare which is at this instant cast upon his name by the burning metropolis of our last ally.[39] But may no such immortality fall to my lot – let me rather live innocent and inglorious; and when at last I cease to serve you, and to feel for your wrongs, may I have an humble monument in some nameless stone, to tell that beneath it there rests from his labours in your service – 'an enemy of the immortal statesman – a friend of peace and of the people'.[40]

The election was a fairly clean one, and only two deaths occurred. If Canning and Gascogne were described as 'friends of War, Taxes and Famine', this was only to be expected in an election of the period. Nevertheless, Canning cannot have been pleased that his supporters circulated without comment extracts from Brougham's speech of 1810 on his bill to increase the penalties for slave trading. 'The murders committed by these "slavers" were deliberately committed, with motives the most mercenary, the most sordid and the most base . . . those dealers in blood. . . . They ought not to be called "slave traders" but "Liverpool murderers" or "Liverpool suborners of piracy and murder".' A few little songs appealed to the same sentiment:

> *We shipwrights, akin to the true heart of oak*
> *Have cause to remember the terrible stroke*
> *When Roscoe to Parliament took a short trip*
> *A fresh water lubber – the bane of our ship.*[41]

It fell to Canning to thank Brougham for the 'cleanness' of the fight.[42]

The *Liverpool Mercury* summed it up: 'The few electors who are to be found in the middle ranks of society, and those, in general, whose labour does not require a combination of hands, and who, therefore are more likely to think for themselves, compose those worthy two-fifths who espoused the cause of the

unsuccessful candidates. Had the ropers, coopers, riggers, shipwrights and others been allowed to follow their own inclinations
the order would have been reversed.'[43]

This view must be taken with some caution, as pressure could
be exerted by American merchants for the Whigs as well as by
the West Indians against them. The 1818 poll book which pro-
vides a detailed breakdown of occupations shows only one group
– the shoemakers – discrepantly pro-Whig and another – the
'Gentlemen, Merchants and Brokers' – discrepantly against them.
There was little bribery in the 1812 election as the funds of
neither side ran to such an expense. The election of 1830, where
it was much in evidence, saw an expenditure more than ten times
that of 1812.

Canning followed up his election with a period of celebration.
He wrote to his mother about 'a round of turtle dinners which
began on Sunday, and are not to be terminated till Wednesday
next'.[44] After Liverpool he proceeded to Warrington and thence
to Manchester. Here he renewed his onslaught against parliamentary reform, declaring emphatically that Great Britain lived
under 'a limited monarchy, not a crowned republic'.[45]

He was delighted with his success. In a letter to his mother he
reflected on his own career:

> I do not complain, however, of the occupation for it certainly
> has been most gratifying and glorious beyond my most sanguine
> dreams of popular ambition. I may have looked to be a Minister
> – but I hardly ever thought that it would have fallen in my
> way to come in so close contact with so large a portion of the
> people, and to be so received.[46]

The representation of Liverpool involved constituency obligations which Canning had hitherto avoided. The town had a
parliamentary office in London with which Canning kept close
contact. As a member for a pocket borough, he had only been
responsible for his views to himself. He now had to answer to
his Liverpool supporters. He replied to John Drinkwater, who
was objecting to a local measure: 'I know not what to answer to
your observations upon the Dock Bill, and the Loan. It is quite
impossible for me (I think) to presume to exercise my individual
judgement upon a measure, proposed as it should seem, by a

great majority of the Town and sanctioned by Act of Parliament.'[47]

Canning found himself firmly involved with the West India interest. To conserve grain supplies and eliminate the huge sugar mountain which protectionist policies had created, Parliament had confined distillation to sugar. Canning had to join himself to the Liverpool West Indians agitating for a continuance of the ban against grain distillation.[48]

Many of Canning's supporters had become financially involved in the sugar trade to Caribbean islands taken during the war. They were naturally alarmed at the prospect that the islands might be returned, for then their sugars would be excluded from the British market by a prohibitive duty. Canning joined in the agitation which culminated in Britain's retention of the Dutch colonies of Demerara, Essequibo and Berbice.[49] Many merchants were involved in the Danish island of St Croix, and Canning opposed its sudden restoration.[50] When it was finally returned to the Danes, a temporary relaxation of the heavy duties which would otherwise have been imposed on its produce was obtained.[51]

There were a variety of other mercantile issues on which there were strong feelings in Liverpool. The largest was the opening of the East India monopoly in which Liverpool obtained a share in 1813. Canning took a full part in the parliamentary debates of that year. The trade to South America was important for some, and Canning joined in the pressure put upon the British Government to attempt to secure some more permanent relaxation of their monopoly from the Spaniards.[52] Canning asked for a renewal of the parliamentary grant for the Company of Merchants Trading to Africa[53] and joined in the local agitation for an international abolition of the slave trade which the local West Indians were clamorous in demanding, for being deprived of the trade themselves, they did not want others to enjoy it. Canning presented the local petitition on the subject in July 1814, and perhaps had the pleasure of joining in an agitation which by implication strongly criticized Castlereagh for not having done more to prevent the resurrection of the French slave trade.

As a Member of Parliament, there was an obligation on Canning to look after the individual interests of his constituents. Canning's personal prominence made him more powerful than most back-benchers in this regard, and he was able to ask the Prime Minister if he could bring all cases regarding the town of

Liverpool directly before him.[54] Canning was not short of personal cases. Susannah Storey wrote to him early in 1814. She was the widow of William Storey, sixteen years in the 27th Foot. She had one son with Wellington, one with the Light Dragoons in the East Indies, one a mariner on HMS *Sussex* and one she had not heard of for two years, but whether he was 'in prison or serving his Majesty I cannot say'.[55] It is hardly surprising that she wanted a pension. Canning asked for further details.

Some personal cases involved those who had fallen foul of the law. Canning asked the Home Secretary Sidmouth to recommend one Edward Rogers to the royal mercy. He had been sentenced to transportation for warehouse breaking. Sidmouth declined to intervene because of the aggravated nature of the offence, and because 'he was before tried for a similar offence, but acquitted by the jury, leaving however in the minds of the court, a perfect conviction of his Guilt'.[56]

Cases involving the armed services were frequent. One Michael Burns wrote to Canning in 1814 complaining that his son had enlisted whilst drunk, was taken as a deserter, and was then at Cowes awaiting shipment to the East Indies. Despite the fact that those six of the petitioners who had voted in the 1812 election had voted for Canning and Gascogne, Canning 'answered discouragingly'.[57]

There was also the lunatic fringe. One gentleman, who described himself as 'a Danish bourgeois of St Thomas', claimed credit for a variety of political and military projects including the union of Norway with Sweden (which Canning regarded as disgraceful) and the capture of Guadeloupe. There was 'a conspiracy to stifle my services, as impudent as impotent', and he wanted Canning 'to promote, as in honor and justice you are bound, a National Donation to me. . . .'[58]

In general Canning would attempt to assist those who had helped his own election. Prior to the extensions of the franchise later in the century, the voter was in a privileged position as regards his claim upon the public bounty. In a town like Liverpool there were a large number of jobs, particularly connected with the docks, to which the Government appointed those recommended by the local MPs. Gascogne and Canning would take turns in making such nominations. In April 1814 we find Charles

Arbuthnot complying with Canning's request to make William Higgett the Riding Surveyor of Hawkers and Pedlars at Liverpool.[59] In November Arbuthnot accepted Gascogne's and Canning's nominees for posts at the port of Liverpool. A roper and a shipwright respectively they had both split their votes between Canning and Gascogne in 1812.[60]

Where requests were for public jobs outside Liverpool, and in particular promotion in the armed services, no such success could be guaranteed, for all other MPs would be putting forward similar requests. In reply to a Mr Woodward who made such a request – for promotion for his son who was a lieutenant in the navy, Canning complained that he had had so many such requests since he became MP for Liverpool that they were now piled high on Lord Melville's table (Melville was First Lord of the Admiralty). Woodward pleaded that his son had voted for Canning in 1818, but the latter replied that in the previous three years he had made sixteen applications to the Admiralty for promotion, and all but two remained unfulfilled.[61]

Nevertheless, to preserve his political position, it was always necessary for Canning to appear to be doing something. T. W. Croker sent a letter to him refusing the discharge of a petitioner's son from the navy. He concluded, 'I suppose the applicant is a constituent,' and so 'the proof that you endeavoured to obtain the discharge will probably be most agreeable to the worthy voter.'[62]

In practice the treatment of petitioners depended on their importance. Canning could hardly refuse a request he received in May 1814 to ask Lord Melville to allow Captain Macleod, who directed the Impress Service at Liverpool, to keep his commission. The request was supported by eight leading Liverpool associations headed by the West Indian, the Ship Owners and the Portugal and Brazil Associations.[63] Canning's leading supporters often addressed him in peremptory terms. In 1819 H. B. Hollinshed and John Bolton insisted that a Captain Bamber be appointed a landing waiter immediately, as they felt a strong obligation to him and he was most distressed at not being on the list. Captain Bamber was informed of his appointment at once.[64] In 1821 Hollinshed supported the similar claims of one supporter whose father had had a banking house, but 'Misfortunes however have rendered it necessary for the family to seek employment.'[65]

Usually such requests were partisan, but occasionally political opponents linked hands to secure a common aim. In 1821 the Comptrollership of the Customs at Liverpool fell vacant. The local candidate supported by Lord Sidmouth had made himself 'generally obnoxious' in the town, and there was a further danger that the London Board of Customs would appoint an outsider. The town rallied round a Mr Stanley. William Ewart and John Gladstone joined forces with Thomas Leyland, Canning's opponent at the 1816 by-election, and the Whig East Indian firm of Cropper, Benson & Co.[66]

Canning often had to work with Gascogne to defend the interests of the town. Together they supervized the progression of the Liverpool Gas Light Bill in 1818 and secured the amendments to it which leading interests in the town desired. It was important to demonstrate one's keenness in this regard, and in 1818 Canning had to write to the mayor to explain his apparent passiveness when Gascogne had already given notice of an amendment to a bill which affected local interests.[67] Occasionally there were difficulties between them, and in 1822 Gascogne complained of Canning's taking more than his fair share of customs places.[68] In 1815 Canning had to attempt to intervene from Portugal in an affair in which Lord Liverpool had insulted Gascogne by a letter to Gladstone on the property tax, and the General's party were as a result cavorting with the Whigs. In general Canning and Gascogne got on better than their widely differing politics on many issues might have led one to expect.

Given the variety of economic interests in Canning's party at Liverpool, differences arose between them. In 1821 there was an agreement that high-quality East Indian clayed sugar should bear an extra duty of 5s per cwt. Gladstone, still fundamentally an East Indian though becoming more deeply involved in the West, proposed amendments which would have allowed sugar to be refined to a point just marginally below the duty standard. The West Indians were naturally angry and S. R. Lushington wrote from the Treasury to ask Canning to reconcile the parties as both interests existed at Liverpool. He added, 'We have endeavoured to hold the scales equally here between the two parties and I share, I believe, the common fate of all arbiters, of being thought to neglect both.'[69]

The early nineteenth century was a great age for clubs, and in

December 1812 the Canning Club was founded to 'support those
Principles which recommended that illustrious statesman, the
Right Honourable George Canning, our choice as a Member of
Parliament for this Borough'. Many prominent citizens of Liverpool were members and the Lady Patroness was Hollinshed's
daughter. The club was a success, meeting regularly in a cycle at
the homes of members. Essentially, however, its function was
social rather than political.[70]

After the first excitement had worn off and Canning had got
used to the prestige of being Member for Liverpool, it is difficult
to say whether he really appreciated his new role. One cannot
imagine Canning deeply involved in the minutiae of patronage
at the local docks and the contrast with his period as a minister
must have been galling. This helps to explain the growing disillusionment with his own position which crept upon Canning in
1813.

Canning feared that one of the purposes of the 1812 election
was to remove his friends from Parliament. In September he
wrote that the Ministry were 'cock-a-hoop', expecting a very good
Parliament with very few of his friends in it. He himself feared
the worst and felt somewhat guilty at his own responsibility for
'such a martyrdom'.[71] J. W. Ward argued that the attempt to
reduce his support in Parliament would fail, and he proved
correct.[72] The Treasury opposed Charles Ellis at Seaford in vain,
and while they succeeded in driving Huskisson from Harwich,
he managed to win Chichester instead. Canning attempted to get
Sturges-Bourne back into Parliament. Worcester, he urged, would
only cost £3-£4,000 and failing that there was Honiton.[73] In fact
Sturges-Bourne had been thinking of leaving Parliament for some
time because of parental opposition to his political conduct.[74] He
was to return three years later. In the event Barrington Blackford
returned for Newtown, Canning's cousin of the same name for
Sligo, Hylton Jolliffe for Petersfield, R. H. Leigh for Wigan, and
Granville for Staffordshire as well as Ellis and Huskisson. Apart
from Sturges-Bourne, John Dent, Bootle Wilbraham and William
Taylor disappeared.

Canning returned to Parliament with an amazing degree of
confidence. He wrote to Wellesley: 'Our object, I apprehend . . . is
to force the present Ministry to a capitulation – not to put the

whole garrison to the sword. . . . I think it desirable that the terms
on which their lives are spared should not be *so* absolutely disgraceful as to make them unuseable hereafter'.[75]

Canning would have had little sympathy with the individual
members of the Ministry. His Oxford rival was Prime Minister,
his rival for the mantle of Pitt was Foreign Secretary, and there
were a large number of ministers for whom Canning had scant
respect – notably Westmoreland, Buckinghamshire, Mulgrave
and Camden. Furthermore, the new Home Secretary was Canning's old enemy Viscount Sidmouth, but here there had been
something of a reconciliation. It arose over the murder of the
Duke d'Antraigues by his valet. As he had been the source from
whom Canning had learnt of the secret terms of the Treaty of
Tilsit, he naturally feared that the Duke might have papers which
compromised individuals on the continent very seriously. On
22 July he went through them with Sidmouth at the Home Office,
and the latter offered Canning a reconciliation which he gladly
accepted. 'It may be at least a question', said Canning to Granville,
'whether he be not the party that has a right to complain.' He
then went on to compare him favourably with Castlereagh who
could 'neither feel nor feign'.[76]

No one was quite sure what position Canning would adopt in
the session of 1813. The Whigs thought it worth-while to consult
him on the possibility of an amendment to the address on the
Catholic question,[77] though in fact Canning used the opportunity
to call for a vigorous prosecution of the war.[78] The Dean of
Christchurch, who knew him very well, was not sure that 'some
nitrous cloud of politics may not hurry him off, like Milton's
Satan, to very strange regions.'[79]

The two major issues which arose during the session were the
Catholic and East India questions. Canning had supported the
Catholics in the previous year, considering that the King's madness excused him from Pitt's promise not to raise the subject
during the King's life. Canning was not in favour of Grattan's
policy of unqualified repeal of all discriminatory measures against
the Catholics and he attacked the petition presented early in 1813
as 'violent and ill-conceived'.[80] On 2 March he nevertheless supported Grattan's motion for a committee on the Catholic claims
and this was carried by 264 to 224 votes. In committee on the
ninth he strongly supported the resolution on the expediency of

removing disabilities and this was carried by 186 to 119. In May he introduced into the bill various securities for the Protestant establishment, embracing the appointment of commissioners to report on the nomination to episcopal vacancies. The crucial vote came late in May on a motion to eliminate from the bill the clause that allowed Catholics 'to sit and vote in Parliament'. Canning wrote that the vote would be close and those opposed to the measure hoped to win by securing thirteen 'doubtfuls' to add to the 283 votes they expected, against 291 on the Catholic side. The vote when it came was 251 to 247 against Grattan and Canning, and the bill, its most important clause having been eliminated, was dropped by its supporters.[81]

In 1813 the charter of the East India Company came up for its twenty-year renewal. Canning's constituents had strong views on this question, for hitherto all East Indian trade had been through the Company in London. It was clear that the Company was not going to retain its monopoly of the trade to India, and much of the debate centred round the problem of the China trade. Merchants in the outports wanted to have the opportunity to share in both. Canning was in a difficult position. He wrote to Granville that he was not himself convinced that opening the trade of China was a necessary adjunct to opening that of India, but felt that his supporters would insist on it and he would go with them.[82] Creevey watched the situation with amusement, feeling that Canning would not come up to Gladstone's mark on the question.[83] In Parliament Canning dithered and attempted to compromise. On 31 May he strongly defended the Company's administrative role in India, while at the same time remaining fairly equivocal on the question of the China monopoly. On 14 June he stated, fairly courageously, that he did not wish to see the China trade opened at the present time, but that he would support an amendment from Ponsonby to limit the operation of the charter to ten years. This was defeaed by 137 to 61.[84] In the event the Company kept the China trade till the next renewal in 1833, but Canning's equivocal stance does not seem to have harmed him in Liverpool. His friend John Gladstone took immediate advantage of the new law in sending the first ship from Liverpool to India.

One of the main military developments since Parliament had last met was the American declaration of war provoked by Britain's Orders in Council[85] and insistence on the right of search. Furthermore, frontiersmen saw Canada as an obstacle to American expansion. Canning had been a supporter of the policy which led to war. Of the right of search he had declared unequivocally, 'We are by ancient, unquestioned, and uninterrupted usage, and by the law of nations, as it is now understood, in the possession of the right.'[86] When the war was debated in February 1813 Canning rose to speak at the same time as James Stephen. His *amour-propre* bolstered by the general expression of a preference for himself, he urged the vigorous prosecution of the war. The address being debated 'would do much to teach the Americans a lesson which would probably induce them to bring the war to a speedy termination'.[87] Privately he nevertheless criticized the conduct of the war.

On other debates Canning was fairly predictable. Against the Government he supported a sinecure offices bill, but he had done that before. When the Prince of Wales' affairs were debated Canning attempted to quieten controversy as he had no desire to see this particular issue, which was personally embarrassing, raised.

In 1813 Canning found himself involved in the affairs of Lady Hamilton, Nelson's erstwhile mistress. Canning and George Rose had seen Nelson on the *Victory* before he sailed for the campaign which ended at Trafalgar. Nelson's family had been lavishly rewarded by the state, and Lady Hamilton claimed that on the *Victory*, Canning and Rose had assured Nelson that she would receive financial support. The issue had been raised in 1809 and Canning had replied to Rose that he was willing to help, but did not think the Secret Service Fund appropriate, for 'here is a service published not only in Lady Hamilton's memorial and known to every person whom she has solicited, but printed in extracts of a will registered in Doctor's Commons, and accessible to all mankind'. Between 1809 and 1812 it was scarcely conceivable that anything could be done for her, as Perceval's strong evangelical views could scarcely have accommodated what he would have regarded as a state subsidy for sin. In 1813 Lady Hamilton renewed her approaches, and was furious that Canning denied any such promise as she credited him with having made on board the *Victory*. She called his reply to Rose the 'most infamous falsehood raised against mine honour'.[88] Nothing was done for the lady in Parliament, and it remains of interest to speculate on the reactions of Wilberforce and Stephen had any such proposition been made.

As the year 1813 progressed Canning grew increasingly despondent at his own political prospects. In July, a visit from Wellesley-Pole, younger brother of the Marquess, impelled him to take the decisive step of setting free his party. They might, he told the Speaker, 'follow him as a friend, but not as a leader'.[89] It is difficult to fathom Canning's motives for this. The views of Wellesley-Pole were never considered by anyone as being of much relevance, and he was not really a Canningite at all. Lady Bessborough suggested that Canning was getting rid of his friends so as to be rid of 'encumbrances' who would have to be found office if Canning joined the Ministry.[90] It is certainly true that the Cabinet was at this time considering ways whereby Canning might be re-admitted, but in fact no one was found to make way for him. On the other hand, a year later when Canning left for Lisbon, he was most solicitous for the future well-being of his friends. Certainly they were surprised at the turn of events and J. W. Ward compared the event to a sudden eviction from an agreeable coach party, leaving no other alternative but to wait for the ministerial conveyance.

Canning grew increasingly gloomy. 'No proposition of any kind', he wrote to Granville, 'has been or is likely to be made to me.'[91] Above all, he began to grow sensible of the opportunity he had thrown away the previous year. The war was drawing to a successful conclusion, and it was to be his rival Castlereagh who would help make the peace settlement which would re-draw the map of Europe. He sadly mused on events: 'I am afraid no possible combination of circumstances can place me again where I stood in July last year: and it is no use to reflect where I might have been had the "tide" of that time being "taken at its flood".'[92] Lady Bessborough wrote that Canning lamented at 'having refused the management of the mightiest scheme of politics which this country ever engaged in, or the world ever witnessed, from a miserable point of etiquette, one absolutely unintelligible (so I have been almost uniformly told) at a distance of more than six miles from Palace Yard'.[93] Relations with his friends grew strained, and Granville, while conceding the justice of Canning's disappointment at having no hand in the great work, also complained that this had given Canning's feelings a most 'unjust

asperity'. In reply Canning referred gloomily to 'the short remainder of my political life'.[94]

Canning was not very active in the subsequent parliamentary
session. In November 1813 he was obliged to go to town for
the marriage of his cousin Miss Leigh, and he used the opportunity
to speak on the war. Of Napoleon he declared: 'His efforts have
been exhausted; his monarchy was reduced to sink our commerce;
but rising with ten-fold vigour it has defied his puny efforts, never
to be repeated.' In May he defended Britain's fulfillment of her
treaty obligations to Sweden even though he lamented the necessity of supporting the imposition of union on the unwilling Nor-
wegians. In June he applauded the Treaty of Paris ending the war,
with the exception of the clauses allowing France a limited revival
of her slave trade. His final speech was on 4 July, supporting the
augmentation of the grant to the Prince of Wales[95] and his final
appearance was on the twenty-fifth, when he was forced to come
to town to present the Liverpool petition against the slave trade.
Later in the year Canning complained to Huskisson that for two
years the Opposition had never pressed the Government too hard
for fear of forcing them into an alliance with himself.[96]

In the Spring of 1809 Canning purchased Gloucester Lodge
at Old Brompton on the outskirts of London. He hoped the
distance from the city would be such as to enable his family to
join him, for George's health remained a considerable problem.
In practice they had to remain at Hinckley. Canning's establishment was still large and in 1810 he paid the tax on male servants
for a butler and valet, two footmen, and one under-butler, coach-
man, under-coachman, porter, gardener (employing two others)
and a foot-boy. Canning also rented a flat in Albany for sleeping
late in winter.

In December 1812 his fourth child was born. This was Charles,
or 'Carlo', later to be Governor-General of India and known as
'Clemency Canning'. The health of his eldest continued to deter-
iorate and in November 1813 Granville spoke of him as 'gradually
wasting away'.[97] The clearance of the French from southern
Europe presented him with the opportunity to take his son to a
warmer clime where he might recover his health, and the diminu-
tion of his own political prospects inclined him increasingly in this
direction. In early 1814 he asked Frere about the suitability of

Spain, but Frere refused to be drawn into a firm opinion because of the disruption of war.[98]

Canning's own routine meanwhile continued much as usual. In November 1813 he left town for Hinckley and then proceeded to Crewe Hall for Christmas. He spent New Year in Liverpool and then visited a variety of friends, arriving back in Gloucester Lodge on 22 March. Visits to the Ellises first at Claremont and then at Sunning Hill followed. In April one finds him dining with the Princess of Wales, Grattan, Plunkett, Boringdon, Granville and others. May represented the usual routine of dinners with politicians and diplomats, and visits to the House of Commons and the Liverpool office. June was much the same, except for a short break to go to Oxford to take the degree of Doctor of Law and a visit to the theatre to see Keane in Othello.[99] Throughout the period he was planning a radical change in his career.

Since the breakdown of the 1812 negotiations politics had not been happy for Canning. By his own stubbornness he had put himself out of the innermost circles of politics at the very time when its prizes were most glittering. The end of the European war was placing in the hands of his great rival Castlereagh a major part in the re-shaping of Europe while he could only watch from the sidelines, wielding a waning influence and gnawing the ends of old plots. By the middle of 1814 his disillusion was complete and he wrote to Granville that he had, in his 'nearly extinct state neither means nor disposition to meddle in anything of politics any more'.[100] Coincident with this disillusionment was the problem of the health of his eldest son, and the necessity of his living in a healthier climate. He had already asked Frere his opinion of Spain as a suitable place. The solution to the problem came from Liverpool's generosity. Through Ellis he offered Canning the Embassy at Lisbon on 6 July, promising, as Canning told his wife, to raise it into 'a great, splendid, anomalous situation, wholly out of the line of ordinary missions . . . a sort of outwork of England'.[101]

Canning was very favourably inclined to the proposal, and there only remained the problem of his own friends, whom he was unwilling to leave in the lurch, or see drift to the Whigs. He wanted, as he told Sturges-Bourne, to put them in connection with Government.[102] The easiest request was for an Earldom for Boringdon. This would have come about in 1809 had it not

appeared unseemly to bestow it upon one so recently and notoriously cuckolded. Liverpool agreed to a Viscounty for Leveson-
Gower but with more reservations. The major claim for office was
for Huskisson to become Treasurer of the Navy or Master of the
Mint. Liverpool agreed, provided that Rose resigned amicably.
Two seats at the India, Admiralty or Treasury Boards were agreed
easily for Ward, Sturges-Bourne or Binning, and the India Board
without pay for 'Bobus' Smith. Promises of future preferment
were agreed for Kensington, Blackford, Jolliffe, Leigh, Patten,
Broadhead, Littleton and Canning's cousin George. Despite
differences which sprang from Rose's reluctance to quit office,[103]
the arrangement was on the whole a successful one. Canning himself was surprised at Liverpool's acquiescence, which was probably due to a combination of basic generosity with fear of what
Canning's old party, leaderless and perhaps looking to the somewhat mistrusted Huskisson, might do in the absence of Canning
himself.

The departure took place in early November, whereupon the
ship, the *Leviathan,* was immediately becalmed in Portland Roads,
giving an opportunity for a visit by Princess Charlotte, the Bishop
of Salisbury, Lady Ilchester, and several others.[104] The calm did
not last and the travellers were met with a violent storm in the
Bay of Biscay which produced a rumour of their having been lost
at sea.[105] The worst, wrote Canning cheerfully, was that he had
lost his hat in a high wind. At the end of the month they left the
ship, paying £40 for tips and lighters, and Canning presented his
£2,000 letter of credit to Messrs Sealy and Goodall in Lisbon.
Almost immediately he was struck down with a fierce and
debilitating attack of gout which did not leave him until the end
of the month.[106] The only positive advantage of this was that it
enabled him to read, at half a volume per day, Richardson's long
and astonishingly popular novel *Clarissa,* given to him by Lady
Liverpool to read on the ship. The gout he blamed on his having
fought off sea-sickness and leaving off a flannel waistcoast when
he arrived.[107]

The accommodation problem was solved for Canning when he
moved into a suite in a palace given to Wellington. However, he
was immediately horrified at the level of prices in Lisbon, two to
three times that of London, and complained he would be ruined,
being unable to keep expenses below £100 per week. Much to

Canning's pleasure, Charles Ellis and his family also came to Portugal, but this happy event was marred by the illness and death of George Ellis, with whom Canning was also very close, and this cast a pall over 1815. In the summer Canning's family went to Cintra, which Canning described as being 'as cool as a grotto and beautiful beyond anything that I ever saw, except perhaps the Lakes'.[108] His son George was further south, at Caldas, for his health. Canning commented, 'Ph-h-h-h-ugh ph-ugh-h-h-h-ugh. Phhh-hh-ugh-h-h. How hot it is.'[109]

In Lisbon Canning was immediately struck by the formality of the Portuguese court. Of Don Miguel de Forjaz he was immediately suspicious, considering him determined 'to oppose a vigorous resistance to the first British Minister that should come here after the peace'.[110] In January he wrote that they had become friends and that Forjaz came to play whist in the evening, and as Canning played so badly he lost, 'which of course contributes to his good humour'. In fact first impressions were to prove more accurate.[111]

The Lisbon Embassy was a somewhat peculiar position. The Royal Family had fled to Brazil in 1807 and the delays in communication between Rio and Lisbon made it difficult to get any decisions from the royal ministers in the latter. British representatives in Lisbon were remote from the intrigues of Rio and could only bemoan the activities of what they regarded as the anti-British faction led by the Marquis d'Aranjo. Furthermore, in Lisbon relations were fouled by a total difference of view on the Portuguese slave trade and by tensions over Lord Beresford's command of the Portuguese army which Forjaz wanted for himself. The former issue was partially salved by Britain's agreement to pay £300,000 in return for the suppression of the Portuguese slave trade north of the equator. Canning's relations with Forjaz nevertheless ran into continual difficulties. He constantly complained of delays in their correspondence as letters piled up unanswered.[112]

From April a more serious issue arose to befoul relations, and that was Napoleon's escape from Elba, and re-installation at Paris as Emperor. Canning's own view was that nothing 'short of complete success'[113] should be accepted as a riposte, and he was naturally sympathetic to Wellington's insistence that Portugal supply troops to fight in Flanders. Britain offered every assistance to Portugal in this regard, including offers of transport and free

clothing for their troops, but by 22 May the Portuguese had not
yet agreed to deliberate on the question, as they had not had
official notice of the proclamation of accession.[114] In June Canning
threatened Forjaz that the transports provided by Britain would
go home, but Forjaz called the bluff in such a way that Canning
could only suggest a final appeal to Rio as an alternative to imple-
menting his threat. The Portuguese government, he complained,
is 'neither tractable in peace nor available in war'.[115]

The attitude of the Portuguese probably resulted from a combination of wounded *amour-propre* at the autocratic manner in
which Britain was apparently behaving, realization that war in
Flanders was remote from Portuguese interests and general confusion resulting from the division of functions between Rio and
Lisbon. Canning saw little but hypocrisy and anti-British intrigue
in the conduct of the Portuguese, and in July he wrote bitterly to
Forjaz that while he rejoiced at Wellington's victory, it was
'mortifying that Portugal should stand forth in the face of Europe
the only power that has directly declined to take any part in the
contest'.[116]

Canning kept closely in touch with general political affairs.
He wrote to Lord Liverpool on subjects of the day in a style of
constructive criticism. He did not like the Peace with America
arranged at Ghent, though felt it politically necessary to avoid
clamour against the income tax. On the latter he criticized the
Government for being too weak in their expression of support for
it, considering that its defeat would be 'one of the most serious
misfortunes that can befall the country'. He followed the negotiations at Vienna, bemoaning the Russian acquisition of Poland
but conceding there was nothing to be done about it. He strongly
objected to the non-restoration of the Bourbons in Naples. 'Is it',
he asked, 'to be the only victim among the Crowned Heads being
so far as steadiness and fidelity go, the least deserving among
them, of such a fate?' It was his love of legitimacy probably more
than fear of making Prussia too powerful that made him applaud
the preservation of Saxony despite its support for Napoleon.[117]

The great events that were shaking Europe must have made
Canning feel himself cut off and redundant in Portugal, especially
given the brick wall he was knocking against with the local
authorities in Lisbon. Furthermore, Canning was sensitive to
accusations that the Lisbon position was a corrupt job and was

at pains to boast that he had reduced the expenses of the mission to under £1,000 per week. Indeed back in England there were such wild accusations as one that Mrs Canning never went out in her chair 'without two running footmen'.[118] Accusations of this sort were to persist throughout Canning's life as exemplary of the corruption of the system.

As early as April 1815, when it seemed clear that the Portuguese Court had no immediate intention of quitting Rio, Canning had submitted his resignation. He was nevertheless keen to insist that he had no intention of reversing his abdication in 1813 and landing, like Bonaparte, 'at Falmouth by surprise'.[119] He assured Liverpool that he was not responsible for the lamentations in Britain for his absence.[120] The return of Napoleon changed the situation for Canning and in June he was convinced that he would have to wait till October when a military concert may have been reached between Portugal and the allies and Sir John Beresford returned to take over some of his functions.[121] Relations with Portugal did not get any better and he was pleased to be able to say in July that his mission had been 'terminated, or suspended till Portugal comes to her senses'.[122] Thereafter Canning largely confined himself to complaints about the Portuguese: 'In war . . . no help; in peace . . . a restless, impatient untruthful ally – meditating only how to throw off the burthen of the alliance.'[123] Canning gradually slipped off the burden of office until his letter of recall which he received in October[124] enabled him to concentrate on his family, particularly the health of his eldest son, and await events.

In England, Canning had largely resigned his affairs, including his constituency responsibilities, to Huskisson, who probably knew more than anyone except Mrs Canning and Charles Ellis of Canning's real intentions and ambitions. In February 1816 the Earl of Buckinghamshire, President of the Board of Control for India, died. Huskisson wrote immediately to Liverpool stressing that Canning had on his departure expressed his interest should any vacancy arise in the Cabinet during his absence.[125] The office was one of the most junior in the Cabinet and far, far below Canning's pretensions of 1809 and 1812. Nevertheless, when Liverpool responded to Huskisson's suggestion with an invitation to take the position, he accepted after only brief (for Canning) hesitation. Canning was nothing if not a political animal and was fundamentally aware that he could not be really content in any other milieu.

The political situation in England was by no means ideal for Canning. Frere wrote to him gloomily of the political power of Castlereagh and the general political instability, fearing that 'the fundholders and landholders would go on alternately halloing the mob against each other till the rabble would be constituted compleat masters of the state'.[126] Furthermore, the political position of the Government was weak and in March they were substantially defeated on a motion to keep the income tax in operation. Consideration of the Government's weakness probably influenced Liverpool in his decision to recall Canning.

Before Buckinghamshire's death, Canning had already planned a return to England after which he intended to return to Portugal to take young George to try the waters at Barages in France. Of his stay in Portugal he commented that he had 'found in the delightful idleness and abstraction from all worldly concerns, which belong to this corner of Europe, all the charm that you foretold to me'.[127] His acceptance of office changed his plans and he determined to establish his family immediately at Bordeaux, where he was received very well and stayed long enough to demonstrate his taste by purchasing seven cases of Chateau Margaux 1811 at a price of 5s per bottle. Leaving his family he proceeded to England where, after visiting his mother in Bath, he went on to Liverpool for his re-election as MP, required by law on his assumption of paid office. By the middle of June he was back in Gloucester Lodge.[128]

Canning issued his first election circular from Saltram on 25 May 1816. He was opposed by a Radical-Whig called Thomas Leyland, with Thomas Green again Chairman of the Opposing Committee. The election was vigorously fought and much was made of the supposed corruption involved in Canning's position at Lisbon.

> *Fourteen thousand a year is a very fine thing*
> *For a trip to a Court without any King*

'Is it to Colonel Williams,'[129] replied a Canning broadsheet, 'with his stock of waste paper on Parliamentary Reform, that famishing families are to look for subsistence? Constitution, Commerce and Canning.'

In fact, the election was never in doubt. Canning's own party were firm and he was proposed by Bolton and seconded by Hollinshed. The poll proceeded despite the suggestion of Leyland's proposer that they withdrew because of insufficient support and by the fifth and final day Canning had a majority of 1,280 to 738.[130] He could now return to London to recommence, at a much lower level, his interrupted ministerial career.

8
THE RETURN TO OFFICE

Finally successful over the French abroad, Britain in 1815 moved rapidly into a period of dislocation and strife at home. The important political issues were now domestic and many of them concerned the preservation of public order in a new period of internal danger.

The Cabinet which Canning joined in 1816 still contained many people of whom he had a low opinion. Castlereagh continued as Foreign Secretary, his old enemy Sidmouth was Home Secretary, and even Camden, responsible for much of the bungling of 1809, was still there. Two of Sidmouth's supporters were there also. One, Nicholas Vansittart, was Chancellor of the Exchequer, and for him Canning and his friends reserved a fair degree of largely unjustified contempt. The other, Bragge Bathurst, was Chancellor of the Duchy of Lancaster. The Lord Chancellor, Eldon, and the Lord Privy Seal, Westmoreland, were deeply suspicious of Canning and remained so till he died. Also suspicious was Earl Bathurst, the much underrated Colonial Secretary.

The combination of an uncongenial Cabinet with the feeling of being charged with a second-hand job as President of the Board of Control for India made Canning fairly gloomy as to his own situation and prospects and force one to appreciate the depth of commitment to politics which had made him accept the job on those terms. At the end of 1817 he wrote to his wife who was ill, wishing her ailments upon himself 'who am living a sort of postscript after the real volume of my life is closed'.[1]

The Board of Control for India had been set up by Pitt's India Act of 1784 to provide the Government with a general political

control over Indian affairs, whilst leaving in the hands of the East
India Company the patronage of which Fox's ill-fated measure of
the previous year would have deprived them, and in theory full
management of the commercial concerns of the Company. At the
head of the affairs of the Company was the Court of Directors,
presided over by a Chairman and Deputy Chairman and elected
by the proprietors of East India stock. The Court operated through
a number of committees, the most important of which was the
Secret Committee, which transmitted the orders of the Board to
India. The proprietors themselves had little real power and the
1784 Act prevented them from vetoing any measure agreed
between the Court and the Board of Control. The apex of the
Indian triangle was the Governor-General in India possessed of
a power of instant action which could not be exercised by those
in far-distant Britain before the construction of a telegraph link.

The years between 1784 and 1816 had seen various struggles
for control between the Court, the Board and the Governor-
General. The net result had been a gradual weakening of the
Court. The appointment to all the major political offices and
military commands fell early to the Board and when the latter
was headed by Henry Dundas there had been a co-operation
between the Board and the Governor-General, Wellesley, which
largely ignored the Court and resulted in an expansionist policy
in India which the pure Company interest did not want. Even
many of the commercial decisions of the company were being
controlled by the Board to some extent, while the Company
suffered a further blow to their power with the loss, in 1813, of
their monopoly of trade to and from India.

In the year before Canning took office at the Board of Control
there had been a great deal of tension and conflict between the
Chairmen, Charles Grant and Thomas Reid, on one hand, and
the Board. This had reached the stage of a breach in personal
contact which, however, was restored by the Directors when
Canning took office on 20 June 1816. The Governor-General was
Lord Moira, soon to become Marquess of Hastings. He had gone
to India shortly after his unsuccessful attempts to form a Government in 1812, a leading motive behind his departure being his
desire to pay off his enormous debts.

There were twelve members of the India Board presided over
by Canning. Liverpool, Castlereagh, Bathurst, Sidmouth and

G

Vansittart were there *pro-forma*. There were also Lord Teign-
mouth the Evangelical former Governor-General, Viscount
Lowther, John Sullivan, Viscount Apsley (son of Earl Bathurst)
and finally two Canningites, Lord Binning and Sturges-Bourne.
In practice, however, most of the business was conducted directly
between the President and the two 'Chairs', or through the Secret
Committee with the Governor-General.[2]

One of the fringe benefits of Canning's position was a certain
amount of Indian patronage. This was, however, much less in
extent than imagined by many of his friends and relatives, for
the image of India in the eighteenth century as an inexhaustible
gold mine for anyone connected with it had died hard. In 1819 he
wrote angrily to the Rev. Leigh who had requested assistance for
a relative. 'You say "I have the patronage of all India – more in
amount than all the Offices of Government" – Now this is
absolutely and totally the reverse of the truth.' The only patronage
he possessed was the same as that in the hands of the two 'Chairs'.[3]
In his period as President, Canning had twelve 'writerships' as
official positions with the Company were called. Each was estimated to be worth £5,000 but two or three went to the King and
the same number had to be disposed on public grounds. He also
had a large number of 'cadetships' with the Company (for trainee
officials) of which to dispose. Certainly Canning was able to offer
compensation to a Mr Hoper for his financial services to his
friend the Princess of Wales.[4]

The resumption of official duties increased Canning's work
load. His diary frequently records meetings with the Chairmen
and such sundry engagements as visits to the East India College
at Haileybury, as well as meetings of the Secret Committee to
attend, as on 9, 10, 11, 13 and 18 February 1818. Nevertheless
Canning was by no means under such a heavy strain as during
his two periods as Foreign Secretary.[5]

The relative unimportance of India on the domestic scene is
perhaps surprising in view of the size of the country and the
enormous responsibilities inherent in the rule of over a hundred
million people from such a distance. In addition, there was the
international problem posed by fears of foreign involvement with
India, and this consideration made the affairs of Persia and the
Middle East a British concern. The Secret Committee received
regular reports from the President in Baghdad, reporting on such

things as the new organization of the French consulate there, and the probability of war between Persia and the Porte. The diplomatic dimensions of such problems forced co-operation between Canning and Castlereagh, for dealings with the Persian Ambassador, for example, were clearly the responsibility of the latter.[6] In practice, however, Canning's period at the Board of Control was one relatively free from fears of French or Russian interference with India or any of its trade routes.

Canning's relations with the Court of Directors were far better than those of Buckinghamshire, his predecessor, as evidence of which one may cite the readiness of the Company to have Canning as successor to Hastings as Governor-General in India. There were differences of opinion, nevertheless. One of the big issues in British politics as regards India had been the desirability of introducing the Christian religion there. Fearing Hindu resentment, many of the old Company hands favoured the views of Sir Henry Montgomery who declared in 1813 that 'He was more anxious to save the lives of 30,000 of his fellow countrymen than to save the souls of all the Hindus by making them Christians at so dreadful a price'.[7] In 1813 the balance had swung to the Christianizing party and the Thirteenth Resolution on Indian Affairs, passed in the context of the charter renewal, had been a triumph for Wilberforce, who had strong opinions on the question. Canning took a balanced view, with a full awareness of the limits of practicality. In 1817 he told the Bishop of Calcutta he was unwilling to approach the Company for stipends for a limited number of ministers to be ordained in India 'at a time when I am morally certain that it would not be willingly adopted'.[8]

Most of Canning's difficulties with the Court arose on fairly small matters. In 1818 there was a conflict over reversals by the Board of refusals of permission to reside in India by the Court, though in fact this was only nineteen reversals out of eighty-seven refusals since 1813.[9] In 1820 Canning objected strongly to a financial scheme of the Company for setting up a Guarantee Fund.[10]

One of the major issues in Indian affairs was the land-holding system. In Bengal there existed between the cultivators and the Government a middle class of persons known as 'zemindars', who filled the functions of feudal superior and tax-collector but who were generally regarded by Westerners as being fundamentally land-owners. Canning defended from the strictures of the Court the views of Hastings and McLumsden in India that the cultivators had 'suffered from the extortion and rapacity of the Zemindars'. He then, however, expanded his views in a manner typical of his whole philosophy:

> I shall allow myself no other remark than first that in other countries, I believe, the removal of intermediate landholders, or middle-men, (by whatever name known) has been considered (whether wisely or not) as an advancement rather than a degradation; but secondly that I apprehend nothing to be so little useful as reasoning by analogy from Europe to a state of things, of men and of manners so entirely distinct and anomalous, those general maxims of Political Economy, which all enlightened nations indeed possess, and continually recommend to their neighbours, but which, even among the most enlightened, are continually modified and controlled by their own peculiar prejudice or temporary convenience.[11]

Canning's relations with Hastings were not so good as those with the Court. He seems to have believed in a policy combining conciliation and firmness. When a new tax on bottled wine provoked fears of a non-importation agreement at Calcutta, Canning wrote to Liverpool:

> These are little things – but great Empires sometimes hold together or separate from little causes. And I confess I hardly know whether I look with more fearfulness to the extent and composition of the Indian Empire itself, or to the tenure of its connexion with this country. Such as it, that tenure, is, we ought not to impair it for any light cause or from any motive of small fiscal benefit to England.[12]

Consistent in this policy, he agreed with Hastings on the necessity of remedying such deeply-felt grievances as the heavy duty on letters.[13] On the other hand, he felt very strongly as to the unwisdom of Hastings' hasty repeal of Wellesley's legislation for the control of the press.[14]

The period was an important one in the history of India, for Hastings took up again Wellesley's policy of expansion. There was a successful campaign against the Gurkhas from 1814 to 1816, after which Hastings turned his attention to the Pindari robber bands of central India. This quickly led to war against the Mahratta Confederacy which was successfully concluded in 1819. Canning was forced to defend this policy in Parliament, which he did by declaring that he was happy to say that the conflict had not cost the life of a single European officer and stigmatizing the Pindaris as a 'pest'.[15] Rather than applauding these conquests, the Company, more interested in commercial profits, became as deeply hostile to Hastings as they had been previously to Wellesley. Hastings himself, responsible for this major extension of British power, felt bitterly let down by those at home and by Canning in particular, especially as clamour grew for his removal. In February 1821 he wrote to Canning:

> When I observe that latterly there has not been a single measure of mine which has not been captiously misconstrued, I necessarily cast about for the object of such uniform censure.
>
> Now I cannot suppose you, my Dear Sir, to act from any personal ill-will towards me. I take it for granted you are influenced by some consideration of Policy, thoroughly satisfactory to your mind in wishing that I should make way for another.[16]

In fact the British Government did not appreciate the expansionist activities of its far-flung subordinates. Sir Stamford Raffles, who at the same time and with the approval of Hastings, had entered into a treaty for the acquisition of Singapore from the Sultan of Jahore, met bitter obloquy. Thomas Courtenay wrote:

> . . . the conclusion, without any instruction or authority whatever by a gentleman in charge of a subordinate commercial factory, of a treaty by which the British Government is bound to new engagements to a native Prince of Sumatra, appears to the Board to afford a fresh proof of the inconvenience that cannot fail to result from the continuance at Bencoola of a person, however individually respectable, who has in so many instances outstepped his authority.[17]

In fact, Raffles quickly turned Singapore from a swamp into a major trading station.

One can say of Canning's period at the Board of Control that he was an excellent conciliator with the Company and a man with some appreciation of the problems of ruling an empire on the other side of the world. However, the crucial fact was that Canning regarded the job as very much of a backwater and the main streams of his ambition and interests flowed elsewhere.

In 1816 Charles Bagot wrote to Lord Binnings: 'I see plainly that Jacobinism is raising its crest again in a way that it has not done for years – and that is the Antagonist of Canning. It is in his battles with this monster that he is always great and always useful.'[18] The problem arose fundamentally from the economic dislocation resulting from the end of the war, and the 'lower orders' did not have the lobbying power at their disposal which secured the Corn Laws for the farming interest. Wilberforce posed the problem:

> Loyalty of men of property is preserved by self-interest – but on what can we draw for preserving the loyalty, to the constitution I mean, in the lower orders, breathing as they do, an atmosphere of falsehood, profaneness and insubordination in consequence of the swarms of worse than Egyptian plagues which are poisoning and destroying the land from the seditious and irreligious forces, now so actively at work in this country.[19]

Canning was not a laggard in rushing to the defence of the established order. His first speech on returning to the Commons in 1817 was in favour of refusing a hearing to certain petitioners for reform because of the way their petition was worded. He followed this up in March with a speech praising the suspension of Habeas Corpus and declaring for the necessity of the Seditious Meetings Bill, needed because 'there is an unusual degree of inflammability in the public mind; because there are incendiaries abroad who would avail themselves of this extraordinary inflammability to kindle the fires of rebellion in every corner of the Kingdom.' He went on to justify such a bill by declaring that every state must have the means of its own conservation, such as was provided in Rome by the dictatorship.[20]

In August 1819 eleven people were killed when the magistrates ordered to disperse a crowd of fifty to sixty thousand, assembled to hear 'Orator Hunt' at St Peter's Fields, Manchester. Many Whigs were genuinely horrified by this, but Canning merely attacked the 'flagrant misrepresentations of fact, by which the public mind had been worked up to a fearful state of irritation'. He went on: 'The persons, whose machinations are the subject of this debate, and the cause of our being called together at this season, are valueless as motes in the sun-beam, compared with the loyal quiet, unmurmuring millions, who look up to Parliament for protection. Let them not look up to you in vain.' This premature evocation of the silent majority was concluded with a long quotation in Latin as to the responsibility of the Senate for the protection of the State.[21]

Canning strongly defended the 'Six Acts' passed in the wake of the 'Peterloo massacre', declaring that there was never a time 'in which the monarchy was in more danger or the Parliament in greater difficulty than the present'.[22]

Typically, Canning threw himself heart and soul into the fight against Jacobinism, and thus created enemies. In 1817 he went too far in his sarcasm as to the infirmities of a prisoner imprisoned following the suspension of Habeas Corpus. He was answered by an anonymous personal attack entitled 'The Suppressed Letter to the Right Hon. George Canning'. Rashly, and probably wrongly assuming that Philip Francis was the author, he wrote asking for satisfaction if this were the case.[23] A duel with the ageing Radical, had it taken place, would probably have finished his career. On the other hand, Canning was rarely bitter on a personal level and he was utterly disgusted by an attack on his opponent Brougham which appeared in *The Courier,* which he felt 'wholly unjustifiable by any degree of political hostility'.[24] Furthermore, he retained certain more liberal traits, defending the increase in the tea tax of 1819 because it would not affect 'the low-priced teas which are consumed by the poor people',[25] and retaining his support of Catholic emancipation, even though forced to present a petition from his constituents against it.[26]

Canning was readier than his colleagues to believe that the country was settling down. In July 1819 he wrote that 'the real state of the country, in trade and commerce and revenue and means of employment, is now gradually mending. We have passed the worst and if this year passes over without tumult I think we are safe for the time to come.'[27] Unfortunately his prophecy was followed almost immediately by Peterloo. In January 1820 he wrote to his wife that the country was quelled and trade reviving.[28] The following month his diary recorded the unfolding of a plot to murder the Cabinet which has passed down in history as the 'Cato Street Conspiracy'. Canning, along with other members of the Cabinet, learned of this on 22 February. On the twenty-third the Cabinet decided to seize the conspirators at their place of meeting. On the twenty-fourth he wrote: 'Cabinet at Home Department. Examination of witnesses and conspirators. Plot well laid – and sure to have succeeded if not betrayed to us.'[29]

Supporters of the Administration much admired Canning's stand against Jacobinism. In 1817 the Speaker praised his brilliant speech on parliamentary reform, 'not professing to hesitate upon remedies but denying the evil'.[30] However, he was still deeply distrusted, partly for reasons of his suspected opportunism and partly for his attitudes on the Catholic question. His name was dropped from consideration as a possible candidate for Oxford University, something Canning would have loved, when one of the censors threatened to resign.[31] His real importance in the Government was not very great, though an increasingly close relationship with Liverpool helped to offset the distrust of others. In April 1819 he attacked the method whereby the Bank should return to cash payments, but when these proposals were dropped, he was left guessing whether or not this was the result of his representations.[32]

One further public duty in this period is worthy of note. On 22–3 May 1819 his diary recorded, 'Called up at night to attend the Dss of Kent's delivery at Kensington Palace. Got home to bed again by 5.' The King's new grand-daughter was to become Queen Victoria.

Canning did not have much free time to himself in this period, though he managed during the summers to visit friends' homes in southern England. In August 1819 he complained that he had not had a fortnight's holiday since December 1816.[33] Such amusements as he had were rather *ad hoc*, such as taking 'Toddles' and 'Carlo' along with Joan to see the Pantomime at Covent Garden.[34] His health was suffering in the period and his diary records frequent attacks of gout. Instead of riding to town, he now frequently took a carriage. In October 1818 he was upset by a quivering of the eyelid. On the recommendation of 'Alexander the Occulist', he applied leeches, but the remedy proved worse than the disease as the leech bites swelled and spread.[35]

At this time Canning's second son commenced a naval career, a 'violent passion' for which he had conceived on his voyage from Lisbon, and Canning took him down to the naval academy in

Portsmouth in January 1817.[36] Relations were never really good
between Canning and this black sheep of the family and were soon
to take a sharp turn for the worse. However, in general Canning's
relations with young people were excellent and a close friendship
existed between him and Lord Howard de Walden, the son of
Charles Ellis. It is clear that Canning was approached by him on
a highly personal matter early in 1817, for he replied to his young
friend: 'There it goes – into the fire – and I assure you, nobody
has seen it – nor heard any part of it – You have nothing to fear
in writing to me without reserve.'[37] Not so good were his relations
with his own relatives, continually plaguing him for preferment.
'My cousin Garvagh's object', he wrote in 1819, 'that *I* should
propose and insist upon his being elected one of the Representative Peers of Ireland! Liverpool says it's impossible. So be sure it
is.'[38]

In August 1819 Canning took his wife and two younger children abroad. On Saturday 14 August he got up at 6 am in time
to write ten letters before breakfast at 7 am and took an Admiralty
Barge at 8.30. Sailing from Woolwich they reached Rotterdam
on the seventeenth and proceeded through Holland to reach a
'good inn' at Cologne on the twenty-fifth. Thence they proceeded
down the Rhine by boat to Bonn and to a 'delectable inn' at
Ingelheim. Through Germany they proceeded to Switzerland and
Italy, enabling them to attend the opera in Milan on 22 September. From Genoa they went by boat to Naples, taking excellent
apartments at the 'Gran Brettagna'. On 11 October he went to
Pompeii, where there had been much excavation in the previous
century to the loss of later and better equipped archaeologists, and
on the fifteenth he went up Vesuvius, setting out at 1 pm to reach
the top by sunset and then back by 9 to 10 pm – 'a fatiguing day,
but for once well worth the trouble'.

In Naples he had the opportunity to discuss diplomatic affairs
with the British minister, Sir William A'Court, and then he proceeded northward, arriving at Rome on the twenty-fourth where
he was much put out to receive an urgent summons to return
to England, for Parliament was to meet in November in the wake
of the Peterloo cases. Canning nevertheless allowed himself a
few days in Rome, leaving his card with Cardinal Consalvi, the
Secretary of State, and meeting, by chance, Sir Thomas Lawrence
in St Peter's. On the twenty-seventh he wrote, 'Went by appoint-

ment to the Pope at ½ p 9 – fine old man, and very civil.' He
followed this with visits to the Capitol, the Colosseum, the Pan-
theon and a visit to Diocletian's Baths with the Duchess of Devonshire. It is interesting to note that in this period the Englishman
abroad was never short of fellow countrymen of his acquaintance,
such was the general urge to travel on the conclusion of the French
Wars.

On 30 October Canning left his family in Rome and proceeded
rapidly northwards with a virtually non-stop trip of thirty-eight
hours to Florence. Here he met another large group of English
friends before proceeding via Turin to cross the Mt Conis Pass
at night into France. On 15 November he dined with Sir Charles
Stuart, the British Ambassador in Paris. He spoke with the
French Prime Minister, Decages, and left his card with 'Mon-
sieur', the future Charles x. On the nineteenth he crossed the
Channel, being sick for the entire thirteen hours of the crossing,
and by the twentieth was back at the India Board, after which
he dined with Liverpool, Huskisson and Arbuthnot to discuss
the draft of the King's speech. The following day he was laid low
with another major attack of gout.[39]

Canning took an early opportunity to visit his eldest and ailing
son, George. Their relationship was a close one, as can be gauged
by a letter written by the latter in 1817. His leg, he declared, was
much better, and 'as to your kind enquiries after Livy, he is much
obliged to you for them, and assured you, thro' me, that he never
was better in his life, and he confidently hopes to be able to entertain you in handsome style on your arrival. Now Goodbye, My
Dear Papa, until you and I meet, when I do not think we shall
need Mr Livy's company to enliven us.'[40] Early in 1820 young
George's health started taking a dramatic turn for the worse.
'George gets steadily worse,' wrote Canning on 27 March 1820.
On twenty-ninth, 'George worse. The decay gradual but sure.
Consciousness nearly gone.' On the thirty-first 'George breathed
his last at 2.30 am –

> *Nor was to the bow'ry of bliss conveyed*
> *A purer spirit or a more welcome shade.*'[41]

His malady, wrote Canning to his mother, 'was in effect nothing
else than the breaking up of a frame so weak that the wonder
rather is that it should have lasted so long . . . God's will be done!

Never was human being of 19 so prepared for heaven.'[42] To his wife he wrote: 'If I did not know my own dearest love's religious faith and firmness of mind, I should begin at a great distance from the sad intelligence which I have to communicate to her in this letter – and should go through a long detail of the variation of poor dear George's illness before I came to its fatal termination.'[43]

The funeral was on 6 April at the New Churchyard in Kensington, and Canning then went to visit his mother in Bath. In May he was struck down by a violent attack of gout which kept him in bed till 4 June.

In this period Canning had twice to defend his parliamentary seat at Liverpool. In April 1818 Canning received a fresh requisition from six hundred of his Liverpool supporters which, he said, he couldn't refuse.[44] 'Everything seems to promise a quiet contest – though (for Gascogne at least) a severe one,' he wrote to his wife.[45] Canning arrived at Liverpool on 17 June and addressed a large crowd from John Bolton's balcony before proceeding to the town hall and thence to the Canning and Backbone Clubs. Canning was at the hustings at 8.30 for the commencement of polling the following day.[46] The challenge to Gascogne and Canning came from Earl Sefton, a large property-owner and a man better able to hold together the Whigs and the Radicals than most others.

As might be expected, Canning used the election for a vigorous enunciation of his principles. Could, he asked, 'this election itself . . . recur annually, accompanied with an extension of the suffrage to half a million of persons more than now enjoy it, without infinite and intolerable mischief?' (Cries of No, No!) The franchise was a right, and such a term implied a principle of limitation.

> The reformers are wise in their generation. They know well enough – and have read plainly enough in our own history – that the prerogative of the Crown and the privileges of the peerage would be as dust in the balance against a preponderating democracy. They mean democracy and nothing else. And give them but a House of Commons constructed on their own principles – the peerage and the throne may exist for a day, but may be swept away from the face of the earth by the first angry vote of such a House of Commons. . . . The constitution of this country is A MONARCHY, controlled by two assemblies.[47]

Canning also turned to the economic problems faced by the country. The war, he explained, had opened channels of commercial enterprise and brought a prosperity peculiar to itself that atoned in some measure for its evils. The removal of this stimulus was the cause of 'temporary stagnation ... insidiously imputed to national exhaustion'.

As usual, the election produced its stock of squibs and songs. Apart from their regular stand-by, 'Hearts of Oak', the Canning party produced:

> *Old cock-fighting Sefton declares he will stand*
> *Backed by Rushton, Tom Green, and the Jacobin Band.*
> *He flatters himself that with friends such as these*
> *The nation to reform and the mob to please.*

To the air 'John Anderson, my jo John', the Sefton party had

> *John Gladstone now, my jo John,*
> *Ere we were first acquent,*
> *We baith were Whigs, ye know, John*
> *To power we had not bent.*[48]

In the voting Gascogne and Canning pulled quickly ahead. The Seftonites tried to seize the tactical advantage of securing another voting bar by nominating another candidate called Heywood, whereupon the Canningites replied by nominating Bolton. After the first two days the votes fell fairly levelly, but Gascogne retained his lead of about 150 over Sefton, and on the twenty-fifth Canning was elected with 1,654, Gascogne with 1,444 and Sefton came third with 1,280. The chairing took place on the twenty-sixth and was followed for Canning by dinner at the Boltons. On the twenty-seventh he called on the Gladstones at Seaforth and on 1 July went round Liverpool with William Ewart. Thence he went via Welbeck and Cheltenham to visit his mother at Bath and on 11 July travelled all the 108 miles back to Gloucester Lodge in one day.[49]

The election of 1820 was a quieter affair, following the death of the King and catching the Whigs unprepared and perhaps out of funds after the strenuous contest of 1818. The day before he left for Liverpool, Canning did not even know whether there would be a contest.[50] He arrived in Liverpool on 9 March to face derisory opposition from two Radicals, Peter Crompton and

Thomas Leyland, who polled 345 and 125 respectively against 1,635 for Canning and 1,532 for Gascogne. The chairing took place on the sixteenth and on the eighteenth Canning took the opportunity of making a major speech. 'What', he asked, 'was the situation of the country in November 1819? Do I exaggerate when I say that there was not a man of property who did not tremble for his possessions?' As for Peterloo, he compared the right of the crowd to gather at Manchester and that of the citizen to live unmolested. 'Can the decision by possibility be other than that the peaceful and industrious shall be protected, the turbulent and mischievous put down?' He finally attacked the regular opposition for being prepared for a certain degree of co-operation with Radical reformers, when the real question was whether one was 'for or against the institutions of the British Monarchy'.[51]

On 20 March Canning left Liverpool to go to Welbeck and thence to the death-bed of his son. He was never again to contest a Liverpool election. The holding of a seal of the importance of Liverpool was a triumph for Canning, for 'placemen', as ministers and others thought to be bought by office could be described, were not popular in the counties and open boroughs. Part of his success is explained by his assiduous cultivation of his local supporters, and readiness to support their interests. He jealously guarded the patronage of the town, writing that 'A Liverpool place could not be given to a non-Liverpudlian except for the *express* purpose of losing the election.'[52] In 1821 he insisted that the Liverpool Customs must go to his supporters even if Government, through fear of being accused of partiality, wished to hand the decision over to the Commissioners of Customs. If not, the seat would be lost on his departure from it.[53] Also, Canning was fortunate in having as his leading supporters men such as Bolton and Gladstone who did not intrigue behind his back, and who knew exactly the degree of legitimate influence contemporary norms of political morality allowed them to bring to bear.

Before he went to Liverpool for re-election a new storm had begun to break over Canning's career. He had always had a close relationship to the Princess of Wales. She was now living abroad, and the stories of her conduct were such that the Regent sent a Commission to Milan in 1818 on the basis of whose report he became convinced of her adulterous conduct, particularly with one Bartolommeo Bergami, a handsome Italian attendant. Canning was one of the few points of contact between the Princess of Wales and her husband. In August 1819 he had gone to Carlton House to show the Regent a letter which he had received from the Princess asking Canning to tell her husband that she intended to come to England.[54]

The crisis came to a head when the Princess nominally became Queen with the death of George III in 1820. This coincided with renewed disillusionment with office on Canning's part. On 28 January 1820 he had an interview with Liverpool in which he stressed his dissatisfaction with his position and unwillingness to keep it for long. Liverpool acknowledged its inadequacy to Canning's pretensions, and the possibility was raised of Canning becoming Governor-General of India.[55] On 6 February, nevertheless, Canning had been induced to stay in office for a year in order to secure Hastings' recall.[56] Clearly he was disillusioned with Government, especially because of the ascendancy of 'Endymion' (Castlereagh) over 'The Magdalen' (Liverpool). It was now too late to set the former aside.[57]

One of the first things the new King insisted upon was a divorce from his wife. On 10 February the Cabinet learned of the King's 'determination to look for other servants if we do not agree to bring forward a Bill of Divorce'. 'Be it so,' added Canning. The same day the Cabinet decided not to agree to divorce, and by expressing a united determination on the matter forced their opinion on the King. On the fourteenth, Castlereagh had a long talk with him and found him 'rather softened'. Finally, the day after George III's funeral, he agreed to give up the divorce.[58]

Ministers' plans were for Caroline to live permanently abroad in return for a generous financial settlement. To this, the King forced them to add the elimination of the Queen's name from the liturgy. Canning was unhappy about this but prepared to agree provided it was not linked with a penal process, which it might appear to prejudge.

If Caroline had been wise, matters would have rested there. In fact, she set out for England to claim her rights as soon as she heard of the death of George III. A desperate attempt by the Government to buy her off through the mediation of Henry Brougham failed, and on 6 June the Queen arrived in London to meet with the rapturous support of the crowd.

News that the Queen was definitely coming reached Canning

on 5 June, and he immediately explained his doubts and difficulties to Liverpool at dinner. He had a sleepless night on 6 June, followed by a day of reflection on the seventh which he concluded by going to Parliament and making a vigorous speech in defence of government policy. Liverpool approved of the speech but the King was furious at certain expressions of warmth towards the Queen which revived George IV's old fears that Canning and his wife had been lovers.

The Cabinet was in fairly continuous session for the next few weeks. Nothing came of a project by Canning for pacification by means of an Act of Parliament, and negotiations between the Cabinet and the Queen broke down on 18 June. Canning had already offered his resignation on the fourteenth but this was refused. On the nineteenth, Canning called on Wilberforce to discuss the possibility of a parliamentary motion calling on the Queen to accept the settlement and not insist on the restoration of her name in the liturgy. Wilberforce's real motive was undoubtedly fear of the effects on public morality of revelations of sexual misconduct in high places. After vacillating for three days, he brought forward his motion on 22 June. Canning gave it strong support, and the motion was carried by 391 to 124.[59]

The project turned out to be a failure for when the Queen met the parliamentary delegation to receive their resolution she gave a flat refusal. Clearly, the growing evidence of popular support was hardening her attitude. This crisis provoked Canning into again offering his resignation to the King. However, the latter professed himself satisfied and Canning remained. The King nevertheless told Wellington, on the basis of that conversation, that he 'had almost made Canning confess to his former *extreme intimacy* with the Queen'.[60] This probably arose from Canning's request not to take further part in the proceedings, but to leave them to those 'without personal acquaintance or intercourse of kindness with the accused party'.[61] It is easy to see how the King's mind, somewhat distraught in this jumble of affairs, had exaggerated the cause of Canning's reluctance.

In Canning's mind there was now clearly no alternative but a trial,[62] and in this he would take no part. Fortunately, despite the King's feelings towards him, he gave him this permission and reiterated it in July.[63] The Cabinet decided to proceed by bringing a bill of Pains and Penalties against the Queen in the House of

Lords. They also decided to introduce into it a divorce clause, which Canning, immediately breaking his rule of taking no part in proceedings, promptly attacked.[64]

Meanwhile, the Queen, perhaps growing anxious at the turn affairs had taken, approached Canning by means of Sir Robert Wilson and John Hookham Frere, intimating that she was prepared to accept the terms she had rejected. Canning said he could do nothing, advising her that the only thing now that would serve would be unconditional submission.[65] If Canning's position in the Government had been difficult before the Queen's affair arose, it was now even more untenable. His prospects of office were even more limited, and in July he told Liverpool he could not consider becoming Home Secretary because that office was so closely involved in the Queen's business. He could only keep his present office because of its remoteness from the affair.[66]

With the Queen's trial due to start on 17 August, Canning felt it would be wiser to leave the country and visit his family. On 9 August Canning left the Nore (a sandbank in the middle of the Thames where the fleet used to anchor) and arrived at Flushing the same night. Passing through Brussels, Burgundy and Switzerland he proceeded to Verona, where he saw the amphitheatre and went to the play. He wrote to his mother from Venice, 'Decay and desertion are sadly perceptible. It must have been a magnificent city in its day.'[67] He then took his family into Austria and southern Germany, admiring the 'Mountains and Rivers and Pine Forests' between Villach and Rastadt, where there being no beds available. 'The females lay down in their cloaths. I slept in the carriage till day-break.' At Halleim they saw the saltmines, and then went back through Salzburg, Munich, Strasbourg and Nancy to Paris, where they stopped. Canning lived a fairly active social life here and kept in touch with the diplomatic situation through Sir Charles Stuart. On 8 November he went to the Assize Court to see the trial of a man accused of murdering his lover's husband, then to the Opera.[68]

In England the political temperature had risen. The King was the object of mockery and hatred, portrayed in prints as a disgustingly fat old lecher. As Frere commented: 'The whole nation *knows what he is.*'[69] The anti-Queen faction had little publicity, though one cannot but be amused by one poem which circulated:

> *Sweetest Queen, we thee implore*
> *Go away, and sin no more,*
> *But if that effort be too great,*
> *Go away at any rate.*

Canning kept in touch with the situation at home, even discussing it with Peel in Paris on 31 October, and putting his view that there was no alternative but acquittal. Canning himself was already considering resignation, and commented of Peel, 'Surely he cannot take office if I go out.'[70] He kept in close touch with Granville and Huskisson, the former urging him to stay away till the affair had passed.[71] Canning continued to reiterate his own view: 'The Bill will not pass . . . We ought to have told the King from the beginning, "Sir, Divorce is IMPOSSIBLE!" "What if she comes, if she raves, if she insults?", etc. etc. "Yes, Sir, in *any* case DIVORCE IS IMPOSSIBLE".'[72] In a letter to Liverpool, he compared the affair to that of the Duke of York in 1809. 'If Parliament once seats itself in the moral chair, and pronounces upon private delinquency, where will its intermeddling stop?'[73] Above all, he urged the bill would not pass, and it should now be given up by Liverpool himself, *in toto*.[74]

In practice Canning proved to be an accurate prophet. Granville thought that the revelation that the Queen had spent the night under the same tent as Bergami would prove decisive against her,[75] but when the bill came to its second reading on 6 November there was only a majority of twenty-eight which dropped to nine on the third reading. These votes clearly showed the impossibility of carrying it through the House of Commons and Liverpool dropped the measure. Canning returned on 18 November to a London rejoicing in the Queen's escape from her hated traducers.

The King himself was naturally furious at the turn of events, and particularly hostile to Canning whose supporters in the Lords had voted against the measure. Furthermore, all his old feelings as to Canning's exact relationship with the Queen were revived. Holland commented on Canning's conduct in 1820 that 'so far from rescuing his character from reproach, it seemed to imply some secret or mysterious reason that disqualified him for a judge or an accuser'.[76]

It was not a happy time for Canning to return, and indeed he left his family in Paris, perhaps fearing their exposure to a scandal which to some extent touched himself. He believed that, having been beaten, ministers should not, as they seemed intent on doing, pursue the matter of the liturgy. In addition, he believed the King was plotting against the Ministry.[77] On 22 November he saw the King, but was clearly not satisfied with the outcome, for on the twenty-fourth he wrote to his wife that he wanted to withdraw from 'a position become utterly untenable'. The Government should have resigned after the Lords vote, or given in on everything.[78] Canning spent the next few days in consultation with others. On the twenty-eighth he dined *tête-à-tête* with Liverpool, on the twenty-ninth with Huskisson and on the thirtieth with Charles Ellis, who played an important role in this crisis in Canning's life, for fundamentally Canning trusted him more than anyone else. On 1 December there was another unsatisfactory audience with the King, after which Canning and Ellis went down to visit Liverpool at Walmer Castle. On the seventh he had a long discussion with Liverpool on resignation. 'He,' wrote Canning, 'vehemently against – but after discussion, I think acquiescent.'[79]

On 9 December, Liverpool wrote to Arbuthnot, saying he feared that Canning's determination had been taken. It arose, he thought, out of the personal *awkwardness* of his position, and that 'when he stated his difficulties to the King, the King did not express the least anxiety to help him'.[80] Canning sent off his resignation to the King on the thirteenth. The House of Commons business, he urged, would now be so mixed with the question that he could 'not absent himself from them, without appearing virtually to abandon the Parliamentary duties of his station'.[81] The resignation was very different from that of 1809 or the crisis of 1812. Canning kept himself on good terms with Liverpool, whom he found 'friendly and understanding', and was frightened at the language of some of his supporters such as Titchfield, who was speaking of Canning going out and then overthrowing the Government. This, he felt, would 'ruin all'.[82]

He wrote to his mother that his resignation arose from his inability to remain in office and uninvolved. He intended to go to Paris before Parliament discussed the question and not come back till it was over. 'An acquaintance of 22 years and habitudes of confidence during the first ten years of them make it impossible for me to be a prosecutor of the Queen.' On the other hand, he could not turn against the King.[83] On 2 January 1821 Canning met the Chairs for the last time, and before leaving England on 17 January, he took the opportunity to write to Liverpool again on the subject of the Queen. In fact, the affair of the Queen died down with remarkable suddenness as ministers played the affair quietly, leaving the Opposition free to overplay their hand. Above all, the Queen forfeited a great deal of popularity by the acceptance of £50,000 per year and a house. A brief resurgence occurred on 19 July when the Queen unsuccessfully attempted to gain access to the coronation. Within a month, however, she was dead, and with her the entire issue. 'She had great and good qualities – with all her faults,' wrote Canning sadly.[84]

Canning's trip to Paris took five days, and the expenses of a gentleman travelling in the age before railways can be gauged from the fact that the entire trip cost £72, including £12 12s for the boat fare.[85] In Paris he moved in high political circles, meeting the Prime Minister, Villèle, together with Baron Pasquier, sometimes described as 'father of the French mercantile marine,' and Talleyrand.

Of course there had been other issues throughout this period apart from India, internal security and the Queen, many of them illustrative of Canning's basic attitudes. Of the bill to protect child operatives in cotton factories, Canning commented that he was neither a friend nor opposer of the measure. 'The only prejudice he felt was the conviction resulting from all speculations on political economy, in favour of non-interference in contracts.'[86] On Brougham's motion for a commission on the education of the poor, he declared: 'I am not hostile to the inquiry but I oppose the motion of the Hon. and learned gentleman because I think that the blind and headlong zeal with which he pursues a favourable object, has suggested to him a course opposed to the established practice of the House, and which, if adopted, would go near to overturn the fixed banners of the constitution.'[87]

When Lyttleton produced his regular motion for the abolition of state lotteries, he conceded that to remove temptation from the lower orders, the one-sixteenth share in a ticket might follow the one-sixty-fourth and one-thirty-second into oblivion, but he was not prepared to deprive the Government of £300,000 p.a.[88] In 1820 he supported the disfranchisement of the borough of

Grampound for corruption but opposed the transfer of the seats to Leeds.[89] In 1821 a member asked for a commission to investigate Robert Owen's industrial settlement at New Lanark. While speaking highly of Owen, Canning opposed the motion on the grounds that his plan depended on drawing the population together in masses which destroyed individuality(!), that it would not work on a more extended scale, and that Parliament should pause before giving its blessing to a community ideal not based on Christianity.[90] Canning's knowledge of the industrial system was clearly somewhat limited.

Perhaps it is easy to see why Canning was so distrusted. His views were often expressed in such a different way from others that his enemies were infuriated while those on his own side remained distrustful. However, there was one issue on which Canning was not equivocal, and that was Catholic emancipation. While Canning was in Paris in February 1821 he heard that William Plunket had carried a motion to bring in an Emancipation Bill. Canning returned to London to speak in favour of the second reading. Britain and Ireland, he declared, had come closer together and only an isthmus remained: 'Shall we not rather cut away at once the isthmus that remains, allow free course to the current which our artificial impediments have obstructed, and float upon the mingling waves the arc of our common constitution?'[91] The vote was carried by 254 to 243 and a subsequent amendment to exclude from the privileges to be accorded to Catholics the right to sit in Parliament was lost by 223 to 211. Canning wrote to his mother that he had done enough on the question for the while. 'I do not mix in every debate of detail, but wait for the opportunities, where there is a great difficulty to be met or a considerable impression to be made.'[92] While it was a great achievement for the pro-Catholics to secure the passage of the bill in the Commons, which they had done by 2 April, it was doomed in the House of Lords with the opposition of the Prime Minister, the Lord Chancellor and the Home Secretary.

In April, Canning returned to his family in Paris, going the round of balls, which he disliked, for the sake of Harriet and his young nephew and the Ellises.[93] In June he brought his family back to England.

At this period in Canning's career there seemed two options open to him. The first was to wait for a renewed offer from the

Government, which, given Liverpool's obvious willingness to have him back, seemed likely; the second was to take up the possibility already mooted the previous year of succeeding Hastings in what Wilberforce called 'the first in true importance of all the offices under the Crown',[94] the Governor-Generalship of India.

Canning wrote to his wife early in April that he saw his own future as being all risk and no gain. 'What does the reputation of being the first speaker in the House of Commons do for me? Nothing.' He was too old to try new combinations. Huskisson, and all the Government and Tories, wanted him to take any office to make 'their House of Commons less disgraceful to them – and play second fiddle to the end of my days. But they are mistaken.'[95] Ten days later he added: 'At 51 one must consider one's last card as being to be played – and with a view not so much to indefinite advance, as to secure retreat.'[96] He did not seem to have a clear role. He wanted to promote a bill to put the English Catholics on the same footing as the Irish, but many of the Irish leaders preferred their grievances rather 'than to take what they can get gradually and quietly.' In April he was upset when 'no adversary and no audience' prevented him from speaking in a debate on parliamentary reform.[97]

Various projects, the most realistic of which was for Canning to go to the Admiralty in place of Melville, were mooted. It was even said that Liverpool had told Castlereagh of his wish to retire, and that in this case, with Castlereagh as Prime Minister, Canning could be Foreign Secretary.[98] In fact all these schemes fell foul of the King who reiterated his flat refusal to have anything to do with Canning. Indeed on 16 June 1821 Canning called on Liverpool for a general discussion of old times, only to hear afterwards through Charles Ellis and Cecil Jenkinson that Liverpool had just received a letter intimating the King's resistance to Canning's return, which had driven him 'distracted'.[99] Relations between the King and Liverpool were at their lowest ebb, and Canning was loth to impose himself on Liverpool, especially after the latter was laid low in June by the death of his wife. On 22 June Canning wrote to Liverpool that the King's dislike of the proposed arrangements was 'the talk of the town'. He begged Liverpool 'not to let any consideration for me endanger the stability of the administration and least of all your situation in it ... I would

rather remain out of His Majesty's Service indefinitely than re-
enter it against his wishes.'[100] 'All arrangements', wrote Canning
on 5 July, 'are for the present at an end . . . If ever it be resumed,
it must be on *their* part of course – and I must judge of a new
matter.'[101]

Liverpool wrote a tortured letter to Bathurst, saying that the
King could exclude someone from his Cabinet, but it was most
unwise. There were no public grounds to justify such exclusion.
'You say that there is nothing in the present state of Europe that
makes *Mr Canning's* services necessary – I would ask whether in
the internal state of this country there are not many circumstances
which render it highly advisable at least that the Government
should have the assistance of every person of great talents and
sound principles who can be obtained.' Furthermore there was
fear of the accusation: 'Mr C. out of office by the Personal
Exclusion of the King, agreed by the Government.'[102]

The autumn found the issue still hanging fire and the King
still in a foul humour with the Government. On the King's return
from Ireland in September, Liverpool was even refused an
audience with him.[103] Mrs Arbuthnot recorded in September that
the King was resolved that nothing would induce him to admit
Canning to the Cabinet again.[104] Liverpool told Arbuthnot that
if the King was determined to break with his ministers, it would
be over Canning.[105]

A temporary solution appeared to Liverpool in the form of
providing Canning with a position which did not bring him into
contact with the King until such time as Hastings left India. The
King certainly welcomed the Indian proposition, or, as Canning
wrote, 'jumped at the solution', despite Hastings' obvious unwillingness to resign.[106] However, Liverpool and Wellington were
anxious for Canning's return to office. The Duke was particularly
worried by the threat posed to the country by the Whigs, bringing
in their train the Radicals who would dominate them and subvert
the Government.[107] In fact, Canning was unlikely to accept any
such humiliating proposition. Ellis bet Titchfield at 'three to one
on' that Canning would refuse it.[108] In practice the project
collapsed in confusion as Canning realized that he could do
nothing against the firm opposition of the King and began to try
to reconcile himself to the prospect of India.

From the financial point of view the project was exceedingly attractive. The Governor-General's salary was £25,000 p.a., exchanged at a rate which made it worth £30,000. This could be compared with the sum of £5,400 paid to a Secretary of State. Canning's own financial position had gradually deteriorated. An income of £3,000 per year on leaving office in 1809 had become £740 by 1821 if he allowed for all the interest payments due to his wife.[109] The purchase of his farm at Deeping had been a major financial mistake, but fundamentally his income was not sufficient to support his station. Furthermore, he felt deeply that he had an obligation to leave his wife's fortune in the same state as he found it. In liquid form it was now only a sixth of its former extent. In addition, he had interminable requests from his mother's family for assistance, to which he replied by upbraiding them for ingratitude and acknowledging no obligations except to his mother herself. In addition, he pointed out that his own Irish estate was encumbered and inalienable.[110]

Two problems existed. The first was the attitude of Hastings who, after first intimating through his agent Colonel Doyle that he wished to resign, then proceeded to exhibit wounded dignity and suggested that Canning and the Court of Directors, with whom he had never been popular, were plotting against him. It eventually became clear early in 1822 that India was to be available. The second problem was the attitude of Joan, who was very averse to the whole project, as was his daughter Harriet. His wife's brother-in-law, the Duke of Portland, was nevertheless clear that from a financial point of view he had a duty to his children to take the position.[111]

Underneath, Canning had a deep reluctance to leave the British political scene and was relieved to tell Leigh in December 1821 that he did not have to say yes or no for a year.[112] To Joan he wrote that he would not go to India unless she wanted it – but he did point out the awful state of his own financial affairs.[113] In fact there seemed little alternative. The King seemed prepared to facilitate his going to India or indeed anywhere.[114] Castlereagh, it was said, was keen to have him go immediately rather than have his help in the ensuing session.[115] In April 1822 Canning had the almost unique honour to be adopted unanimously by the Court as Governor-General and his departure seemed certain. He only wished to wait in England to explain affairs to Hastings, who had been offended by the way matters had been handled, or perhaps for something to turn up.

Meanwhile, Canning continued his parliamentary life. In April 1822 he strongly attacked Lord John Russell's plan for parliamentary reform in a speech replete with classical allusion.[116] He also successfully introduced a bill to allow Catholic peers to sit in the House of Lords, but this was eventually thrown out in the upper chamber by 171 votes to 129.

Early in August 1822 Castlereagh, or Lord Londonderry as he had become, cut his throat in a fit of mania in which he believed he was being blackmailed as a homosexual. Canning clearly saw that this would have enormous implications for the Government, but nevertheless continued as normal, going up to Liverpool for the round of 'convivial duties' connected with his coming departure.[117] The onus now fell heavily on Liverpool. Canning wrote to his wife that the Prime Minister's weakness was manifest. Indeed, if anyone were to drop down in a fit or was shot in his presence, he would sneak away in his carriage, perhaps calling another to attend, 'Yet he and he alone has the confidence of the country – and there is no other member of the Government upon whom I could for a moment rely.'[118]

On 25 August Canning wrote to Granville discussing 'what the K and his faction may do'. He commented that Eldon would try to prevent any proposal. He still thought he would go to India, for 'there is nothing in domestic politics to tempt one – and as to foreign politics – what is there remaining but the husk without the kernel?'[119] In fact the King had already written to Liverpool insisting that Canning still go to India. On 3 September Canning wrote that office would be untenable for any length of time because of 'the enmity of the King, the jealousy of the colleagues and the real and incurable difficulties of the country ... the acceptance will plunge me back again into the miserable circle of worn-out politicians from which I thought I had escaped'. Against this, there was 'Toddles' to consider, who was most unwilling to go to India – but 'she must make her hay, for my sun will not shine very long'.[120]

Meanwhile Liverpool, Wellington and Peel were convinced of the necessity of bringing in Canning to add strength to the Government. Peel recommended strongly to the King that Canning get all of Castleragh's inheritance – *viz.* the Foreign Office and the lead in the House of Commons. The King accepted the latter but demurred at the former.[121] Wellington wrote to the King on the seventh, stressing the need for Canning's accession to the Government. On all lines of policies he was in agreement with other ministers, and to the King's arguments about honour he replied that the King's honour consisted in 'acts of mercy and grace'.[122] On 8 September the King agreed, and Canning was offered the two positions. 'I would that the offer had not come,' he wrote to his mother; 'The sacrifice of personal interest which I make to public duty is enormous.' As to expenses, he said later, 'the continuance in such an office . . . is private ruin.' [123] The King reconciled himself to the worst with a good grace, and received Canning in a friendly interview on the sixteenth. One cannot really believe that Canning was distressed at the outcome of events.

Canning's political enemies were by no means so pleased. If Canning were to have all that Londonderry possessed, wrote Grey, 'it is in fact giving him the Government of the country.'[124] The Speaker was worried by his Catholic principles which 'must be mischievous to the constitution if he persists in them, of which, nevertheless, from his recent speech at Liverpool, there may be some doubts.'[125] Mrs Arbuthnot wrote that 'Mr Canning is a sort of volcano. We never have been and never shall be free from intrigues while he remains among us.'[126]

One of the anxieties to anyone aware of Canning's past history was that he would try to use his entry to the Government to force a re-construction of the Government along lines agreeable to himself. Liverpool wrote to Arbuthnot that 'Canning assured me he had no object but Huskisson and Backhouse. It is not however the less material that he should be warned against the danger of any attempts such as those meditated on former occasions.'[127] In an undated draft of 1822, Canning wrote to his wife: 'Do not let us fall into the traces of 1812 dearest love! The fatal decision which blasted all my prospects – threw away the goodwill of the Sovereign, the Ministry, and the House of Commons, and for-feited for me the most splendid situation in this country – in Europe – and in history, was founded upon a few cross words, and cold looks operating upon a temper vexed and tired with conflicting discussions.'[128]

In practice, however, Huskisson proved a problem. In mid-

1821 dislike of government arrangements had induced him to attempt to submit a threatened resignation through Canning until sharply told by Canning himself that this was not the proper procedure.[129] Now he showed himself not satisfied with the Presidency of the Board of Trade unless it carried with it a seat in the Cabinet. This, Huskisson told Canning on 3 October, would be wholly unacceptable.[130] Liverpool declared that no-one could have behaved worse than Huskisson, in 'endeavouring to force himself into a Cabinet against the wishes of the King and his own friends'.[131] Wellington was angry at Canning, suspecting he had not spoken earlier about Huskisson's determination to be in the Cabinet so as to force Liverpool to admit him. An inter-related problem was the future of Nicholas Vansittart, Chancellor of the Exchequer. Liverpool respected him, but Canning urged on Huskisson that Vansittart's removal was such a public object that he would never be forgiven if he upset the arrangement by insisting on an alternative involving himself.[132] In fact, Vansittart was replaced by Frederick Robinson, later to be Canning's successor as Prime Minister; but Liverpool wrote to Vansittart saying his own career would not be of much longer duration, and as he did not want to see Vansittart left out in the cold, he offered him the Chancellorship of the Duchy of Lancaster.[133]

Ellis added his influence, pressing Huskisson to recollect Canning's 'fatal mistake' of 1812, only to get a reply indicating that Huskisson was thinking of giving up politics altogether.[134] Finally Canning wrote on 3 January saying that the King had no objection to Huskisson personally, but was only worried at the size of the Cabinet. Huskisson accepted the inevitable in an ungracious manner;[135] he little thought, wrote Canning to Arbuthnot, 'when he was kicking and struggling, how other people's feelings were to be tried'.[136]

Canning's decision to stay in Government raised the problem of his parliamentary seat. On 17 September Hollinshed had written to him saying he could be returned again 'without any trouble from our respectable opponents'.[137] Gladstone urged him not to leave until the next general election.[138] Canning replied that he did not want to continue as he would be less efficient and less impartial, though, if they insisted, he would remain.[139] As his successor he suggested Huskisson, at which Gladstone, who had been canvassing support for himself, immediately withdrew.[140]

The nomination was kept fairly quiet till May when Gladstone introduced Huskisson to an enthusiastic reception at the Canning and Backbone Clubs. Huskisson was returned in an easy victory over Sefton's heir, Lord Molyneux, by 236 votes to 31.

Canning found himself a seat at Harwich, a seat far less demanding on its member being heavily dominated by the Government. Here he succeeded Vansittart, raised to the peerage as Lord Bexley, creating a gap which Canning promised the non-electors of the town to fill.[141] The borough representation in fact required a great deal of work for Canning and his co-member J. C. Herries. There was a vast amount of patronage work, a great deal of it involving one Philip Hart whose father desired for him instant promotion to the rank of lieutenant. The correspondence on this question alone was interminable.[142] There were also normal local duties such as the contribution of £400 to the Church,[143] though both he and Herries refused to be Vice-Presidents of the local Bible Society. In 1825 Canning wrote to Melville at the Admiralty, 'I did not trouble you half so much on account of Liverpool as I am obliged to do on account of Harwich'.[144]

By the death of Castlereagh, Canning had finally achieved his ambition of combining a useful office with the lead in the Commons. Apart from anything else, this was an enormous work load to take on which undoubtedly contributed to his early death. Certainly Canning did not show much pleasure at his new eminence. To Frere he wrote that he had arrived at this position 'ten years too late for enjoyment, and perhaps for advantage to the country'. He often felt he wished he had taken the Indian job 'and wish myself governing some eighty or a hundred millions in the shades of Barrackpore'.[145] He was wrong. He would not have been happy away from the British political scene, for if Canning often felt difficulty in living with it, he would have found it quite impossible to live without it.

9

FOREIGN POLICY: THE REALITY OF POWER

Speaking at Liverpool on 30 August 1822, Canning declared:

> Gentlemen, in the times in which we live there is (disguise it
> how we may) a struggle going on – in some countries an open,
> in some a tacit struggle – between the principles of monarchy
> and democracy. God be praised that in that struggle we have
> not any part to take. God be praised that we have long ago
> arrived at all the blessings that are to be derived from that
> which alone can end that struggle beneficially – a compromise
> and intermeddling of those conflicting principles.[1]

This attitude, however reasonable in the context of British
politics, was not widely shared by the continental statesmen with
whom Canning had to deal as Foreign Secretary. The French
Revolution had initiated a period of change in the borders and
constitutions of Europe. The victorious allies at Vienna, and particularly Alexander of Russia – gradually retreating into his own
mystical world – had set against this a rigid pattern; and it was
their intention, though one in which Britain did not participate,
to defend the new authoritarian status quo by force of arms. To
settle matters of general interest, a congress system was set up –
to which Britain was agreeable. This was part of the Quadruple
Alliance to which Britain was a signatory along with Russia,
Prussia and Austria. The only other obligation Britain accepted
was to prevent a revival of the Napoleonic system in France.

The differing attitudes of the former allies to the degree of
policing required by the new Europe was quickly revealed in
1820 when revolution broke out in Spain, Portugal, Naples and

Piedmont and constitutional regimes established. Britain looked on as that in Naples was destroyed by Austrian arms. Canning spoke strongly against intervention in defence of the Neapolitan constitution. 'Was it not romantic', he asked, 'to talk of embarking the country, not on account of duty, alliance, or obligation, but merely as a matter of sympathy and feeling, in a war in which she had neither interest nor concern?'[2] He nevertheless insisted that the argument did not apply to Spain where, troops, about to be despatched to Spanish America to attempt to suppress the secessionists had revolted under the leadership of one Riego and imposed a constitution on the unwilling Ferdinand VII. 'El Desiderado', as the King had been known during the French occupation of Spain, had little to be said for him on the credit side from the time he betrayed his own father in 1808 till his death, twenty-five years of blood and treachery later. The new regime established in Spain in 1820 was a running sore for Prussia, Austria and particularly Russia who feared the contagion of democratic principles and waited for an opportunity to restore the status quo.

Britain made it absolutely clear that it wanted no part in any nineteenth-century version of the Brezhnev doctrine. The Cabinet declared in May 1820 that 'The notion of revising, limiting, or regulating the course of experiments of casting anew their government in which several states of Europe were then engaged, either by foreign force or foreign council' was 'as dangerous to avow as impossible to execute'.[3] Britain's opposition prevented any immediate intervention in Spain and she refused to participate in the conference at Troppau in October 1820 which reasserted the rights of Russia, Prussia and Austria to overthrow revolutionary governments if necessary.

The government position which Canning inherited was thus one with which he was fully in accord. Above all, he had a full appreciation of the underlying turbulence of Europe – a 'heaving and struggling between conflicting principles'. The optimal position, he urged, was one of neutrality between them.[4]

Canning inherited a Foreign Office which, like other departments of state, was gradually becoming more professional, but where the system of appointment allowed for great dilatoriness on the part of officials. He described the attachés of his day as 'a couple of dozen of young men scattered over Europe owing no allegiance and taking diplomacy only as a subsidizing to amusement'. It was he who began the system of direct appointment of attachés by the Foreign Secretary and the system of paid attachéships, already foreshadowed by Castlereagh.[5] Many of the small staff in the Foreign Office were true professionals, starting as lowly clerks at £100 p.a. and gradually working their way up the system. The system was in a period of transition and one of the problems Canning and other ministers had to face was the mixed ability and enthusiasm of those under them.

As with other offices he had held, a major drag on Canning's time concerned patronage problems. The clamour was incessant and the jobs few. In 1825 he told Gladstone that there were 400 applications for consulships on his list.[6] Even the issue of passports was the personal responsibility of the Foreign Secretary, and one Canning took seriously. 'If *any* person may *claim* a passport,' he wrote to Lord Holland, 'with my discretion ends my responsibility. I should then open a small stall for distributing them at Charing Cross.' If he gave them indiscriminately to all comers, he might as well not give them at all.[7]

There were two main aspects of the international situation which faced Canning on his assumption of office in September 1822. Britain had agreed to join in a Congress at Verona which had as its main purpose a solution to the problems which had arisen in the Near East with the revolt of the Greeks against the Turks in April 1821. This was a question of enormous interest to Russia, which had traditionally cast its geopolitical eyes to Turkey and the Mediterranean and also because the Greeks were their co-religionists. It had already been decided that Wellington represent Britain at the congress. The other problem was a worsening of the Spanish situation, where Ferdinand's failure to re-establish his personal rule had driven the country into the hands of democratic extremists who seemed likely to lead it into war with France.

The possibility of intervention in Spain hung over the Verona Congress. Pressing most strongly for it was Czar Alexander who was prepared to march an army of 150,000 into Piedmont to be used as required to maintain stability in Europe, but Mettenich and the other allies balked at something which could constitute a threat to themselves. It was nevertheless clear to Wellington that secret negotiations had been proceeding between the French and Ferdinand VII and the Spanish royalists.[8]

In France the Government was under strong pressure for war. The British Ambassador, Charles Stuart, analyzed the Chamber of Deputies as consisting of 144 extreme right, 115 centre right, 97 extreme left and 66 centre left. The Government of the moderate right was thus in a weak position to face the clamour from the extreme right for war, and furthermore Stuart argued, they intended to conduct the next election in a spirit of friendship to that extreme right.[9] Meanwhile, the Prime Minister Villèle repeated his opinion that the summoning of an extraordinary session of the Cortes in Spain must be followed by a declaration of war against France, though that did not in fact occur. Hearing in Paris the clamours against Villèle's moderation, as well as reports of French troop movements on the Spanish border, Stuart became gloomy as to the prospects for peace.[10]

On 20 October the French minister submitted a paper asking the allied powers firstly, if France should need to withdraw her minister from Spain, would the other allied powers do the same? Secondly, if France should be at war with Spain, what countenance would the allies give her? And thirdly, if France required it, what assistance?

The continental allies replied that they too would withdraw their ministers and would give France every countenance and assistance. Britain refused to reply to a hypothetical case, and would not be party to any note to Spain containing menaces as regards its internal affairs. The Czar wanted a treaty among the allies before they left Verona, and for the Spanish Government to be informed 'that the continuance of the Spanish system is inconsistent with the happiness and prospects of Spain, and the safety of France or of any other country in Europe'.

Wellington wrote that Austria and Prussia did not want war but could not separate themselves from Russia and felt they must be consistent with their former attitude to Naples. He feared that the allied ministers sitting together in Paris would act with the ultraroyalists in pushing France towards war. The only alternative was 'moderate but firm language' towards Spain.[11]

Clearly a variety of domestic and international factors were leading to intervention. On 19 November Wellington wrote that the Austrian minister had expressed more strongly than before 'his sense of Necessity that the three great Military Powers should pronounce against the Spanish Revolution and should withdraw their ministers'.[12]

Tension was now rising between Britain and the allies, especially as it was feared that Britain was fitting out a naval armament for the West Indies which would take over Cuba. Canning insisted that it was to protect British trade from pirates acting under the flags of Spain and her rebel colonies.[13] Villèle was also worried by what Canning called the 'wholly unfounded' allegation that Britain was secretly treating with Spain and getting commercial advantages in return for her assistance at Verona.[14] Wellington referred to this distrust as being general amongst the allies there.[15]

In Paris, Villèle was meanwhile putting forward a variety of conditions for peace. He declared that he did not care what system of government operated in Spain, but insisted on the security and life of the King, the mediation of France between Spain and her colonies and permission to convey a prince to Mexico or Peru, with the presumable intent of establishing a Bourbon dynasty.[16] Canning objected strongly to the tone Villèle had taken, especially where he declared France would not submit to territorial or commercial advantages to Great Britain, especially, added Canning, as Britain had not declared it would not submit to the establishment of a French force in Spain.[17]

Meanwhile, Britain did its best to produce a conciliatory attitude to Spain by sending Lord Fitzroy Somerset with suggestions as to constitutional reform, and an insistence that Britain would not go to war in their defence. The overture came to nothing, for after the allies had withdrawn their ministers from Madrid, Spain took a firm stand and refused all concessions to France. Chateaubriand the French foreign minister, instructed the Spanish Ambassador to leave.

That war was inevitable was made clear by the French King's speech of 28 January. 'A hundred thousand French are ready to march,' he declared. 'Let Ferdinand be free to give his people the institutions they cannot hold but from him,' at which words it is said that the Russian Ambassador, Pozzo di Borgo, joyfully threw his hat in the air.[18]

By demonstrating both the seriousness of the war risk and the odiousness of the principles in vogue on continental Europe, the speech provoked a strong reaction in Britain and there were voices urging war.

Canning still continued to work anxiously for peace. He told Bagot in St Petersburg to try and get the Emperor to use his influence at Paris for peace, because the grounds now cited by France were quite different from those provided for in the defensive engagements laid down in the Procès Verbal agreed by the continental allies at Verona.[19]

At home, the Government put forward a stronger line in the King's Speech in February lest their weakness might precipitate hostilities.[20] Public opinion was certainly very hostile to the French Government and the Spanish King. As Canning had pointed out in the previous year, if Mettenich was as ill-advised to put in conflict the two abstract principles of monarchy and democracy, 'he could not have done it with more disadvantage than in the person of Ferdinand VII.'[21] Canning tried to imply abroad that public opinion at home might force them into war, and publicly spoke of the possibility of the latter in a speech at Harwich on 11 February.[22]

In fact, the British Government did not intend a war which could embroil her with all Europe. Reconciling herself to the inevitability of events, Britain confined herself to laying down certain conditions for French action: that she did not establish a permanent military occupation of Spain, that she did not take over any Spanish colonies and that Portugal was inviolate.[23]

The Duc d'Angoulême had already left Paris to command the French forces, and the invasion commenced in early April. There was little resistance and Madrid fell quickly, though Cadiz held out for a few months. Restored to his full power Ferdinand showed his vengeful nature by executing his political opponents to an extent which horrified the French. It fell to Canning to defend government policy in Parliament on 14 April, expressing the hope that Spain would emerge successful.[24] A censure motion was moved some days later but failed miserably.

Nevertheless these events cannot but be seen as a major diplomatic disaster for Britain. It should have been clear late in 1822 that a variety of forces were pushing France to war. She had the goodwill of the continental allies urging her on. Internally there were the ultra-royalists with their hatred of democracy as such. There was the historic desire of France to dominate the affairs of Spain and, above all, there was the wish by the Bourbon regime to prove itself to a nation which still remembered its Napoleonic triumphs. A more militant line by Britain before February 1823 when France was already committed might have stayed the allies in their course and allowed British pressure within Madrid to produce an acceptable settlement. By making it fairly clear that Britain would not go to war, Canning had thrown away the ace before the start of the game.

There were many who applauded his conduct. Frere rejoined that Britain had been kept out of what would have been called 'Canning's War'.[25] The King would certainly have been hostile to a more militant attitude and as late as 17 April warned Canning to be 'extremely cautious' in his language.[26]

To Frere Canning wrote, 'I do not deny that I had an *itch* for war with France, and that a little provocation more might have scratched it into an eruption.' However, better reason prevailed and he looked back on his actions with satisfaction. 'Never was the Country so completely satisfied with the course taken by Government.'[27] Three years later, however, he put a very different interpretation on events. Why, he replied to Ellis, did he not resist effectively in 1823? 'My answer is that I was *beaten* here – as Villèle was in his Cabinet in France. Why did I not resign? Because I was not six months in office, because I had not yet met Parliament as minister – because my resignation would not have been understood . . . because "the love of Peace" was the nation's "passion".'[28]

One thing Canning did set himself to do after this crisis was to get rid of Stuart from Paris, for whom he had hardly a good word. In August he referred to one of his despatches as being 'not deficient in that obscurity which characterizes the great part of Sir Charles Stuart's communications'.[29] Liverpool said that 'a naked Recall – however just – appears to me to be full of difficulty.' A peerage, he added the next day, would be impossible for it would be a precedent. 'Consider what a number of poor Peers would be there added to the Peerage.' This would be a much greater evil. He should be offered St Petersburg on the assumption he would refuse.[30] Stuart was not in fact recalled till October 1824 and re-accredited the following year.

Another aftermath of the crisis was Canning's growing hostility to the French. In October 1823 he insisted, 'Surely, surely it is a general rule in time of peace to equal if not outnumber the French forces on all naval stations.'[31] His dislike for Villèle grew.

Huskisson said that 'Canning considers him as inoculated with much of the trickery and insincerity of the old French school wherever England is concerned ... by this respect he goes quite as far as Talleyrand in giving him credit for insincerity and *lying* as a part of his resources.'[32]

The Spanish crisis was a major rebuff for Canning and British diplomacy. If one accepts the account of events given by Canning to Ellis – and they were far too close for lies – then it was also a political setback for Canning. All of this goes to explain the readiness with which Canning in future crises was prepared to defy opinion at home and abroad and, if need be, threaten to resign to get his way. As for Spain, Canning could do little further except urge that government bounty should be given to refugees from Ferdinand's white terror. He could nevertheless ensure that in future he was the master rather than the victim of events.

The slave trade was an important question for Canning to face as Foreign Secretary, for he had the dual task of persuading British public opinion that he was doing his best to secure an international abolition and at the same time he had to negotiate with the governments concerned, all of whom were dragging their heels, at the least, on the issue. There can be no doubt as to Canning's own commitment to abolition, but it was to be over forty years after his death before changing attitudes and economic circumstances brought an end to the Atlantic trade.

When Britain abolished the slave trade in 1807 the omens seemed good for a general and universal abolition. Denmark had led the way by abolishing the trade in 1800, and the United States used the first opportunity allowed by the constitution to abolish it from 1808. The Spanish and French trades were interrupted by the war, so as to leave Portugal as the only power still vigorously maintaining the trade, and this was largely south of the equator. To the north, the trade was virtually suppressed.[33]

The ending of the war threatened a revival of the trade, particularly by France, and it became a major aim of British diplomacy to prevent this. The first Treaty of Paris of 30 May 1814 allowed the French slave trade to recommence for five years. Public opinion was mobilized by the African Institution, founded in 1807 in the interest of abolition, and according to Thomas Clarkson, about 1,370 petitions were signed by 1,375,000 persons.[34] The West Indian interest allied themselves with the abolitionists, for having been deprived of the trade themselves they clearly wanted to deprive their economic rivals of it as well. All others who had been opposed to the abolition in 1807 now linked hands against the trade, even including Eldon, whose 'opinion of the impolicy of what we have done makes me wish to prohibit it to other nations.'[35] The Government in 1814 was somewhat shocked by the intensity of feeling on the subject. Castlereagh commented: 'The nation is bent upon this object. I believe there is hardly a village that has not met and petitioned upon it; both Houses of Parliament are pledged to press it: and ministers must make it the basis of their policy.'[36] Public pressure on the Government to achieve a universal abolition was a most important diplomatic factor throughout the period.

The initial idea of ministers and abolitionists was to achieve abolition by international agreement. This at first seemed a promising approach as Czar Alexander was favourable and discussed the question in depth with Clarkson. However, as he became more interested in the problem of Jacobinism the Czar's enthusiasm waned. All that emerged was a pious declaration at the Congress of Vienna against the slave trade, reiterated at Verona eight years later. The non-slave trading powers were not interested in the question, and in 1817 the Austrian and Prussian Ambassadors in London were instructed not to take a line on the slave trade unfavourable to Spain and Portugal.[37] It thus became clear that it was only through the medium of bilateral negotiations that the trade could be abolished.

The public reaction to the first Treaty of Paris quickly convinced the British Government that more steps had to be taken to prevent the revival of the French slave trade. The Government started thinking in terms of offering the French compensation, and in September 1814 Liverpool instructed Wellington to offer the French an island, Trinidad, he suggested, or preferably two to three million pounds sterling.[38] Negotiations were slow as the French colonists, who were clamorous against the measure, were also ardent Bourbonites, and nothing had been achieved before the return of Napoleon from Elba. With the possible intention of winning British support he abolished the slave trade, which gave Britain the leverage to press abolition successfully on the Bourbons when they were restored for a second time. The trade was allowed a short period of grace.

However, abolition in law was to prove very different from abolition in fact. By the middle of 1814 the trade was getting under way again and developed rapidly after the restoration. Senegal and Gorée were given back to France and quickly became centres of the trade. 'The hoisting of the white [Bourbon] flag on the ramparts of St Louis and Gorée was at once the signal for commencing the slave trade without any limitation,' wrote one resident.[39] Not even the least appearance of secrecy was retained, declared another.[40]

The French did not wish to end the slave trade. 'They hate the abolition as Frenchmen', wrote Canning, 'because they know the measure was forced upon them by us; they dread the enforcement of it because they believe it would be advantageous to us.'[41] In 1822 Thomas Babington wrote, 'No Member of the Ministry cares a fig for the abolition of the slave-carrying trade while many are really interested in its continuance.'[42]

It was clear that merely getting a foreign government to pass an abolition law was insufficient. In addition continual pressure had to be brought to bear upon them to enforce it, and additional treaty arrangements were necessary to enable the British navy to police it. The development of the latter policy was eventually to turn the British navy into the major force suppressing the slave trades of all other countries. Canning in 1820 had not liked the idea of this policy. He wrote to his mother that Britain had no more right to punish foreigners for slave-trading than to sit in their courts for any other crimes.[43] In fact the so-called 'mixed commission' courts were already in existence, which gave British officials that right in certain cases.

The French Prime Minister in 1822 when Canning became Foreign Secretary was Villèle, a man with colonial connections, and the ministry was much less concerned than the preceding ministry of Richelieu to concede anything fresh on the subject, least of all a right to the British navy to search ships carrying the French flag. It was argued that public opinion alone would have prevented the latter concession,[44] and Villèle made it absolutely clear that the French King would never allow British vessels the right to arrest French vessels with slaves on board.[45]

The French flag thus became popular with slave traders of all

nations, who usually kept a variety of flags and papers to prove
the most convenient nationality as the case arose. Canning's main
problem was thus to persuade the French to tighten their laws
and to enforce them more vigorously. In fact Britain made interminable representations to the French without satisfaction. In
October 1822 Stuart complained of an outrage committed by the
crews of three French slavers against the boats of H.M.
Iphigenia.[46] In November Canning instructed him to complain
that a French brig of war had captured several vessels obviously
employed in the slave trade, but let them go because they did
not actually have slaves on board at the time.[47] In March 1823
Canning sent papers to the French foreign minister, Chateaubriand, to show that the trade was being carried on to a greater
extent than in any former period.[48] The Governor of Sierra Leone
reported that at Gallinas, fourteen French vessels received slave
cargoes in four months.[49]

In fact, the French were most loth to co-operate. French subjects were engaged in the trade, wrote Stratford Canning, 'to an
extent which reflects discredit, if not on the motives of the
French Administration, at least on the efficiency of its measures.'[50]
Stuart wrote that the defensive tone adopted by the French ministry and the way they gave their measures a character of concession
destroyed every hope of their making vigorous efforts.[51] In May
1823 Canning wrote a bitterly sarcastic letter implying that France
had no intention of giving up the trade.[52]

There were several reasons why France did not wish to abolish
the trade. It was extremely profitable, especially for the Atlantic
ports and above all Nantes. At the latter port, said Stuart, the law
was a dead letter.[53] The British consul there did not dare confide
information on the subject to the ordinary mail.[54] There was
French national pride which objected to moral dictation from the
other side of the Channel. This feeling was strongest on the right,
which dominated the Chamber of Deputies in this period. Finally
there was the feeling that Britain was merely being hypocritical.
It was felt that her real motive in wishing to suppress the trade
was to stop the underdeveloped lands in the West becoming
competitors to the British West Indies, much of which was suffering from soil exhaustion and consequently higher unit production
costs. The French were also aware that the British Governor of
Mauritius, Farquhar, had tolerated the slave trade in this highly

profitable sugar-growing area, and while Britain regarded the allegation as ludicrous, and instead attacked the Governor of the nearby French Îsle Bourbon (Reunion Island) for the same thing,[55] it was eventually shown to have been the case.

Canning got little satisfaction from continually asking his Ambassador to bring infractions of their own laws to the attention of the French Government, when it was obviously to so little effect. Stronger laws were enacted by the French in 1827, but the problem of enforcement remained. In fact, nothing was done till after the July Revolution when a Government of a very different complexion took office with the Duc de Broglie, a leading abolitionist, prominent. He was later Foreign Minister. The Anglo-French Conventions of 1831 and 1833 included a limited right of search but this had been out of the question in Canning's time.

In America, the abolition law of 1808 was not wholly effective, and it became British policy to press for more stringent measures. The most obvious of these was the mutual right of search, but this was wholly anathema to the Americans. In 1822 John Quincy Adams, the Secretary of State, declared it to be 'inadmissible from its very nature, degrading to the National character and only *calculate*d to make slaves of the American people'.[56]

The American Government and especially the Senate certainly included those who were secretly sympathetic to the trade, but unlike in France, there were many abolitionist officials. In Paris, the US minister, Albert Gallatin, worked very hard, partly on his own initiative, to get France to tighten her laws. On the other hand, Americans were very sensitive for historic reasons where questions of the British navy arose.

When Canning took office it was absolutely clear that America would not accept the idea of the right of search or mixed commission courts.[57] However, they were prepared to accept a compromise solution whereby the slave trade would be made piracy by the law of nations and offenders handed over to their own courts. In response Britain rushed a Slave Trade Piracy Act through Parliament, even though they regarded it as superogatory.[58] In fact, after the terms of the Treaty had been arranged, the Senate refused to agree to the inclusion of American coastal waters in its provision for a right of visit. Canning was furious at what he regarded as a gross breach of diplomatic etiquette, even by American standards, and commented: 'This mode of dealing with a Treaty is certainly not new on the part of the United States.'[59] The new Secretary of State, Henry Clay, tried to justify the change by a reference to a treaty with Colombia which said the same,[60] but almost immediately President Adams decided it was not expedient to continue the negotiation for the moment.[61]

At the same time, delicate commercial negotiations were going on between Britain and the United States. From 1822 Britain had relaxed the system of mercantile controls long imposed on the West Indies. They were to be allowed to export their produce directly to Europe in British ships and West Indian ports were opened to American ships. Unfortunately this did not satisfy the Americans, who insisted on the admission of their own goods to the colonies on the same terms as Britain's own. An American proclamation of 24 August 1822 proceeded to levy discriminatory duties against British ships from the West Indies. Negotiations were fairly long and drawn-out. 'With the Americans,' sighed Huskisson, 'to exhaust concession is only to provoke new and more preposterous pretensions.'[62]

In 1825 a British Act of Parliament allowed for the levying of counteracting tonnage and duties on vessels from countries which levied extra duties on British vessels and goods other than their own. When a settlement was near, complained Canning, 'the American Commissioner has put forth new pretensions which ours has very properly resisted.'[63] In fact negotiations did break down and under the 1825 Act, an Order in Council of July 1826 levied an extra ninety-four cents per ton on US ships.

Canning had a fairly large degree of disdain for the Americans, mainly because their diplomatic brashness offended his sense of how things ought to be done. He disliked the susceptibility of their foreign policy to popular pressure and regarded them as unreasonable people with whom to negotiate. Perhaps above all, he was looking into the future and not liking what he saw.

The return of Ferdinand VII to Spain removed any hopes that that country would willingly abolish the slave trade. However, on the British Government's initiative,[64] £400,000 was given to Spain in 1817, in return for an abolition treaty whereby Spain abolished the trade north of the equator immediately and that south of it by May 1820. Above all, the treaty established the mutual right of search between Britain and Spain, and mixed commission courts to try infractions of the law.

The full operation of the treaty came at the same time as the period of constitutional rule, and there was genuine hope of Spanish co-operation. Useful additional articles were added to the treaty, including one which allowed condemnation of a slaver without slaves on board.[65]

The return of absolutism thwarted these hopes. Furthermore, the existence in Cuba of large quantities of fertile virgin soil, ideally suited to the cultivation of sugar, made infractions of the law economically attractive, and the British Government got continual reports of these. In July 1824 the Ambassador, William A'Court, reported on two slavers fitting out in Madrid.[66] Canning told A'Court that the slave trade at Havana was carried on with 'publicity' and 'impunity'.[67] A large quantity of information came from the British commissioners in Havana, who complained of continual infractions. In 1824 Commissioner Kilbee told Canning there were forty-four departures from Havana for Africa, compared with ten in 1823. In less than two months, he said in February 1825, over nine vessels had landed 2,642 negroes at Cabanas or its immediate neighbourhood.[68]

The only slight success for the British Government, at least on paper, was to secure from the Duke of Infantado's new government in 1826 a ratification of the additional articles made 'during the latter end of the constitutional anarchy'.[69] In fact the only way to suppress the Spanish slave trade was pressure in Cuba. There, said Canning, he was sorry to observe the trade was as 'unremitting as ever'.[70] Such complaints as were made were met by either flat denials,[71] or counter-complaints of British complicity in the trade, or usurpation of power by the commissioners.[72]

Much of the blame would appear to rest with the Captain-General of Cuba, Francisco Dionisio Vives, but he clearly does not seem to have displeased his masters in Madrid by tolerating the trade. Canning wrote to Frederick Lamb, who had replaced A'Court as Ambassador: 'It is almost with despair of any useful results, that I direct you to communicate with the Duke del Infantado on this subject.'[73] Shortly afterwards he learned of the spectacular incident of the slave ship *Minerva*, chased into Havana by HM *Pylades*. When demand was made for examination by the mixed commission, the authorities refused this because the ship had not actually been captured. Meanwhile, 'Boats full of slaves were seen to hurry from this vessel.'[74]

The Portuguese slave trade might have been curtailed more effectively had Britain chosen to take advantage of her power and paramountcy there in the latter half of the French war. The failure cost £300,000 – the sum Britain agreed to pay Portugal for the abolition of the slave trade north of the equator in 1815. In 1817 Mixed Commission Courts were set up in Sierra Leone and Rio de Janiero. As Portugal did not abolish the trade south of the equator till 1836, it was spared for the period the lies and evasions to which the French and Spaniards had to resort. Had Portugal imposed a full abolition, there is no reason to believe it would have been effective. Enormous profits could be made by slave dealing in Brazil, and the governors of Portuguese settlements in Africa were large slave dealers.[75]

The declaration of Brazilian independence in 1822 gave Britain a potential influence. Wilberforce urged that a slave-trading Brazil should not be recognized. Canning qualified his agreement with this by declaring that the Government would have to take 'the commercial as well as the moral feelings of the country with us'.[76] In fact an abolition treaty was secured with Brazil in 1826 in accordance with which Brazil passed an Anti-Slave Trade Law in 1831, but a subsequent decline in the import of slaves is to be attributed rather to a depression of the sugar market.[77]

The continuance of the Portuguese and Brazilian slave trades provided further ammunition for those who wished to accuse Britain of hypocrisy in its attempts to abolish the trade. She might, said John Quincy Adams, 'by a word put a stop to the prosecution of that trade by Portugal and Brazil. Both of these countries must submit to the declared will of Great Britain.'[78] In fact, all Britain could have obtained was stronger legal guarantees which would probably have been worthless in the face of opposition from local officials. The economic forces behind the trade can be gauged from the estimate of a million slaves imported to Brazil between 1831 and 1870.[79]

Whereas many Spanish-Americans may have ignored British policy toward the slave trade, they regarded her formal recognition of the independence of the South American republics as the hall-

mark of their nationhood, and honoured George Canning himself
as its donor.

In 1822, most of Spanish America had to a large extent succeeded in asserting their independence from Spain, a fact which
had enormous repercussions on a Europe obsessed with the problems of legitimacy and the preservation of the status quo. Being
the most liberal of the European states, it was to Britain that the
nascent republics looked most for diplomatic support. Shortly
after assuming office, Canning was approached by Lord Holland
who told him that application had been made from the Columbian
republic to 'some private English gentlemen' to negotiate their
independence from the Spanish Government. 'At that time,' said
Lord Holland, 'they determined to communicate no part of it
to Lord Londonderry from a persuasion well- or ill-founded
that he was hostile to both these governments, or at least to any
amicable understanding between them.' The same did not apply
to Canning so they were willing to tell him.[80] Canning agreed to
see their communication but promised only that he would not
use it to the disadvantage of the Columbians.[81] A subsequent leak
was vigorously denied by Canning and proved to be the responsibility of Sir Robert Wilson, one of the persons approached by
the Columbians, who had told the French Prefect of Police.[82]

It was clear that the independence of Spanish America had
enormous repercussions for Britain. Liverpool himself had said
much earlier that it must alter Britain's whole commercial policy.[83]
Indeed Britain had already established a large number of links
with Spanish America by means of commercial houses scattered
throughout the country, a fact which did not go unnoticed in
continental Europe. In December 1822 Villèle told Liverpool that
France could not agree to the further extension of British commercial supremacy there. 'I confess', said Canning, 'I long to tell
M de Villèle . . . that we *will* trade with the late Spanish American
colonies, whether France likes it or not.'[84]

Canning's reaction was to try to evolve a common policy with
the United States which had already recognized Buenos Aires,
Mexico, Colombia and Chile. This was rendered difficult by the
large amount of mutual suspicion existing between the two
powers, especially because of Britain's uneasiness at possible
American ambitions in Cuba. Canning wrote, 'The possession by
the United States of both shores of the channel through which

our Jamaica trade must pass ... would amount to a suspension of that trade, and to consequent total ruin.'[85] One historian has commented that American policy in the 1820's 'was to maintain the Spaniards as tenants at will on the island until the rightful owner was ready to step in'.[86]

In practice negotiations with the United States broke down. America distrusted British intentions, and eventually insisted on an immediate recognition of Spanish-American independence. Canning was not prepared for this at that stage and turned to Europe, inviting the French minister, Polignac, to discuss the question. Potentially there were even more sources of distrust with France as both powers feared the military preparation of the other in the Caribbean. Melville, the First Lord of the Admiralty, feared 'that the secret views of the French Government may be at variance with their profession of moderation, and a desire to continue at peace'.[87]

The Conference between Canning and Polignac was held between 9 and 12 October 1823. Britain put four main points: she would assist negotiation between Spain and her colonies; she would be neutral in a conflict between them; she would view the intervention of a third party, on the Spanish side, as a new question; and finally, she could not bind herself not to recognize the independence of the Spanish-American Republics. Polignac agreed with Canning about the impossibility of restoring Spanish America to its former subjection. He also denied any intention on France's part to annexe any part of South America or to take any military part in the suppression of the republics.[88] Metternich had already acknowledged the unrealistic nature of any such project when he told Sir Henry Wellesley that Spain would be foolish to try to recover her colonies and would be well-advised to keep Cuba and use it as a channel for Mexican trade.[89]

Meanwhile the United States set its hand to the affair. For some time they had been worried by the turn of European politics. In 1821 the Czar had issued a 'ukase' prohibiting all foreign vessels from approaching within a hundred Italian miles of the north-west coast of America, the Aleutian and Kurile Islands and the east coast of Siberia. This extraordinary claim caused anger to Britain, and Canning wrote to Bagot in St Petersburg on the need for common action between Britain and the United States on the subject.[90] On top of this, America was appalled by the suppression of constitutional government in Spain, and the prospect, however remote, of a concerted attempt to restore Spanish power in her ex-colonies. The result was President Monroe's declaration to Congress of 2 December 1823 stating United States opposition to the interference of European powers in the affairs of the American continents. Canning was opposed to that part of the Monroe Doctrine which declared American opposition to any European establishment in non-occupied parts of the continent. However, the declaration for non-interference must have pleased him as he had previously sounded Rush about the disposition of the United States Government to join in any steps Britain might take to prevent a hostile enterprise on the part of European powers against Latin America.[91]

The Polignac Memorandum gradually became public in the first part of 1824. Copies were despatched to Latin America where it won for Canning the widest acclaim. Coming in conjunction with the Monroe Doctrine, it marked a watershed in the history of Latin America, for both the major land and the major maritime powers with which they were concerned now fundamentally recognized their independence.

British policy was causing unease in Europe. On the one hand she appeared to be moving towards a recognition of triumphant revolutionary principle; on the other she was suspected of secretly aiming at commercial advantage. Even Grey thought this when he told Lord Holland: 'When we now talk of recognizing the independence of South America we but too plainly show that we have no views but to our trading interests. In short the whole policy of our Ministers is that of stock-jobbers and commercial speculators.'[92] There was the difficult task of justifying British policy in continental Europe. Canning told his ambassadors to explain it, but not allow themselves to be provoked, and let feelings subside.[93]

Relations between Britain and Latin America were now excellent. Canning praised the Mexicans: 'They would give us anything we asked – but we asked nothing but the Abolition of the Slave Trade and they immediately proposed a law abolishing it.'[94] There were already British consular representatives in Latin America and in October 1824 commissioners were sent out to Mexico and Colombia to discover whether the commitment to independence was irrevocable, and to report on the internal and external security of those states. Lionel Hervey quickly provided satisfactory answers to these questions concerning Mexico, though there was some trouble with the indecisive and rather uninformative reports of Colonel Hamilton from Colombia.[95]

Canning meanwhile could get little satisfaction from Spain, whose new regime was not inclined to reconcile itself to the reality of the South American situation. An offer of mediation by Britain in January 1824 came to nothing, as did an offer of a naval guarantee for Cuba in return for recognition in May. As it was realized that the whole impact of Canning's policy could in the end lead to nothing but recognition, the opposition of the King became apparent. He did not wish to break ranks with his fellow monarchs. He regarded the Liberator Bolivar as a sort of trans-Atlantic version of the Irish nationalist, O'Connell.[96] Furthermore, his dislike of Canning spilled over into a rejection of his policies. A furious row occurred in April 1824 when Canning joined Whig politicians and representatives for the Latin American states at the Lord Mayor's Banquet. He had not wished to let the affair fall completely into Whig hands and had even urged Liverpool to attend, though the latter was 'out of town'. The King began intriguing with foreign ambassadors, indicating his dislike of his own Foreign Minister and anticipating his removal.

Meanwhile the first decisive step was taken in July 1824 in a move which meant effectively the recognition of Buenos Aires, the most settled of the Latin American countries and the one with which Britain had always had the closest links. On 23 July the Cabinet accepted a memorandum in favour of the negotiation of a commercial treaty and instructions to that effect were sent off in August.

The American colonies, Canning told Frere in the same month, were 'severed beyond all doubt from their respective mother countries for ever'.[97] The only question then remaining was what steps Britain should take in the light of this new situation, and, most importantly, Liverpool himself was coming round to the view that we should only 'consider our own interest, and that interest should lead us to establish an influence in the Spanish colonies as far as we can do it, consistently with good faith, and our past professions'.[98]

In this crisis, the French King Louis XVIII died and was succeeded by his more absolutist brother, Charles X, in whom Can-

ning judiciously expressed 'undoubting confidence'.[99] Personally
inconvenienced by being forced to cut short a trip to Ireland, and
politically by the fact of the new reign, Canning commented:
'Whatever may have been the merits of the K. to France's life, he
has effaced them all by the inopportuneness of the moment which
he has chosen for leaving it.'[100] George IV immediately sent the
Earl of Westmoreland, who shared his views on the South
American question, to discuss it with the new king.[101]

The Cabinet met for the first time in three months on 1 December 1824. Canning and Liverpool were now working together on
the South American question, and the latter supported the memorandum which the former had drawn up urging recognition. In
the minds of both of them it was clear that the recognition of
Spanish America partly resulted from and was intrinsically connected with the French occupation of Spain. Canning regarded
the attempts of Wellington, Westmoreland and Eldon to separate
the two questions as simply dishonest[102] at a time when Britain
was unable to get any assurances from the French about the
withdrawal of their troops. It was thus in his most famous speech
made a year later (12 December 1826) that Canning declared:
'Contemplating Spain, such as our ancestors had known her,
I resolved that if France had Spain, it should not be Spain with
the Indies. I called the New World into existence to redress the
balance of the Old.'

The other underlying diplomatic factor which weighed particularly heavily with Liverpool was the attitude of the United States.
In December 1824 Liverpool wrote to Wellington: 'I am con-
scientiously convinced that if we allow these new states to consolidate their system and their policy with the United States of
America, it will in a very few years prove fatal to our greatness,
if not endanger our safety.'[103]

However, France was the most immediate problem, and with
Granville confirming from Paris that the French would not withdraw from Spain, Liverpool and Canning managed to get the
agreement of most of the Cabinet to a memorandum urging the
recognition of Colombia and Mexico by way of commercial
treaties. Even Peel, who in the middle of the year had been hostile,
was now generally favourable, and Wellington was left to lead the
group of four other Cabinet 'ultras' in opposition to recognition.
The memorandum was then sent to the King whom Liverpool

saw and judged disinclined to make serious problems. Canning
wrote to Granville, 'The fight has been hard, but it is won. The
deed is done. The nail is driven. Spanish America is free; and if
we do not mismanage our matters sadly, she is English, and
Novus saeclorum nascitur ordo. You will see how nobly Liverpool
fought with me on this subject.'[104]

In fact the King attempted to upset the decision with the assistance of Wellington who, Canning felt, was behind the King's
change of heart, recognizing several of his phrases in an angry
letter received from Windsor. On 17 December the King wrote
to Wellington saying he intended to be 'very short and very
preremptory' with Canning. 'You are the only person in whom
I can completely confide, and the only one upon whom I do, and
that I can *entirely depend.*'[105] Furious with the turn of events,
Canning was dissuaded from a contemplated resignation by Liverpool, who urged that the important thing was that the King *did*
what they wanted and 'we ought to let him grumble a little for
consolation.' 'He saw that not once but twenty times the King
had wished and intended to get rid of him [Liverpool] and had
pledged himself to others to do so – That when he knew the K.
less he used to feel, as I do now, a determination to bring the
matter to a point; but that the K. always saved him the trouble, by
stopping short, just when the point came near.'

In fact, the King was reasonable when he saw Canning. When
Bathurst tried to say he was for recognition of Mexico but against
that of Colombia, the King shut him up after the first part of his
sentence. He would, thought Canning, be gradually reconciled,
even though 'it sanctions what he conceives to be a revolutionary
principle. It cuts him off from his dearly beloved Metternich . . .
and it exposes him to the risk of having a cocoa-nut coloured
Minister to receive at his Levee'.[106]

On the 31 December 1824 Canning wrote to British ministers
abroad giving them information about the commercial treaties
with Mexico and Colombia. Chile was not being so recognized
because of insufficient information, nor Peru because a large
Spanish garrison was still holding out there. He insisted that
'Spain has refused to listen to repeated offers of mediation on the
part of Great Britain, although uniformly accompanied by conditions eminently favourable to Her Interests.'[107] Canning then
wrote to the British ministers in Latin America giving them full

power to treat and put commercial intercourse 'on a regular and permanent footing' provided they could satisfy the Government on the finality of the renunciation of the political connection with Spain and on internal and external security.[108] The Colombian representatives were authorized to waive the provision for free worship of British subjects if it really did constitute a threat to internal security, while entering into a secret article looking forward to the building of Protestant churches when these difficulties were removed.[109]

> Canning described his triumph to Frere on 8 January 1825: I did, while I lay in my bed at the Foreign Office with the Gout knawing my great toe, draw the Instructions for our Agents in Mexico and Columbia which are to raise those States to the rank of Nations.... The thing is done ... an act which will make a change in the face of the World almost as great as that of the discovery of the Continent now set free. The Allies will fret; but they will venture no serious remonstrance. France will fidget, but it will be with a view of hastening after our example. The Yankees will shout in triumph, but it is they who lose most by our decision.

The great danger of the world was a division between Europe and America, republican and monarchist. Now Britain had stepped in and planted herself in Mexico. If, he added, he had been turned out on the issue, he would have returned with all the commerce and manufacturing interests of England at his heels. He must nevertheless be cautious, as his opponents might want revenge.[110]

On 31 December, he had written to his wife that tomorrow he must see the allied ambassadors 'to hear what they will not like to hear – our determination respecting South America.' 'The Holy Allies were grumpy of course,' he added on the third, 'but took the thing better than I expected.'[111]

The reception of the news in the European capitals could hardly have been expected to be ecstatic. In Berlin the Prussian Minister Count Bernstorff told Clanwilliam that he regretted the decision for widening the rift between Britain and her continental allies, for extinguishing the hope (which he must have realized was ludicrous) of a pro-Spanish reaction in the colonies, and for its effects in St Petersburg and Vienna on discussions concerning the Greek question.[112] Later, Bernstorff apologized for the lang-guage of Baron Maltzahn, the Prussian minister in London, on the question. Clanwilliam took this with a pinch of salt, believing that Maltzahn had no other instructions but 'that of conforming himself in every respect to the Austrian and Russian ambassadors'.[113] He blamed the reaction on the acceptance of Metternich's view that Britain would not act so quickly.[114]

In fact the issue was not to be settled so easily as Canning had thought in early January. The King himself was in constant contact with foreign ambassadors on the question and despite the fact that Wellington had now reconciled himself to events, was still trying to upset the decision, which he did by writing to Liverpool on the subject on 27 January. Fortunately the strong attitude taken by Canning and Liverpool, who even reached the point of reading out letters of resignation, swung the Cabinet round to universal support, and in Canning's words, put the question 'beyond the reach of shuffling and change'. 'Cabinets – Cabinets – Cabinets,' he wrote at 6.30 pm on 1 February, 'day after day and till about this hour'. The King's activities 'cost us and lost us three whole days – besides our temper'. There was in addition the problem that the King had been seeing the Russian and Austrian ambassadors, Esterhazy and Lieven. If it went on, said Canning, he would have to warn him that he had no constitutional right to see foreign ministers except in Canning's presence.[115]

In fact the King, warned by Wellington of Canning's popularity and incapable of forming a Ministry agreeable to himself without Liverpool, had no alternative but to back down, though ungraciously. 'I hear that though very angry,' wrote Canning on the fourth, 'HM does not intend to return any answer. He therefore will *not* tell me that I have lost his confidence. So we shall jog on.'[116] In fact the battle was over. On the tenth, Canning wrote to his wife that Esterhazy had written to Metternich saying that Canning's policy was fixed and irrevocable, that the country would bear no other, and that Metternich must make up his mind whether he would come close to England on Canning's grounds or throw himself at the feet of Russia. He nevertheless added a codicil that Esterhazy might have shown him this letter in order to mystify George and Stratford Canning.[117]

The whole issue might have blown up into a major constitutional crisis. Metternich, wrote Canning, 'the greatest rogue and

liar on the continent, perhaps in the civilized world', had been
intriguing with Lieven to try to change the policies of the British
Government by getting rid of him. If forced, Canning went on,
he would have resigned and declared in the House of Commons
that he had been driven out by the Holy Alliance. He would have
attacked the relationship of foreign ministers with the King, and
'If after such a denunciation and the debates which would have
followed, the Lievens and Esterhazys did not find London too
hot for them, then I know nothing of the present temper of the
English nation.'[118]

One of the problems underlying the whole crisis was the attitude
of France. In December Canning had written to Bathurst that
the French Government 'have but two rules of action; to thwart
us whenever they know our object, and when they know it not,
to imagine one for us, and set about thwarting that.'[119] The problem was a delicate one. War with France, said Liverpool rather
strangely, would be war with the United States, and this would
be very dangerous before we had established ourselves with the
South American states.[120] There was the additional complication
that France still nurtured hopes of reconquering Haiti, independent now for over twenty years. Joan Canning, who was in Paris,
kept contact with Villèle. 'M.O.L [my own love]'s conference
with V[illèle] has done more good than fifty conferences of Allied
Ministers.' 'I have no doubt', he added, that 'Russia will come
threatening upon him. But he may surely appeal to the feelings
manifested in France – and to the physical impossibility of
making any impression on us.' Meanwhile, Britain would try to
keep the new states in a temper to receive France kindly. Again,
on 9 March, he asked his wife to explain his views to Villèle.[121]
In fact there was little France could do about the British initiative
in Latin America, despite their fears of the grand commercial
and geo-political ambitions of their ancient rival.

British recognition of the Latin American states went ahead,
and in November 1825 Señor Hurtado of Colombia arrived as
the first accredited envoy. 'And so behold,' wrote Canning, 'the
New World established, and if we do not throw it away, ours.'[122]

A slight problem existed regarding the recognition of Brazil,
for here Britain enjoyed friendly relations with metropolitan
Portugal which she was most loath to jeopardize. 'We are convinced', Canning had written in 1823, 'that in some shape or other

Brazil will maintain its independence.'[123] Canning had two distinct interests here. Brazil was a monarchy under the son of the Portuguese King, which had nevertheless declared its independence. He argued that 'the conservation of monarchy in any portion of South America will tend to break the shock of that inevitable divorce by which the New World was about to be divorced from the Old.' This was a typical Canning argument, but more practical was the consideration that Britain's commercial treaty with Brazil expired in February 1825 and its abrogation would be 'a matter of the most serious detriment to our merchants.'[124] Britain's main aim in this conflict was to play a mediating role between Brazil and Portugal. To this end, Sir Charles Stuart was accredited on a special mission to Brazil early in 1825. This, said Canning, would surprise everybody and astound Villèle. 'I consider it as the greatest coup that was ever devised.'[125] To the European powers, Canning insisted through his cousin Stratford that the fullest possible separation existed in fact between Portugal and Brazil, and that Britain wanted to narrow a breach for which she was not responsible.[126]

The French also had their fingers in the same pie, and their representative offered to recognize Brazilian independence in return for commercial privileges for France.[127] It was nevertheless Stuart who obtained the treaty in August 1825 which was ratified in Lisbon in November. This was a triumph for Canning in asserting Britain's world diplomatic role and was to be followed shortly by a commercial treaty with the slight embarrassment that the terms of the instructions of Lord Ponsonby, who was sent to negotiate, were revealed in a London paper before he left Plymouth.[128] In addition Britain gained certain engagements regarding the abolition of the slave trade, albeit in practice they proved fairly nominal.

It is to Canning's credit that in the crisis over Latin America he was prepared to reconcile himself more quickly than any others to a wholly new status quo. In addition, it must be said that underlying his own policies was a highly realistic assessment of Britain's political and commercial advantage yet combined with appreciation of the reaction of others. There was also the fear of the activities of other powers. 'We shall never', wrote Canning in August 1823, 'acquiesce in the establishment of a preponderating influence in these colonies; much less in the appropriation of any portion of them by any other power.'[129] Above all perhaps, was Canning's underlying distrust and dislike of the policy of the United States. In July 1826 he wrote to Liverpool 'that the ambitious and overbearing views of the States are becoming daily more developed, and better understood in this country'.[130]

To complete his triumph, Canning was able to congratulate himself that he had acted honourably throughout. Britain might, he told his wife, have made any bargain it pleased with the South American states as a condition of recognition. In fact, all they had wanted was to put themselves on as favourable a footing as everyone else. She had even been willing to give 'a decided priority to Spain' if she had agreed.[131]

In practice, the political and commercial effects of Britain's actions were great. British trade and investment in South America developed rapidly and has remained an important aspect of the nations' economic life. Above all, for Canning, as directly responsible for South American independence and the surge in trade, he had fully revenged himself for the humiliation of 1823 abroad and asserted himself, with Liverpool's help, as irreplaceable at home.

In April 1821 Greece followed the Danubian principalities of Moldavia and Wallachia into revolt against the Turks and appealed to the courts of Europe for support:

> We invoke therefore the aid of all civilized nations of Europe, that we may the more properly attain to the goal of a just and sacred enterprise, reconquer our rights, and regenerate our unfortunate people. Greece, our mother, was the lamp that illuminated you; on this ground she reckons on your active philanthropy. Arms, money, and counsel, are what she expects from you. We promise you her lively gratitude, which she will prove by deeds in more prosperous times.[132]

By the time Canning took office in 1822, Sultan Mahmud had wholly failed to suppress his rebel subjects and a vicious war was in progress replete with atrocities on both sides. Not unnaturally, the affair had international consequences of the first importance. Russia hovered on the sidelines, sympathetic to her Greek co-religionists and politically hostile to the Turks, but unwilling to sanction the principle of rebellion. Austria, fearing the principle

of national independence as wholly inimical to the entire existence
of a multinational empire such as her own, used its diplomatic
powers to delay events in the hope that eventually the Turks'
military success would bring an automatic solution to the problem. In Britain, the issue was complicated by the existence of a
large amount of popular feeling for the Greeks with lobbying
power through the establishment of a London Greek Committee
and most famously witnessed by the death of Lord Byron at
Missolonghi fighting for the Greeks.

Quickly disillusioned by the obvious Russian unwillingness to
participate in the conflict on her behalf, many Greeks looked to
England in general and Canning in particular for support. He was
known to be a bitter enemy of Metternich and sympathetic to
South American Independence. What they underestimated was
the high priority in British foreign policy given to the preservation
of friendly relations with the Turks.

Canning was torn between conflicting aims. On one hand, he
did not want to see a military defeat from the Greeks. On the
other, the severance of diplomatic relations between Russia and
Turkey raised the possibility of war between these powers which
could be dangerous in numerous ways, not the least of which
being the establishment of a strong Russian domination over the
Turkish Empire such as was temporarily brought about by the
Treaty of Unkiar Skelessi ten years later. All these influences
impelled Canning to play a mediating role.

Apart from the Greek question, there were strong differences
between Russia and Turkey over the principalities of Wallachia
and Moldavia and the Black Sea. In Constantinople, it was the
task of the British Ambassador Strangford to effect a reconciliation, but apart from the enigma of Russia's real aim there was a
problem in persuading the Porte to adopt measures to deprive the
Russians of an excuse for war. Granville declared that he was
controlled by the fanaticism of his subjects.[133]

Strangford's negotiations in Constantinople continued through
the summer of 1823, keeping Nesselrode, the Russian foreign
minister in touch with their progress.[134] To Metternich's horror,
Britain had meanwhile granted belligerent rights to the Greeks.
Canning justified the latter by declaring: 'The character of
Belligerency is not so much a principle, as a fact: a certain degree
of force and consistency, acquired by any mass of Population

engaged in war, entitles that population to be treated as a belligerent.'[135]

Metternich himself was playing a delaying game, fundamentally wanting a settlement of the non-Greek issues involved in order to avoid a Russo-Turkish war, while delaying the Greek question until the Turks had solved it militarily. He declared that he saw no point in a Russian diplomatic presence in Constantinople until Russia's first pretensions in the Black Sea were solved, while the Greek question should be solved by the allies in concert after the return of a Russian minister to the Turkish capital.[136]

Meanwhile the Czar met the Austrian Emperor at Czernowitz and promised to send a representative to Constantinople, while taking no steps on the Greek question till after he had consulted the other European powers.[137] Canning wrote urgently to Strangford forbidding him to attend the meeting. He was becoming increasingly suspicious of Russian motives, blaming the influence of Tatischev over the Czar. They would, he felt, try to break off the negotiations, first over the principalities, and if that failed, on the Greek question.[138] He nevertheless gave a warm welcome to the Russian intention to restore direct relations with Turkey when he learned of it. He had already made it clear that Strangford could not go on indefinitely conducting Russian diplomacy, while the negotiations were protracted until the war party at St Petersburg gained the upper hand.[139]

In January 1824 the Czar produced a memorandum on the Greek question urging the division of the country into three autonomous principalities over which the Turks would possess rights of garrison and tribute. A similar arrangement already existed in Moldavia and Wallachia. In addition, he invited the European powers to a conference on the question, which Canning determined to boycott until the Russian promise to send a representative to Constantinople was realized. This took a longer time than anticipated, as Turkish troops were slowly withdrawn from the principalities. Nevertheless, the Turks reacted less violently to the Greek memorandum than might have been expected and a minister was nominated in August, though not sent.

Meanwhile, to Canning's delight, the Greeks themselves rejected the Czar's memorandum and asked for British assistance. This rebuff to continental diplomacy was such as could have been expected to strengthen Canning's own resolution. He reiterated his insistence on the presence of a Russian ambassador at Constantinople and joined to it a demand that Russia would declare that it would not use force against the Turks. Russia's reaction was to break off communications with Britain on the Greek question.[140]

In February 1825 Canning defended British policy. Britain was not prepared to accept the mere nomination of a Russian minister at Constantinople for the fact of establishment. Indeed British envoys declared abroad that this was regarded as a matter 'of national faith and honour' from the moment Strangford had been authorized to announce it at Constantinople. He stressed the importance of the rejection of the Russian plan by the Greek provisional government and poured scorn on Nesselrode's claim that this did not represent the wishes of the Greeks.[141] A plan anathema to both belligerents could hardly be the basis of a settlement.

In November 1824 Canning wrote to Sir Henry Wellesley that Britain engaged in the Greek-Turkish question not so much for hope of a successful issue as to support Metternich in his endeavour 'so to manage it as to render it harmless'.[142] By December his attitude had changed. Strangford was rightly convinced that the Porte would listen to no offers of intervention, while the Greeks would have nothing short of independence. Thus Metternich's policy, said Canning, was to gain time and inspire in the Russian Emperor a hope of success he did not share himself and enable the latter to impose a similar 'illusion' on the Russian people. To follow this policy, Britain would have to give false reasons for her conduct to Parliament and people. 'In the broad daylight of Parliament,' he went on, 'no British minister could venture a declaration by which the truth should be knowingly altered or concealed.' Nevertheless, a declaration of a sincere desire to intervene for the good of both parties combined with a frank disavowal of force might eventually operate on one party or the other. This would also 'gain time – which, it is impossible not to agree with Prince Metternich in believing to be, in complications apparently so hopeless, the safest, the steadiest and most effectual unraveller of difficulties which cannot be instantly solved.' However, Britain could not be an indifferent spectator of so great a change as the break-up of the

Ottoman Empire. The difference with Meternich he attributed to a difference in principles.[143]

Metternich was not happy with British policy. He strongly objected to the British concession of belligerent rights to the Greeks, especially as in the British view this entailed a Greek right of search of neutral vessels, for Britain had always rejected the principle of 'free ships, free goods'.[144] Bernstorff dutifully raised an objection to belligerent rights in Berlin.[145] Metternich argued that the Porte had made private overtures indicating he would not reject allied overtures to bring pacification to Greece. Above all, Austria would never co-operate in securing the total independence of Greece, but would try to get her rights under the sovereignty of the Porte. 'The cause of the Sultan was not one which stood in opposition to the Sovereign of Christendom, but, on the contrary ... was the general cause of Monarchs against rebellious subjects.'[146] By early January Metternich was sufficiently angry with British lack of response to 'threaten' Russian hostilities against Turkey.[147]

Meanwhile the Czar's conference had not been the expected success. Not appreciating Metternich's tactic of delaying events, he was surprised not to be generally authorized to use force against Turkey. Furthermore, he was furious that Metternich had openly boasted of his ability to manage him.[148] With the failure of the conferences, the Czar turned back to Great Britain in the hope that a separate arrangement regarding Greece might be made between the two powers. In October 1825 the Ambassador, Lieven, was accordingly authorized to open the question in London.[149]

In October 1825 Stratford Canning, cousin of the Foreign Secretary, was accredited to Constantinople. He was to urge on the Porte the dangers of the situation, that Russia was only prevented from crying out for war by the pacific disposition of the sovereign. The Turks must think in terms of the pacification of Greece: 'Every success of the Turkish army renders the Greeks more and more objects of sympathy and compassion, and every failure contributed to place Turkey in the light of a more tempting and easy prey.' Britain's good offices were to be stressed because of her freedom from engagements regarding the affairs of Turkey and Greece. Stratford was especially charged to counter French influence in Constantinople by hinting at their double-dealing.

Were the French officers who were sent to Egypt to drill and
discipline the troops of the Pasha sent there 'with the purpose of
preparing those troops to fight against the Greeks in the Morea
and not with the design of aiding the Pasha to set up for himself
an independent principality in Egypt.' Were Generals Roche
and Fabouier sent to join the Greek armies to persuade them to
return to their allegiance to the Porte?[150]

Canning had long made it clear that Britain herself did not
contemplate in any case the use of force towards either party.[151]
In 1825 events occurred which might have shaken that resolution.
The Sultan called on the Pasha of Egypt, nominally his vassal,
to assist him to suppress the Greeks, and the Pasha sent his son,
Ibrahim, who proceeded throughout 1825 with the ruthless and
effective subjugation of the Peleponnese.

Faced with a major military crisis the Greeks turned to Britain.
In June Canning was asked for protection for all the provinces
brought under the Greek administration.[152] In September Canning
had a conference with the Greek deputies who asked his advice
as to a suitable monarch, hinting at the King's brother, the Duke
of Sussex. Canning stressed Britain's neutrality and historic
friendship with Turkey, which could be upset by the placing of
a prince friendly to Britain on the Greek throne. This could lead
to a general war. There would come a point in the contest where
Britain could make herself useful 'by promoting a fair and safe
compromise' though this might be something short of independence. The deputies replied that 'The Greeks must now either be
entirely independent or perish.' Canning went on to justify the
imminent British Declaration of Neutrality, made because of the
participation of the King's subjects in the Greek contest contrary
to the law of the land.[153] In October Canning rejected a proposal
that Greece should become a British protectorate on the grounds
that this 'would be, in effect, to make war upon the Porte'.[154]

Meanwhile, Britain was beginning to hear reports of the activity
and policy of Ibrahim Pasha, which indicates it was one of turning
the Peleponnese into a purely Muslim province by forced conversion, extermination and deportation of the population to North
Africa. At first sceptical, Canning became shaken by the seriousness of these reports, and in February 1826 Stratford Canning
was told to tell the Porte that if there were further confirmations
of these reports, Britain would 'not permit the execution of a

system of depopulation which exceeds the permitted violence of war and transgresses the conventional restraints of civilization.'[155]

In December 1825 Czar Alexander died and was succeeded by a younger brother Nicholas, the rightful heir Constantine having renounced the throne to remain as Grand Duke of Poland. Strangford, now Ambassador in St Petersburg, was told that he must not do less in the way of mourning than the French Ambassador.[156] To win the support of the new Czar and also impress British policy upon him before the political lines of the new regime hardened, Wellington was sent to take a message of condolence and congratulation to the new Emperor.[157] Russia had meanwhile been plunged into internal disruption by army-led rebellions known as the Decembrist Rising. This later made Canning fear that Nicholas might follow a warlike policy in order to keep his army 'distracted abroad'.[158] At the same time, a new problem was created by Strangford, who on his own initiative had put forward a proposition for renewed concert amongst the allies on the Greek and Turkish question at the same time as Stratford Canning was declaring in Constantinople Britain's intention to keep herself free from any such engagements. Canning issued a very strong rebuke, making it quite clear he would not tolerate diplomats' changing policies.[159]

The new Czar was more interested in the general claims of Russia against Turkey than in the Greek question specifically. The whole situation had become more fluid as military defeats had led the Greeks to indicate that they would be prepared to settle for something short of independence. The Russian Government took the opportunity to strike while the iron was hot by sending an ultimatum to Constantinople demanding the settlement of various long-standing issues, the complete evacuation of the principalities and the release of Serbian deputies held by the Turks.[160] The Greek question was not mentioned. Stratford Canning was told to press upon the Turks the seriousness of the ultimatum and get them to concede the points regarding the principalities and the Serbian deputies. Canning was not however prepared to go along with certain other demands regarding the execution of the Treaty of Bucharest of 1812, for Britain could not force compliance with a Treaty 'they not only suspect but know the other party not to intend to execute'.[161]

In practice the Sultan was happy with the shift of Russian

policy away from Greece. On 25 May Canning received news
that the Turks had complied with the terms of the ultimatum.[162]
Canning congratulated his cousin on the success of his support for
the Russian ultimatum.[163] The settlement, known as the Convention of Akkermann, was eventually reached in October 1826.

Meanwhile the lowering of the Greek terms provided an opportunity for some form of agreement on the Greek question which
Wellington achieved with the Russian Government in April
1826. This Protocol provided for an autonomous Greece under
Turkish suzerainty leaving to the Turks a say in the nomination
of Greek rulers. Mediation was to be offered to the Turks, against
the refusal of which an unspecified form of intervention was
threatened.[164] The agreement was by no means what the Greeks
officially asked for in their approach to Britain sent on 29 April,
especially with regard to Turkish nomination of Greek rulers, and
the absence in the Protocol of any British guarantee for the final
settlement. However, Canning declared that it gave to Greece
everything but the absolute independence she could only have
after a long and bloody struggle.[165] As for the Turks, Stratford
Canning was told to impress upon them that they should not
nurture the idea that Nicholas had given up the idea of interference on behalf of the Greeks.[166]

Meanwhile, the Protocol hung fire for some time. Canning
wished to achieve the co-operation of Paris and turn the Protocol
into a treaty, despite the opposition of Wellington. Negotiations
dragged on in an atmosphere of suspicion, though Charles x was
a genuine hellenophile. From September to October 1826 Canning himself was in Paris, and Villèle agreed to co-operate putting
the Protocol of April into operation. Fear of Russia, Canning felt,
was the pervading sentiment in Villèle's mind.[167] There was also,
however, a great amount of mutual suspicion between the British
and the French. In June 1827, Canning, now Prime Minister,
received information concerning the dealings of the French with
the Pasha of Egypt. Canning referred to 'the appearance of
crooked policy and contradictory engagements which make this
intelligence important and in some degree alarming'.[168] Nevertheless, a treaty was eventually agreed on 6 July 1827, very much on
the lines of the Protocol. However, a secret article provided for
the three powers to prevent hostilities between the Greeks and

Turks if mediation was refused.[169] Instructions were sent to naval forces in the Mediterranean.

Canning was satisfied with the Treaty. Above all he had out-witted Metternich who had been completely left in the cold in the negotiation and who was now powerless to prevent an outcome of events which he did not wish. Canning commented that he could either join the Treaty, or not join, in the face of all the world, a concert which the world generally approved.[170]

The *dénouement* occurred after Canning's death. On 20 October a general engagement broke out between the Turkish and allied navies, as a result of which the Turkish navy was wiped out, depriving their forces in Greece of support from Egypt. To some extent the battle was the result of the personal decision of the British Admiral Codrington and its policy became a bitterly decisive issue back in England. It was nevertheless on the basis of that battle that Greek independence was established.

Canning deserves congratulation on his handling of the Eastern Question. By playing the straight role of honest broker he had ensured a central place for Britain in the settlement of the various issues involved. He had outwitted Metternich and made France play second fiddle. He had, for the moment, avoided a Russo-Turkish war and at the same time secured Greek independence, which was a cause to which he had a certain degree of commitment. If there is to be criticism levied at his policy it is at the extension of Russian influence in the Balkans and Mediterranean and at the weakening of the only power which presented any effective check. However, this is probably unfair, for the fundamental Russo-Turkish conflict involved far wider issues than those with which Canning could be concerned, had long preceded his period in office, and were to continue as major problems for a further fifty years.

Portugal had not escaped the general wave of revolutions which swept some of the smaller European states in 1820. The establishment of a constitutional regime inspired King John to return from Brazil, leaving his son Dom Pedro there, in order to save his throne. However, though he himself was prepared to accept the constitutional regime, his wife and second son Dom Miguel were not, and the movement of the constitutionalist assembly towards extremes gave them their chance to force the King to abolish the constitution, albeit with the promise of another.

It was clear that Portugal was split into two hostile camps, and it was natural for the constitutional party frightened by the French invasion of Spain, to turn to Britain for assistance. Nevertheless, the appeal for assistance by Count Palmella, the Portuguese Foreign Minister, in July 1823, met no response from Britain, loth to involve herself in an internal matter.

The crisis re-emerged the following spring when the King decided to summon the Portuguese Cortès. Miguel determined to use this as an excuse for a coup and after some arrests, Palmella and Subserra, the pro-French Minister of War, were forced to flee to a British warship in the Tagus. The French Ambassador, Hyde de Neuville, meanwhile promised Subserra to supply French troops to help suppress Dom Miguel, and even gave instructions to the French commander at Badajoz to march into Portugal. The French commander fortunately desisted from obeying the Ambassador in what would have been a highly provocative step.[171]

In Portugal itself the affair temporarily fizzled out when John was persuaded to take refuge on a British warship whence Miguel, losing his nerve, approached him and asked for forgiveness. Subserra, however, had taken refuge in the same warship, and was able to re-establish his influence over the King, as a result of which the British Ambassador, Thornton, was prepared to listen sympathetically to a request for British troops to provide a counteracting influence. However, Canning felt that the request was designed to provoke a refusal, after which French troops could be introduced.[172]

On 2 July the request for six thousand troops was formally lodged by the Portuguese minister Villa Real with the British Government. The Cabinet, Canning said, did not think that they had that number of troops to spare, but he drew the King's attention to the Portuguese suggestion that George IV might send his Hanovarian troops.[173] The King proved agreeable to this, but it became unnecessary when Canning was able to get assurances from the French that they themselves would not send troops.[174]

There remained the problem of the Spanish Government's eyeing with the greatest hostility schemes for the establishment of constitutional rule in Portugal. Before leaving Spain to replace Thornton in Lisbon, Sir William A'Court had warned the Spanish

Government against any interference in the arrangements His Most Faithful Majesty had 'in contemplation for the good of his people and for the tranquility of His Kingdom'. The Spanish Ambassador had remonstrated against the assembly of the Cortès, alongside the ministers from Russia, Prussia and Austria. 'The orders clearly come', wrote Canning, 'from the Conference of the "Allied Continental Ministers"' at Paris and particularly Pozzo di Borgo – 'the soul of that conference and the master spirit of all the intrigues that are going on in the South of Europe.'[175] To Liverpool he wrote in December that 'Portugal appears to be the chosen ground on which the Continental Alliance have resolved to fight England hand to hand, and we must be prepared to defeat them, under every imaginable form of intrigue or intimidation, or be driven from the field.'[176]

Canning then faced a two-fold problem. He had to preserve Portugal from the intrigues of Spain and the Holy Alliance, and he also had to preserve British influence in the country as against that of France. In November he was angered when Palmella asked Spain and France to revise the course of a negotiation Britain had been carrying on on Portugal's behalf for two years regarding Brazil.[177] In January A'Court successfully intrigued to get rid of the pro-French Ministry and particularly Subserra. Canning called it 'the blow . . . which is to bring back Portugal within the legitimate influence of her old ally'.[178] 'France is full of jealousy about Portugal,' he wrote on the twenty-first, 'which is exceedingly foolish, because Portugal is, always has been, and always will be, English, so long as Europe and the world remain in anything like their present state.' It was, he added, foolish of Polignac and Villèle to believe that Britain stuck to Portugal because of trade. In fact 'in our new course of extended and liberal commercial principles' the treaties with Portugal were 'clogs'.[179] A'Court's task was made easier by the departure of the French Ambassador Hyde de Neuville. He had fallen foul of his own government and had been given leave of absence which he chose to take up on 4 January, two days before he would have received orders telling him to stay. Canning gleefully wrote that 'Nothing could equal Polignac's astonishment and rage at hearing that Hyde de Neuville, whom he thought fixed anew on the banks of the Tagus, was happily landed at Brest.'[180]

On 21 January King John dismissed his pro-French Ministry

and replaced it with one which was pro-British. The re-establishment of British power enabled Britain to conclude successfully the negotiations between Brazil and Portugal. Despite the fact that Canning refused to supplement naval assistance in the Tagus with the British troops requested by King John, British influence remained supreme, and with Miguel safely exiled in Vienna, the country remained free from internal disruption.

King John died on 10 March 1826. His legitimate successor was Dom Pedro, Emperor of Brazil, who appreciating that it would be unrealistic to attempt to be King of Portugal as well, renounced the throne of Portugal in favour of his eight-year-old daughter, with his sister Isabella as Regent. At the same time, he gave to Portugal a farewell present of a constitution.

This news naturally caused anger amongst the absolutist monarchies of Europe at the same time causing internal dissension in Portugal. By August deserters from the Portuguese army were crossing the Spanish border and re-forming as units loyal to Dom Miguel with the support of the Spanish authorities, to some extent urged on by De Moustiers, the French Ambassador. The crisis was boiling during Canning's sojourn in Paris in September and October 1826, but it seemed that firmness was likely to induce France to put the necessary pressure on Ferdinand to disarm the Portuguese ultras.

On 19 October Canning heard that Miguel had taken the oath to the constitution, and this information took the edge off the crisis. However, the Spaniards remained obdurate and the news soon came that he had taken this oath with reservations.[181] By mid-November the hostile intentions of the Spaniards were fairly apparent. Canning wrote to Melville on the tenth that naval reductions were out of the question.[182] Meanwhile Ellis was carrying out negotiations for Canning privately in Paris. Canning told him to reply to Frenchmen who urged the consideration of *amour propre blessée* with the consideration 'how the *"amour propre"* of this country has been *"blessée"* for three years, not by words but by deeds'. The Opposition were urging that Portugal should have been defended by resistance to the French at the Pyrenees, or at least by a threat to blockade Cadiz.[183] Canning was quite clear that Britain had an obligation to defend Portugal which could not be avoided without breach of faith.[184]

On 22 November casual incursions of Miguelists into Spain

became a regular invasion, news of which, together with a request for assistance from Palmella, now Ambassador in London, reached England on 3 December. Canning did not press a decision immediately but awaited events. Two days later he learned from Frederick Lamb, now Ambassador in Madrid, that the Spanish Government had denied responsibility for the invasion and promised redress. Canning considered the despatch to have given a respite from the dangers of 'such a war as the next war in Europe will be'. However, he stressed the necessity of France forcing Spain to recognize the Portuguese Regency.[185] It nevertheless quickly became apparent that Spain was not going to desist from support of Miguel, and that France was unwilling to force her. Canning wrote on the eighth, 'Mr Villèle's notion of treating Spain like a child is very harmless when the sports of the child are so. But when the child tosses firebrands into the neighbouring house, one forgets the imbecility in the mischievousness of the prank.'[186]

On 9 December, re-informed with fresh reports of the Miguelist invasion, the Cabinet met and decided on action. By the time the question was debated in Parliament on the twelfth, 5,000 troops were already mobilized and news had already been despatched to Lisbon. This would arrive, said Canning, on the twenty-first or twenty-second. If the interval of a week proved crucial, he would not forgive himself for not pressing a decision on Sunday the third.[187]

The crisis gave Canning the opportunity for one of the great speeches of his career in the King's Message respecting Portugal. He went into a long account of Britain's political and commercial ties with that country. He demonstrated that the events that had occurred constituted a *casus foederis* leaving Britain no alternative but to act:

This, then, is the case which I lay before the House of Commons. Here is, on the one hand, an undoubted pledge of national faith – not taken in a corner – not kept secret between the parties – but publicly recorded amongst the annals of history in the face of the world. There are on the other hand, undeniable acts of foreign aggression, perpetrated, indeed, principally through the instrumentality of domestic traitors, but supported with foreign means, instigated by foreign councils, and directed to foreign ends.

Regarding the Portuguese constitution, all he would declare as an English minister was 'May God prosper this attempt at the establishment of constitutional liberty in Portugal! and may that nation be found as fit to cherish and enjoy its new-born privileges, as it has often proved itself capable of discharging its duties amongst the nations of the world'. This was the clearest assertion ever made that Britain not only objected to the principle of interference as laid down by the Holy Alliance but also to the objects to which that interference was directed. Canning concluded:

> Let us fly to the aid of Portugal by whomsoever attacked, because it is our duty to do so; and let us cease our interference where that duty ends. We go to Portugal, not to rule, not to dictate, not to prescribe constitutions, but to defend and to preserve the independence of an ally. We go to plant the standard of England upon the well-known heights of Lisbon. Where that standard is planted, foreign dominion shall not come.[188]

There was an amendment to allow more time for consideration moved by Sir Robert Wilson, but the only objection in principle came from Henry Bright, a Whig West Indian planter, who denied that any *casus foederis* had arisen. However, Henry Brougham strongly defended Canning's policy, urging the Government to act steadily up to the principles it avowed. Canning's policy was supported by an overwhelming majority in the House.

The news of the intervention of British troops reached Portugal on 18 December and their actual arrival later in the month stiffened Portuguese loyalist resistance to the point that they were able to expel the Miguelists in January. Britain's immediate worry was the reaction of the French, but in fact the Foreign Minister Damas made a very friendly speech. Clearly there was cause for apprehension, for Spain had interfered in Portugal on the same principles as France had interfered in Spain. In fact underlying Anglo-French relations at this time, in the opinion of Canning, was the attitude of Villèle and the fact that he had the support of the King. This, thought Canning, was the only factor behind Anglo-French friendship.[189]

Still, felt Canning, Metternich was casting jealous eyes towards Spain, 'moving heaven and earth to overthrow the Portuguese constitution' which was incompatible with 'the monkish government of Spain.' He was worried about the brother of a man in Metternich's employ, who had gone to Portugal 'at the head of a little detachment of Jesuits.'[190]

In practice, only a temporary stability had been brought to Portugal. As his twenty-fifth birthday approached, Miguel was encouraged in his ambitions by Metternich. Returning to Portugal in February 1828 he became Lieutenant-general of the Kingdom and in July was crowned King. The Wellington Administration, which had no such prejudices in favour of constitutional arrangements as had Canning's, merely stood by. There followed a war between Pedro and Miguel till the former, returned from Brazil, was eventually successful in 1833.[191]

Canning's policy was looked to after his death for inspiration. Palmerston quoted it against the Government in 1829. Lord William Russell used it to press Grey into stronger action in 1832, declaring 'Canning is held up against you as a bolder and more liberal man.' Naturally Grey in reply had no good word for Canning's policy.[192]

In general, it would be fair to criticize Canning's policy on the grounds that being wholly geared to outside intervention in Portugal, it did not really recognize the imminence of a genuine civil war.

Canning's foreign policy was based firmly on British national interest as traditionally seen. In the Near East, this was the balancing of contending parties. In Portugal it was the defence of a traditional ally. In Spain, where there was a rebuff, it was the old policy of preventing too close an alliance with France. Failure here underlay the recognition of Latin-American independence.

It was Canning's good fortune that many of Britain's policy aims could be dressed up in idealistic terms. To a large extent this was justified as regards the slave trade, for the popular pressure which so affected government policy on this issue was idealistically generated. As regards South America, Portugal and Greece, policy to which can be seen as having idealistic overtones, no other explanation but British national interest is required.

Canning had a firm grasp of the realities of power, and after the

Spanish crisis, had the experience to gain his aims by diplomatic means. If he shared the idealism of Whig support for the Greek and Portuguese causes, this hardly affected his policies. It would have been a contradiction of his whole philosophy to judge overseas institutions by moral abstractions and then make this the basis of British policy. On the other hand, it would have been equally inconsistent to make the sanctity and immutability of existing governments and institutions into an absolute. However, Canning's flare for oratory could give his policies the appearance of an idealistic base which they did not possess. As Grey said: 'The only difference between him and Castlereagh seems to me to be that he can make brilliant speeches, and with a hypocritical profession of better views, put forward the same base policy.'[193]

A recent historian has written: 'To be sure, the difference between Castlereagh and Canning was primarily a question of emphasis.'[194]

If there is greatness in Canning's foreign policy it does not lie in the originality of his thinking but rather in the occasional flare in its execution and the invariable brilliance of its exposition.

Paradoxically, just as Canning's enemies amongst the Whigs were cynical about his policies, so his enemies amongst the Tories were deeply suspicious that they were tinged with Radicalism, especially regarding the independence of Latin America. There were many in the Cabinet whom he could not trust, including Wellington. In January 1825 Canning wrote that he was keeping Villèle's correspondence to himself, as he could not rely on secrecy if Westmoreland knew. To make up for this he would show the occasional despatch to the King.[195] Canning's trump card, sufficient to outwit any opposition, was the strong support of Liverpool on nearly all foreign policy questions. 'It is incalculable', wrote Canning, 'what an impediment and perplexity our strict union (L's x mine) upon the grand subjects of foreign policy is to the sighers after the Continental school'.[196]

The policy of rejecting such continental entanglements, especially one so obnoxious as the Holy Alliance, was nevertheless not a novel one. It was the normal state of British foreign policy. Had Castlereagh lived, differences would have been marginal.

The atmosphere of diplomacy in this period was one of mutual suspicion arising from fear of internal and external political convulsion. There was tremendous fear that the post-war tranquillity was transitory, and even Canning once admitted to Frere that he was sometimes given to apocalyptic feelings. There were not lacking those who saw the apocalyptic passages in the Twelfth Book of Daniel as referring to the Congress of Verona.[197] This fear and suspicion had its expression in the building up of large spy networks in this period. Britain by no means eschewed this kind of activity, though perhaps they were not as good as others at it, and there does not seem a British equivalent of Russia's feat in copying Britain's Code 22 when Stratford Canning was in Warsaw.

In continental Europe this suspicion had further expression in co-operation between the powers for the preservation of internal security. Thus in 1823 Prussia sent a German demagogue, Vith Doring, under arrest to Austria, Metternich declaring that he would send him back when they got the information they wanted out of him.[198] Britain took no part in this. In 1824 Britain complained bitterly to the Prussian Government of the arrest of a Mr Stickney: 'The charge of having disseminated papers in Switzerland or Italy ... would not, if true, justify the detention of a British subject by the Prussian Government.'[199] At the request of Jeremy Bentham, in 1822 Canning made the strongest complaints regarding the arrest of an Englishman by the French Government on the grounds that he was carrying seditious letters.[200]

One amusing anecdote of Canning's period as Foreign Secretary must be recounted. On 26 January 1826 Britain signed a trade treaty with France sweeping away discriminatory duties. As no agreement could be reached with the Netherlands, two Orders in Council put an additional twenty percent levy on Dutch vessels and merchandise. Canning told Bagot, British minister in the Netherlands, of this on 31 January, accompanying it with a despatch in cipher. On 3 February Bagot replied that he was unable to decipher it because he only possessed cipher 'S'. On 6 February, Canning preserving a tone of urgency, supplied ciphers 'T' and 'V'. Bagot and Second Secretary Tiemey were up 'till cock-crow' transcribing the despatch which read:

Sir,

> *In matter of commerce the fault of the Dutch,*
> *Is offering too little and asking too much.*

The French are with equal advantage content.
So we clap on Dutch bottoms just 20 per cent.
(Chorus) – 20 per cent, 20 per cent
(Chorus of English Custom House Officers and French
*   Douaniers):*
(English) – We clap on Dutch bottoms just 20 per cent
(French) – Vous trapperez Falck[201] *avec 20 per cent.*

I have no other commands from His Majesty to convey to your
Excellency to-day.
  I am, with great truth and respect Sir,
  Your Excellency's most obedient humble servant,
                                          George Canning.[202]

'I could have slain you!' wrote Bagot to Canning, 'but I got
some fun myself, for I afterwards put the fair de-cypher into
Douglas's[203] hands, who read it twice without moving a muscle,
or to this hour discovering that it was not prose, and returned it
to me declaring that it was 'oddly worded'; he had always had
a feeling that the despatch must relate to discriminatory duties.'[204]
  Such lighter moments in Canning's Foreign Office career were
rare. He was constantly under the strain of knowing he had
enemies plotting against him. He even told Sir George Warrender
that when he took the Foreign Office he probably wouldn't hold
the job for six months.[205] Furthermore, throughout the period
Canning's health, particularly his gout, was worsening, and above
all, he was exhausted by the sheer amount of work involved in
being both Foreign Secretary and a Member of the House of
Commons. Parliament itself was overworked, he complained in
August 1827: 'Seven hours per day, four days per week, seven
weeks from Whit,' made worse by 'the utter uninterestingness
of the greater part of the discussions'. He even admitted that the
two jobs ought not to be combined, but he 'would rather die'
than consent to 'their separation in his person.'[206]

THE DEMISE OF TORY ENGLAND

Canning's position as Leader of the House of Commons brought him in contact with the whole range of political affairs. A problem he was faced with very shortly after taking office was that of West Indian slavery.

Prior to 1807 there had been a strong political campaign in Britain against the transatlantic slave trade. This had sprung again into existence in 1814–15, geared to making this abolition international. The abolitionist leaders had at first thought it was unnecessary to turn their attention to the issue of slavery itself, for they argued that with the opportunity of future importation removed, slave owners would have to improve the treatment of their slaves in order to keep up numbers. As a result, and over the years, the slaves would gradually be transformed into a free peasantry.

The years 1815 to 1822 demonstrated there had been a fallacy in the abolitionists' thinking, but they at first responded to atrocious examples of continuing ill-treatment in the West Indies by merely insisting that an illegal importation was continuing. They were loth as a body, and especially Wilberforce, to actually overturn the basic institution of a society.

Nevertheless, by 1822 it was clear that affairs could not continue indefinitely without the re-mobilization of the huge body of abolitionist opinion which existed in the country. The spark came from Liverpool where an abolitionist society was founded in 1822 at the inspiration of James Cropper, a Quaker East India merchant. Strong elements within the East India interest had sound economic reasons for opposing slavery, for sugar could be grown cheaper by free labour in the East, but was discriminated against by a higher tariff to protect that of the West. In 1822 the relaxation of the mercantilist system to allow direct trade between the West Indies and the United States and certain parts of Europe weakened the case for maintaining those parts of the mercantilist system which favoured the West Indians.

In response to the call for the abolition of slavery, the old leaders of the movement began organizing in late 1822 and reformed themselves as 'the London Society for mitigating and gradually abolishing the state of slavery throughout the British Dominions'. Wilberforce passed the leadership of the movement on to Thomas Fowell Buxton, MP, a fellow evangelical who had caught his attention with his activities in various philanthropic organizations and in the campaign for the amelioration of the harsher provisions of the criminal law.

By the time Canning came to grips with the question, the movement was pursuing the same strategy as the earlier campaign against the slave trade. A mass organization of local corresponding societies had sprung into existence led by men experienced in the techniques of pressure group politics. At the same time, a vigorous parliamentary onslaught on slavery was planned.

On 15 May 1823 Buxton raised the subject in Parliament. He urged no immediate abolition 'but such preparatory steps, such measures of precaution, as, by slow degrees, and in the course of years, first fitting and qualifying the slave for the enjoyment of freedom, shall gently conduct us to the annihilation of slavery'. His final resolution was for the gradual abolition of slavery as fast as was consistent 'with a due regard to the well-being of the parties concerned'.[1]

It fell to Canning to deal with the issue. Despite his former liberal position on the slave trade, his friendship with Charles Ellis, John Gladstone and Lord Dudley – all prominent West Indians – made him suspect to the abolitionists. 'Would that poor Lord L. [Londonderry] had at least lived,' lamented Stephen, 'till Canning was clear of the Lizard.'[2] Wilberforce too feared that Canning was 'becoming more our enemy than formerly'.[3]

In practice, the issue was not immediately the political dynamite expected. On 22 April Ellis had chaired a meeting of the London Committee of West India Merchants and Planters which put forward a very moderate line, setting up a sub-committee which recommended a whole variety of fairly substantial changes in the institution of slavery to be recommended to the local assemblies in the West Indies. Only one of these recommendations – the bestowal on the slaves of the right to purchase their freedom at a fair valuation – was not accepted by the general committee.[4]

Canning was meanwhile playing a subtle role. A Quaker petition on the subject which had preceded Buxton's resolution failed, complained Wilberforce, to spark off anything 'because of Canning's skill and the good generalship of his troops'.[5] Faced with Buxton's resolution and armed with the moderate reaction of the London West Indians, Canning proposed an amending proposition to the effect that amelioration of the condition of the slaves was expedient, and this would prepare them for the enjoyment of civil privileges as soon as was compatible with the well-being of the slaves, the safety of the colonies and a 'fair and equitable consideration of the interests of private property'.[6]

The Government thus embarked, in a wave of general approval, on a policy of putting pressure on West Indian assemblies to improve the condition of the slaves. The mettle of direct interference, raising as it did the whole question of colonial autonomy posed so drastically in regard to the old American colonies, had not been grasped. Twenty-four years earlier, nevertheless, Canning had given warning of what to expect from such a policy when he had declared: 'Trust not the masters of slaves in what concerns legislation for slavery. However . . . their laws may appear, depend upon it they must be ineffectual in their operation.'[7]

The actual execution of the policy was in the hands of the Colonial Secretary, Lord Bathurst, who sent a circular letter to the colonial governors urging the adoption of various reforms, and in particular the provision of religious instruction for the slaves, the acceptance of the evidence of slaves in court and security for their property.

Meanwhile, Buxton and other abolitionists met Canning on 10 June. In a friendly atmosphere, a fair measure of agreement was reached as to detailed reforms. As regards the actual abolition of slavery, Canning distinguished two methods. The first was the purchase by slaves of their own freedom; the second, the liberation of children born after a certain day. The latter, he argued, could not be given without the former, but he would not concede either until a fuller knowledge was gathered of the provisions in Spanish law regarding 'compulsory manumission', as it was known.[8]

This atmosphere of co-operation was suddenly broken when a slave revolt broke out in Demerara on 18 August 1823. West Indian society lived in perpetual fear of a re-occurrence of the bloody servile war which had ravaged Haiti thirty years earlier and were quick to blame the agitation of the slave question for the outbreak. Any spirit of co-operation that existed in the West Indies immediately faded. The Governor of Jamaica wrote that 'There is at the present moment so much irritation and such a desire to resist all the propositions of Government that I fear most of the suggestions which under other circumstances would have been agreed will now encounter serious opposition.'[9]

The abolitionists were shaken by the event and by a sudden turn of popular feeling against them. The Government also changed tack. Chinnery, Canning's private secretary, 'stated openly and loudly' that the insurrection in Demerara had been instigated by Wilberforce, Buxton & Co. . . .'[10] 'Sad intelligence from Demerara,' wrote Canning. 'I had a spiteful pleasure in communicating it to Wilberforce.'[11] He told the latter, 'I am sure you do not doubt my sincerity as to the good of the blacks, but I confess I am not prepared to sacrifice all my white fellow countrymen to that object.'[12] Canning and Huskisson immediately resigned from the abolitionist-dominated African Institution.

The Demerara revolt nevertheless created a situation which the Government simply could not ignore, and it would appear that they seriously considered a policy of direct interference to prevent the situation getting out of hand. Liverpool himself had shed the anti-abolitionist views he had held as a young man and in 1815 wrote to Stephen that he was in no way 'hostile to a system for the gradual improvement of the condition of the negroes in the West India Islands by Parliamentary Enactment if it cannot be otherwise obtained'.[13] The issue was now firmly posed. In January 1824 Canning wrote to Liverpool: 'Your view of the W.I. question is of must aweful importance. It is one which has been present to my mind for the last two months and upon which I have thought but not spoken with anyone.'[14]

Underneath there lay two great fears. The first was that of the slavery question getting out of hand both politically in Britain and physically in the West Indies. The second was fear that antagonized West Indian colonies might seek the protection of the United States. In April 1823 Ellis had warned that little would be needed 'to induce all the resident proprietors – with the concurrence of too many of the absentees – to connect themselves with any country strong enough to protect them'.[15] Lord Harrowby urged the existence of a strong America party in Jamaica and that 'nothing short of the absolute extinction of hope could have justified Parliament from taking into its own hands the business of internal legislation for the colonies in the first instance – whether in the past is another question.'[16]

There was furthermore a general doubt as to Britain's legal rights in this regard. With the example of America clearly in mind, Liverpool wrote that he considered the arguments for the right to tax the colonies stronger than those for the right to impose internal legislation upon them. However, above all, a firm decision had to be taken.[17] Consideration was given to the possibility of sending a Commission of Inquiry to the West Indies as a prelude to British legislation, but in fact, at whose urging it is not clear, the whole issue was quickly dropped. The Colonial Under-Secretary, Wilmot Horton, described it as 'much too delicate to be mooted'[18] and the Government reverted to its original policy of merely putting pressure on the West India assemblies. As to the legal question involved, Canning declared in Parliament in March that 'transendancy is the *arcanum* of empire, which ought to be kept back within the *penetralia* of the constitution. It exists, but it should be veiled.'[19]

There were two aspects to the policy all governments pursued until 1831. There existed a number of colonies in the West Indies, notably Demerara and Trinidad, which did not have legislative assemblies, and in these crown colonies, the Government proceeded to introduce changes in the slave system by Order in Council. One for Trinidad was passed in 1824 and the Government hoped it would serve as a model to which the other colonies could be persuaded to adapt.

Meanwhile the abolitionists had recovered from their setback of the previous August, receiving an enormous boost by the trial and death sentence imposed on John Smith, a Demerara missionary, on the charge of inciting the slaves to revolt. Government was quickly conscious of the renewed pressure. 'You know the saints,' (as the abolitionist leaders were known), sighed Canning in March, 'I cannot get on with them or without them.'[20] In March 1824 it fell to Canning to present command papers on slavery to Parliament, including the Trinidad order. He laid out three possible lines of action for the Government to impose its will on the West Indies. These were direct force, harrassment by fiscal regulations and 'the slow and silent course of temperate but authoritative admonition'. The latter was to be followed, and Canning voiced an optimism he can hardly have felt when he declared that they should soon learn that 'the planter of Jamaica is anxiously employed in emulating the endeavours of the Government in Trinidad to improve the condition of the negroes.'[21]

Debates on slavery and allied topics became a regular feature of parliamentary life. Brougham raised the case of the missionary, Smith; Dr Lushington that of two free coloureds illegally deported from Jamaica. In 1825 Buxton moved a resolution on the affair of a missionary named Shrewsbury whose chapel in Barbados had been destroyed by infuriated whites. Wilmot Horton, the under-secretary, blundered badly in declaring his hope that this would be a warning to missionary societies, and Canning had quickly to intervene to save the debate from taking a disastrous turn. He countered Buxton's demand that Barbados be mulcted for the rebuilding of the chapel by drawing attention to two unfortunate precedents for such a course of action – the aftermath of the Porteus Riots in Edinburgh and the Boston Port Bill. He then moved an amendment expressing outrage at the 'scandalous and daring violation of the law'. Unfortunately he expressed himself so strongly he antagonized the West Indians, and came under strong attack from Ralph Bernal and William Manning. He must have been thankful when Buxton ended the debate by withdrawing his motion.[22]

The Government was meanwhile growing angry at the lack of response to their policies and the increasing militancy of the West Indians. In 1826 the merchants and planters appointed a special committee to draw up an Address to Colonial Legislatures, pointing out to them the situation in which they were placed and urging reforms, but when this was presented to the normal standing committee, it was rejected.[23] It was clear that little helpful legislation could be expected from the West Indies and in February 1826 the Cabinet agreed that Canning would tell the Commons that the West Indians would be given another year; that 'if the result is still unsatisfactory, we will, in the next session, propose measures to Parliament for effectually redeeming the pledges given by the House of Commons by their Resolutions of May 1823'.[24]

It thus seems likely that but for the government instability of the succeeding four years and the imminence of greater problems, decisive action might have been taken much earlier than it was. During Canning's brief period as Prime Minister the subject was scarcely raised except one particular aspect of it – the allegation that an illicit slave trade was being continued in the island of Mauritius. A select committee was set up on this question but the illness of Buxton delayed its operations so that the truth of the allegations was not demonstrated for two years.

The abolitionists were suspicious of Canning's administration. After his death, Brougham wrote 'as to *our* peculiar question – he was a very *incubus* on us. I must fairly say that I regarded him as our very worst adversary on all that related to W.I. affairs . . .' He was 'one who attempted to have the same object in view – and pretended to be waddling towards it by another and more roundabout road – while he was in reality running in the very opposite course.'[25]

This assessment was unfair. Canning had West Indian friends, but Ellis and Dudley were well-balanced and reasonable. The quotation should be taken not to illustrate Canning's views on the West Indian question but rather his ability to inspire unmerited distrust. As to the question itself, there is no doubt he had a clear wish to see the end of slavery, but also a very firm grasp of the real problems involved.

Canning's opinions on 'the Catholic Question' were clear: he had long made his support of Roman Catholic claims perfectly apparent. The issue was not one on which a commonly agreed government viewpoint could be reached as the Cabinet was deeply divided. The Cabinet members in the Commons supported emancipation with the strong exception of Robert Peel, while in the Lords, Liverpool himself led most other Cabinet members in opposition to concession. The issue was an open one in the Government, whose members were free to take whichever side of the issue suited them. Liverpool, despite his own markedly hostile views, attempted to balance the two factions and prevent the Government's breaking up.

Until 1823 the Catholic Question had been essentially a debating point in the British Parliament, but in that year an organization known as the Catholic Association was founded in order to bring popular pressure to bear on the issue from Ireland. The leading light in this effort was Daniel O'Connell, an Irish barrister.

The organization quickly alarmed the Government, raising as it did the spectre of conflict between organized Catholics and organized Protestants. 'Mr O'C appears to be going very near the wind,'[26] wrote Canning in November 1823, and throughout 1824 the problem of what to do about the Catholic Association occupied much of the Government's time. In June Canning referred to their proceedings as being nicely balanced between legality and illegality.[27] In December 1824 an unfortunate attempt by the Irish Attorney-General to prosecute O'Connell struck even the King as being awkward in its coincidence with the recognition of Colombian independence. 'There is a fatality attending Plunkett's prosecutions,' complained Canning.[28] In January 1825 they proceeded to push a bill through Parliament to suppress the Catholic Association along with militant Protestant organizations.

Canning strongly defended the need for this measure, for if they had not put it forward, the Protestants would have forced it upon them, he declared.[29] He spoke strongly for it in Parliament, assisted, he felt, by the 'injudicious violence' of Brougham on the other side. His speech, he wrote, 'has had the good fortune of pleasing all parties ... when I say all parties, I of course do not mean the Associationists.'[30] He was very optimistic as to the effects of the measure. He felt that in six months O'Connell and the Catholic Association would 'be with Spa Fields and Manchester, and the Protestant fanatics ... will, I hope, have shrunk back into their shell.'[31] Hardly could a more inaccurate forecast have been made, for within five years the reorganized Catholics had reduced Ireland to an ungovernable state.

The side Canning had taken in this dispute clearly could have led to suspicions as to the stability of his pro-Catholic principles, even though he asserted to Granville that none of their friends had been deceived by the attempt to confuse the Catholic Question with the Catholic Association.[32] Indeed his principles were immediately put to the test when Sir Francis Burdett raised the substantive issue in Parliament.

The Speaker himself had written of the expectation that Canning would in Brougham's phrase 'sneak out of his former part of advocating Roman Catholic Emancipation'.[33] Canning was in a quandary. He was convinced of the utter impolicy of raising the question at that stage, which he declared to be 'against all reason and comon sense', yet in practice he saw he would have to attend, otherwise others also would hold back and he would be blamed for the result.[34]

On 28 February, suffering from gout and leaning on a stick, Canning reiterated his well-known views in favour of emancipation.[35] The motion was carried by thirteen votes and proceeded over the next few months to go through all its stages in the Commons. Canning began to grow optimistic. 'I am a very good Catholic still,' he wrote cheerfully to his wife on 9 March. On the eleventh he wrote, 'I really begin to hope that we have a chance of settling the Cath Q this year.'[36] In fact, much of the support for emancipation was less than whole-hearted. Huskisson wrote to J. W. Croker that 'Securities may be expedient for allaying the apprehension of our English friends and I know that some of the new converts are so thin-skinned as to require a pretty thick security plaster to keep them steady in their seats.'[37]

The inevitable defeat for the measure in the House of Lords, opposed as it was by all the leading Cabinet members there, depressed Canning. The issue had already threatened to break up the Government in April when Peel had told Liverpool that he could no longer tolerate his position as the only 'Protestant' minister in the Commons, but had been persuaded to withdraw by Liverpool's demonstration that this must break up the Government.[38] After the Lord's defeat, Canning tried to bring the question to an issue within the Cabinet, declaring it could not remain 'in abeyance'.[39] On 27 May the Speaker declared that Canning had said twice recently that he had considered the effect of resigning over the Catholic Question, but had decided on staying on as most advantageous to it.[40]

The Parliament had been elected in 1820 and as 1825 drew on it became clear that a dissolution could not be long delayed. This raised special problems for the Catholic Question, for it was generally accepted that the pro-Catholic case was unpopular in England, and in an election held at a time when the issue was widely agitated, it was to be feared that many Catholics would be

forced to commit themselves to the anti-Catholic side. 'It is clear',
wrote Canning, 'that if there is to be another session of this
Parliament the Catholic Question must be kept in abeyance – I
see no way of keeping it so – and to myself personally no credit-
able one (supposing it mooted – which it will infallibly be by the
Jacobin Catholics) than that I should move the previous question
upon it.'[41] Nevertheless, to Plunkett he urged the totally variant
argument that the Catholics should be quiescent so that the
House of Lords might yield if the Commons reiterated its
opinion.[42] This was presumably designed simply to prevent
agitation. In practice, Canning's views were not seriously regarded
by the Irish Catholic leaders, but those of Brougham were, and
he also urged that a delay could be useful.[43]

In May 1826 the Parliament was dissolved, and the elections
gave a great opportunity to the Protestant party. In the interval
between elections the main method of exercising pressure was
through petitions – but here the Protestant party had not had it
all its own way. In 1825 Fitzwilliam wrote to Grey that the
English Bar had petitioned for Catholic emancipation, with nine-
tenths of them signing, and 'this one petition overbalances the
hundreds from the Tailors, Butchers, Bakers, etc., etc., coming
from Glasgow and other places.'[44] In an election it was nevertheless the latter group that had to be satisfied. 'Roman Catholics are
dear to us as fellow subjects,' declared James Wilson at York,
'but they profess a religion hostile to the State.'[45] Such sentiments
were wrung from candidates standing for election in the more
open boroughs and counties up and down the country. There
could be no question that the Parliament elected in the summer
of 1826 was more Protestant than its predecessor. As English
opinion polarized one way, in Ireland the Catholic organizations
were growing in strength. Huskisson wrote that influence there
had passed wholly into the hands of priests and separatists.[46] It
should have been clear to any analytical mind that in the near
future the Government would have to take the issue into their
hands.

The role of putting forward the Catholic Question in Parliament
had fallen to Sir Francis Burdett, who wrote to Huskisson, Canning being absent due to ill-health, early in 1827. He saw that
his friends thought that the question should be brought forward
as soon as possible and they wanted Burdett to give notice for

the twenty-second, subject to Canning's health.[47] Canning had caught a bad cold at the Duke of York's funeral after lending his cloak to his aged and implacable enemy Lord Eldon to stand upon. Huskisson replied that there was little chance of the twenty-second, due to Canning's health, especially as the Corn Question must have precedence.[48] Canning himself approved of Burdett's course of bringing forward the Catholic Question by way of resolution rather than a bill in the House of Commons, but felt that a decent interval should elapse after the death of the Duke of York on 5 January.[49] The Duke of York, who was a younger brother of the King, had made himself extremely popular in 'no-popery' circles by a stunningly vicious attack on the Catholic claims.

On 17 February 1827 the whole political situation was changed when Lord Liverpool, recovering at Bath from a severe illness of the previous year, was struck down by a sudden stroke. Canning was quite clear that the Catholic Question should not be put off because of government uncertainty. The peers, however, would not change their minds on the subject without a decent interval for saving appearances.[50] Huskisson replied that those who were to move the question were divided. The dissensions among the Opposition continued, he wrote on the twenty-fifth. The 'makers and lovers of mischief' including Thomas Creevey, Earl Sefton, John Cam Hobhouse and Douglas Kinnard were 'indefatigable in their endeavours to sway Burdett to put off his motion. He is not, I am told, shaken, but those who wish him to persevere are not without their apprehensions. He is ... fond of procrastination and consequently more ready to listen to those who recommend delay.'[51] Clearly tactical reasons dictated by the government crisis and the possibility of a Whig return to office were the factors considered by those pro-Catholics urging delay.

Burdett went ahead with his motion and the debate took place on 5 and 6 March. Canning spoke in favour of the motion but spoiled the effect of his speech by a vicious attack on Sir John Copley, the Master of the Rolls, who had drawn the material for his speech from a pamphlet by the High-Church Protestant Dr Philpotts,[52] addressed to Canning.[53] Mrs Arbuthnot commented that Canning had treated Copley with the 'greatest possible insolence and contempt'.[54] The probable fact is that Canning had been made unusually irritable and touchy by his bad health.

The outcome of the debate illustrated the change in the complexion of the Parliament, for the motion was lost by 276 to 272. This was a clear regression on the situation that had existed in 1825, and this despite the fact that the resolution was couched in the most 'milk and water style' to catch young and unpledged voters.[55] It turned the attention of the pro-Catholic party to the problem of how the motion could ever be got through Parliament without Government backing. This problem had faced the anti-slave trade party thirty years previously when they discovered that even the general approbation of the Commons was not enough to carry a bill against a determined opposition without Government support.

In April Canning himself became Prime Minister, leading a largely pro-Catholic administration. In the Cabinet there were only three 'Protestants': Lyndhurst, as Sir John Copley had become, as Lord Chancellor; the Marquess of Anglesey as Master-General of the Ordnance and Lord Bexley (Nicholas Vansittart) as Chancellor for the Duchy of Lancaster. The accession of strong elements from the Whigs into the Government provided a strong pro-Catholic influence because they were by now fairly heavily committed to emancipation.

In Protestant circles wild rumours spread. The Speaker recorded that 'In Lancashire, the Roman Catholics talk of not paying their tithes now that Mr Canning is First Minister, and the Roman Catholic priests tell their people that they shall have mass in the Protestant churches next year.'[56] In practice Canning was still faced with heavy anti-Catholic sentiment in Parliament, in the country and from the King. He himself was absolutely unwilling to make the issue a government question, even though two years earlier he had briefly urged this. Instead he followed a policy like Liverpool's of leaving the question open in the Government, and this despite the fact that all the strong Protestant ministers of Liverpool's day had refused to serve under him.

When the future Government was still in doubt, Canning had made his position on the issue quite clear. 'I am morally certain,' he wrote to Huskisson, 'that an attempt to force the question upon this country by a Government united on this point and for this purpose would be the prelude to another catastrophe like that of the India Bill of 1784.'[57] Clearly Canning feared that the King would turn out a pro-Catholic ministry and allow an exclusively

Protestant successor to appeal to the country on the platform of
'Church and King' which had been so popular in 1807 and whose
potentialities had been demonstrated in 1826.

Had Canning lived it is unclear what eventually would have
happened for he would have been faced with the same dilemma
which was to face the former anti-Catholic Wellington; namely
the impossibility of governing Ireland without emancipation, and
the impossibility of the Lords' agreeing to it without government
pressure. In practice the King would probably have been able
to turn out the Canningites and appeal to the old Protestant
ministers, but this is in the realm of speculation. What is undoubted is that despite the fact that Catholic emancipation had
been a major aim of his career, Canning found that as Prime
Minister he could not further it and was not prepared to try.
It nevertheless almost certainly was the case that Catholic emancipation could only have been achieved by a 'Protestant' Ministry.

The autumn of 1825 saw the height of a speculative boom with
banks providing easy credit and speculation encouraged by the
opening of South America to British investment. Huskisson had
long warned of the dangers of a bank crisis and financial crash,
and Liverpool had spoken openly on the subject, warning investors
that they could not expect the Government to rescue them from
the consequences of their own folly.

In September Huskisson wrote to Canning on the subject,
blaming the Bank of England for its 'greedy folly' and arguing
that only a good harvest had prevented the stoppage of cash payments. He was nevertheless afraid of the autumn and urged an
immediate dissolution of Parliament before the crisis broke.[58]

In late November the boom burst, and Huskisson wrote grimly
that the Bank had much to answer for,[59] blaming them for an
over-supply of credit. Gladstone wrote to Canning from Liverpool
complaining of the evils that had come upon them, saying that
some were blaming the free trade system itself, but he did not
agree. Canning replied that what had happened was 'rather
sudden than surprising'.[60]

Meanwhile a large number of small banks had gone out of
business as the crisis of confidence produced a panic run. Canning
suspected that the old school of bank directors were hoping to
force the Government to sanction a suspension of cash payments,
but that if this were done 'we never should have a tolerable

currency again.'[61] The Cabinet sat from 9 pm till 2 am and refused
to sanction this step.

Prompt support from the Bank of England stopped the immediate panic but left the underlying problem for the Government to
face in the new year. Despite the fact that it antagonized their
own country supporters, Liverpool put forward a measure to
abolish small currency notes. Canning stood by Liverpool loyally
and spoke up strongly for it on 10 February and again on the
twenty-seventh, to circumvent a technical expedient to which
the country banks were resorting to evade the new law.[62] A slight
incident occurred between Liverpool and Canning when the
former did not say he intended to allow the Bank of England to
go on issuing £1 notes until 10 October. Canning complained of
this, but still stood loyally by Liverpool. The measure was successful thanks to the support of strong elements from the Opposition.

Meanwhile the shortage of money which had been created
caused pressure for the issue of Exchequer Bills. Liverpool, rigor-
ously orthodox in the face of the crisis, and perhaps somewhat
smug that he had foreseen it coming, vigorously resisted this
measure and threatened to resign rather than yield. Despite his
own misgivings Canning stood by him, even though the issue
looked likely at one stage to bring the Government down.[63]
Perhaps he was influenced by Frere who urged him: 'Do not let
it be said that you are like the two Doctors in *Gil Blas* fighting
about the prescription while the poor little Grocer is dying of
the dropsy.'[64] In fact the discovery of some more money in the
Bank of England cellars eased the crisis and by March the whole
economic situation was much improved.

The financial crisis had serious repercussions throughout the
economy in 1826. Distress in the manufacturing areas impelled
the more liberal members of the Government to ease the problem
by relaxing the Corn Laws of 1815 which prevented the import
of foreign corn when the domestic price fell below the high level
of eighty shillings per quarter.

Already there were signs of opposition to the Corn Laws as
they stood from within the Cabinet. Their principles of monopoly
and preference were inconsistent with the relaxations of British
navigation laws that were being undertaken at the time and quite
contrary to the spirit voiced by Huskisson in 1825 when he
declared: 'Whenever you give a free scope to capital, to industry,

to the stirring intelligence and active spirit of adventure, which so strongly marks the present times, you are in fact opening new roads to enterprise and affording new facilities to the interchange of the productions of the different regions of the earth.'[65]

In September 1825 Canning wrote to Huskisson asking if it would be convenient to get rid of the Corn Question that session. Liverpool thought it would, but Wellington felt otherwise.[66] In fact Wellington's argument that they could not force a measure through Parliament which was so antagonistic to the position of the landed interest, who after all were the Government's main supporters, eventually persuaded Liverpool.

The following year the situation was considerably more grave, and the Government was forced to two emergency measures of releasing up to 300,000 quarters of wheat stored in warehouses at a reduced duty, which was acceptable in the crisis, and also granting the Government a discretionary power to import a further 500,000 quarters, which was far less acceptable.[67] It was upon Canning, who had to defend the measure in the Commons, that the wrath of the country gentlemen, already antagonized by the prohibition of small currency notes and made suspicious by the progress of the Catholic Question, fell. Furthermore, it was from the Whig opposition that Canning drew his support on these questions, thus illustrating the growing irrelevance of the old party division to the main issues of politics and making it absolutely clear that it was only Lord Liverpool who held the Tory coalition together in the face of these crises.

In the second half of 1826, with the election safely out the way, the Government again turned its attention to the possibility of a more permanent measure than the temporary expedients of earlier in the year. In August Liverpool told Canning that he agreed with Huskisson and himself as to the need for an early discussion of the Corn Question by the Cabinet. In practice, however, the policy was largely evolved by Liverpool, Canning, Huskisson and Robinson, the Chancellor of the Exchequer.

Huskisson himself drew up a paper on the subject. Liverpool agreed with him that 60s was a remunerative price. Certainly his local farmers were satisfied with protection up to that level. However, the country gentleman would expect a protection of 25s up to a price of 55s or even 60s. He therefore agreed with Huskisson's principle of a sliding scale of duties but suggested that these alter by 2s for every 1s up and down rather than the 1s per 1s suggested by Huskisson. He was going to have a full discussion on the subject with Canning on Friday.[68] By November there was basic agreement that there should be a 20s duty at 60s which should vary 2s for every 1s rise or fall in price.[69]

While Canning was still working on the last details and slight alterations in the measure, Lord Liverpool suffered his stroke. Huskisson suggested to Canning that it might 'be better not to stir the questions'.[70] The loss of Liverpool, he urged, made a very material difference to the chance of getting a corn bill through the House of Lords. 'He had devoted himself, heart and soul, to its success. It was so understood by many who would have made almost any sacrifice to have kept him at the head of the Government.'[71]

Nevertheless, the decision was to go ahead with the measure. Canning laid the plan before Parliament on 1 March. There were fears that the agriculturists might link up with the Whigs to overturn the measure, or at least postpone it,[72] but in fact the bill had proceeded through all three readings by the middle of April.

By the time the measure reached the House of Lords, Liverpool's old coalition had finally collapsed, Canning was Prime Minister, and Wellington and the High Tories were in Opposition. Despite the fact that Wellington had been in the Cabinet that approved the measure, whether by deliberation or by accidental misunderstanding of what Huskisson told him, he moved an amendment which was both destructive to the measure in principle and fatal to its progress in practice, by entrenching on the principle that the Lords could not initiate the suggestion of higher taxation.

In February Huskisson had written that Lord Liverpool was vital for the Corn Question, for if he did not support the bill personally, how would the House of Lords react to a lukewarm or an insidious member of the Government fighting for it?[73] The prophecy came true. Canning's Government was short in talent in the House of Lords with only Lord Chancellor Lyndhurst having real talent. Certainly there was no one of the necessary stature to oppose Wellington, and in early June his amendment was carried and later insisted upon.

The King fully backed Canning in the crisis and the usual pressures were brought to bear. In May Canning had told the

King through Sir William Knighton that Lord St Helens' proxy was held by Lord Digby, an enemy to the corn bill, and that the Government could not tolerate a Lord of the Bedchamber voting against the measure.[74] After Wellington's amendment, three members of the royal household were forced to resign for supporting it.[75] Canning was furious at Wellington and his 'disastrous amendment'.[76] He had 'greatly lowered his high estimation by his trickery upon the Corn Bill'.[77]

The Government was now faced with a problem of what to do about corn, and the parliamentary session was accordingly prolonged. Canning's expedient was to allow the quantity of corn then in bond, together with a small quantity expected from Canada, to come into consumption under the rules and conditions of the bill that had failed.[78] He had already denied any attempt to alter the corn laws by 'a side wind' when so accused by the High Tory Lethbridge,[79] and the measure was a temporary expedient to last only till 1 May following. Canning's introduction of this measure on the eighteenth was his last parliamentary speech. He promised that next session he intended to carry a new measure.[80] He could not have known the irony that it was to be Wellington's administration which would introduce a sliding scale. The measure was not seriously opposed though C. C. Western, a Whig representative of the landed interest, moved an amendment which would have made 70s the pivotal point for the duties to rise or fall, but this was lost by 238 to 52. The measure accordingly became law. Canning used the opportunity to attack the opposition peers, furious as he was at the setback and already a dying man. Sir Joseph Yorke told him, 'P.P. Canning, if you do not keep your friends you will lose your place.'[81]

One of the main subjects on which the Opposition chose to attack the Government was expenditure of public money among its supporters. Radical pamphleteers made this the main subject of their attack on the 'system' or 'the thing' as they called it. The 'Black Book' publishers regularly went through the entire House of Commons testing the patronage received by every Member of Parliament and his family in devastating terms. The Bathurst family was placed with £18,423 from eight different sources. Of Thomas Courtenay it declared: 'Secretary To the East India Board (Parl. Report), £2,200; Agent to the Cape of Good Hope (Parl. Paper No. 377), £5,600; Principal Registrar to the Land

Tax, salary unknown. The Cape Agency, though put down at
£600, is supposed to nett £4,000 a year in all. He has also four
relations, three of them sisters, who have £900 in pensions. He is
returned to Parliament by 36 electors of a rotten Devonshire
borough.' As the Black Book declared elsewhere, 'Retrenchment
and Reform are convertible terms; whatever tends to one must
lead to the other.'[82]

In Parliament the cause of retrenchment was put ably and
effectively by Joseph Hume, the Radical Member for Aberdeen,
who, declared the Black Book, had 'done more for the country in
the last two sessions than the Whig party since the Revolution of
1688.'[83] The problem for the Government was that to hold
together a parliamentary majority required that patronage had to
be used effectively. Under a continued onslaught this had gradually diminished since Burke's time, or even earlier, and the failure
of the system of control was to be fully demonstrated in 1830
when the Wellington Administration both failed to win an election
and were then subsequently defeated in the Commons. The
parliamentary reform which followed urgently came to fill a
vacuum rather than to overthrow an established system.

In the 1820s the Government, and hence Canning, were at
pains to defend what patronage remained from a parliamentary
onslaught. In 1826 Huskisson wrote to Canning that the state of
the country was better, 'but the Revenue is bad, and we shall be
worried to death with proposals of retrenchment. They will be
listened to, as they always are when the country is of sorts.'[84]
Canning of course had a dual responsibility to defend items of
diplomatic expenditure, such as the Austrian Loan Convention.[85]

The Government could do little against a House of Commons
so hostile on the issue. In 1824 Liverpool was loth to raise the
project of having a second Colonial Under-Secretary, as it 'might
revive the ill-humour of the House of Commons' and indeed raise
the entire question of whether a third Secretary of State (for
War and the Colonies) was necessary at all.[86] After a debate in
the House of Commons in April 1826 Canning complained of
'a phalanx of lawyers against us' and insisted that the offices of
Treasurer of the Navy and Master of the Mint would never again
be considered as available 'for the general business of the Government'.[87] Even the peerage could not be readily used as a source of
political reward. Liverpool wrote in July 1826 that 'our last batch

of Peers I have reason to know is so unpopular, that I am not prepared to add to the number.'[88] Perhaps the best illustration of what was happening to the system was the fact that when Charles Arbuthnot came to retire, having effectively managed the Government's patronage for many years, there was no adequate reward that the Government felt they dared offer him.

There were of course a large number of other issues on which Canning had to defend government policy. He felt obliged to speak on the Aliens Act, despite its unpopularity, because he felt it was right.[89] He urged a government initiative on criminal law reform because of the dangers of leaving the question in the hands of the opposition.[90] He had to defend Government from Burdett's motion attacking delays in the Court of Chancery.[91] All these illustrate the vast range of issues that fell within the purview of the Leader of the House of Commons and demonstrate what an enormous task it was to perform, especially when held in conjunction with the Foreign Office. On one issue, soon to be of great importance, we do not know Canning's opinion. In 1825 he was approached by Hollinshed from Liverpool to ask him if he would join the opposition to the Liverpool-Manchester Railway – 'a scheme that can never answer, will only deface the country and be an extreme nuisance'. Canning replied that he never attended on private bills, had refused to see the railroad deputation 'and on the same ground ... must decline entering with you into any discussion of the subject'.[92]

One of the features of the latter part of Liverpool's administration was Canning's reconciliation with the King. The latter had bitterly opposed Canning's entry into the Cabinet in 1823. 'He is wild with the idea,' wrote Arbuthnot to Liverpool, '... that Canning never leaves you for a moment at rest, and that by assiduity, by perseverance, by insinuation and by every tool and weapon he can use, he continued to pervert your better judgement and turn you in all things, to his own purposes.' Liverpool of course vigorously denied the accusation.[93]

After Canning's inauspicious inauguration as Foreign Secretary there followed the bitter conflict with the King over South American independence. Talking of kings, wrote Canning to Frere early in 1825, 'there is one who if he know how, would send me to any court or country so that he could get me out of his own. And yet, I take my oath, I serve him honestly and have saved him, in spite of himself, from a world of embarrassments in which a much longer entanglement with Prince Metternich and his Congresses would have involved him.'[94]

The reconciliation began at an audience late in 1825 when the King told Canning that Esterhazy had confessed that he was ashamed of the way Canning had been treated. Esterhazy confirmed this.[95] In 1826 Canning's affability and genuine kindness succeeded in turning the King's affections towards him to such a degree that in the middle of the year the King asked Canning if he could do him any service in appreciation for his work. Canning was not prepared to ask for a peerage for himself, but secured one for Charles Ellis, who became Baron Seaford. Canning referred to him as 'a person who – after my own family – is the nearest to me in the world.'[96] The King was happy to comply, partly in order to make sure that Canning would by every means in his power contribute to his own peace and comfort. In fact the peerage caused something of a political storm. In November 1826 Canning praised the enormous kindness of the King in an unfortunate affair involving Canning's son-in-law, Lord Clannicarde, and a high-stake gaming session in which one gentleman lost £6,000 at loo, following which legal action was threatened.[97] In December 1826 the King wrote to Canning praising his 'great and splendid exertions the other evening in the House of Commons'.[98]

Throughout this period Canning had many personal problems with his son William. As early as 1817 he wrote to him sternly saying that 'no progress in study can make amends to meanness and falsehood'.[99] However, the real problem proved to be that young William had inherited his maternal grandfather's gambling instinct without his skill. First evidence of this predisposition came in 1818 when Canning found William at home one Sunday learning the thirty-nine Articles by heart, only to discover it was for a guinea bet.[100] Canning himself was not averse to gambling as such, and his diary for 7 January 1819 records his expenditure of £27 18s 0d on a lottery ticket.

The lottery, so soon to be abolished, was a very pervasive feature of the period. The press was filled with advertisements such as the one published in 1820, in which 'Brittania' sits beside a table on which is piled bags of gold, surmounted by a Union Jack and a poem:

> *When riches invite, don't you think he's a cake*
> *Who careless looks on while his neighbours partake,*
> *And as two Twenty Thousands,* all sterling, *one day*
> *Must decide, let me ask, is it wise to delay?*[101]

In 1821 Canning complained bitterly on receiving a letter from William's Captain. 'New debts and bills! and an unsatisfactory account from William himself. I am perplexed what to do with him – there is no sense of truth – or point of honour.'[102]

On 16 October 1821 he recorded a long and satisfactory talk with William, but the reformation was not long-lasting. In January 1822 William wrote a pleading letter to his father begging forgiveness, listing debts mounting to £426, mainly billiards or cards.[103] Canning agreed to pay that part of the debt which was borrowed, but wrote grimly 'a poor gamester is only a rogue who has played to win another's money having none of his own to pay, if he loses. For such I have no compassion.' He insisted on the separation of one debt which William had tactfully described as 'partly billiard, partly borrower'.[104]

Canning felt that the best thing for William was to be transferred to an obscure naval station. From the Admiralty, J. Barrow replied that 'The only obscure home station is that on the west coast of Ireland, where I suppose the Beings they meet with are generally half savage.'[105] February found Canning agreeing to pay even William's gaming debts, except for £47 to a Billiard Table Keeper. He authorized immediate payment of a £3 5s 0d debt to a midshipman. Canning warned William that he would cut him off financially if there were any re-occurrence, and that the only thing he could expect in his own right was the small and precarious income from his Irish estate.[106]

In fact Canning discovered that even while William was discussing his debts with him, he was still frequenting the London gaming tables. He nevertheless agreed to pay the new debts, which involved £400 in six weeks to ten persons. In May Canning wrote again grimly, 'I have received your letter. The less that I say of the contents the better. Except that I may as well tell you at once that of the two monstrous and profligate debts which you disclose to me, I will neither now nor ever pay one farthing.'[107]

Young Canning's naval career was not living up to his father's expectations either. In November he went on a week's absence without leave, claiming that the note refusing leave had slipped through a hole in his pocket. He was returned on board by police. Canning wrote to Captain Dawkins insisting on exemplary punishment.[108]

Relations improved slightly in the subsequent years and Canning agreed to make up William's pay by two-thirds. However, 1826 finds still more debts and Canning writing to his son that 'short memories are very inconvenient for persons whose statements are not literally correct.'[109] William was drowned at sea in 1828, a year after Canning's death.

As if Canning did not have enough to worry about with William, he also had his maternal relations. He refused to interfere in a case where the ship of one of these had been taken off its station. The man had quarrelled with virtually every officer on board and was said to be relying on Canning. He relied in vain.[110]

Much more satisfactory were the affairs of his daughter Harriet. In the spring of 1824 she met Lord Clanricarde and in February 1825 they became engaged. He, said Canning, was 'young – sufficiently rich, very noble (for it is one of the oldest peerages in Ireland) and well-spoken of by all his contemporaries at Eton and at Oxford'.[111]

The marriage took place shortly afterwards, and in February 1826 Harriet gave Canning a grand-daughter. With the marriage in prospect Canning launched Clanricarde on a Foreign Office career, putting him in the same office with C. Ellis' son, Howard de Walden.[112]

Canning had a certain amount of opportunity to travel in this period. In August and September 1823 he visited the Gladstones at Liverpool and went up to Lowther Castle in Cumberland. In October he went to the West Country. In September 1824 he managed a trip to Ireland and had hoped to follow this with a trip via the Lakes to Scotland to see his friend Sir Walter Scott,[113] but the death of Louis XVIII necessitated a curtailment to the trip. In September and October 1826 he made his final visit to Paris.

Through the period one gets a very great impression of Canning's tremendous weariness. On 3 May 1823 he wrote to his mother, 'I am as well as anyone can be after three nights' debate and three nights' speaking in a House as hot as a conservatory.' On the tenth he said, 'I am well but wearied.' On 14 June he added, 'I am worn to death with fatigue mental and bodily.' In the Parliamentary session he complained on 2 August, 'one's day closes at 4 and one's night lasts till 2. The exhaustion is almost too much to bear.'[114]

The situation did not improve. In 1825 he complained of a situation 'when one passes forty hours in one debate – without time for sleeping and eating (though I do very little of either) between.'[115] 'My Dear Mother,' he wrote the following day, 'I am tired to death.'[116]

All this left Canning very little free time. In January 1825 he wrote to Frere apologizing for not writing at all during 1824 saying this was want of time, even though the parliamentary session was neither arduous nor long.[117] 'Your highness knows,' he told Esterhazy, 'that during the session I cannot be sure of dining at all! Except on Saturdays and Sundays.'[118] His friend Bootle Wilbraham nevertheless said that Canning was in a better situation than Castlereagh had been in, having Robinson as Chancellor of the Exchequer where his situation forced him to speak and hence relieve Canning of some of his Parliamentary burdens.[119]

In addition to the tiredness there was Canning's general ill-health and in particular his perpetual gout, which he often had to ignore in order to speak in Parliament. His right hand was often badly affected, making him unable to write. Despite all this he could often be reasonably light-hearted. 'Here comes Mr Owen of Lanark for another interview,' he wrote to Frere, 'his purpose being to show that nothing but the establishment of his parallelograms can cure the evils of the world, and especially of Ireland. I won't see him.'[120]

It is undoubted that hard work combined with a constitution that was basically not very robust were pushing Canning rapidly towards the grave in these years. In 1827 when a stroke removed Liverpool from the office which had long been Canning's ambition it was ironic that he was already a dying man.

It was Lord Liverpool's achievement that he held together a coalition of the most strongly divergent views. There was a wide gulf between Canning and his friends on one hand, and such as the Lord Chancellor on the other, and there was a continual struggle between them. After Lord Liverpool's stroke it was quickly apparent that many members of the old Administration would not serve under Canning at the same time as it was evident that no Ministry could be formed without him.

A period of intrigue opened immediately. The Duke of Buckingham whose offer of support in return for Canning's clearing the way for his return to office had been curtly rejected by the latter in 1826,[121] tried to persuade Wellington to use his influence against Canning. Indeed he was so confident of success that he wrote to Bathurst asking for the Governor-Generalship of India when the latter had become Prime Minister.[122] An atmosphere of doubt and false rumour hung over British politics whilst men turned their eyes to Windsor to see which way the King would move.

The King was in a quandary, probably secretly hoping that Liverpool would recover and then resolve the situation. When Wellington, to whom the eyes of Protestants were increasingly turning, saw him on 22 March, the King was utterly non-committal. However, the necessity of action impelled itself upon him when a message came from Lady Liverpool that her husband had been able to signify that he wished to resign.

The King saw Wellington and Canning on 28 March and declared his wish to keep the Cabinet as at present but with a Protestant peer at its head. Furthermore, it was clear that he wished to evade his responsibility by letting the Cabinet choose such a First Minister: a proceeding which Canning and Peel both found unconstitutional, on which grounds Canning withheld this communication from the Cabinet.[123] Meanwhile chances of holding the Cabinet together were slipping away as Canning insisted on the substantive power of Prime Minister while Peel indicated clearly that he was not prepared to serve under Canning. This was a blow, for Canning regarded Peel in a very different light from the other Protestant ministers, describing him as 'certainly the most efficient Secretary of State for the Home Department that the country ever saw, and the most able and honest minister'.[124]

Meanwhile in Parliament, George Tierney moved that no further supplies should be granted until there was a new minister. Canning was forced to reply, in a voice indistinct through illness, admitting only that Liverpool had resigned but being unable to say anything about what Ministry would replace him.[125]

There followed a week of intensive discussion among members

of the Cabinet while the King remained silent. Peel refused to budge from his position, being unable to accept a pro-Catholic Prime Minister. No-one was clear how the situation would resolve itself and in this atmosphere a great deal of mutual suspicion grew up, especially between Canning and Wellington, who had at this stage still not committed himself to refusing to serve should Canning become Prime Minister. The search for a Protestant peer who would be sufficiently a cipher to satisfy Canning, however forlorn as a project in any circumstances, had no chance of success when the King himself was merely sitting on the sidelines await-ing events. Certainly Wellington himself, whom the King eventu-ally suggested was wholly unsuitable, and Canning too, made this so very clear that eventually the King told Canning to attempt to reconstruct Liverpool's Administration, but without explicitly nominating him as Prime Minister.

Wellington was immediately infuriated at Canning's assump-tion that he was to head the Administration and angered by Canning's arrogance of tone. He resigned at once, and despite the King's attempts to persuade him to reconsider, he remained adamant.[126] An avalanche of resignations ensued from the Protes-tant side. Those of Eldon and Westmoreland were to be not only expected but welcomed. That of Bathurst was a genuine blow and Canning replied offering him the Home Office. Bathurst answered: 'Since writing my letter, resignations have followed to an extent of which I had not the smallest conception. Under these circum-stances, I cannot but refuse the offer.'[127]

A more surprising blow came with the resignation of Canning's former friend, the pro-Catholic Melville. He wrote that he was happy to serve provided Canning could keep Lord Liverpool's Government together, but 'the separation is to be an extent of which I was not before aware, and I really feel that I could not do justice to your Government if I were to continue in office.'[128] Bexley too resigned but the King asked to meet him after church on Good Friday. 'He kept me near three hours complaining of the desertion of his Protestant counsellors as casting a suspicion on his principles, as well as embarrassing his measures,' wrote Bexley. 'He ended by commanding me as his personal servant in the Duchy (of Lancaster) not to leave him.'[129] He agreed to stay. A host of resignations from minor offices totalling an estimated forty-one on 13 April also occurred.[130]

It is difficult to estimate how much this huge wave of persons voting with their feet against Canning was really a reaction to his Catholic principles or more a personal revulsion. Huskisson drew the shrewd parallel of asking what would have happened if Londonderry, also a pro-Catholic, had succeeded Liverpool in 1822. The clear implication is that the Protestants would have overcome their scruples and supported someone far more agreeable to them on general and personal grounds than Canning.[131]

The King was not a man to appreciate the desertion of his own servants in the face of his own will and, even though he had strong reservations about Canning as First Minister, the expressed opposition to this reinforced his resolution. On 12 April he received Canning who, according to Wellington, stood with a watch in his hand giving the King half an hour to make him Prime Minister, for in that time the writ for the appropriate by-election had to be moved.[132]

Canning had then to build his administration from the remnants of Liverpool's coalition. Huskisson agreed not to cause any trouble, promising to stay at the Board of Trade, though without waiving higher pretensions for the future.[133] Robinson stayed, becoming Viscount Goderich and Secretary of State for War and the Colonies. Canning's West Indian friend Lord Dudley became Foreign Secretary. Harrowby stayed on as Lord President of the Council, and Charles Wynn as President of the Board of Control. Though a 'Protestant', Sir John Copley joined the administration as Lord Chancellor, forgetting his row with Canning in the Commons of a month previously. The Duke of Portland, Canning's wife's brother-in-law, became Lord Privy Seal. Viscount Palmerston became Secretary at War.

Altogether it was not a very impressive collection of names and was widely regarded as somewhat humorous. It was quickly evident that to stand in Parliament it would have to attract some support from the Whigs, and negotiations to that effect began almost at once.

There was no united view amongst the Whigs as to what they should do in this situation. Grey wrote to Holland on 14 April, 'I certainly have a rooted distrust of Canning and I certainly would take no place in an administration of which he is at the head.'[134] He also used the opportunity to express his view that he took it as axiomatic that no son of an actress should become

Prime Minister of England. He tried to persuade others of his view and to keep the Whigs from coalition as he had in 1809 and 1812. To Fitzwilliam, richest of the Whig aristocracy, he wrote of his deep distrust of Canning's character, principles, temper and discretion,[135] only to receive a dusty reply in which Fitzwilliam spoke of his determination 'to give every support in my power to Canning's administration'.[136] When Sir James Scarlett became Attorney-General, Fitzwilliam promptly returned him again for the borough of Peterborough.[137]

Most surprising of all perhaps was the attitude of Brougham, who had had many parliamentary clashes with Canning. He wrote to Holland that our 'object is to keep out the ultras and not let them back. . . . Lord Sefton (no friend of Canning or coalition) is full of this and has written strongly. I find with 2 or 3 exceptions all our friends view things in this light.' A coalition with Canning to form a liberal Government was expected of them.[138]

The substantial negotiations to achieve this junction were conducted by Canning with Lord Lansdowne. Canning played the affair fairly cleverly, not appearing to be too over-anxious lest the Whig price should become too high. On 19 April Canning and Lansdowne met at the house of Lord Carlisle and conversed for three hours, and Lansdowne received a long account of certain aspects of the Liverpool Administration and Canning's position in it. Lansdowne was invited to join the new Government, but warned of the King's desire to keep the high administration in 'Protestant' hands. When they met again, Lansdowne agreed that the Cabinet would not have to take up a position on the Catholic Question, and that the subjects of repeal of the Test and Corporation Acts and parliamentary reform should not be brought forward. However, he insisted on the 'Catholic' composition of the Irish Government, on which the King was adamant. Having been 'driven from point to point', commented the Whig James Abercromby, he had 'at last taken shelter under a Protestant Lord Lieutenant'.[139]

The breakdown of the negotiations caused dissension amongst the Whigs. Brougham had already threatened 'violent and factious opposition' and had already organized a group of followers who were in favour of linking with Canning. Under pressure from all sides, Lansdowne gave up his insistence on 'Catholic' government in Ireland and negotiations re-opened. Canning and Lans-

K

downe met again on the twenty-sixth and from then on the Whigs
began to trickle into office. The Duke of Devonshire, who had
done much to bring the negotiations to a successful conclusion,
agreed to become Lord Chamberlain. On 27 April Canning was
able to write that arrangements for his Administration were
complete, and that Lord Lansdowne and his friends agreed to
accede to the Government without taking office at once.[140]

A series of stop-gap appointments were made to bridge the time
before the full entry of the Whigs. Canning wrote urgently to his
friend Sturges-Bourne imploring him to become Home Secretary,
and insisting that his whole administration depended on it.[141]
Lansdowne himself eventually replaced him on 16 July, entering
the Government along with Carlisle as Lord Privy Seal and
George Tierney as Master of the Mint.

The Whigs were badly split by Canning's Ministry, between
those like Brougham who gave it full support, those who remained
in opposition with Grey and those who followed Viscount Althorp
into a position of neutrality. There was naturally a great deal
of bitterness. Brougham, declared Grey, 'I believe to be the Devil
incarnate. . . . He will stick at nothing to carry his own points, and
will sacrifice friends, principles, and everything that is most
sacred for his own advancement.'[142]

Canning was triumphant. He wrote to Wellesley: 'The Protestant part of the Government did me the honour to think that they
could not make an administration without me but wished to have
me as cheap as possible – to task me to the utmost for their
support in the H of C, and to the F.O. but to place over me a
Protestant master.' He had nevertheless been determined to
inherit Liverpool's position or retire. As for his Government, it
had an immense majority in the House of Commons.[143] One of
Canning's remaining problems was to provide the King with the
'Protestant' Administration he had promised him for Ireland; for
Wellesley, the Catholic Lord-Lieutenant, wanted to stay there.
Canning eventually conceded he could stay no later than the
following January.[144]

As First Minister, Canning faced a Parliament whose old
divisions had been broken down and he was in no risk of defeat
in the Commons. Nevertheless, party feelings ran high on the
part of the ultras, and at one point Canning lost his temper in
answering Sir Edward Knatchbull.[145] On 4 May Canning des-

cribed events to the King. The only occurrence of the previous evening had been 'a foolish and furious ebullition from Sir Thomas Lethbridge which produced nothing but laughter and a very violent little speech from Lord Castlereagh which produced no effect whatever.' His aim, he declared, was to force the new opposition to come to a regular attack.[146]

The session was a fairly active one. On 7 May Canning announced his intention to have a committee of finance to consider the whole state of the revenue. On the fourteenth he had to face a suggestion from Hume to place some limitations on the prerogative of creating peers. Canning naturally replied with a strong defence of the prerogative and a categorical refusal to consider the question. On 28 May Lord John Russell proposed the disfranchisement of Penrhyn, against which corruption had been proved, and the transfer of its seats to Manchester. Canning opposed this, but his Whig supporters were not prepared to follow and, with the absence of many Tory anti-reformers, carried the day. Canning attempted to brush off the incident, but it must have been fairly worrying for the future stability of his Government.

On 31 May Russell returned to the attack, with a motion for the repeal of the act against blasphemous and seditious labels. This was one of the Six Acts and clearly a potentially divisive issue. Canning nevertheless refused to weaken his expected position, declaring that repeal would not help the 'natural liberty of the press. . . . They had now all the advantages of a free press, purged from some of the mischief which the law under discussion was specially provided to meet.'

On 1 June, Canning introduced the budget. The estimated income of the year was £54.6 million and expenditure only £51.81 million. He referred glowingly to 'that constant accumulation of wealth – that continual tendency to increase'.[147]

It was apparent that his situation in the Commons was for the moment at least relatively secure, though the destruction of his Corn Bill in the House of Lords illustrated he had great problems elsewhere. With the King his relations continued to improve. In July he dutifully told Canning that Wellington had paid a visit to the Royal Lodge, for which he received Canning's thanks.[148] With the King's Private Secretary, Knighton, relations were not so good; and on 5 June Canning angrily asked him how information known only to the two of them had reached the press. 'Is not this astounding?' he asked. 'Can you in any way account for it?'[149]

Canning's position was nevertheless precarious. The old Tories inspired vicious press attacks upon him. As time drew on, the Whigs grew somewhat disgruntled with their relatively lowly position in the Administration, Brougham in particular hankering after office. Furthermore, they continued to obey their own whip and remained fundamentally outside Canning's control.

Meanwhile Canning's health continued to worsen. He never fully recovered from the cold he had caught at the Duke of York's funeral, and as the year went on his entire health began to collapse. On 31 July he returned to Chiswick House, lent him by the Duke of Devonshire, after visiting the Foreign Office. He declined a dinner invitation from Lord Holland in order to allow his lumbago time to dissipate.[150] On 2 August he was able to conduct three hours business with J. C. Herries, one of the Secretaries of the Treasury. The following day he was declared to be in imminent danger and after five days of intense pain, he died on 8 August 1827. 'I feel deeply for Canning,' wrote the abolitionist Zachary Macaulay. 'O that he had attended to the things belonging to his peace. And yet he had moments of thoughtfulness. When he had no cabinet meetings or cabinet dinner, he would have prayers and a sermon on a Sunday.' As for his death, a physician had commented that he had seen nothing so agonizing.[151]

His young son 'Carlo' was accompanied by two of the King's brothers and the Duke of Portland as they laid him to rest in Westminster Abbey alongside William Pitt. Vast crowds lined the way and packed the Abbey, remaining quiet and respectful in marked contrast with the overt glee shown by some at the funeral of Castlereagh five years previously.

Canning's death created an immediate problem for the Government. Brougham argued strongly that it could be kept going and urged Holland that: 'One thing is ever to be kept in mind by us. Canning was the great and indeed only obstacle to the *outs* coming in again – Therefore we must hold the door faster than ever against them.'[152] The King decided to keep the Ministry going as far as possible and on 13 August 1827, Goderich kissed hands as Prime Minister. The Administration might have seemed to have a good chance. For some the removal of Canning was the removal of a stumbling block. C. C. Western wrote that he felt far less antipathy to the Administration now Canning was gone.[153] Goderich, however, proved to be not strong enough for the task in hand and resigned his commission before even meeting Parliament. Wellington and Peel returned in January to make a vain attempt to restore the situation as it had existed under Lord Liverpool.

Many political and diplomatic problems remained outstanding at his death. Greece was still, in Huskisson's words, 'a kettle of very nasty fish',[154] and the Portuguese problem was basically unsolved. Catholic emancipation looked no nearer, though sudden developments in Ireland were soon, ironically, to force it upon Wellington and Peel. The Corn Bill was not law, and it too was left to be put forward in a different form by those who had rejected Canning.

The King was deeply grieved at Canning's loss and offered Mrs Canning a peerage, which she accepted, becoming Lady Canning. The immediate future was marred by a vicious row with Huskisson, whom she regarded as a traitor for taking office under Wellington. Canning's mother had died earlier in the year and his aunt, Mrs Leigh, in 1826. His son William followed him in 1828, but young 'Carlo' grew up to be Governor-General of India. If Canning himself had accepted the post he might well have lived many more years.

Perhaps the single most important effect of Canning's death was that it cleared the way for the parliamentary reform of which he was the implacable opponent. The ultra-Tories did not realize their inability to resist this on their own and did all in their power to destroy the one man who could have effectively barred it. As it happened, many of Canning's own supporters drifted over to the Whigs, and Palmerston and Goderich were to find high office in Grey's Government. Had Canning lived, the breakdown of the non-Whig parties which occurred between 1828 and 1830 would have happened in a different form, and with very different results.

POSTSCRIPT

George Canning combined ambition, brilliance and wit with a devastatingly exact control of the English language which was based on a firm classical grounding. His use of words was masterly, whether to dissect an opponent or enunciate high-flown sentiments. As might be expected, this led to a wide contrast in attitudes to him, ranging from bitter hostility to semi-adulation.

His own language often carried him beyond the realities of politics in which he lived. One can contrast his sentiments about monarchy in the abstract with his personal dealings with the King. One can look at his speeches in defence of Portugal and contrast them with his actual dealings with the Portuguese. Such contrast could be called hypocrisy, but in Canning's case it bespoke an innate sense of the fitness of things based not so much on abstract principles but rather on their historic development and potentialities.

Canning's importance can be looked upon in several ways. He was Foreign Secretary at two crucial periods and played an important part in decisions which shaped Europe and America. He was at the forefront of British policy-making on the domestic front at certain times in his life. He was particularly important in building up support for Catholic emancipation so that it could become a realistic policy.

Perhaps more important than either of these was his role in the development of political groupings. Canning became a focal point for those who sat happily neither with the old Tories nor with the Whigs with their factious and élitist attitudes. He provided a philosophy for those who saw that some moderate reforms were required, without basing their demand for them on a critique of the existing system as such. In doing so, he effectively broke up the political system as soon as he re-entered it in 1822 by developing for the Tories the choice of living with him or being over-run without him. Only Lord Liverpool could have held these elements together without fission and the old system effectively broke up on his departure.

In his own philosophy, Canning was essentially a follower of Burke. While ready to see the case for reform made on grounds of necessity, he was not prepared to deduce this necessity from abstract criteria. Still less was he prepared to look at society as if it were a blank sheet on which the casual philosopher could inscribe his own musings. His philosophy was anti-Radical for Radicalism was flawed by the very insistence on rationality which it claimed as its hall-mark of acceptability. This philosophy he expressed cogently in a prose which was at once vigorous, exact, and replete with nuances of which many are sadly lost in contemporary and cruder usage.

APPENDIX

Selected List of British Ministers Abroad, 1822–7

Austria
Sir Henry Wellesley 1823–31

Brazil
Sir Charles Stuart 1825–6 (Special Mission)
Baron Ponsonby 1826 (Special Mission)
Robert Gordon 1826–8

France
Sir Charles Stuart 1815–24
Viscount Granville 1824–8

Portugal
Sir Edward Thornton 1823–4
Sir William A'Court 1824–8
Sir Charles Stuart (Special Mission) 1825

Prussia
Earl of Clanwilliam 1823–8

Russia
Sir Charles Bagot 1820–4
Stratford Canning (Special Mission) 1825
Viscount Strangford 1825–6
Duke of Wellington (Special Mission) 1826
Duke of Devonshire (Special Mission) 1826

Spain
Sir William A'Court 1822–4
Frederick Lamb 1825–7

Turkey
 Viscount Strangford 1821–4
 Stratford Canning 1826–7

United Netherlands
 Earl of Clancarty 1817–24
 Viscount Granville 1824
 Sir Charles Bagot 1824–32

United States of America
 Stratford Canning 1820–3
 Charles Vaughan 1823–5

NOTES

The prefix 'Harewood' is used to indicate the Canning Papers owned by the Earl of Harewood and preserved at Sheepscar Branch Library, Leeds. The prefix is followed by the box number. Other abbreviations are used as follows:

BM Add Mss	British Museum, Additional Manuscripts
CPD	Cobbett's Parliamentary Debates
Dropmore	Manuscripts of Sir John Fortescue preserved at Dropmore (Historical Manuscripts Commission)
Hans.	Parliamentary Debates, New Series (Hansard)
HMC	Historical Manuscripts Commission
NLS	National Library of Scotland
Parl. Hist.	Parliamentary History
PRO	Public Record Office
PRO-FO	Public Record Office – Foreign Office
SRO	Scottish Record Office
TRHS	Transactions of the Royal Historical Society

CHAPTER I

1 20 July 1683.
2 *Poems by George Canning of the Middle Temple, Esq.* (London, 1767), p. 22.
3 Canning, *Poems*, p. 34.
4 Canning, *Poems*, p. 6.
5 Robert Bell, *The Life of the Rt Hon. George Canning* (London, 1846), p. 31.
6 Bell, *Life of George Canning*, p. 29.
7 Canning to his mother, 19 October 1782. Harewood 2.
8 Canning to his mother, 28 May 1783. Harewood 2.
9 Canning to his mother, 22 September 1792. Harewood 2.

10 Canning to his mother, 25 May 1795. Harewood 2.
11 *Life of Wilberforce*, ed. R. I. and S. Wilberforce (London, 1838), vol. 5, p. 139.
12 Lord Holland, *Further Memoirs of the Whig Party, 1807–21, with some miscellaneous reminiscences* (London, 1905), p. 317.
13 Dorothy Marshall, *The Rise of George Canning* (London, 1938), p. 11.
14 Sir Richard Hill, *An Address to Ladies of Fashion containing some particulars relating to Balls; and a few occasional hints concerning Play-houses, Card Tables, etc.* (London, 1761).
15 *The Microcosm*, no. 2, 2nd edition (London, 1788), p. 17 ff.
16 *The Microcosm*, no. 34.
17 *The Microcosm*, nos 11 and 12.
18 *The Microcosm*, no. 5.
19 Marshall, *The Rise of George Canning*, p. 10.
20 Canning to his mother, 13 June 1786. Harewood 2.
21 Frere to Canning, n.d. (1788). Harewood 64.
22 Canning to the Rev. Wm. Leigh, 24 November 1787. Harewood 12.
23 Canning to the Rev. Wm. Leigh, 24 November 1787. Harewood 12.
24 Canning to the Rev. Wm. Leigh, 24 November 1787. Harewood 12.
25 Canning to the Rev. Wm. Leigh, 24 November 1787. Harewood 12.
26 John F. Newton, *Early Days of the Rt Hon. George Canning, First Lord of the Treasury and Chancellor of the Exchequer, and some of his contemporaries* (London, 1828), pp. 20–1.
27 Newton, *Early Days of . . . George Canning*, p. 22.
28 Canning to the Rev. Leigh, 26 September 1788. Harewood 12.
29 Holland, *Further Memoirs, etc.*, p. 317.
30 Henry, Lord Brougham, *Historical Sketches of Statesmen who flourished in the time of George III* (London, 1855), p. 357.
31 Marshall, *The Rise of George Canning*, p. 24.
32 Canning to his mother, 27 December 1789. Harewood 2.
33 Canning to the Rev. Leigh, 28 May 1791 and 12 December 1792. Harewood 12.
34 Canning to the Rev. Leigh, 28 May 1791. Harewood 12.
35 Canning frequently went to Wanstead to visit his uncle's widow Hetty Canning and her family.
36 Canning's Diary, 2 March, 26 and 29 April, and 21 June 1792. Harewood 29 (d).
37 Marshall, *The Rise of George Canning*, p. 29.

38   Lord Granville Leveson-Gower, *Private Correspondence, 1781–1821*, ed. by his daughter-in-law, Castalia, Countess Granville (London, 1916), vol. 1, p. xxiii.
39   Canning to his mother, 9 November 1789. Harewood 2.
40   Canning to the Rev. Leigh, 27 July 1788. Harewood 12.
41   Canning to his mother, 30 March 1786. Harewood 2.
42   Canning to his mother, 8 June 1791. Harewood 2.
43   Canning to his mother, 13 June 1791. Harewood 2. The green-room is a room for actors to meet socially.
44   Canning to his mother, 22 March 1794. Harewood 2.
45   Lord Edmund Fitzmaurice, *Life of William, Earl of Shelburne* (London, 1876), vol. 3, pp. 474–5.
46   Canning to Lord Crewe, 25 May 1791. Canning Papers, William L. Clements Library, Ann Arbor, Michigan.
47   Sir Charles Petrie, *George Canning*, 2nd edition (London, 1946), p. 27.
48   Colonel Norman Macleod to Charles Grey, 30 November 1792. Grey Papers, University of Durham, box 41:1.
49   Canning to Pitt, 25 July 1792, enclosed with diaries. Harewood 29 (d).
50   Pitt to Canning, 28 July 1792. Harewood 30.
51   *The Journal of Elizabeth Lady Holland*, ed. the Earl of Ilchester (London, 1908), vol. 1, p. 123.
52   *Journal of Elizabeth, Lady Holland*, vol. I, p. 217.
53   E. B. Wilbraham, 1771–1853: MP for Westbury, 1795–6; Newcastle-under-Lyme, 1796–1812; Clitheroe, 1812–18; Dover, 1818–28; cr. 1st Baron Skelmersdale, 1828.
54   The Duke of Brunswick had led an abortive invasion of France on behalf of Austria and Prussia in 1792. The repulse of this force at Valmy on 20 September 1792, commented Goethe, marked the beginning of a new age in world history.
55   Canning to E. B. Wilbraham, 4 December 1792. Quoted in Josceline Bagot, *George Canning and his Friends* (London, 1909), vol. 1, p. 30 ff.
56   Diary, 20 November 1792. Harewood 29 (d).
57   Canning to the Rev. Leigh, 27 April 1793. Harewood 12.
58   Pitt to Canning, 21 and 29 June 1793. Harewood 30.
59   Canning to the Rev. Leigh, 28 June 1793. Harewood 12.
60   Canning to the Rev. Leigh, 9 November 1793. Harewood 12.
61   Diary, 26 and 27 July and 24 to 27 August 1792. Harewood 29 (d).
62   Diary, 5 and 7 August 1794. Harewood 29 (d).
63   Parliamentary History, 31 January 1794, vol. 30, p. 1317 ff.

64 Canning to his mother, 3 February 1794. Harewood 2.
65 Bagot, *George Canning and his Friends*, p. 47 n.
66 Parl. Hist., 10 April 1794, vol. 31, p. 254 ff.
67 Canning to his mother, 2 April 1794. Harewood 2.
68 Parl. Hist., 29 February 1792, vol. 29, p. 918 ff. One unfortunate
    howler, nevertheless, was his forecast that 'Poland, since her
    revolution, was likely to become a power of no inconsiderable
    consequence' (col. 924).
69 Canning to the Rev. Leigh, 27 March 1792. Harewood 12.
70 Parl. Hist., 2 April 1792, vol. 29, pp. 1124–33. The next forty
    years were however to show that hopes of a self-sufficient slave
    population were in vain.
71 P. J. Rolo, *George Canning* (London, 1965), p. 27.
72 Diary for 1792. Harewood 29 (d).
73 Diary, 1 September 1793. Harewood 29 (d).
74 Parl. Hist., 17 May 1794, vol. 31, p. 535.
75 Diary, 8 November 1793. Harewood 29 (d).
76 Canning to Baron Crewe, 24 November 1792. Canning Papers,
    Ann Arbor, Michigan.
77 Marshall, *The Rise of George Canning*, p. 70 ff.
78 Canning to E. B. Wilbraham, 4 December 1792. Quoted in
    Bagot, *George Canning and his Friends*, p. 32.
79 Canning to E. B. Wilbraham, 4 December 1792. Quoted in
    Bagot, *George Canning and his Friends*, p. 37.
80 Canning to Baron Crewe, 24 November 1792. Canning Papers,
    Ann Arbor, Michigan.
81 *Journal of Elizabeth, Lady Holland*, p. 217.
82 Rolo, *George Canning*, p. 25.
83 Canning to Sir Walter Scott, 26 July 1811. Scott Papers, NLS
    Mss 3880:206.
84 Lady Stafford to Leveson-Gower, 1 November 1794. *Leveson-
    Gower Private Correspondence*, vol. 1, p. 100.
85 Canning to his mother, 29 April 1794. Harewood 2.
86 Lady Bessborough to Leveson-Gower, August 1798. *Leveson-
    Gower Private Correspondence*, p. 217.
87 Gabrielle Festing, *J. H. Frere and His Friends* (London, 1899),
    p. 113.
88 Marshall, *The Rise of George Canning*, p. 120.
89 A full account of this amusing but grossly overplayed incident
    is given in Bagot, *George Canning and his Friends*, pp. 70–116.
90 Marshall, *The Rise of George Canning*, pp. 127–8.
91 Marshall, *The Rise of George Canning*, p. 132.
92 Diary, 24 February to 8 March 1794. Harewood 29 (d).

CHAPTER 2

1 Canning to the Rev. Leigh, 4 January 1795. Harewood 13.
2 Parl. Hist., 30 December 1794, vol. 31, p. 1026.
3 Parl. Hist., 30 December 1794, vol. 31, p. 1009.
4 Parl. Hist., 21 March 1795, vol. 31, p. 1406.
5 Diary, 26 February 1795. Harewood 29 (d).
6 Diary, 16 and 24 June 1795. Harewood 29 (d).
7 Canning to the Rev. Leigh, 28 October 1795. Harewood 13.
8 Diary, 2 November 1795. Harewood 29 (d).
9 Diary, 2 to 6 January 1796. Harewood 29 (d).
10 Canning to Auckland, 12 August 1796. Auckland Papers, BM Add Mss 34454:42.
11 Canning to Boringdon, 21 August 1796. Quoted in A. G. Stapleton, *George Canning and His Times* (London 1859), p. 38.
12 Canning to Auckland, 16 August 1797. Auckland Papers. BM Add Mss 34454:126.
13 Canning to Auckland, 22 January 1797. Auckland Papers, BM Add Mss 34454:45.
14 Canning to the Rev. Leigh, 26 May 1796. Harewood 13.
15 Canning to Pitt, 1 July 1799. Harewood 30.
16 Canning to his mother, 31 January 1795. Harewood 2.
17 Windham Papers. BM Add Mss 37844:267.
18 Canning to Leveson-Gower, 29 July 1796. Marshall, *The Rise of George Canning*, p. 160.
19 Pitt to Chatham, 4 September 1796. Earl Stanhope, *Life of the Right Honourable William Pitt* (London, 1862), vol. 2, p. 381.
20 Canning to his mother, 6 June 1795. Harewood 2.
21 George Ellis to Canning, 18 October 1796. Harewood 62.
22 Malmesbury to Grenville, 27 October 1796. *Diaries and Correspondence of James Harris, First Earl of Malmesbury*, 2nd edition (London, 1845), vol. 3, p. 281.
23 Malmesbury to Pitt, 11 November 1796. *Malmesbury Diaries and Correspondence*, vol. 3, p. 294.
24 Malmesbury to Grenville, 28 November 1796. *Malmesbury Diaries and Correspondence*, vol. 3, p. 313.
25 Grenville to Malmesbury, 11 December 1796. *Malmesbury Diaries and Correspondence*, vol. 3, p. 327.
26 Malmesbury to Canning, 27 November 1796. *Malmesbury Diaries and Correspondence*, vol. 3, p. 310.
27 Pitt to the King, 9 April 1797. Stanhope, *Life of Pitt*, vol. 3, Appendix IV–V.
28 Canning to the Rev. Leigh, 10 April 1797. Harewood 13.
29 Diary, 10 May 1797. Harewood 29 (d).

30 Stanhope, *Life of Pitt*, vol. 3, p. 53.
31 Stanhope, *Life of Pitt*, vol. 3, p. 53.
32 Diary, 12 and 22 to 24 June 1797. Harewood 29 (d).
33 Canning to George Ellis, 13 July 1797. *Malmesbury Diaries and Correspondence*, vol. 3, pp. 381–3.
34 Canning to Malmesbury, 20 July 1797. *Malmesbury Diaries and Correspondence*, vol. 3, pp. 400–1.
35 Canning to George Ellis, 8 August 1797. *Malmesbury Diaries and Correspondence*, vol. 3, pp. 435–9.
36 '*Nous sommes encore a tâtonner.*' Grenville to Woronzour, 22 July 1797. The Manuscripts of J. B. Fortescue, presented at Dropmore (Historical Manuscript Commission, 1892–7), vol. 4, p. 335.
37 Buckingham to Grenville, 4 September 1797. Dropmore, vol. 4, p. 368.
38 Malmesbury to Canning, 14 August 1797. *Malmesbury Diaries and Correspondence*, vol. 3, p. 446.
39 Malmesbury to Canning, 14 August 1797. *Malmesbury Diaries and Correspondence*, vol. 3, p. 447.
40 Malmesbury to Canning, 29 August 1797. *Malmesbury Diaries and Correspondence*, vol. 3, p. 498.
41 Malmesbury to Canning, 29 August 1797 (different letter). *Malmesbury Diaries and Correspondence*, vol. 3, pp. 496–7.
42 G. Lefebvre, *The Directory*, tr. R. Baldick (London, 1964), p. 84.
43 Stanhope, *Life of Pitt*, vol. 3, p. 60.
44 Malmesbury to Pitt, 9 September 1797. *Malmesbury Diaries and Correspondence*, vol. 3, p. 520.
45 Canning to George Ellis, 18 October 1797. Harewood 62.
46 Diary, 3 October 1798. Harewood 29 (d).
47 Pitt to Grenville, 6 October 1798. Dropmore, vol. 4, p. 337.
48 Canning to the Rev. J. Sneyd, c. March 1799. Bagot, *George Canning and his Friends*, vol. 1, p. 146.
49 *The Diary of the Rt Hon. William Windham, 1784–1810*, ed. Mrs Henry Baring (London, 1866), pp. 400–1.
50 Canning to the Rev. Sneyd, c. March 1799. Bagot, *George Canning and his Friends*, vol. 1, p. 146.
51 Canning to Leveson-Gower, 10 September 1799. *Leveson-Gower Private Correspondence*, vol. 1, pp. 257–9.
52 Diary, 8 October 1798. Harewood 29 (d).
53 Canning to Grenville, 1 April 1799. Dropmore, vol. 4, p. 514.
54 Canning to his mother, 18 March 1795. Harewood 2.
55 Diary, 9 May 1797. Harewood 29 (d).

56 Diary, 26 May 1797. Harewood 29 (d).
57 Parl. Hist., 12 November 1795, vol. 32, p. 301.
58 Parl. Hist., 26 December 1798, vol. 34, p. 125; 13 February
     1800, vol. 34, pp. 1469–71.
59 Canning to Pitt, 23 October 1798. Harewood 30.
60 Parl. Hist., 13 March 1797, vol. 33, p. 106.
61 Parl. Hist., 11 December 1798, vol. 34, p. 67.
62 Parl. Hist., 11 December 1798, vol. 34, p. 45.
63 Canning to his mother, 4 February 1795. Harewood 2.
64 *The Anti-Jacobin*, No. 20, 26 March 1798, vol. 1, p. 157.
65 *The Anti-Jacobin*, No. 1, 20 November 1797, vol. 1, p. 7.
66 Marshall, *The Rise of George Canning*, p. 179. See *The Poetical
     Works of Robert Southey* (Paris, 1829), p. 706.
67 *The Anti-Jacobin*, No. 1, 20 November 1797, vol. 1, p. 8
68 *The Anti-Jacobin*, No. 32, 18 June 1798, vol. 1, p. 252.
69 *The Anti-Jacobin*, No. 5, 11 December 1797, vol. 1, pp. 36–8.
70 *The Anti-Jacobin*, No. 11, 22 January 1798, vol. 1, pp. 83–4.
71 *The Anti-Jacobin*, No. 13, 5 February, 1798, vol. 1, p. 97.
72 *The Anti-Jacobin*, No. 12, 29 January 1798, vol. 1, pp. 92–3.
73 *The Anti-Jacobin*, No. 3, 30 November, 1797, vol. 1, p. 20 ff.
74 Canning to the Rev. Leigh, 30 November 1797. Harewood 13.
75 *The Anti-Jacobin*, No. 19, 19 March 1798, vol. 1, p. 150.
76 *The Anti-Jacobin*, No. 4, 4 December 1797, vol. 1, p. 29.
77 *The Anti-Jacobin*, No. 23, 16 April 1798, vol. 1, p. 180 ff.
78 *Burlesque Plays and Poems*, ed. H. Morley (London, 1885),
     p. 199.
79 *Burlesque Plays and Poems*, p. 203.
80 *Burlesque Plays and Poems*, p. 209.
81 Festing, *J. H. Frere and His Friends*, p. 30.
82 *The Anti-Jacobin*, No. 2, 27 November 1797, vol. 1, pp. 15–16.
83 *The Anti-Jacobin*, No. 36, 9 July 1798, vol. 1, p. 282 ff.
84 Marshall, *The Rise of George Canning*, p. 195.
85 Canning to Leveson-Gower, 22 August 1799. *Leveson-Gower
     Private Correspondence*, vol. 1, p. 255 ff.
86 Bagot, *George Canning and his Friends*, vol. 1, p. 158 n.
87 Namier and Brooke, *History of Parliament (1754–90)*, vol. 3,
     p. 414.
88 Capt. Keith Scott, *Scotland, 1118–1923* (London, 1923).
89 Edinburgh Consistorial Court Records, SRO CC 8/5/12. James
     Sutherland was restored to the family title of Lord Duffus in
     1826.
90 *Scots Magazine* (1776), p. 163.
91 Joan Scott's wealth was such as would attract the adventurer.

In 1799 a Mr John McLean wrote from an accommodation address to the Lord Chancellor complaining that his offers of marriage had been rebuffed, and he wanted Lord Lough-borough's advice as to how he might prosecute Miss Scott. (J. McLean to Lord Loughborough, 12 November 1799. NLS, Melville Papers, Ms 1056:107.)

92 Arther Paget was a diplomat and an MP. In 1809 he married the wife of Canning's friend Lord Boringdon after an affair which ended in the latter going to Parliament for a divorce.

93 Canning to Lady Susan Ryder, 15 August 1799. Harewood 29. Lady Susan was the wife of Dudley Ryder, heir to the Earldom of Harrowby.

94 Canning to Lady Susan Ryder, 21 and 24 August, and 20 September 1799. Harewood 29.

95 Canning to Lady Stafford, 12 May 1800. *Leveson-Gower Private Correspondence*, vol. 1, pp. 279–80.

96 Festing, *J. H. Frere and His Friends*, pp. 31–2.

97 Lady Malmesbury to the Rev. Sneyd, early 1801. Bagot, *George Canning and his Friends*, vol. 1, p. 127.

98 Charles Ellis to Canning, 12 July 1800. Harewood 62.

99 Canning to his wife, 8, 13 and 29 November and 3 December 1800. Harewood 18.

100 Canning to his wife, 14 November 1800. Harewood 18.

CHAPTER 3

1 *The Later Correspondence of George III*, ed. A. Aspinall (Cambridge, 1963–70), vol. 3, p. 2144 n.

2 Buckingham to Grenville, May 1800. Dropmore, vol. 6, p. 221/L.

3 *George III*, ed. Aspinall, vol. 3, p. 2108.

4 Pitt to Canning, 10 December 1799. Harewood 30.

5 Parl. Hist., 11 December 1798, vol. 34, p. 67.

6 Parl. Hist., 11 December 1798, vol. 34, p. 45.

7 *George III*, ed. Aspinall, vol. 3, p. 2065 n.

8 Canning to Leveson-Gower, 19 November 1799. *Leveson-Gower Private Correspondence*, vol. 1, p. 273.

9 Canning to Pitt, 23 November 1799, and Pitt to Canning, 3 December 1799. Harewood 30.

10 Canning to the Rev. Sneyd, 6 January 1800. Bagot, *George Canning and his Friends*, vol. 1, pp. 159–61.

11 Parl. Hist., 25 January 1800, vol. 34, p. 1261.

12 Canning to Frere, 2 December 1800. Festing, *J. H. Frere and His Friends*, p. 35.

13   Canning to Windham, 31 December 1799. *The Windham Papers*, ed. The Earl of Rosebery (London, 1913), vol. 1, p. 148.
14   Canning to Mornington, 24 Aguust 1800. Wellesley Papers, BM Add Mss 37295:5-32.
15   Canning to Frere, 16 September 1800. Festing, *J. H. Frere and His Friends*, p. 33.
16   *Diary of William Windham*, p. 432.
17   Leveson-Gower to Canning, 14 September 1800. Harewood 65.
18   Pitt to Grenville, 2 November 1800. Dropmore, vol. 6, p. 372.
19   Canning to Pitt, 20 November 1800, and Pitt to Canning, 22 November 1800. Harewood 30.
20   Parl. Hist., 27 November 1800, vol. 35, pp. 644-7.
21   *George III*, ed. Aspinall, vol. 3, p. 2276 n.
22   Canning to Pitt, 29 July 1800. Harewood 30.
23   Canning to Pitt, 29 July 1800. Harewood 30.
24   Canning to Pitt, 11 January 1801. Harewood 30.
25   The argument is analogous to that of Lord Durham forty years later that it was safe to concede responsible government in Canada provided the French majority in Lower Canada was swamped by the English in Upper Canada.
26   Canning to Pitt, n.d. (1798). Harewood 30. Canning was at Ashbourne from 17 July to 2 August (Diary).
27   John Fitzgibbon, Earl of Clare, Lord Chancellor of Ireland and leader of the High Protestant faction.
28   Canning to Windham, 23 October 1798. Windham Papers, BM Add Mss 37844:273/4.
29   Parl. Hist., 23 January 1799, vol. 34, pp. 224H, 235, 237.
30   Parl. Hist., 22 April 1799, vol. 34, pp. 958H, 976.
31   *George III*, ed. Aspinall, vol. 3, p. 2339 n.
32   Festing, *J. H. Frere and His Friends*, p. 41.
33   *George III*, ed. Aspinall, vol. 3, p. 2357.
34   Pitt to Canning, 15 February 1801. Harewood 30.
35   Canning to Pitt, 8 March 1801. Harewood 30.
36   *Diary and Correspondence of Charles Abbot, Lord Colchester*, ed. by his son (London, 1861), vol. 1, p. 224.
37   Canning to Newbolt, 7 February 1801. Harewood 64.
38   Festing, *J. H. Frere and His Friends*, p. 43.
39   Leveson-Gower to his mother, 7 February 1801. *Leveson-Gower Private Correspondence*, vol. 1, p. 290.
40   Lady Stafford to Leveson-Gower, 19 February 1801. *Leveson-Gower Private Correspondence*, vol. 2, pp. 96-7.
41   Pitt to Canning, 26 April 1801. Harewood 30.
42   Canning to Pitt, 10 September 1801. Harewood 30.

43 Parl. Hist., 18 April 1800, vol. 35, pp. 211–12.

44 *Journal of Elizabeth, Lady Holland*, vol. 2, p. 52.

45 Bagot, *George Canning and his Friends*, vol. 1, p. 163.

46 A. B. Rodger, *The War of the Second Coalition, 1795–1801* (Oxford, 1964), p. 279.

47 Canning to Grenville, 7 October 1801. Dropmore, vol. 7, p. 54.

48 Festing, *J. H. Frere and His Friends*, p. 59.

49 The possibility of Bonaparte either changing his system or being overthrown 'would', said Canning, 'be too provoking a piece of good luck for this wretched, pusillanimous toad-eating administration'. Festing, *J. H. Frere and His Friends*, pp. 69–70.

50 Leveson-Gower to Canning, 17 October 1801. Harewood 65.

51 Canning to Sturges-Bourne, 25 October 1801. Canning Papers, Ann Arbor, Michigan.

52 Canning to Pitt, 21 October 1801. Canning Papers, Ann Arbor, Michigan.

53 Pitt to Canning, 26 October 1801. Canning Papers, Ann Arbor, Michigan.

54 Canning to Windham, 20 April 1802. Windham Papers, BM Add Mss 37844:284.

55 Windham to Canning, 24 April 1802. Windham Papers, BM Add Mss 37844:288.

56 Parl. Hist., 11 May 1802, vol. 36, pp. 754, 777, 828.

57 Canning to Windham, 23 May 1802. Windham Papers, BM Add Mss 37844:294.

58 *Journal of Elizabeth, Lady Holland*, vol. 1, p. 218.

59 *George III*, ed. Aspinall, vol. 2, p. 1514 n.

60 *The Canningite Party*, ed. A. Aspinall (TRHS, 1934), pp. 180, 184.

61 Canning to Leveson-Gower, 13 November 1798. *Leveson-Gower Private Correspondence*, vol. 1, pp. 226–7.

62 Festing, *J. H. Frere and His Friends*, p. 36.

63 Canning to Frere, 7 November 1802. Festing, *J. H. Frere and His Friends*, p. 61.

64 The phrase *Leze-Medecine* is explained by Canning's continual reference to Addington as 'The Doctor', thus reminding everyone of the profession of the latter's father. Given Canning's own parentage this was extraordinarily presumptuous. *Leveson-Gower Private Correspondence*, vol. 1, p. 315.

65 Philip Ziegler, *A Life of Henry Addington, First Viscount Sidmouth* (London, 1965), p. 106.

66 Canning to Frere, 11 April 1802. BM Add Mss 38833:104.

67 *The Poetical Works of the Rt Hon. George Canning*, MP,

Secretary of State for Foreign Affairs (London, 1823), p. 36.
68 Canning to Frere, 1 to 7 June 1802. Festing, *J. H. Frere and His Friends*, p. 79.
69 Canning to Frere, 1 to 7 June 1802. Festing, *J. H. Frere and His Friends*, p. 84.
70 Canning to Leveson-Gower, 27 January 1802. *Leveson-Gower Private Correspondence*, vol. 1, p. 325.
71 Canning to Frere, 28 August and 7 September, 1802. Festing, *J. H. Frere and His Friends*, p. 86.
72 Buckingham to Grenville, 1 November 1802. Dropmore, vol. 7, p. 122.
73 *Diaries and Correspondence of the Rt Hon. George Rose*, ed. L. V. Harcourt (London, 1860), vol. 1, pp. 490–2.
74 *Rose Diaries and Correspondence*, vol. 1, pp. 457–60.
75 Stanhope, *Life of Pitt*, vol. 3, p. 421.
76 *Rose Diaries and Correspondence*, vol. 2, p. 7.
77 Diary, 15 March 1803. Harewood 29 (d).
78 Canning to Pitt, 7 February 1803, and Pitt to Canning, 10 March 1803, Harewood 30.
79 Festing, *J. H. Frere and His Friends*, pp. 91–2. He was of course right.
80 Pitt to Canning, 2 and 10 March 1803. Harewood 30.
81 Paper in Pitt's handwriting given to Canning, dated 8 November 1802. Dropmore, vol. 7, p. 123.
82 *Colchester Diary and Correspondence*, vol. 1, p. 417.
83 Festing, *J. H. Frere and His Friends*, p. 71.
84 Festing, *J. H. Frere and His Friends*, p. 67.
85 Diary, 26 February and 27 May 1802. Harewood 29 (d).
86 Parl. Hist., 27 May 1802, vol. 36, p. 854.
87 Canning to Wilberforce, 5 February 1802. Harewood 80 (a).
88 Ziegler, *Addington*, pp. 151–2.
89 Frere to Canning, 2 February 1802. Harewood 64.
90 Parl. Hist., 7 May 1802, vol. 36, p. 654.
91 Parl. Hist., 23 November 1802, vol. 36, p. 959H.
92 Colonel MacMahon to Northumberland, 27 November 1802. *The Correspondence of George, Prince of Wales*, ed. A. Aspinall (London, 1963–8), vol. 4, p. 690.
93 Parl. Hist., 8 December 1802, vol. 36, p. 1070H.
94 Parl. Hist., 11 March 1803, vol. 36, p. 1195.
95 Parl. Hist., 11 March 1803, vol. 36, p. 1387.
96 T. Grenville to Lord Grenville, 30 May 1803. Dropmore, vol. 7, p. 170.
97 Ziegler, *Addington*, p. 187.

98   Parl. Hist., 11 March 1803, vol. 36, p. 1386.
99   Parl. Hist., 11 March 1803, vol. 36, p. 1533.
100 Not all were inclined to Canning's views. He complained later that 'Bootle shirked and Boringdon voted with the Government in the Ho[use of] Lords!!! after joining for the last two months as heartily as heart could desire, in the cry against the Dr. No matter. I am glad he has been brought to the test.' Festing, *J. H. Frere and His Friends*, pp. 95–6.
101 *Colchester Diary and Correspondence*, vol. 1, pp. 422–3.
102 *Colchester Diary and Correspondence*, vol. 1, p. 430 (1 July 1803).
103 Canning to Frere, 9 June 1803. Festing, *J. H. Frere and His Friends*, p. 95.
104 Festing, *J. H. Frere and His Friends*, p. 98.
105 Canning to Pitt, 10, 17 and 22 November 1803. Harewood 30.
106 Pitt to Canning, 20 November 1803. Harewood 30.
107 Festing, *J. H. Frere and His Friends*, p. 102.
108 Canning to Pitt, 1 December 1803. Harewood 30.
109 Pitt to Canning, 5 and 25 December 1803. Harewood 30.
110 Canning to Pitt, 27 January 1804. Harewood 30.
111 T. T. Pratt, 1759–1840. First Marquess Camden, Lord Lieutenant of Ireland, 1795–8; Secretary of State for War and the Colonies, 1805—6; Lord President of Council, 1805–6, 1807–12.
112 Canning to Leveson-Gower, 19 February 1804. *Leveson-Gower Private Correspondence*, vol. 1, p. 446.
113 *Cobbett's Parliamentary Debates*, vol. 1, pp. 752, 805, 927, 949.
114 Pitt to Canning, 9 April 1804. Harewood 30.
115 Canning was in the minority on two votes on the Irish Militia Bill, 125 to 54 votes and 100 to 42 votes.
116 CPD 2:57, 2:263, 2:311–19.
117 Canning to Frere, 12 July 1802. Festing, *J. H. Frere and His Friends*, p. 47.
118 Frere to Canning, n.d. (1804). Harewood 64.
119 Canning to Frere, 17 August 1802. Festing, *J. H. Frere and His Friends*, pp. 52–3.
120 Diary, 18 September 1801. Harewood 29 (d).
121 Festing, *J. H. Frere and His Friends*, p. 55.
122 Festing, *J. H. Frere and His Friends*, p. 54.
123 Diary, October 1801. Harewood 29 (d).
124 It was his friend John Dent who had suggested the two-shilling tax on dogs.

CHAPTER 4
1   Parl. Hist., 23 May 1803, vol. 36, pp. 1408, 1484.

2   *Colchester Diary and Correspondence*, 6 May 1804, vol. 1, p. 505.
3   Stanhope, *Life of Pitt*, vol. 4, pp. 191–2.
4   Canning to Pitt, 9 May 1804, and Pitt to Canning, 14 May 1804. Harewood 30.
5   *George III*, ed. Aspinall, vol. 4, p. 2866 n.
6   At first the office was held by Addington's brother-in-law, Charles Bragge.
7   Diary, 14 May 1804. Harewood 29 (d).
8   *Colchester Diary and Correspondence*, vol. 1, pp. 529–30.
9   Lady Bessborough to Leveson-Gower, 29 December 1804. *Leveson-Gower Private Correspondence*, vol. 1, p. 505.
10 Lady Bessborough to Leveson-Gower, 8 February 1805. *Leveson-Gower Private Correspondence*, vol. 2, p. 11.
11 Lady Bessborough to Leveson-Gower, February 1805. *Leveson-Gower Private Correspondence*, vol. 2, p. 19.
12 Canning to the Rev. Sneyd, 4 February 1805. Canning Papers, Ann Arbor, Michigan.
13 T. Grenville to Lord Grenville, 8 November 1804. Dropmore, vol. 7, p. 237.
14 *Rose Diaries and Correspondence*, vol. 2, p. 270.
15 Diary, 4 January 1805. Harewood 29 (d).
16 *George III*, ed. Aspinall, vol. 4, p. 3002 n.
17 Canning to Lady Stanhope, 1 January 1805. Stanhope, *Life of Pitt*, vol. 4, p. 244.
18 Diary, 15 January 1805. Harewood 29 (d).
19 Canning to Leveson-Gower, 25 February 1805. *Leveson-Gower Private Correspondence*, vol. 2, pp. 28–32.
20 Canning to Leveson-Gower, 16 April 1805. *Leveson-Gower Private Correspondence*, vol. 2, p. 58.
21 CPD 3:621, 4:176, 5:519.
22 *George III*, ed. Aspinall, vol. 4, p. 3068 n.
23 Lady Bessborough to Leveson-Gower, 10 April (June?) 1805. *Leveson-Gower Private Correspondence*, vol. 2, pp. 55, 82.
24 Canning to his mother, 9 April 1805. Harewood 6.
25 CPD 4:298.
26 CPD 4:341.
27 Diary, 11 April 1805. Harewood 29 (d).
28 CPD 4:381.
29 CPD 4:381–2, 4:562.
30 *George III*, ed. Aspinall, vol. 4, p. 3085 n.
31 The vote was later reversed.
32 Buckingham to Grenville, 13 June 1805. Dropmore, vol. 7, p. 278.

33 Ziegler, *Addington*, p. 239.

34 Canning to his mother, 1 August 1805. Harewood 6.

35 Pitt to Bathurst, 27 September 1805. Bathurst Papers (Historical Manuscripts Commission, vol. 76, 1923), pp. 49–50.

36 *Rose Diaries and Correspondence*, vol. 2, p. 249.

37 Canning to his mother, 12 November 1805. Harewood 6.

38 Canning to Lady Bessborough, 3 December 1805, vol. 2, p. 140.

39 Canning to the Rev. Sneyd, 8 January 1806. Canning Papers, Ann Arbor, Michigan.

40 Diary, 14 January 1806. Harewood 29 (d).

41 Diary, 15 January 1806. Harewood 29 (d).

42 Diary, 18 January 1806. Harewood 29 (d).

43 Festing, *J. H. Frere and His Friends*, p. 106.

44 Lady Bessborough to Leveson-Gower, 23 January 1806. *Leveson-Gower Private Correspondence*, vol. 2, p. 162.

45 Melville to Canning, 23 January 1806. Harewood 77.

46 Canning to the Rev. Leigh, 25 January 1806. Harewood 17.

47 Canning to the Rev. Leigh, 22 February 1806. Harewood 17.

48 Diary (printed). Harewood 29 (d).

49 Canning to Leveson-Gower, 29 January 1806. *Leveson-Gower Private Correspondence*, vol. 2, pp. 169–73.

50 *George III*, ed. Aspinall, vol. 3, p. 2125 n.

51 Canning to Leveson-Gower, 25 February 1806. *Leveson-Gower Private Correspondence*, vol. 2, p. 181.

52 *The Poetical Works of . . . George Canning*, p. 46.

53 *Rose Diaries and Correspondence*, vol. 2, pp. 262–3.

54 Canning to his mother, 14 March 1806. Harewood 6.

55 CPD 6:298–306.

56 Diary, 23 February 1806. Harewood 29 (d).

57 *The Poetical Works of . . . George Canning*, p. 46.

58 See note 60.

59 Canning to E. B. Wilbraham, 6 April 1806. Bagot, *George Canning and his Friends*, vol. 1, pp. 230–1.

60 Canning spoke criticizing Windham's military reforms on 6, 10 and 17 March, 17 and 30 April, 6 and 30 May, and 6 June 1806. CPD 6:357, 368, 463–5, 793, 967. CPD 7:28, 454, 543.

61 Dropmore, vol. 8, p. 148.

62 CPD 7:618 f., 649 f.

63 CPD 7:913–14.

64 Canning to the Rev. Leigh, 24 July 1806. Harewood 17.

65 Lady Bessborough to Leveson-Gower, 10 May 1806. *Leveson-Gower Private Correspondence*, vol. 2, p. 195.

66 Wellesley to Grenville, 27 July 1806. Dropmore, pp. 210, 212–13, 248.
67 Leveson-Gower to Canning, 23 May, 15 September and 13 December 1806. Harewood 65.
68 Diary, March 1806. Harewood 29 (d).
69 *George III*, ed. Aspinall, vol. 3, p. 2291 n.
70 Canning to his wife, 21 February 1807. Harewood 22.
71 *George, Prince of Wales*, ed. Aspinall, vol. 6, p. 2288 n.
72 Canning to Huskisson, 30 November 1806. Harewood 67.
73 Perceval to Canning, 29 November 1806. Harewood 33.
74 A. G. Stapleton, *George Canning and His Times*, p. 96.
75 Wellesley to Grenville, 13 September 1806. Dropmore, vol. 8, p. 331.
76 Canning to Wellesley, 16 September 1806. Dropmore, vol. 8, p. 337.
77 Canning to Lowther, 26 September 1806. BM Add Mss 37295: 77–9.
78 Lady Bessborough to Leveson-Gower (?), October 1806, 28 October 1806. *Leveson-Gower Private Correspondence*, vol. 2, pp. 220, 222.
79 Grenville to Wellesley, 16 October 1806. BM Add Mss 37295: 95–8.
80 Wellesley to Grenville, 12 October 1806, and Grenville to Wellesley, 16 October 1806. Dropmore, vol. 8, pp. 380, 387–8.
81 Buckingham to Grenville, 19 February 1807, Earl Temple to Grenville, 24 February 1807. Dropmore, vol. 9, pp. 53, 54.
82 Canning to his wife, 16 February 1807. Harewood 22.
83 Canning to his wife, 27 February 1807. Harewood 22.
84 Canning to his wife, 6 and 9 March 1807. Harewood 22.
85 Canning to his wife, 10 March 1807. Harewood 22.
86 Canning to his wife, 10 March 1807. Harewood 22.
87 Canning to his wife, 14 March 1807. Harewood 22.
88 CPD 8:44 f., 373 f., 411.
89 Canning to his wife, 19 and 23 March 1807. Harewood 22.
90 Denis Gray, *Spencer Perceval, The Evangelical Prime Minister, 1762–1812* (Manchester 1963), p. 80.
91 Lady Bessborough to Leveson-Gower, 30 June 1806. *Leveson-Gower Private Correspondence*, vol. 2, p. 206.
92 Festing, *J. H. Frere and His Friends*, p. 207.
93 Gray, *Spencer Perceval*, p. 82.
94 Canning to his wife, 16 February 1807. Harewood 22.
95 Canning to his wife, 28 February, 11 March 1807. Harewood 22.
96 CPD 9:62.

97 CPD 8:857–8.
98 Perceval to Sidmouth, 14 March 1807. Perceval Papers, BM Add Mss 49184:97.
99 Canning to his wife, 5, 11, 12 and 14 March 1807. Harewood 22.
100 *Colchester Diary and Correspondence*, vol. 2, p. 100.
101 Melville to Canning, 7 March 1807. Harewood 77.
102 Canning to his wife, 17, 19, 20, 22, 23 (two letters), 24, 25 and 28 March 1807. Harewood 22.
103 *The Poetical Works of ... George Canning*, p. 48. *Cabinet Edition of the British Poets* (London, 1851), vol. 4 (Canning), pp. 12–13.

CHAPTER 5
1 Canning to Granville, 1 and 17 April 1807. PRO Granville Papers, 30/29/8/4.
2 6 April 1807. Harewood 31.
3 Canning to Melville, 26 March 1809. SRO, Melville Castle Muniments, GD 51/1/116.
4 Canning to Mulgrave, 18 July 1808. Harewood 31.
5 CPD 9:341/7.
6 Dropmore, vol. 9, p. 134.
7 Canning to the Rev. Leigh, 27 April 1807. Harewood 17.
8 Canning to the Rev. Leigh, 6 October 1809. Harewood 17.
9 British Museum, Tracts 1850 d 26.
10 Canning to the Rev. Leigh, 27 June 1807. Harewood 17.
11 *George III*, ed. Aspinall, vol. 4, pp. 3430, 3448.
12 Mulgrave to Canning, 6 May 1807, and Canning to Mulgrave, 5 May, 1807. Harewood 31. Canning to Castlereagh, 5 May 1807. Harewood 32.
13 Canning to Alopeus, 18 June 1807, FO 65:73; Canning to Granville, 16 May 1807, PRO 30/29/8/4.
14 G. B. Garlike to Canning, 4 July 1807. FO 22:52.
15 Canning Memos, 10 and 11 July 1807. Harewood 41 (a); Canning to Granville, 9 June 1807. PRO 30/29/8/4.
16 D'Antraigues to Canning, 21 July 1807. Harewood 51 (b).
17 Canning to Granville, 21 July 1807. PRO 30/29/8/4.
18 Alopeus to Canning, 1 August 1807, and Canning to Alopeus, 5 August 1807. FO 65:73.
19 Garlike to Canning, 25 and 28 July 1807. FO 22:52.
20 *George III*, ed. Aspinall, vol. 4, p. 3511 n.
21 Canning to his wife, 1 August 1807. Harewood 22.
22 Canning to his wife, 26 August 1807. Harewood 22.
23 Canning to the Rev. Leigh, 11 September 1807. Harewood 17.

24 *George III*, ed. Aspinall, vol. 4, p. 3539 n.
25 Canning to Leveson-Gower, 12 August 1807. PRO 30/29/8/4.
26 *Memorials of . . . Admiral Gambier* (London, 1861), 2:17/19.
27 *George III*, ed. Aspinall, vol. 4, p. 3535.
28 Canning to Leveson-Gower, 29 September and 2 October 1807. PRO 30/29/8/4.
29 Canning to his wife, 22 August 1807. Harewood 22.
30 FO 65:73.
31 Canning to Chatham, 14 November 1807; Chatham to Canning, 15 November 1807. Harewood 31.
32 *George III*, ed. Aspinall, vol. 4, p. 3562.
33 *George III*, ed. Aspinall, vol. 4, p. 3560.
34 S. Walpole, *Life of Spencer Perceval* (London, 1874), vol. 1, p. 269.
35 Canning to Strangford, 22 October 1807. FO 63:56.
36 Canning Memo. Perceval Papers, BM Add Mss 49177:150.
37 Canning to his wife, 26 August 1807. Harewood 22.
38 Canning to Leveson-Gower, 5 November 1807. PRO 30/29/8/4.
39 Canning to Strangford, 7 November 1807. FO 63:56.
40 Canning to Strangford, 12 November 1807. FO 63:56.
41 FO 63/72:166 ff.
42 Canning to the Admiralty, 26 November 1807. FO 65:73.
43 Canning to the Rev. Leigh, 19 December 1807. Harewood 17.
44 R. Dundas to Canning, 6 June and 20 August 1807. NLS Ms 59:6, 25.
45 Canning to Leveson-Gower, 12 August 1807. PRO 30/29/8/4.
46 Canning to Leveson-Gower, 5 November 1807. PRO 30/29/8/4.
47 Camden to Canning, 20 September 1807. Harewood 31.
48 Mulgrave to Canning, 1 January 1808. Harewood 31.
49 Westmoreland to Canning, 5 November 1807. Harewood 31.
50 Canning Memos, August to September 1808. Harewood 41a.
51 19 November 1807. PRO–FO 73:44.
52 C. Stuart to Canning, 8 February 1808. Harewood 58.
53 Canning Memo, 12 July 1808. Harewood 41 (a).
54 Canning to Perceval, 16 January 1808. Harewood 32.
55 Canning to Portland, 6 November 1808. Harewood 32.
56 Canning to Chatham, 6 July 1809. Harewood 31.
57 Canning to Chatham, 4 August 1808. Harewood 31.
58 Canning Memo, June 1808. Harewood 41 (a).
59 Canning to Castlereagh, 24 July 1808. Harewood 32.
60 *Leveson-Gower Private Correspondence*, vol. 2, p. 321.
61 Canning Memos, 21 and 26 July 1808. Harewood 41 (a).
62 W. Hinde, *George Canning* (London, 1973), p. 200.

63   Canning to Chatham, 17 September 1808. Harewood 31.
64   Canning to Perceval, 17 September 1808. Harewood 32.
65   Canning to Perceval, 17 September 1808 (different letter from above). Harewood 32.
66   Huskisson to Canning, 19 September 1808. Harewood 67.
67   Canning to Portland, 30 December 1808. Harewood 32.
68   Canning to Castlereagh, 24 September 1808. Harewood 32.
69   Perceval to Canning, 20 September 1808. Harewood 33.
70   *George III*, ed. Aspinall, vol. 5, p. 3730.
71   Mulgrave to Canning, 23 October 1808. Harewood 31.
72   *Diary of Sir John Moore*, ed. G. J. V. Maurice (London, 1904), vol. 2, p. 202.
73   Portland to Canning, 31 December 1808. Harewood 33.
74   Walpole, *Life of Perceval*, vol. 1, p. 347.
75   Canning to Castlereagh, 11 December 1808. Harewood 32.
76   Canning to Portland, 30 December 1808. Harewood 32.
77   Canning to Castlereagh, 7 January 1809. Harewood 32.
78   9 January 1809. Bathurst Papers (Historical Manuscripts Commission), p. 84.
79   Canning Memo., 28 January 1809. Harewood 41 (a).
80   Canning Memo., 10 February 1809. Harewood 41 (a).
81   Canning Memo., 24 February 1809. Harewood 41 (a).
82   Martin de Garay to Canning, 12 March 1809. Wellesley Papers, BM Add Mss 37386:297.
83   Canning to Wellesley 12, August 1809. Wellesley Papers, BM Add Mss 37386:251.
84   Canning to Wellseley, 27 August 1809. Wellesley Papers, BM Add Mss 37287:167.
85   Wellesley to Canning, 15 August 1809. Wellesley Papers, BM Add Mss 37286:281–98.
86   Canning to Martin de Garay, 20 July 1809. Wellesley Papers, BM Add Mss 37286:107.
87   Canning to Wellesley, 12 August 1809. Wellesley Papers, BM Add Mss 37286:257–69.
88   Wellesley to Canning, 2 and 15 September 1809. Wellesley Papers, BM Add Mss 37287:235–46, 353–87.
89   Canning to de Garay, 20 July 1809. Wellesley Papers, BM Add Mss 37286:107.
90   Canning to Castlereagh, 28 December 1808. Harewood 32.
91   James Burke in PRO-FO 72/81:20.
92   Canning to Wellesley, 18 July 1809. Wellesley Papers, BM Add Mss 37286:94.

93 Canning to Wellesley, 12 August 1809. Wellesley Papers, BM Add Mss 37286:253–6.
94 Canning to Wellesley, 16 September 1809. Wellesley Papers, BM Add Mss 37288:3–11.
95 Canning to Wellesley, 27 August 1809. Wellesley Papers, BM Add Mss 37287:165–6.
96 Lord Wm. Bentinck to Canning, 25 June 1809. Harewood 58.
97 Canning to Portland, 21 March 1809. Harewood 33.
98 Mulgrave to Canning, 29 July 1809. Harewood 31.
99 CPD 9:700 ff., 1027 ff.; Canning to his wife, 1 August 1807. Harewood 22.
100 *George, Prince of Wales*, ed. Aspinall, vol. 6, p. 2520.
101 Portland to Canning, 22 February 1808. Harewood 32.
102 *George III*, ed. Aspinall, 1 July 1807, vol. 4, p. 3487.
103 *George III*, ed. Aspinall, 18 July 1807, vol. 4, p. 3487 n.
104 *George III*, ed. Aspinall, vol. 5, p. 3594 n. Palmerston, recently arrived in Parliament, was an admirer of Canning.
105 15 June 1806. CPD 11:889–90.
106 *Journal of Elizabeth, Lady Holland*, vol. 2, p. 239.
107 Canning to Richmond, 27 May 1808. Harewood 31.
108 25 May 1808. CPD 11:573.
109 *George III*, ed. Aspinall, vol. 5, p. 3832.
110 24 February 1809. CPD 12:1098.
111 6 March 1809. CPD 12:1202.
112 Canning to Portland, 5 March 1809. Harewood 32.
113 15 March 1809. CPD 13:593 ff.
114 Canning to the Rev. Leigh, 10 May 1808. Harewood 17.
115 Canning to Portland, 13 June 1809. Harewood 33.
116 Canning to his mother, 30 May 1809. Harewood 7.

CHAPTER 6
1 Castlereagh to the King, 1 October 1809. *George III*, ed. Aspinall, vol. 5, p. 3980.
2 Canning to Portland, 24 March 1809. Harewood 33.
3 Portland to Canning, 4 April 1809. Harewood 33.
4 Portland to Canning, 28 April 1809. Harewood 33.
5 Canning to Portland (twice) and Portland to Canning, 5 May 1809. Harewood 33.
6 Portland to Canning, 10 May 1809. Harewood 33.
7 Canning to Portland, 13 and 18 June 1809. Harewood 33.
8 Portland to Canning, 18 June 1809. Harewood 33.
9 Perceval to Canning, 25 June 1809. Harewood 33.
10 Canning to Portland (first letter), 27 June 1809. Harewood 33.

11 Canning to Portland (second letter), 27 June 1809; and Portland to Canning, 28 June 1809. Harewood 33.

12 Perceval to Canning, 28 June 1809. Harewood 33.

13 Canning to his wife, 5 July 1809. Harewood 23.

14 Canning to his wife, 12 July 1809. Harewood 23.

15 *George III*, ed. Aspinall, vol. 5, p. 3919.

16 Canning to Perceval, 14, 16, 17 and 18 July 1809. Harewood 33.

17 Portland to Canning, 18 July 1809. Harewood 33.

18 Canning to Portland, 18 and 20 July 1809; and Portland to Canning, 20 July 1809. Harewood 33.

19 Perceval to Canning, 28 and 29 August 1809. Harewood 33.

20 Perceval to Canning, 28, 29, 30 and 31 August; and Canning to Perceval, 28, 29 and 31 August 1809. Harewood 33. Canning to his wife, 4 and 30 August 1809. Harewood 23.

21 Canning to Portland, 2 September 1809; Portland to Canning, 3 and 7 September 1809; and Perceval to Canning, 5 September 1809. Harewood 33.

22 Perceval to Canning, 7 and 8 September 1809. Harewood 33. Liverpool to Canning, 8 September 1809. Liverpool Papers, BM Add Mss 38243:145.

23 Hinde, *George Canning*, p. 223.

24 Canning to Portland, 12 September 1809. Harewood 33.

25 *George III*, ed. Aspinall, vol. 5, p. 3960.

26 Canning to his wife, 15 September 1809. Harewood 23.

27 *George, Prince of Wales*, ed. Aspinall, vol. 6, p. 2600.

28 12 September 1809. *The Huskisson Papers*, ed. Lewis Melville (London, 1931), p. 62.

29 Canning to Perceval, 16 September 1809. Harewood 33.

30 Walpole, *Life of Perceval*, vol. 1, pp. 374–5.

31 F. Rose to G. Rose sen., 17 September 1809. NLS Ms 3649.

32 Walpole, *Life of Perceval*, vol. 2, p. 7 ff.

33 Castlereagh to Canning, 19 September 1809. Copy, Royal Archives 14669.

34 Canning to Castlereagh, 20 September 1809. Copy, Royal Archives 14669.

35 C. Ellis to Mrs Leigh, 21 September 1809. Harewood 62.

36 Canning to his wife, 20 September 1809. Harewood 23.

37 Canning to his mother, 21 September 1809. Harewood 7.

38 Canning to the Mrs and Miss Leigh, 21 September 1809. Harewood 17.

39 *The Morning Post*, 22 September 1809; *The Morning Chronicle*, 24 September 1809.

40 Canning to the King, 22 September 1809, Royal Archives

14674; The King to Canning, 23 September 1809, Royal Archives 14675.
41 Portland to Canning, 22 September 1809. Harewood 33.
42 Canning to Perceval, 21 September 1809 and 1 October 1809; and Perceval to Canning, 29 September 1809 and 2 October 1809. Harewood 33.
43 Canning to The Rev. Leigh, 11 October 1809. Harewood 17.
44 Mr Cooke to Auckland, 25 September 1809. *The Journal and Correspondence of William, Lord Auckland, with a preface, etc.* (London, 1860–2), vol. 4, p. 326.
45 *Auckland Journal and Correspondence*, vol. 4, p. 327.
46 *George III*, ed. Aspinall, vol. 5, p. 3979.
47 Canning to Sheridan, October 1809. Canning Papers, Ann Arbor, Michigan.
48 Canning to Sturges-Bourne, 2 October 1809. Canning Papers, Ann Arbor, Michigan.
49 Canning to Perceval, 2 October 1809. Harewood 33.
50 *The Morning Post*, 2 and 14 October 1809; *The Morning Chronicle*, 14 October 1809.
51 Canning to his mother, 18 October 1809. Harewood 7.
52 Canning to his mother, 19 November 1809. Harewood 7.
53 G. Canning, *A Letter to the Earl Camden, containing . . . a narrative of the transaction connected with the late duel, etc.* (London, 1809).
54 Huskisson to Canning, 4 October 1809. Harewood 67.
55 Canning to his wife, 26 October 1809. Harewood 23.
56 *Auckland Journal and Correspondence*, vol. 4, p. 333.
57 *Colchester Diary and Correspondence*, vol. 2, pp. 209–10.
58 Liverpool to M. Wallace, 23 September 1809. Liverpool Papers, BM Add Mss 38243:247.
59 G. Ellis to Sir Walter Scott, 23 September 1809. NLS Ms 870: 16 ff.
60 *George, Prince of Wales*, ed. Aspinall, vol. 6, p. 2631 n.
61 Grey to Holland, 3 and 9 October 1809. Grey Papers, University of Durham, Box 35.
62 *Leveson-Gower Private Correspondence*, vol. 2, p. 321.
63 Grey to Holland, 11 November 1809. Grey Papers, University of Durham, Box 35.
64 The Princess of Wales to Perceval, 6 October 1809. Harewood 28 (a).
65 Canning to Wilbraham, 19 December 1809. Bagot, *George Canning and His Friends*, vol. 1, p. 344.

66 Perceval to the Princess of Wales, 5 October 1809. Harewood 28 (a).
67 Canning to his wife, 19 September 1809. Harewood 23.
68 G. Rose to F. Rose, 28 October 1809. NLS Ms 3795:200–4.
69 Canning to his wife, 26 October 1809; Canning to Perceval, 28 October 1809. Harewood 23. Perceval to Canning, 30 October 1809. Harewood 33.
70 Bagot, *George Canning and His Friends*, vol. 1, pp. 340–1.
71 Canning to his wife, 23 October 1809. Harewood 23.
72 See Note 65.
73 See Note 58.
74 *Auckland Journal and Correspondence*, vol. 4, p. 330.
75 See Note 65.
76 Canning to Leveson-Gower, 13 October 1809. PRO 30/29/8/5.
77 Lonsdale to Rose, 3 December 1809. NLS Ms 3795:206–7.
78 S. H. Romilly (ed.), *Letters to Ivy from the first Earl of Dudley* (London, 1905), p. 82.
79 *Letters to Ivy*, p. 87.
80 Frere to Canning, 29 November 1809. Harewood 64.
81 Canning to his wife, 2 December 1809. Harewood 23.
82 T. Grenville to Grenville, 17 March 1810. Dropmore, vol. 10, p. 20.
83 *George III*, ed. Aspinall, vol. 5, p. 4142.
84 *George III*, ed. Aspinall, vol. 5, p. 4113 n.
85 Canning to Bagot, 10 April 1810. Bagot, *George Canning and his Friends*, vol. 1, p. 350.
86 Canning to Sturges-Bourne, 22 June 1810. Canning Papers, Ann Arbor, Michigan.
87 Canning to Wellesley, 30 June 1810. Wellesley Papers, BM Add Mss 37295:316–7.
88 Wellesley to Perceval, 23 July 1810. Wellesley Papers, BM Add Mss 37295:346.
89 Castlereagh to Perceval, 4 September 1810. Walpole, *Life of Perceval*, vol. 2, pp. 152–3.
90 Canning to Perceval, 26 September, 4 October 1810. Wellesley Papers, BM Add Mss 37295:401, 409. Perceval to Canning, 30 September, 4 October 1810. Ibid., 401 ff. Canning to his wife, 10 March 1810. *George III*, ed. Aspinall, vol. 5, p. 4108 n.
91 Dropmore, vol. 10, pp. 55, 58.
92 Canning to his wife, 2 February 1812. Harewood 25.
93 31 December 1810. Perceval's fifth Resolution on the Disposal of Household Offices amended by 226 to 213 and 217 to 214.
94 *George, Prince of Wales*, ed. Aspinall, vol. 7, p. 2816 n.

95 *George, Prince of Wales*, ed. Aspinall, vol. 7, p. 2801 n.
96 Canning to Bagot, 15 June 1811. Bagot, *George Canning and his Friends*, vol. 1, p. 370. Canning to Huskisson, 25 July 1811. Harewood 67. Canning to Leveson-Gower, 29 July 1811. PRO 30/29/8/5. Canning to Huskisson, 18 September 1811. *The Huskisson Papers*, ed. Melville, pp. 69–71.
97 Dropmore, vol. 10, pp. 161, 165.
98 Canning to his wife, 9 January 1812. Harewood 25.
99 Canning to his wife, 2 February 1812. Harewood 25.
100 Canning to his wife, 6 February 1812. Harewood 25.
101 Canning to his wife, Fragment, 1812. Harewood 25.
102 Canning to his wife, 9 February 1812. Harewood 25.
103 Dropmore, vol. 10, pp. 216, 222.
104 Dropmore, vol. 10, pp. 243, 244.
105 *George III*, ed. Aspinall, vol. 5, p. 4074 n.
106 *Letters to Ivy*, p. 90.
107 Canning to his wife, 21 November 1809. Harewood 25.
108 CPD 15:205–7, 581.
109 *George III*, ed. Aspinall, vol. 5, p. 4105 n.
110 29 March 1810. CPD 16:324–52.
111 CPD 15:715–43.
112 *George III*, ed. Aspinall, vol. 5, p. 4208.
113 CPD 16:540–1.
114 CPD 16:715–18, 740.
115 *George III*, ed. Aspinall, vol. 5, p. 4138 n.
116 CPD 16:1092.
117 CPD 17:191 ff., 156 ff.
118 CPD 16:776.
119 *Journal of Elizabeth, Lady Holland*, vol. 2, p. 272.
120 15 May 1810. CPD 16:1089 ff.
121 *George III*, ed. Aspinall, vol. 5, 4080 n.
122 Huskisson to Canning, 17 August and 10 October 1810. Harewood 67.
123 Huskisson to Canning, 5 July 1811. Harewood 67.
124 8 and 13 May 1811. CPD 19:1076 ff.; 20:94 ff.
125 Canning to Wellesley, 5 May 1811. Wellesley Papers, BM Add Mss 37295:472.
126 Memo (n.d.). Perceval Papers, BM Add Mss 49177:258.
127 3 March 1812. CPD 21:1139–50.
128 Canning to his wife, 8 January 1812. Harewood 25. 3 February 1812. CPD 21:514–47.
129 Canning to his wife, 4 February 1812. Harewood 25. Canning to Wellesley, 15 April 1812. Wellesley Papers, BM Add Mss 37296:314–15. CPD 21:1035–9; 22:1012 ff.; 23:55.

130 CPD 22:1175.
131 *Letters to Ivy*, p. 158.
132 Liverpool Papers, BM Add Mss 38193:13 ff. Wellesley Papers, BM Add Mss 37296:334 ff.
133 Canning to Wellesley, 16 May 1812. Wellesley Papers, BM Add Mss 37296:326.
134 CPD 23: 266 ff.
135 Canning to Wellesley, 23 May 1812. Wellesley Papers, BM Add Mss 37296:427–9. Canning to Liverpool, 23 May 1812; Liverpool to Canning, 24 May 1812; Canning to Liverpool, 24 May 1812; Melville to Canning, 23 May 1812. Harewood 61.
136 Canning Memos, 23 and 24 May 1812. Harewood 61.
137 Canning Memos, 26 and 27 May 1812. Harewood 61.
138 Canning and Leveson-Gower, 1 June 1812. PRO 30/29/8/5.
139 Grenville to T. Grenville, 12 May 1812. Dropmore, vol. 10, p. 246.
140 Grey to Grenville, 15 May 1812. Dropmore, vol. 10, p. 251.
141 Grey to Wellesley, 2 June 1812. Harewood 61.
142 Grey and Grenville to Wellesley, 3 June 1812. Harewood 61.
143 Canning to Wellesley, 5 and 6 June 1812. Wellesley Papers, BM Add Mss 37297:127, 129.
144 Canning to Leveson-Gower, 7 June 1812. PRO 30/29/8/5.
145 Frere to Canning, 12 June 1815. Harewood 64.
146 11 June 1812. CPD 23:437 f.
147 22 June 1812. CPD 23:633.
148 Liverpool to Canning, 15 June 1812. Liverpool Papers, BM Add Mss 38568:18.
149 Canning to his mother, 4 July 1812. Harewood 7.
150 *The Huskisson Papers*, ed. Melville, p. 81.
151 Liverpool to Canning, 22 July 1812. Liverpool Papers, BM Add Mss 38568:20 ff.
152 *Leveson-Gower Private Correspondence*, vol. 2, p. 437.
153 C. D. Yonge, *Life and Administration of the 2nd Earl of Liverpool* (London, 1868), vol. 1, p. 410.
154 *Leveson-Gower Private Correspondence*, vol. 2, pp. 438, 443.
155 Canning to Leveson-Gower, 1 August 1812. PRO 30/29/8/5.
156 Canning to his mother, 3 August 1812. Harewood 7.
157 *Leveson-Gower Private Correspondence*, vol. 2, p. 444.
158 *Leveson-Gower Private Correspondence*, vol. 2, p. 441.

CHAPTER 7
  1 *A Complete List of the 1,425 Burgesses who Polled at the Late Liverpool Election* (Liverpool, 1802), p. 48.

L

2 E. Williams, *Capitalism and Slavery* (London, 1964), p. 34.
3 T. Barnes, *History of the Commerce* . . . [*of*] *Liverpool* (Liverpool, 1852), p. 609.
4 Barnes, *History of the Commerce* . . . [*of*] *Liverpool*, pp. 631–2.
5 *History of the Election* . . . *Liverpool, 1806*, p. 27. Barnes, *History of the Commerce* . . . [*of*] *Liverpool*, p. 507.
6 *The Poll, etc.* (Liverpool, 1830), p. 81.
7 Figures drawn from 1818 poll book.
8 *The Poll, etc.* (Liverpool, 1790), pp. 22–3.
9 *A Compendious and Impartial Account* [*of the*] *Liverpool Election, 1806*, p. vi.
10 *A Collection of Addresses* . . . [*from the*] *Liverpool* . . . *Election* (May, 1807), p. 10.
11 *A Collection of Addresses*, p. 11.
12 *An Impartial Collection of Addresses, Songs, Squibs, etc.* . . . *Liverpool* [*Election*], *1812*, p. 5.
13 BM Add Mss 29862:123–4.
14 Canning to Drinkwater, 24 February 1812. Liverpool Record Office, HQ 920 CAN.
15 Canning to his wife, 10 March 1812. Harewood 25.
16 Canning to Drinkwater, 25 and 30 May, 8 June 1812. Liverpool Record Office, HQ 920 CAN.
17 Canning to Leveson-Gower, 17 August 1812. PRO 30/29/8/5.
18 Canning to Drinkwater, 15 September 1812. Liverpool Record Office, HQ 920 CAN.
19 Canning to Drinkwater, 25 September 1812. Liverpool Record Office, HQ 920 CAN.
20 Canning to Sturges-Bourne, 27 September 1812. Canning Papers, Ann Arbor, Michigan.
21 Canning to Sturges-Bourne, 3 October 1812. Canning Papers, Ann Arbor, Michigan.
22 W. Roscoe to T. Attwood, 10 October 1812. Liverpool Record Office, Roscoe Papers.
23 Canning to Wellesley, 17 October 1812. Wellesley Papers, BM Add Mss 37297:179–80.
24 Canning to Leveson-Gower, 7 October 1812, enclosing Canning to Requisitioners, 4 October 1812. PRO 30/29/8/5.
25 Creevey to Roscoe, n.d. Liverpool Record Office, Roscoe Papers, 1070A.
26 Brougham to Roscoe, 4 July, 25 September 1812. Liverpool Record Office, Roscoe Papers, 489, 494.
27 Creevey to Roscoe, 21 February 1813. Liverpool Record Office, Roscoe Papers, 1071.

28 *The Liverpool Mercury*, 11 September 1812.

29 *The Liverpool Mercury*, 20 October 1812.

30 Brougham to Roscoe, 29 September 1812. Liverpool Record Office, Roscoe Papers, 494.

31 Roscoe to Gloucester, 17 September 1812. Liverpool Record Office, Roscoe Papers, 1781.

32 *The Liverpool Mercury*, 2 October 1812.

33 Canning to his mother, 12 October 1812. Harewood 7.

34 *An Impartial Collection of Addresses, Songs, Squibs, etc. ... Liverpool [Election], 1812*, p. 89.

35 *The Poll, etc.* (Liverpool, 1812), p. 62.

36 Canning to Wellesley, 19 October 1812. Wellesley Papers, BM Add Mss 37297:181.

37 *The Speeches and Public Addresses of George Canning during the late election in Liverpool* (Liverpool, 1812), p. 13.

38 *Canning Speeches and Public Addresses* (Liverpool, 1812), p. 27.

39 The news of the burning of Moscow had just been received.

40 *The Speeches delivered during the Election at Liverpool ... by Henry Brougham*, pp. 24–5.

41 *An Impartial Collection of Addresses, etc. ... Liverpool [Election], 1812*, pp. 48, 105, 119.

42 *Canning Speeches and Public Addresses* (Liverpool, 1812), p. 21.

43 *The Liverpool Mercury*, 23 October 1812.

44 Canning to his mother, 23 October 1812. Harewood 7.

45 *Canning Speeches and Public Addresses* (Liverpool, 1812), p. 37.

46 Canning to his mother, 9 November 1812. Harewood 7.

47 Canning to Drinkwater, 27 November 1812. Liverpool Record Office, HQ 920 CAN.

48 Canning to Liverpool, 1 December 1812. Liverpool Papers, BM Add Mss 38193:24–5.

49 Canning to Liverpool, 28 December 1813. Liverpool Papers, BM Add Mss 38193:730–1.

50 Canning to Liverpool, 27 January and 28 February 1814. Liverpool Papers, BM Add Mss 38193:733–5.

51 N. Vansittart to Canning, 11 June 1814. Liverpool Record Office, Parliamentary Office/27.

52 F. Robinson to Canning, 16 June 1814. Liverpool Record Office, Parliamentary Office /29.

53 Canning to Liverpool, 20 May 1813. Liverpool Papers, BM Add Mss 38193:26–7.

54 Canning to Liverpool, 13 November 1812. BM Add Mss 38568:32–3.

55 S. Storey to Canning, 13 January 1814. Liverpool Record

Office, Parliamentary Office /1.

56 Sidmouth to Canning, 16 February 1814. Liverpool Record Office, Parliamentary Office /3.

57 Michael Burns to Canning, 20 February 1814. Liverpool Record Office, Parliamentary Office /23. 1812 Poll Book.

58 T. Codd to Canning, 16 and 30 April, 2 June 1814. Liverpool Record Office, Parliamentary Office /11, /12, /13.

59 C. Arbuthnot to Canning, 22 April 1814. Liverpool Record Office, Parliamentary Office /14.

60 C. Arbuthnot to Canning and Gascogne, 7 November 1814. Liverpool Record Office, Parliamentary Office /55.

61 Canning to R. Woodward, 14 and 18 July 1821. R. Woodward to Canning, 17 July 1821. Liverpool Record Office /91-3.

62 T. W. Croker to Canning, 19 September 1814. Liverpool Record Office, Parliamentary Office /47.

63 T. Gladstone and others to Canning, 28 May 1814. Liverpool Record Office, Parliamentary Office /24.

64 H. Hollinshed and T. Bolton to Canning, 12 January 1819. Liverpool Record Office, Parliamentary Office /72.

65 C. Clarke to Canning, 18 August 1821. Liverpool Record Office, Parliamentary Office /94.

66 Mr Stanley to Canning, September 1821. Wm. Ewart to Canning, 6 September 1821. Liverpool Record Office, Parliamentary Office /95-6.

67 Canning to Gascogne, 20 and 22 March 1818. Liverpool Record Office, Parliamentary Office /416.

68 Gascogne to Canning, 23 June 1822. Liverpool Record Office, Parliamentary Office /97.

69 S. R. Lushington to Canning, 23 June 1821. Liverpool Record Office, Parliamentary Office /89.

70 Minute Book, Liverpool Record Office, 329 CAN 1.

71 Canning to Leveson-Gower, 27 September 1812. PRO 30/29/8/5.

72 *Letters to Ivy*, p. 169.

73 Canning to Sturges-Bourne, 27 September and 3 October 1812. Canning Papers, Ann Arbor, Michigan.

74 Sturges-Bourne to Canning, June 1810. Canning Papers, Ann Arbor, Michigan.

75 Canning to Wellesley, 19 November 1812. Wellesley Papers, BM Add Mss 37297:187-8.

76 Canning to Leveson-Gower, 18 August 1812. PRO 30/29/8/5.

77 Grey to Grenville, 1 November 1812. Dropmore, vol. 10, p. 299.

78 30 November 1812. CPD 24:61.

79 Dr Cyril Jackson to Sidmouth, 4 February 1813. George Pellew, *The Life and Correspondence of the Right Hon. Henry Addington, First Viscount Sidmouth* (London, 1847), vol. 2, p. 303.
80 *Colchester Diary and Correspondence*, vol. 2, p. 417.
81 CPD 24:1041 ff.; 25:245, 1107; 26:88, 213, 360 ff. Canning to Wellesley, 25 May 1813. Wellesley Papers, BM Add Mss 37297:203.
82 Canning to Leveson-Gower, 11 January 1813. PRO 30/29/8/5.
83 T. Creevey to W. Roscoe, 21 January 1813. Liverpool Record Office, Roscoe Papers, 1071.
84 CPD 26:472 ff., 636–7.
85 These were repeated before news of the declaration of war was received.
86 A. Stapleton, *George Canning and his Times*, p. 149.
87 CPD 24:649.
88 Canning to Rose, 24 July 1809 and 17 February 1813. Lady Hamilton to Rose, 4 March 1813. *Rose Diaries and Correspondence*, vol. 2, p. 263 ff.
89 *Colchester Diary and Correspondence*, vol. 2, p. 434.
90 *Leveson-Gower Private Correspondence*, vol. 2, p. 470.
91 Canning to Leveson-Gower, 30 July 1813. PRO 30/29/8/5.
92 Canning to Leveson-Gower, 9 August 1813. PRO 30/29/8/5.
93 *Leveson-Gower Private Correspondence*, vol. 2, p. 484.
94 Leveson-Gower to Canning, 26 October 1813. Canning to Leveson-Gower, 29 October 1813. Harewood 65.
95 CPD 27:144, 850; 28:447.
96 *The Huskisson Papers*, ed. Melville, p. 93 ff.
97 *Leveson-Gower Private Correspondence*, vol. 2, p. 493.
98 Frere to Canning, 28 April 1814. Harewood 64.
99 Diary, November 1813 to July 1814. Harewood 29 (d).
100 Canning to Leveson-Gower, 26 June 1814. Granville Papers, PRO 30/29/8/5.
101 Diary, 6 July 1814. Harewood 29 (d). Canning to his wife, 14 July 1814. Harewood 25.
102 Canning to Sturges-Bourne, 19 July 1814. Canning Papers, Ann Arbor, Michigan.
103 Canning to Sturges-Bourne, 29 July 1814. Canning Papers, Ann Arbor, Michigan.
104 Canning to Liverpool, 9 November 1814. Liverpool Papers, BM Add Mss 38193:46.
105 Canning to Liverpool, 29 November 1814. Liverpool Papers, BM Add Mss 38193:751.
106 Canning to the Rev. Leigh, 25 November, 9 December and

31 December 1814. Harewood 17. Diary, 3 December 1814. Harewood 29 (d).

107 Canning to Liverpool, 29 December 1814. Liverpool Papers, BM Add Mss 38193:53, 69.

108 Canning to Bagot, 14 July 1815. Bagot, *George Canning and his Friends*, vol. 2, pp. 5–6.

109 Canning to the Rev. Leigh, 11 August 1815. Harewood 17.

110 Canning to Liverpool, 23 January 1815. Liverpool Papers, BM Add Mss 38193:69.

111 Canning to Liverpool, 30 January 1815. Liverpool Papers, BM Add Mss 38193:80.

112 Canning to Forjaz, 11 February and 29 March 1815. Harewood 98.

113 Canning to Liverpool, 29 June 1813. Liverpool Papers, BM Add Mss 38193:87.

114 Canning to Forjaz, 1 May 1815. Harewood 98. Canning to Beresford, 22 May 1815. Harewood 98 (b).

115 Canning to Beresford, 14 and 16 June 1815. Harewood 98 (b). Canning to Liverpool, 24 June 1815. BM Add Mss 38193:92.

116 Canning to Forjaz, 5 July 1815. Harewood 98.

117 Canning to Liverpool, 14 January and 17 March 1815. BM Add Mss 38193:65.

118 Canning to Huskisson, 15 April 1815. Harewood 67.

119 See Note 118.

120 Canning to Liverpool, 24 June 1815. BM Add Mss 38193:89.

121 Canning to Huskisson, 17 June 1815. Harewood 67.

122 Canning to Beresford, 8 August 1815. Harewood 98 (b). Canning to Liverpool, 8 August 1815. BM Add Mss 38568:48.

123 See Note 122.

124 Canning to Beresford, 7 October 1815. Harewood 95 (b).

125 Huskisson to Liverpool, 5 February 1816. Harewood 67.

126 Frere to Canning, 6 March 1815. Harewood 64.

127 Canning to Frere, 27 January 1816. BM add Mss 38833.

128 Diary, June 1816. Harewood 29 (d). Canning to Leveson-Gower, 28 May 1816. PRO 30/29/6.

129 Colonel Williams was a Radical pamphleteer who seconded Leyland.

130 *An Impartial Collection of Addresses, Songs, Squibs, etc. . . . Liverpool [Election], 1816. The Poll, etc.* (Liverpool, 1816).

CHAPTER 8

1 Canning to his wife, 24 November 1817. Harewood 26.

2 Indian Office Records, E/2/32:343–4.

3 Canning to the Rev. Leigh, 19 March 1819. Harewood 17.

4 Canning to M. Hoper, 9 December 1816, 10 April 1817.

5 E. G., Diary, 8 January, 9 to 13 and 18 February, 28 May 1818. Harewood 29 (d).

6 E. G., T. P. Courtenay to W. Hamilton, 5 December 1816. Canning to the 'chairs' (Chairmen of the Court of Directors of the East India Company), 6 August 1819. India Office Records, F/2/5:6, 396.

7 22 June 1813, CPD 26:828–30.

8 Canning to the Bishop of Calcutta, 24 February 1817. India Office Records, F/2/5:49–52.

9 Canning to the 'Chairs', 22 August 1818. India Office Records, F/2/5:258.

10 Canning to the 'Chairs', 14 January 1820. India Office Records, F/2/5:443.

11 Canning to the 'Chairs', 16 January 1817. India Office Records, F/2/5:110 ff.

12 Canning to Liverpool, 16 September 1818. Vansittart Papers, BM Add Mss 31232:202–5.

13 Canning to Vansittart, 31 October 1817. Vansittart Papers, BM Add Mss 31232:186.

14 Canning to Liverpool, 19 April 1820. Liverpool Papers, BM Add Mss 38193:120.

15 10 April and 15 May 1818. CPD 37:1264; 38:723.

16 Hastings to Canning, 2 February 1821. Harewood 99 (a).

17 Thomas Courtenay to Joseph Dart, 25 March 1819. India Office Records, F/2/5:344.

18 Bagot to Binning, 1 June 1816. Bagot, *George Canning and his Friends*, vol. 2, p. 18.

19 Wilberforce to Liverpool, 16 September 1820. Liverpool Papers, BM Add Mss 38191:276.

20 29 January and 14 March 1817. CPD 35:85, 1114 ff.

21 24 November 1819. CPD 41:192 ff.

22 23 December 1819. CPD 41:1559.

23 *Memoirs of Sir Phillip Francis, KCB*, ed. H. Merivale (London, 1867), vol. 2, p. 409.

24 Canning to Robert Smith, 20 July 1817. Harewood 64.

25 Canning to his mother, 19 June 1819. Harewood 9.

26 Diary, 30 April 1819. Harewood 29 (d).

27 Canning to his mother, 10 July 1819. Harewood 9.

28 Canning to his wife, 7 January 1820. Harewood 26.

29 Diary, 22 to 24 February 1820. Harewood 29 (d).

30 *Colchester Diary and Correspondence*, 29 January 1817, vol. 2, p. 601.

31 *Colchester Diary and Correspondence*, 5 June 1817, vol. 3, pp. 6–7.

32 Diary, 1 to 3 April 1819. Harewood 29 (d).

33 Canning to the Rev. Leigh, 5 August 1819. Harewood 17.

34 Diary, 13 January 1818. Harewood 29 (d).

35 Diary, 18 and 19 October 1818. Harewood 29 (d). Canning to the Rev. Leigh, 21 October 1818. Harewood 17.

36 Canning to his mother, 18 January 1817. Harewood 9.

37 Canning to Howard de Walden, 17 January 1817. Harewood 62.

38 Diary, early July 1819. Harewood 29 (d).

39 Diary, 14 August to 21 November 1819. Harewood 29 (d).

40 G. Canning jun. to Canning, 2 October 1817. Harewood 26.

41 Diary, 27 to 31 March 1820. Harewood 29 (d).

42 Canning to his mother, 31 March 1820. Harewood 9.

43 Canning to his wife, 31 March 1820. Harewood 26.

44 Canning to the Rev. Leigh, 28 April 1818. Harewood 17.

45 Canning to his wife, 16 June 1818. Harewood 26.

46 Diary, 17 and 18 June 1818. Harewood 29 (d).

47 *The Speeches and Public Addresses of the Right Hon. George Canning ... Liverpool Election, 1818* (Liverpool, 1818), pp. 6, 30, 32.

48 *The Speech Book, being a Collection of Addresses, Songs, etc. ... Liverpool Election, 1818.*

49 Diary, 18 June to 11 July 1818. Harewood 29 (d).

50 Canning to his mother, 1 March 1820. Harewood 9.

51 G. Canning, *The Principles and Tendency of Radical Reform* (London, 1820). British Museum Tracts, B.680.

52 Canning to the Rev. Leigh, 16 January 1819. Harewood 17.

53 Canning to Huskisson, 29 October 1821. *The Huskisson Papers*, ed. Melville, p. 125.

54 Diary, 1 August 1819. Harewood 29 (d).

55 Canning to his wife, 28 January 1820. Harewood 26.

56 Canning to his wife, 6 February 1820. Harewood 26.

57 Canning to his wife, 20 February 1820. Harewood 26.

58 Diary, 10 to 17 February 1820. Harewood 29 (d).

59 Diary, 11 to 22 June 1820. Harewood 29 (d). Also Hans. 1: 1297 ff.

60 *Journal of Mrs Arbuthnot*, edited E. Bamford and the Duke of Wellington (London, 1950), vol. 1, p. 25.

61 Canning to his mother, 1 July 1820. Harewood 9.

62 Canning to his wife, 27 June 1820. Harewood 26.

63 Diary, 26 June 1820. Harewood 29 (d). Canning to his mother, 15 July 1820. Harewood 9.

64 Canning to Liverpool, 5 July 1820. Liverpool Papers, BM Add Mss 38193:121–4.

65 Diary, 30 June 1820. Harewood 29 (d). *Journal of Mrs Arbuthnot*, vol. 1, p. 27.

66 Canning to Liverpool, 30 July 1820. Quoted in A. G. Stapleton, *George Canning and his Times*, p. 194.

67 Canning to his mother, 28 August 1820. Harewood 9.

68 Diary, 9 August 1820 ff. Harewood 29 (d).

69 Frere to Canning, 11 October 1820. Harewood 64.

70 Diary, 31 October 1820. Harewood 29 (d).

71 Leveson-Gower to Canning, 8 October 1820. Harewood 65.

72 Canning to Huskisson, 1 October 1820. *The Huskisson Papers*, ed. Melville, p. 111.

73 Canning to Liverpool, 10 October 1820. Quoted in A. G. Stapleton, *George Canning and his Times*, pp. 300–1.

74 Canning to Huskisson, 22 October 1820. Quoted in A. G. Stapleton, *George Canning and his Times*, p. 310.

75 Leveson-Gower to Canning, 13 October 1820. Harewood 65.

76 Lord Holland, *Further Memoirs of the Whig Party, 1807–21*, ed. Lord Stavordale (London, 1905), p. 287.

77 Canning to his wife, 21 November 1820. Harewood 26.

78 Canning to his wife, 24 November 1820. Harewood 26.

79 Diary, 22 November to 7 December 1820. Harewood 29 (d).

80 Liverpool to Arbuthnot, 9 December 1820. *The Correspondence of Charles Arbuthnot*, ed. A. Aspinall, Camden Society 3rd Series, No. 59 (London, 1941), No. 18.

81 Canning to the King, 13 December 1820. Royal Archives, 22520.

82 Canning to his wife, 12 December 1820. Harewood 26.

83 Canning to his mother, 16 December 1820. Harewood 9.

84 Canning to his mother, 10 July 1821. Harewood 9.

85 Diary, 17 to 21 January 1821. Harewood 29 (d).

86 17 April 1818. CPD 38:174.

87 3 June 1818. CPD 38:1245.

88 4 May 1819. CPD 40:98.

89 *Parliamentary Debates*, New Series (Hansard), 19 May 1820, vol. 1, p. 504.

90 26 June 1821. Hans. 5:1324.

91 16 March 1821. Hans. 4:1301.

92 Canning to his mother, 24 March 1821. Harewood 9. In fact he spoke in the Third Reading debate.

93   Diary, April 1821 ff. Harewood 29 (d).
94   Wilberforce to Canning, 30 March 1822. Harewood 80 (a).
95   Canning to his wife, 3 April 1821. Harewood 26.
96   Canning to his wife, 13 April 1821. Harewood 26.
97   Canning to his wife, 20 April 1821. Harewood 26.
98   *Journal of Mrs Arbuthnot*, vol. 1, pp. 82–3.
99   Diary, 16 June 1821. Harewood 29 (d).
100 Canning to Liverpool, 22 June 1821. Royal Archives 22628.
101 Canning to Sturges-Bourne, 5 July 1821. Canning Papers, Ann
     Arbor, Michigan.
102 Liverpool to Bathurst, 27 June 1821. Liverpool Papers, BM
     Add Mss 38289:214 ff.
103 Hinde, *George Canning*, p. 310.
104 *Journal of Mrs Arbuthnot*, vol. 1, p. 119.
105 Liverpool to Arbuthnot, 27 September 1821. *Charles Arbuthnot
     Correspondence*, No. 23C.
106 Canning to Morley, 12 December 1821. A. Stapleton, *George
     Canning and his Times*, p. 324.
107 *Journal of Mrs Arbuthnot*, 4 November 1821, vol. 1, p. 124.
108 Charles Ellis to Huskisson, 20 November 1821. Huskisson
     Papers, BM Add Mss 38743:26.
109 Canning to his wife, 6 April 1821. Harewood 26.
110 Canning to his mother, 16 October 1821. Harewood 9.
111 Diary, 10 November 1821 ff. Harewood 29 (d).
112 Canning to the Rev. Leigh, 8 December 1821. Harewood 17.
113 Canning to his wife, 16 November 1821. Harewood 26.
114 *Journal of Mrs Arbuthnot*, vol. 1, p. 125.
115 H. Legge to C. Abbot, 22 December 1821. *Colchester Diary and
     Correspondence*, vol. 3, p. 240.
116 25 April 1822. Hans. 6:106 ff.
117 Canning to his mother, 28 August 1822. Harewood 26.
118 Canning to his wife, 28 August 1822. Harewood 26.
119 Canning to Leveson-Gower, 25 August 1822. PRO 30/29/8/6.
120 Canning to his wife, 3 September 1822. Harewood 26.
121 C. Arbuthnot to his wife, 2 September 1822 (two letters).
     Charles Arbuthnot Correspondence, Nos 28, 28A.
122 *Journal of Mrs Arbuthnot*, vol. 1, pp. 188–90.
123 Canning to his mother, 14 and 21 September 1822. Harewood
     126.
124 Grey to Lady Holland, 18 September 1822. Grey Papers,
     University of Durham, Box 33:2.
125 *Colchester Diary and Correspondence*, vol. 3, p. 256.
126 *Journal of Mrs Arbuthnot*, vol. 1, p. 195.

127 15 September 1822. *Charles Arbuthnot Correspondence*, No. 29A.
128 Canning to his wife (n.d.), 1822. Harewood 26.
129 Huskisson to Canning, 23 June 1821; Canning to Huskisson, 29 June 1821. Harewood 67.
130 Huskisson to Canning, 3 October 1822. Huskisson Papers, BM Add Mss 38743:223–6.
131 Liverpool to Arbuthnot, 1 and 30 November 1822. *Charles Arbuthnot Correspondence*, Nos 39B, D.
132 Canning to Huskisson, 2 October 1822. Harewood 67.
133 Liverpool to Vansittart, 14 December 1822. Liverpool Papers, BM Add Mss 38291:203–4.
134 Charles Ellis to Huskisson, 23 December 1822; Huskisson to Ellis, 29 December 1822. Huskisson Papers, BM Add Mss 38743:278, 294.
135 Canning to Huskisson, 3 and 6 January 1823. Huskisson to Canning, 6 January 1823. Huskisson Papers, BM Add Mss 38744:2, 6, 9.
136 Canning to Arbuthnot, 10 January 1823. Huskisson Papers, BM Add Mss 38744:19–20.
137 H. B. Hollinshed to Canning, 17 September 1822. Harewood 83.
138 J. Gladstone to Canning, 18 September 1822. Harewood 83.
139 Canning to Hollinshed, September 1822. Huskisson Papers, BM Add Mss 38743:209.
140 J. Gladstone to Canning, 8 October 1822. Harewood 83.
141 Canning to the non-electors of Harwich, 30 January 1823. Harewood 85.
142 Harewood 85.
143 Canning to J. C. Herries, 4 February 1873. Harewood 85.
144 Canning to Melville, 15 August 1825. Harewood 85.
145 Canning to Freres, 7 August 1823. Harewood 64.

CHAPTER 9
1 A. G. Stapleton, *George Canning and His Times*, p. 368.
2 20 March 1821. Hans. 4:1370.
3 A. G. Stapleton, *The Political Life of the Rt Hon. George Canning* (London, 1831), vol. 1, p. 139.
4 Canning to the King, 11 July 1823. Royal Archives 22958. Canning to Frere, 7 August 1823. Harewood 64.
5 S. T. Bindoff, *The Unreformed Diplomatic Service* (TRHS, 1930), p. 146 ff.
6 Canning to Gladstone, 20 October 1825. Harewood 83.
7 Canning to Holland, 4 and 6 March 1824. Harewood 65.

8   Wellington's despatch, 22 October 1822. NLS, Rothesay Papers 6216:337.

9   Stuart to Canning, 3 and 14 October 1822. NLS, Rothesay Papers 6213:646, 733.

10 Stuart to Canning, 17, 21 (two letters) and 24 October 1822. NLS, Rothesay Papers 6213:771–4; 6214:41, 45, 69.

11 Wellington to Stuart, 12 November 1822. NLS, Rothesay Papers 6216:379 ff.

12 Wellington to Stuart, 19 November 1822. NLS, Rothesay Papers 6216:423.

13 Canning to Stuart, 1 December 1822. NLS, Rothesay Papers 6216:457.

14 Canning to Stuart, 1 December 1822. NLS, Rothesay Papers 6216:461.

15 Wellington to Stuart, 21 December 1822. NLS, Rothesay Papers 6216:647.

16 Wellington to Canning, 12 December 1822. NLS, Rothesay Papers 6216:659.

17 Canning to Wellington, 17 December 1822. NLS, Rothesay Papers 6216:677.

18 H. Temperley, *The Foreign Policy of Canning, 1822–27*, 2nd ed. (London, 1966), pp. 77–8.

19 Canning to Bagot, 25 February 1823. PRO-FO 65/138, No. 5.

20 Canning to Charles Ellis, 9 February 1823. Liverpool Papers, BM Add Mss 38568:118.

21 Canning to Sir Henry Wellesley, 16 November 1822. A. G. Stapleton, *George Canning and His Times*, p. 376.

22 Temperley, *Foreign Policy of Canning*, p. 80.

23 Temperley, *Foreign Policy of Canning*, p. 83.

24 14 April 1823. Hans. 8:872.

25 Frere to Canning, 21 April 1823. Harewood 64.

26 *George, Prince of Wales*, ed. Aspinall, vol. 8, p. 3429.

27 Canning to Frere, 7 August 1823. Harewood 64.

28 Canning to Charles Ellis, 26 December 1826. Harewood 62.

29 Canning to Liverpool, 26 August 1823. Harewood 70.

30 Liverpool to Canning, 29 and 30 September 1823. Harewood 70.

31 Canning to Liverpool, 10 October 1823. Harewood 70.

32 Huskisson to Leveson-Gower, 10 November 1825. *The Huskisson Papers*, ed. Melville, p. 194 ff.

33 Macaulay to Grey, 8 August 1814. Grey Papers, University of Durham (Macaulay File).

34 T. Clarkson to Henri Christophe, 26 April 1818. Clarkson Papers, BM Add Mss 41266:37.

35 Opinion of Eldon, *c.* 1807, in Perceval Papers, BM Add Mss 49177:96.
36 Quoted in W. L. Burn, *Emancipation and Apprenticeship* (London, 1937), p. 76.
37 Charles Stuart to Castlereagh, 9 January 1817. NLS, Rothesay Papers 6173:113 ff.
38 Liverpool to Wellington, 7 September 1814. Liverpool Papers, BM Add Mss 38416:332–9.
39 James Hook to S. Cock, 16 October 1822. Harewood 142.
40 John Dodds to William Allen, 16 June 1818. NLS, Rothesay Papers 6189:644.
41 Canning to Wilberforce, 3 October 1822. Wilberforce Papers, Duke University, Box 3:4.
42 T. G. Babington to J. Babington, 30 December 1822. Macaulay Papers, Henry Huntingdon Library, Los Angeles.
43 Canning to his mother, 5 February 1820. Harewood 9.
44 Stuart to Castlereagh, 21 December 1820. NLS, Rothesay Papers 6202:725.
45 Villèle to Stuart, 22 November 1822. NLS, Rothesay Papers 6214:447.
46 Stuart to Canning, 10 October 1822. NLS, Rothesay Papers 6213:677.
47 Canning to Stuart, 1 November 1822. NLS, Rothesay Papers 6216:350. Stuart to Villèle, 7 November 1822. NLS, Rothesay Papers 6214:439.
48 Stuart to Chateaubriand, 28 May 1823. NLS, Rothesay Papers 6219:241.
49 Canning to Stuart, 23 May 1823. NLS, Rothesay Papers 6223:831.
50 Stratford Canning to John Quincy Adams, 29 January 1823. PRO-FO 5/172.
51 Stuart to Canning, 28 July 1823. NLS, Rothesay Papers 6220:357.
52 Canning to Stuart, 22 May 1823. NLS, Rothesay Papers 6219:69.
53 Stuart to Canning, 5 January 1824. NLS, Rothesay Papers 6228:527.
54 D. B. Morris (Consul-General) to Stuart, 9 February 1824. NLS, Rothesay Papers 6225:461.
55 Canning to Stuart, 28 May 1824. NLS, Rothesay Papers 6230:429.
56 Stratford Canning to Londonderry, 29 June 1822. PRO-FO 5/168:296 ff.

57 Stratford Canning to Canning, 31 March and 22 April 1823. PRO-FO 5/176. John Quincy Adams to S. Canning, 24 June 1823. PRO-FO 5/176.
58 Henry Addington to Henry Clay, 9 April 1825. PRO-FO 5/198.
59 Canning to R. Rush, 29 August 1824. PRO-FO 5/194.
60 Clay to Addington, 6 April 1825. PRO-FO 5/196.
61 H. Addington to Canning, 12 April 1825. PRO-FO 5/198.
62 Huskisson Memo, 17 February 1824. Huskisson Papers, BM Add Mss 38766:68.
63 Canning to ? [correspondent unknown], 17 March 1826. Canning Papers, Ann Arbor, Michigan.
64 Clarkson Memo, c. 1820. Macaulay Papers, Henry Huntingdon Library, Los Angeles. Only four MPs voted against the grant.
65 Canning to Havana Commissioners, 16 May 1823. PRO-FO 313/1.
66 A'Court to Canning, 16 July 1824. PRO-FO 185/97.
67 Canning to A'Court, 12 August 1824. PRO-FO 185/97.
68 Kilbee to Canning, 1 January and 25 February 1825. PRO-FO 185/101.
69 Duke of Infantado to F. Lamb, 12 February 1826. PRO-FO 313/2.
70 Canning to Havana Commissioners, 31 July 1826. PRO-FO 313/2.
71 Captain-General Vives to Kilbee, 9 March 1825. PRO-FO 185/101.
71 Canning to F. Lamb, 23 February 1826. PRO-FO 185:107.
72 Conde de la Alcidia to Canning, 8 March 1827; Captain-General Vives to Commissioner Macleay, 25 August 1826. PRO-FO 313/2.
73 Canning to F. Lamb, 21 July 1826. PRO-FO 313/2.
74 Canning to F. Lamb, 10 November 1826. PRO-FO 313/2.
75 C. McCarthy to Bathurst, 26 September 1822. NLS, Rothesay Papers 6223:861.
76 Canning to Wilberforce, 24 and 31 October 1822. Harewood 80 (a); Wilberforce Papers, Duke University, Box 3:4.
77 L. M. Bethell, *The Abolition of the Brazilian Slave Trade* (Cambridge, 1970), pp. 60, 72 ff.
78 H. Addington to Canning, 31 May 1824. PRO-FO 5/186.
79 P. D. Curtin, *The Atlantic Slave Trade* (London, 1969), p. 234.
80 Holland to Canning, 7 October 1822. Harewood 65.
81 Canning to Holland, 9 October 1822. Harewood 65.
82 Canning to Holland, 21 October 1822. Harewood 65.
83 Liverpool to Bathurst, 22 December 1821. Bathurst Papers, HMC, p. 525.

84 Quoted in Hinde, *George Canning*, p. 347.
85 Quoted in Kenneth Bourne, *Britain and the Balance of Power in North America, 1815–1908* (Aberdeen, 1967), p. 64.
86 C. J. Bartlett, *A New Balance of Power: The Nineteenth-century West Indies* (Kingston, Jamaica, 1970), p. 61.
87 Melville to Canning, 19 October 1823. Canning Papers, Ann Arbor, Michigan.
88 Heytesbury Papers, BM Add Mss 41544:228.
89 Sir Henry Wellesley to Canning, 25 July 1823. PRO-FO 7/179.
90 Canning to Bagot, 12 July 1823. PRO-FO 65/138.
91 A. G. Stapleton, *George Canning and His Times*, p. 395.
92 Grey to Holland, 19 March 1824. Grey Papers, Durham University, Box 35, File 2.
93 E. G. Canning to Clanwilliam, 13 February 1824. PRO-FO 64/139.
94 Canning to his wife, 20 March 1824. Harewood 27.
95 Hinde, *George Canning*, pp. 359–60.
96 Arbuthnot to Liverpool, 29 December 1824. Aspinall, *Charles Arbuthnot Correspondence*, p. 63.
97 Canning to Frere, 7 August 1823. Harewood 64.
98 Liverpool to Canning, 27 October 1824. Royal Archives, Geo. Add Mss 15.
99 Canning to Polignau, 21 September 1824. Canning Papers, Ann Arbor, Michigan.
100 Canning to Sir George Warrender, 19 September 1824. Harewood 80 (c).
101 Canning to Liverpool, October 1824. Harewood 70.
102 Canning to Liverpool, 14 December 1824. Harewood 70.
103 Quoted in Bourne, *Britain and the Balance of Power*, pp. 64–5.
104 Quoted in A. G. Stapleton, *George Canning and His Times*, p. 411.
105 The King to Wellington, 17 December 1824. *George, Prince of Wales*, ed. Aspinall, vol. 8, p. 3441.
106 Canning to his wife, 14 December 1824. Harewood 27.
107 Canning to the British minister, 31 December 1824. PRO-FO 7/161.
108 Canning to Colonels Hamilton and Campbell, 3 January 1825. PRO-FO 18/11.
109 Canning to Colonels Hamilton and Campbell, 3 January 1825 (second letter). PRO-FO 18/11.
110 Canning to Frere, 8 January 1825. Festing, *J. H. Frere and His Friends*, p. 265 ff.
111 Canning to his wife, 31 December 1824 and 3 January 1825. Harewood 27.

112   Clanwilliam to Canning, 8 January 1825. PRO-FO 64/143.
113   Clanwilliam to Canning, 28 March 1825. PRO-FO 64/143.
114   Clanwilliam to Canning, 13 March 1825. PRO-FO 64/143.
115   Canning to his wife, 28 January and 1 February 1825. Harewood 27.
116   Canning to his wife, 4 February 1825. Harewood 27.
117   Canning to his wife, 10 February 1825. Harewood 27.
118   Canning to Leveson-Gower, 11 March 1825. PRO 30/29/8/7.
119   Canning to Bathurst, 7 December 1825. Bathurst Papers, HMC, pp. 597–8.
120   Liverpool to Canning, 20 November 1824. Royal Archives, Geo. Add Mss 15.
121   Canning to his wife, 21 January and 9 March 1825. Harewood 27.
122   Quoted in Hinde, *George Canning*, p. 372.
123   Canning to Sir Henry Wellesley, 19 August 1823. PRO-FO 7/179.
124   Canning to Sir Henry Wellesley, 13 August 1824. PRO-FO 7/161.
125   Canning to his wife, 16 January 1825. Harewood 27.
126   Stratford Canning to Canning, 6 May 1825. PRO-FO 65/142.
127   Temperley, *The Foreign Policy of Canning*, p. 221.
128   Canning to Sir Henry Wellesley, 26 April 1862. PRO-FO 7/191.
129   Canning to Sir Henry Wellesley, 19 August 1823. PRO-FO 7/179.
130   Quoted in Bourne, *Britain and the Balance of Power*, p. 61.
131   Canning to his wife, 17 January 1825. Harewood 27.
132   Quoted in Douglas Dakin, *The Greek Struggle for Independence, 1821–33* (London, 1973), p. 59.
133   Leveson-Gower to Canning, 24 December 1821. Harewood 65.
134   Canning to Lieven, 28 August 1823. Harewood 127.
135   Canning to Stratford Canning, 12 October 1825. Wellesley Papers, BM Add Mss 37294:185.
136   Sir Henry Wellesley to Canning, 20 July and 7 August 1823. PRO-FO 7/179.
137   Dakin, *The Greek Struggle for Independence*, p. 153.
138   Canning to Leveson-Gower, 28 December 1823. PRO 30/29/8/6.
139   Canning to Sir Henry Wellesley, 15 September 1823. PRO-FO 7/179.
140   Hinde, *George Canning*, p. 389.
141   Canning to Stratford Canning, 26 February 1825. PRO-FO 65/147. Clanwilliam to Canning, 13 March 1825. PRO-FO 64/143.

142 Canning to Sir Henry Wellesley, 5 November 1824. PRO-FO 7/161.
143 Canning to Sir Henry Wellesley, 5 December 1824. PRO-FO 7/161.
144 Canning to Sir Henry Wellesley, 31 December 1824. PRO-FO 7/161.
145 Clanwilliam to Canning, 29 January 1825. PRO-FO 64/143.
146 Stratford Canning to Canning, 3 and 6 January 1825. PRO-FO 65/147.
147 See Note 144.
148 Hinde, *George Canning*, p. 404.
149 Canning to Stratford Canning, 26 April 1826. PRO-FO 78/140.
150 See Note 135.
151 Canning to Sir Henry Wellesley, 5 December 1824. PRO-FO 7/161.
152 Th. Colocotroni to Canning, 30 June 1825. Wellesley Papers, BM Add Mss 37294:146–7.
153 Memo of the conference, 29 September 1825. Wellesley Papers, BM Add Mss 37294:151 ff.
154 Canning to MM Colocotroni and Miavlis, October 1825. Wellesley Papers, BM Add Mss 37294:179 ff.
155 Canning to Stratford Canning, 10 February 1826. PRO-FO 78/140.
156 Canning to Strangford, 20 January 1826. PRO-FO 65/156.
157 Canning to Strangford, 21 January 1826. PRO-FO 65/156.
158 Canning to Stratford Canning, 10 February 1826, Draft (omitted). PRO-FO 78/140.
159 Canning to Strangford, 10 February and 4 March 1826. PRO-FO 65/156.
160 Dakin, *The Greek Struggle for Independence*, p. 179.
161 Canning to Stratford Canning, 26 April 1826. PRO-FO 78/140.
162 Canning to Lieven, 25 May 1826. Harewood 127.
163 Canning to Stratford Canning, 3 July 1826. PRO-FO 78/140.
164 Dakin, *The Greek Struggle for Independence*, pp. 179–80.
165 Canning to Sir Henry Wellesley, 4 May 1826. PRO-FO 7/191.
166 See Note 161.
167 Canning to the King, 1 October 1826. *George IV*, ed. Aspinall, vol. 3, p. 1256.
168 Canning to Leveson-Gower, 22 June 1827. PRO 30/29/8/12.
169 Dakin, *The Greek Struggle for Independence*, p. 183.
170 Canning to Leveson-Gower, 13 July 1827. PRO 30/29/8/12.
171 Canning to Sir Henry Wellesley, 23 July 1824. PRO-FO 7/161.
172 Hinde, *George Canning*, p. 378.

M

173 Canning to the King, 2 July 1824. *George IV*, ed. Aspinall, vol. 3, p. 1170.
174 See Note 173.
175 Canning to Sir Henry Wellesley, 13 September 1824. PRO-FO 7/161.
176 Canning to Liverpool, 25 October 1824. A. G. Stapleton, *George Canning and His Times*, p. 501.
177 Canning to Sir Henry Wellesley, 26 November 1824. FO 7/161.
178 Canning to Leveson-Gower, 17 January 1825. A. G. Stapleton, *George Canning and His Times*, pp. 507–8.
179 Canning to Leveson-Gower, 21 January 1825. PRO-FO 30/29/8/6.
180 Canning to Leveson-Gower, 25 January 1825. PRO-FO 30/29/8/6.
181 Hinde, *George Canning*, p. 419.
182 Canning to Melville, 10 November 1826. Harewood 77.
183 Canning to Charles Ellis, 26 November 1826. Harewood 62.
184 A. G. Stapleton, *George Canning and His Times*, p. 534.
185 Canning to Leveson-Gower, 5 December 1826. PRO 30/29/8/12.
186 Canning to Grey, 8 December 1826. PRO 30/29/8/12.
187 Canning to Grey, 29 December 1826. PRO 30/29/8/12.
188 13 December 1826. Hans. 16:350–69.
189 Canning to Leveson-Gower, 26 January 1827. PRO 30/29/8/12.
190 Canning to Leveson-Gower, 7 January 1827. PRO 30/29/8/12.
191 H. V. Livermore, *A New History of Portugal* (Cambridge, 1966), p. 271.
192 Lord William Russell to Grey, 21 July 1832, and Grey to Lord William Russell, 28 August 1832. Grey Papers, Durham University, Box 50A.
193 Grey to Holland, 3 February 1825. Grey Papers, Durham University, Box 35:2.
194 Henry Kissinger, *A World Restored* (London, 1957), p. 314.
195 Canning to Leveson-Gower, 21 January 1825. PRO 30/29/8/6.
196 Canning to Leveson-Gower, 17 January 1825. PRO 30/29/8/6.
197 T. Gisborne to T. G. Babington, 18 February 1823. Macaulay Papers, Henry Huntington Library, Los Angeles.
198 Clanwilliam to Canning, 10 May 1823. PRO-FO 64/143.
199 Canning to Clanwilliam, 26 March 1824. PRO-FO 64/39.
200 Canning to Charles Stuart, 8 and 29 October 1822. NLS, Rothesay Papers 6216.
201 Falck was the Netherlands' Minister in London.
202 Canning's despatch to Bagot. Harewood 139 (a).
203 Douglas was the Secretary to the British Embassy at The Hague.

204 Sir Henry Poland, K.C., *Mr Canning's Rhyming 'Despatch' to Sir Charles Bagot* (TRHS, New Series, No. 20, 1905). Also see Harewood 139 (a).
205 Canning to Sir George Warrender, 13 November 1862. Harewood 80 (c).
206 Canning to Frere, 7 August 1823. Harewood 64.

CHAPTER 10
 1 Hans. 9:255 ff.
 2 'The Lizard' is Lizard Point in Cornwall, i.e. safely embarked for India. Stephen to Wilberforce, August 1822. Wilberforce Papers, Catterick.
 3 Wilberforce to Macaulay, 13 October 1823. Macaulay Papers. Henry Huntington Library, Los Angeles.
 4 London Committee of West India Merchants and Planters, minutes of meeting, 22 and 29 April 1823, vol. 5:90, 97, 121,
 5 Wilberforce to Brougham, March 1823. University College, London, Brougham Papers 10959.
 6 Hans. 9:285–6.
 7 Quoted in 'The Anti-Slavery Register', No. 6 (30 November 1825), p. 51.
 8 Buxton to a friend, 13 June 1823. Annotated by Canning. Harewood 142.
 9 Duke of Manchester to Holland, 23 October 1823. Holland House Papers, BM Add Mss 51820.
10 Macaulay to Canning, 6 July 1824. Harewood 142.
11 Canning to Liverpool, 11 October 1823. Harewood 70.
12 Canning to Wilberforce, 11 October 1823. Harewood 80 (a).
13 Liverpool to J. Stephen, 22 March 1815. Liverpool Papers, BM Add Mss 38416:362–3.
14 Canning to Liverpool, 9 January 1824. Harewood 71.
15 Ellis to Huskisson, 3 April 1823. Huskisson Papers, BM Add Mss 38744:202.
16 Harrowby to J. W. Cunningham, 6 February 1824. Macaulay Papers, Henry Huntington Library, Los Angeles.
17 Liverpool to Canning, 9 January 1824. Bathurst Papers, HMC, pp. 560–1.
18 W. Horton to Huskisson, 25 January 1824. Huskisson Papers, BM Add Mss 38745:188–95.
19 16 March 1824. Hans. 10:1106.
20 Canning to Huskisson, 25 March 1824. Harewood 68.
21 16 March 1824. Hans. 10:1064 ff.

22 1b, 23 June 1825. Vol. 13:1285H; 1324–31; 1338–42.

23 London Committee of West India Merchants and Planters, minutes of meeting, 6 July 1826, vol. 5:337.

24 Canning Memo, 26 February 1826. Harewood 142.

25 Brougham to Macaulay, 1827. Macaulay Papers, Henry Huntington Library, Los Angeles.

26 Canning to Peel, 10 November 1823. Peel Papers, BM Add Mss 40311:46.

27 10 June 1824. Hans. 11:1198.

28 Canning to Liverpool, 28 and 29 December 1824. Harewood 70.

29 Canning to his wife, 10 February 1825. Harewood 27.

30 Canning to his wife, 3 and 8 February 1825. Harewood 27.

31 Canning to Frere, 8 January 1825. Quoted in Festing, *J. H. Frere and His Friends*, p. 269.

32 Canning to Leveson-Gower, 18 February 1825. PRO 30/29/8/7.

33 *Colchester Diary and Correspondence*, vol. 3, p. 360.

34 Canning to his wife, 22 and 25 February and 4 March 1825. Harewood 27.

35 28 February 1825. Hans. 12:791.

36 Canning to his wife, 9 and 11 March 1825. Harewood 27.

37 Huskisson to Croker, 16 March 1825. Croker Papers, William L. Clements Library, Ann Arbor, Michigan.

38 Hinde, *George Canning*, p. 397.

39 Liverpool to Arbuthnot, 19 May 1825. *Charles Arbuthnot Correspondence*, ed. Aspinall, p. 69.

40 *Colchester Diary and Correspondence*, vol. 3, p. 390.

41 Canning to Huskisson, 14 September 1825. *The Huskisson Papers*, ed. Melville, p. 193.

42 Canning to Plunket, 25 September 1825. A. G. Stapleton, *George Canning and His Times*, pp. 253–6.

43 Sir James Mackintosh to Lady Holland, 8 October 1825. Holland House Papers, BM Add Mss 51654.

44 Fitzwilliam to Grey, 20 April 1825. Grey Papers, Durham University, Box 14:11.

45 *Speeches and Addresses of the Candidates for the Representation of the County of York, 1826* (Leeds, 1826), p. 51.

46 Huskisson to Canning, 18 August 1826. *The Huskisson Papers*, ed. Melville, p. 210.

47 Sir Francis Burdett to Huskisson, 1827 (n.d.). *The Huskisson Papers*, ed. Melville, p. 210.

48 Huskisson to A. G. Stapleton, 9 February 1827. *The Huskisson Papers*, ed. Melville, p. 215.

49 A. G. Stapleton to Carlisle, 15 February 1827. A. G. Stapleton, *George Canning and His Times*, pp. 259–61.

50 Canning to Huskisson, 23 February 1827. Huskisson Papers, BM Add Mss 38749:129.

51 Huskisson to Canning, 26 February 1827. Harewood 68.

52 In 1829 Philpotts supported the Government in pushing through the Catholic Emancipation Act and received the Bishopric of Exeter from a grateful Wellington.

53 Hans. 16:993 ff. Hinde, *George Canning*, p. 436 n.

54 *Journal of Mrs Arbuthnot*, vol. 2, p. 86.

55 *Journal of Mrs Arbuthnot*, vol. 2, p. 86.

56 *Colchester Diary and Correspondence*, vol. 3, p. 490.

57 Canning to Huskisson, 25 February 1827. Huskisson Papers, BM Add Mss 38749:131. In 1783 the King had used his influence in the House of Lords to throw out his Government's India Bill by letting it be known that any man who voted for it would be considered his enemy. Pitt then formed a Government and successfully appealed to the country on a 'King versus Charles James Fox' platform.

58 Huskisson to Canning, 4 September 1825. *The Huskisson Papers*, ed. Melville, p. 189.

59 Huskisson to [correspondent unknown], 27 November 1825. Harewood 68.

60 Gladstone to Canning, 14 December, and Canning to Gladstone, 18 December 1825. Harewood 83.

61 A. G. Stapleton, *George Canning and His Times*, pp. 230–1.

62 Hans. 14:911.

63 Canning to Leveson-Gower, 6 March 1826. Quoted in A. G. Stapleton, *George Canning and His Times*, pp. 237–9.

64 Frere to Canning, 13 February 1826. Harewood 64.

65 21 March 1825. Hans. 12:1110.

66 Canning to Huskisson, 14 September 1825. *The Huskisson Papers*, ed. Melville, p. 193.

67 Hinde, *George Canning*, p. 402.

68 Liverpool to Huskisson, 25 October 1826. *The Huskisson Papers*, ed. Melville, pp. 210–11.

69 Huskisson to Robinson, 20 November 1826. *The Huskisson Papers*, ed. Melville, pp. 211–13.

70 Huskisson to Canning, 19 February 1827. Harewood 68.

71 Huskisson to Canning, 20 February 1827. Harewood 68.

72 Melville to Canning, 1 April 1827. Harewood 77.

73 Huskisson to Sir Francis Burdett, 12 February 1827. *The Huskisson Papers*, ed. Melville, p. 216.

74 Canning to Sir William Knighton, 18 May 1827. Canning Papers, Ann Arbor, Michigan.

75 Hinde, *George Canning*, p. 454.

76   Canning to Wellesley, 21 June 1827. Wellesley Papers, BM
     Add Mss 37297:358.
77   Canning to Leveson-Gower, 19 June 1827. PRO 30/29/8/12.
78   Canning to the King, 17 June 1827. *George IV*, ed. Aspinall,
     vol. 3, p. 1356.
79   Hans. 15:795.
80   Hans. 17:1337 ff.
81   *Colchester Diary and Correspondence*, vol. 3, p. 516.
82   *The Black Book, or Corruption Unmasked* (London, 1823), pp.
     138, 142, 148.
83   *The Black Book*, p. 165.
84   Huskisson to Canning, 15 October 1826. Harewood 68.
85   EG Hans. 12:1291; 10:500.
86   Liverpool to Bathurst, 5 October 1824. Liverpool Papers, BM
     Add Mss 38299:133.
87   Canning to Liverpool, 11 April 1826. Liverpool Papers, BM
     Add Mss 38193:239.
88   Liverpool to Canning, 10 July 1826. Liverpool Papers, BM
     Add Mss 38301:261.
89   Canning to his wife, 30 March 1826. Harewood 27.
90   Canning to Liverpool, 22 January 1823. Harewood 70.
91   7 June 1825. Hans. 13:1094.
92   Hollinshed to Canning, 17 February, and Canning to Hollins-
     hed, 19 February 1825. Harewood 83.
93   Arbuthnot to Liverpool, 7 October, and Liverpool to Arbuth-
     not, 8 October 1823. *Charles Arbuthnot Correspondence*, ed.
     Aspinall, pp. 45–6.
94   Canning to Frere, 8 January 1825. Festing, *J. H. Frere and His
     Friends*, p. 265.
95   Hinde, *George Canning*, p. 392.
96   Canning to the King, 11 April 1826. *George IV*, ed. Aspinall,
     vol. 3, p. 1234 n.
97   Canning to Leveson-Gower, 28 November 1826. PRO 30/29/
     8/12. Canning to Clanricarde, n.d. Harewood 80 (c).
98   *George, Prince of Wales*, ed. Aspinall, vol. 8, p. 3454.
99   Canning to W. P. Canning, 17 May 1817. Harewood.
100 Diary, 20 December 1818. Harewood 29 (d).
101 Liverpool Papers, BM Add Mss 38282:350.
102 Diary, 29 August 1821. Harewood 29 (d).
103 W. P. Canning to Canning, 19 January 1822. Harewood.
104 Canning to ? [correspondent unknown], 20 January 1822.
     Harewood.
105 T. Barrow to Canning, 23 January 1822. Harewood.

106 Canning to W. P. Canning, 5 February 1822. Harewood.
107 Canning to W. P. Canning, 11 May 1822. Harewood.
108 Canning to Captain Dawkins, 3 November 1822. Harewood.
109 Canning to W. P. Canning, 26 January and 19 December 1824, 15 February and 16 July 1826. Harewood.
110 Canning to his mother, 16 March 1825. Harewood 11.
111 Canning to his mother, 12 February 1825. Harewood 11.
112 Canning to his wife, 10 February 1825. Harewood 27.
113 Canning to Sir Walter Scott, 11 September 1824. NLS, Mss 3899.
114 Canning to his mother, 3 May, 14 June and 4 August 1823. Harewood 10.
115 Canning to his wife, 18 February 1825. Harewood 27.
116 Canning to his mother, 19 February 1825. Harewood 11.
117 Canning to Frere, 8 January 1825. BM Add Mss 38833:336.
118 Canning to Esterhazy, 17 April 1826. Harewood 127.
119 *Colchester Diary and Correspondence*, vol. 3, p. 273.
120 Canning to Frere, 7 August 1823. Harewood 64.
121 Canning to Sir George Warrender, 13 November 1826. Harewood 80 (c).
122 A. Aspinall, *The Formation of Canning's Ministry, February to August, 1827*, Camden Society, 3rd Series, No. 59 (London, 1937), p. 27.
123 *George, Prince of Wales*, ed. Aspinall, vol. 8, p. 3457 n.
124 A. G. Stapleton, *George Canning and His Times*, p. 443.
125 30 March 1827. Hans. 17:164 ff.
126 Hinde, *George Canning*, p. 442.
127 Bathurst to Canning, 12 and 15 April 1827; Canning to Bathurst, 15 April 1827. Bathurst Papers, HMC, pp. 632–3.
128 Melville to Canning, 12 April 1823. Harewood 77.
129 Aspinall, *The Formation of Canning's Ministry*, pp. 90–1.
130 Hinde, *George Canning*, p. 443.
131 Huskisson to Canning, 2 April 1827. Harewood 68.
132 *Colchester Diary and Correspondence*, vol. 3, p. 501.
133 Huskisson to Canning, 17 April 1827. Harewood 68.
134 Grey to Holland, 14 April 1827. Grey Papers, University of Durham, Box 35:2.
135 Grey to Fitzwilliam, 18 April 1827. Grey Papers, University of Durham, Box 14:11.
136 Fitzwilliam to Grey, 22 April 1827. Grey Papers, University of Durham, Box 14:11.
137 Canning to Knighton, 25 April 1827. Canning Papers, Ann Arbor, Michigan.

138   Brougham to Holland, 18 April 1827. Holland House Papers,
      BM Add Mss 51563.
139   A. Aspinall, *The Formation of Canning's Ministry*, pp. 118 ff.,
      133–4.
140   Canning to Gladstone, 27 April 1827. *The Huskisson Papers*, ed.
      Melville, p. 224.
141   Canning to Sturges-Bourne, 26 April 1827. Canning Papers,
      Ann Arbor, Michigan.
142   Grey to Fitzwilliam, 20 October 1827. Grey Papers, University
      of Durham, Box 14:11.
143   Canning to Wellesley, 15 and 22 May 1827. Wellesley Papers,
      BM Add Mss 37297:270, 272.
144   Canning to Wellesley, 7 June 1827. Wellesley Papers, BM
      Add Mss 37297:345.
145   *Journal of Mrs Arbuthnot*, vol. 2, pp. 115–16.
146   Canning to the King, 4 May 1827. *George IV*, ed. Aspinall,
      vol. 3, p. 1342.
147   Hans. 17:589, 783–4, 1049, 1077–81, 1098–114.
148   Canning to the King, 20 July 1827. Royal Archives 25013.
149   Canning to Sir William Knighton, 5 June 1827. Canning Papers,
      Ann Arbor, Michigan.
150   Canning to Holland, 31 July 1827. Harewood 65.
151   Zachary Macaulay to Hannah More, 24 August 1827. Macaulay
      Papers, Henry Huntington Library, Los Angeles.
152   Brougham to Holland, 15 August 1827. Holland House Papers,
      BM Add Mss 51563.
153   C. C. Western to Grey, 14 September 1822. Grey Papers,
      University of Durham, Box 57:9.
154   Huskisson to Croker, 14 October 1827. Croker Papers, Ann
      Arbor, Michigan.

BIBLIOGRAPHY

I. PRIMARY SOURCES

A. Manuscripts

Auckland Papers. British Museum Additional Mss.

Blackwood Papers. National Library of Scotland.

Canning Papers (main collection). Harewood Mss, Leeds Record Office, Sheepscar Branch Library, Leeds.

Canning Papers. William L. Clements Library, Ann Arbor, Michigan, USA.

Canning Club Minute Book. Liverpool Record Office.

Canning Correspondence with George IV. Royal Archives, Windsor Castle.

Consistorial Court Records for the Diocese of Edinburgh. Scottish Record Office.

Croker Papers. William L. Clements Library, Ann Arbor, Michigan, USA.

The Letter Book of Robert Dundas. National Library of Scotland.

Foreign Office Records for 1807–9, 1822–7. Public Record Office.

Granville Papers. Public Record Office.

Grey Papers. University of Durham.

Heytesbury Papers. British Museum Additional Mss.

Holland House Papers. British Museum Additional Mss.

Huskisson Papers. British Museum Additional Mss.

India Office Library, Records for 1816–20.

Papers of the Liverpool Parliamentary Office. Liverpool Record Office.

Macaulay Papers. Henry Huntington Library, Los Angeles, USA.

Melville Papers. National Library of Scotland.

338 *Bibliography*

Peel Papers. British Museum Additional Mss.
Perceval Papers. British Museum Additional Mss.
Roscoe Papers. Liverpool Record Office.
Rose Papers. National Library of Scotland.
Rothesay Papers. National Library of Scotland.
Letters of Sir Walter Scott. National Library of Scotland.
Vansittart Papers. British Museum Additional Mss.
Wellesley Papers. British Museum Additional Mss.
Wilberforce Papers. Duke University, Durham, North Carolina, USA.
Wilberforce Papers. Property of Mr C. E. Wrangh, Rosemary House, Catterick, Yorkshire.
Windham Papers. British Museum Additional Mss.

B. Printed Works

i. Newspapers and Periodicals: the *Anti-Jacobin Review*, the *Liverpool Mercury*, the *Microcosm*, the *Morning Chronicle*, the *Morning Post*, *St James' Chronicle*, *The Times*.
ii. Books (alphabetized according to key word: author, subject or whatever).

The Life and Correspondence of the Right Hon. Henry Addington, First Viscount Sidmouth, ed. George Pellew (London, 1847), 3 vols.
The Correspondence of Charles Arbuthnot, ed. A. Aspinall (London, 1941), Camden Society, 3rd Series, No. 59.
The Journal of Mrs Arbuthnot, ed. Francis Bamford and the Duke of Wellington (London, 1950), 2 vols.
The Journal and Correspondence of William, Lord Auckland, with a preface, etc. (London, 1860–2), vols 1–4.
Bathurst Papers. HMC, Vol. 76. 1923.
The Battle of the Blocks, An Heroic Poem to Fantoccini [on the duel between Lord Castlereagh and G. Canning] (1809).
Ed. S. T. Bindoff and E. F. Malcolm Smith, *British Diplomatic Representatives, 1789–1852* (London, 1934), Camden Society, 3rd Series, vol. 50.
The Black Book, or Corruption Unmasked (London, 1823).
Henry, Lord Brougham, *Historical Sketches of Statesmen who flourished in the time of George* III (London, 1855).

The Correspondence of Edmund Burke, ed. P. Marshall and J. Woods (Cambridge, 1968–70), vols 7–9.

George Canning, *A Letter to the Earl Camden containing . . . a narrative of the transaction connected with the late duel* (London, 1809).

Poems by George Canning of the Middle Temple, Esq. (London, 1767).

The Poetical Works of the Rt. Hon. George Canning, MP, Secretary of State for Foreign Affairs (London, 1823).

Cabinet Edition of the British Poets, Vol. 4 (Canning) (London, 1851).

A. Aspinall, *The Formation of Canning's Ministry, February to August, 1827* (London, 1937), Camden Society, 3rd Series, No. 59.

Josceline Bagot, *George Canning and his Friends* (London, 1909), 2 vols.

Robert Bell, *The Life of the Rt Hon. George Canning* (London, 1846).

John F. Newton, *The Early Days of the Rt Hon. George Canning, First Lord of the Treasury and Chancellor of the Exchequer, and some of his contemporaries* (London, 1828).

A. G. Stapleton, *George Canning and His Times* (London, 1859).

A. G. Stapleton, *The Political Life of the Right Honourable George Canning* (London, 1831), 3 vols.

E. J. Stapleton, *Some Official Correspondence of George Canning* (London, 1887), 2 vols.

Cobbett's Parliamentary Debates.

The Diary and Correspondence of Charles Abbot, Lord Colchester, ed. by his son (London, 1861), 3 vols.

Thomas Creevey, *The Creevey Papers*, ed. the Rt. Hon. Sir H. Maxwell, Bart. (London, 1903), 2 vols.

Mss of Sir John Fortescue preserved at Dropmore (*Dropmore Papers*). HMC, Vols. 2–4, 6–10. 1892–7.

Letters to Ivy from the first Earl of Dudley, ed. S. H. Romilly (London, 1905).

Horace Twiss, *The Public and Private Life of Lord Chancellor Eldon* (London, 1844), 3 vols.

Gabrielle Festing, *J. H. Frere and His Friends* (London, 1899).

Memoirs of Sir Phillip Francis, K.C.B., ed. H. Merivale (London, 1867), 2 vols.

Memorials of . . . Admiral Gambier (London, 1861), 2 vols.

Richard Grenville, Duke of Buckingham and Chandos, *Memoirs of the Court and Cabinets of George* III (London, 1853), 2 vols.

Richard Grenville, Duke of Buckingham and Chandos, *Memoirs of the Court of George* IV, *1820–30* (London, 1859), 2 vols.

The Later Correspondence of George III, ed. A. Aspinall (Cambridge, 1963–70), vols. 2–5.

The Correspondence of George, Prince of Wales, ed. A. Aspinall (London, 1963–70), 4 vols.

The Letters of George IV, ed. A. Aspinall (Cambridge, 1938), 3 vols.

Lord Granville Leveson-Gower (the first Earl Granville), *Private Correspondence, 1781–1821,* ed. by his daughter-in-law, Castalia, Countess Granville (London, 1916), 2 vols.

Parliamentary History, Cobbett's Parliamentary Debates, Hansard (New Series), *1794–1814; 1816–27.*

Sir Lewis Namier and John Brooke, *The House of Commons, 1754–1790* (London, 1964).

Hastings Mss, Vol. 3, Historical Manuscripts Commission, vol. 78 (London, 1934).

The Diary of Henry Hobhouse, 1820–1827, ed. A. Aspinall (London, 1947).

Journal of Elizabeth, Lady Holland, ed. the Earl of Ilchester (London, 1908), 2 vols.

Lord Holland, *Memoirs of the Whig Party* (London, 1852–4), 2 vols.

Lord Holland, *Further Memoirs of the Whig Party, 1807–1821,* ed. Lord Stavordale (London, 1905).

The Huskisson Papers, ed. Lewis Melville (London, 1931).

The Private Letters of Princess Lieven to Prince Metternich, 1820–1826, ed. Peter Quenell (London, 1937).

C. D. Yonge, *Life and Administration of the 2nd Earl of Liverpool* (London, 1868), 3 vols.

[Liverpool Election] *A Collection of Addresses [from the] Liverpool . . . Election, May 1807.*

[Liverpool Election] *A Compendious and Impartial Account [of the] Liverpool Election, 1806.*

[Liverpool Election] *A Complete List of the 1,425 Burgesses who polled at the late Liverpool Election* (Liverpool, 1802).

[Liverpool Election] *History of the Election . . . Liverpool, 1806.*

[Liverpool Election] *An Impartial Collection of Addresses, Songs, Squibs, etc ... Liverpool, 1812.*

[Liverpool Election] *The Speech Book, being a Collection of Addresses, Songs, etc ... Liverpool Election, 1818.*

[Liverpool Election] *The Speeches delivered during the Election at Liverpool ... by Henry Brougham, Liverpool Election, 1812.*

[Liverpool Election] *The Speeches and Public Addresses of George Canning during the late Election in Liverpool.* (Liverpool, 1812).

[Liverpool Election] *The Speeches and Public Addresses of the Right Hon. George Canning ... Liverpool Election, 1818.*

[Liverpool Election] *The Poll, etc.* (Liverpool, 1790, 1818, 1830, etc).

T. Barnes, *History of the Commerce ... [of] Liverpool* (Liverpool, 1852).

Diary of Sir John Moore, ed. G. J. V. Maurice (London, 1904), 2 vols.

Diaries and Correspondence of James Harris, First Earl of Malmesbury, 2nd edition (London, 1845), vol. 3.

Spencer Walpole, *Life of Spencer Perceval* (London, 1874), 2 vols.

Earl Stanhope, *Life of the Right Hon. William Pitt* (London, 1862), 4 vols.

Richard Grenville, Duke of Buckingham and Chandos, *Memoirs of the Court of England during the Regency 1811–1820* (London, 1860), 2 vols.

Diaries and Correspondence of the Right Hon. George Rose, ed. L. V. Harcourt (London, 1860), 2 vols.

Lord Edmund Fitzmaurice, *Life of William, Earl of Shelburne* (London, 1876), vol. 3.

Memoirs and Correspondence of the Most Noble Richard, Marquess Wellesley, ed. R. P. Pearce, Esq. (London, 1846), 3 vols.

Life of Wilberforce, ed. R. I. and S. Wilberforce (London, 1938), 5 vols.

The Diary of the Right Hon. William Windham, 1784 to 1810, ed. Mrs Henry Baring, with a preface by G. Ellis (London, 1866).

The Life and Correspondence of the Rt Hon. William Windham, 1750–1810 (London, 1913), 2 vols.

The Windham Papers, ed. the Earl of Rosebery (London, 1913).
Speeches and Addresses of the Candidates for the Representation of the County of York, 1826 (Leeds, 1826).

II. SELECTED SECONDARY WORKS

Aspinall, A., *Lord Brougham and the Whig Party* (London, 1927).
Aspinall, A., *Politics and the Press, 1780–1850* (London, 1949).
Aspinall, A., *The Canningite Party* (TRHS, 1934).
Bartlett, C. J., *Castlereagh* (London, 1966).
Bartlett, C. J., *A New Balance of Power: The Nineteenth-century West Indies* (Kingston, Jamaica, 1970).
Bindoff, S. T., *The Unreformed Diplomatic Service* (TRHS, 1935).
Bethell, L. M., *The Abolition of the Brazilian Slave Trade* (Cambridge, 1970).
Brock, W. R., *Lord Liverpool and Liberal Toryism, 1820–1827* (Cambridge, 1941).
Bourne, Kenneth, *Britain and the Balance of Power in North America 1815–1908* (Aberdeen, 1967).
Burn, W. L., *Emancipation and Apprenticeship* (London, 1937).
Curtin, P. D., *The Atlantic Slave Trade* (London, 1969).
Dakin, Douglas, *The Greek Struggle for Independence, 1821–33* (London, 1973).
Davis, H. W. L., *The Age of Grey and Peel* (Oxford, 1929).
Feiling, K., *The Second Tory Party, 1714–1832* (London 1938).
Foord, A. S., *The Waning Influence of the Crown, 1714–1830* (Oxford, 1964).
Fulford, R., *The Trial of Queen Caroline* (London, 1967)
Gash, N., *Mr Secretary Peel* (London, 1961).
Gray, D., *Spencer Perceval, The Evangelical Prime Minister, 1762–1812* (Manchester, 1963).
Hill, D., *Mr Gillray, the Caricaturist* (London, 1965).
Hinde, W., *George Canning* (London, 1973).
Kissinger, H., *A World Restored* (London, 1957).
Lefebvre, G., *The Directory*, Trans. R. Baldick (London, 1964).
Livermore, H. V., *A New History of Portugal* (Cambridge, 1966).

Machin, G. I. T., *The Catholic Question in English Politics, 1820–30* (Oxford, 1964).

Mackesy, Piers, *The War in the Mediterranean, 1803–10* (London 1957).

Marshall, Dorothy, *The Rise of George Canning* (London, 1938).

Mitchell, A., *The Whigs in Opposition, 1815–30* (Oxford, 1967).

New, Chester, *The Life of Henry Brougham to 1830* (Oxford, 1961).

O'Gorman, F., *The Whig Party and the French Revolution* (Glasgow, 1967).

Philips, C. H., *The East India Company, 1784–1834* (London, 1961).

Poland, Sir H., *Mr Canning's Rhyming 'Despatch' to Sir Charles Bagot* (TRHS, New Series, No. 20, 1905).

Roberts, Michael, *The Whig Party, 1807–12* (London, 1939).

Rodger, A. B., *The War of the Second Coalition, 1795–1801* (Oxford, 1964).

Rolo, P. J. V., *George Canning* (London, 1965).

Rose, T. Holland, *William Pitt and the Great War* (London, 1911).

Rose, T. Holland, *Canning and the Secret Intelligence from Tilsit* (TRHS, 1906).

Temperley, H., *George Canning* (London, 1907).

Temperley, H., *The Foreign Policy of Canning, 1822–7* (London, 1925).

Webster, Sir Charles, *The Foreign Policy of Castlereagh, 1815–22* (London, 1925).

Williams, E., *Capitalism and Slavery* (London, 1964).

Ziegler, Philip, *A Life of Henry Addington, First Viscount Sidmouth* (London, 1965).

INDEX

Index 349

ministry, 81; Canning on, 98; and abolition of slave trade, 102; in Portland's ministry, 107, 131; opposition to Canning, 125, 279; in Liverpool's ministry, 184; and South America, 231

Ellenborough, Edward Law, 1st Baron, 92

Ellis, Charles Rose, 1st Baron Seaford, 16–17, 25, 51, 66, 248; on Canning, 63, 89; and peace negotiations with France, 66; and Grenville's ministry, 99; and Canning's duel with Castlereagh, 136–7; elected Member for Seaford, 171; in Portugal, 179; supports Canning, 202, 210; and abolition of slave trade, 256, 259, 261; created a peer, 274

Ellis, George, 17, 25, 139; and peace negotiations with France, 33–4, 66; writes for *The Anti-Jacobin*, 40, 43; death, 179

Erroll, Dowager Duchess of, 24

Erskine, D. M., 149, 153

Esterhazy, Prince, 234, 235, 274

Eton College, 4, 5, 9

Ewart, William, 161, 170

Ferdinand I, King of the Two Sicilies, 54

Ferdinand VII, King of Spain, 117, 124, 213, 214, 217, 224, 248

Fitzharris, Viscount, 107

Fitzpatrick, General, 99

Fitzwilliam, Earl, 31, 90, 109, 264, 281

Forjaz, Miguel de, 179, 180

Fox, Charles James, 20, 28, 40, 42–3; relationship with Canning, 4, 17; and schism in Whig Party, 13; opposition to Canning, 39; and war with France, 74–5, 80–1; opposition to Addington's government, 77; and Pitt's second ministry, 81; in Grenville's ministry, 90; and East India Company, 185; death, 95–6, 97

France, at war with Britain, 27–8, 30–8, 40, 55–6; Directory, 34, 35; establishes Parthenopean Republic in Italy, 54; peace negotiations with Britain, 56–8, 64–6; renewal of war with Britain, 72, 74, 75; Britain unsuccessfully tries for peace with, 95; and Treaty of Tilsit, 110–111; economic war with Britain, 114; occupies Portugal, 114–15; intervenes in Spain, 117–18; and Convention of Cintra, 118–19; and the Scheldt expedition, 124–5; slave trade, 167, 219–23; war with Spain, 215–18; and British interests in South America, 235, 236

Francis, Philip, 19, 191

Frederick II, of Prussia, 18, 95

Fremantle, W. H., 126

French Revolution, 12, 13, 212

Frere, John Hookham, 5, 7, 14, 51, 66, 67; on Canning, 23; produces *The Anti-Jacobin*, 40, 43; advises Canning, 73, 84, 153, 176–7, 268; on Pitt, 78; and British invasion of Spain, 121, 122; tries to arrange reconciliation between Canning and Wellesley, 142; and Princess Caroline, 200

Gale Jones, John, 147–8

Gallatin, Albert, 223

Gambier, Admiral, 113

Garlike, Benjamin, 110–12

Garrick, David, 3

Garvagh, Lord, 5

Gascogne, Bamber, 158–9

Gascogne, Isaac, 159–60, 163–5, 168–9, 170, 195–6, 197

George III, King of England, and war with France, 34–5; and Ireland, 61–2; and Pitt, 75, 91; dislikes Fox, 81, 90; insanity, 81, 144–5; and Grenville's ministry, 95, 108; and Catholic question, 100, 103, 108; and Princess Caroline, 102; and Canning's